THE BIBLE AND EARLY TRINITARIAN THEOLOGY

THE BIBLE AND EARLY TRINITARIAN THEOLOGY

EDITED BY

Christopher A. Beeley and Mark E. Weedman

The Catholic University of America Press

Washington, D.C.

The Catholic University of America Press is the publishing division of The Catholic University of America, the national university of the Catholic bishops in the United States.

The paper used in this publication meets the minimum requirements of American National Standards for Information Science—Permanence of Paper for Printed Library Materials, ANSI Z39.48–1984.
∞

Library of Congress Cataloging-in-Publication Data
Names: Beeley, Christopher A., editor.
Title: The Bible and early Trinitarian theology / edited by Christopher A. Beeley and Mark E. Weedman.
Description: Washington, D.C. : The Catholic University of America Press, 2018. | Series: CUA studies in early Christianity | Includes bibliographical references and index.
Identifiers: LCCN 2017033722 | ISBN 9780813229959 (cloth : alk. paper)
Subjects: LCSH: Trinity—History of doctrines—Early church, ca. 30–600. | Trinity—Biblical teaching.
Classification: LCC BT109 .B53 2018 | DDC 231/.04409015—dc23
LC record available at https://lccn.loc.gov/2017033722

CONTENTS

ABBREVIATIONS

ACW	Ancient Christian Writers
ANF	Ante-Nicene Fathers
CCL	Corpus Christianorum, Series Latina
CCSG	Corpus Christianorum, Series Graeca
CCSL	Corpus Christianorum, Series Latina
CPG	Clavis patrum graecorum
CSEL	Corpus Scriptorium Ecclesiasticorum Latinorum
FC	Fathers of the Church
GCS	Die Griechischen Christlichen Schriftsteller der ersten Jahrhunderte
LCL	Loeb Classical Library
LF	Library of the Fathers
NPNF	Nicene and Post-Nicene Fathers
PG	Patrologia Cursus Completus, Series Graeca
PL	Patrologia Cursus Completus, Patrologia Latina
PPS	Popular Patristics Series
PS	Patrologia Syriaca
SC	Sources Chrétiennes
TLG	Thesaurus Linguae Graecae

THE BIBLE AND EARLY TRINITARIAN THEOLOGY

Christopher A. Beeley and Mark E. Weedman

INTRODUCTION

The Study of Early Christian Biblical Interpretation

The past thirty years have seen an unprecedented level of new interest in early Christian biblical interpretation. Arguably for the first time in modern scholarship, the subject has now come into its own. Works on patristic exegesis, early Christian habits of reading and writing, and the complex relationships among biblical interpretation, patristic theology, and the common life of early Christians have proliferated in academic and popular publishing since the 1980s.[1] By contrast with earlier generations, few scholars today would consider teaching early Christian history and theology without giving serious attention to the ways in which church leaders and ordinary believers were frequently reading, hearing, teaching, and responding to the scriptures. Meanwhile, in a parallel development, biblical scholars are now increasingly looking to the reception and interpretation of biblical texts by early Christians as an indispensable part of their work, and some even champion methods of

1. Thanks in large part to this upsurge, the literature on early Christian biblical interpretation is now extensive. Good recent bibliographies can be found in Charles Kannengiesser, *Handbook of Patristic Exegesis*, 2 vols., Bible in Ancient Christianity 1 (Leiden: Brill, 2004); Frances M. Young, "Interpretation of Scripture," in *The Oxford Handbook of Early Christian Studies*, ed. Susan Ashbrook Harvey and David G. Hunter (Oxford: Oxford University Press, 2008), 846–63; and James Carleton Paget and Joachim Schaper, eds., *The New Cambridge History of the Bible*, vol. 1, *From the Beginnings to 600* (Cambridge: Cambridge University Press, 2013). For a popular example of recent interest in the subject, see the IVP Ancient Christian Commentary on Scripture series.

interpretation that align in striking ways with the practices of the first five or six centuries. While historical criticism remains the primary scholarly method in the field of biblical studies, the rise of other approaches to the study of the scriptures is one of the most noteworthy features of recent biblical scholarship.

Although they have not operated in complete ignorance of one another, the fields of biblical studies and early Christian studies have come to approach early Christian biblical interpretation for the most part for their own reasons and within their own intellectual spaces.[2] The aim of this book is to bring these two fields into closer conversation with one another in order to explore new avenues in the relationship between biblical interpretation and the development of early Christian theology. After tracing the emergence of the study of early biblical interpretation in early Christian studies and biblical studies, we note several ways in which they can potentially benefit one another, and we identify the particular contribution this book offers to the current scholarly conversation.

Patristics and Early Christian Studies

The way that scholars approach the study of early Christian theology has changed dramatically in the last few decades. Although earlier habits remain in certain quarters, most scholars today view theology and church life in the patristic period as being deeply involved with the reading, hearing, interpretation, and living practice of the Christian scriptures, to the point that many would now agree with Gerhard Ebeling's remark that the history of the Christian church is virtually synonymous with the history of biblical interpretation.[3]

This perspective is fairly recent in the history of early Christian scholarship, a field that developed as we know it only after the Second World War. While nineteenth-century scholars gave some attention to early Christian use of the scriptures, for most of the twentieth century scholars approached the study of patristic theology chiefly as a set of doctrines articulated by key fig-

2. Both fields continue to maintain distinct scholarly organizations and annual conferences. Only in the last decade did the Society for Biblical Literature make a systematic initiative to develop new program units in patristic theology and exegesis.

3. Gerhard Ebeling, "The Significance of the Critical Historical Method for Church and Theology in Protestantism," in *Word and Faith*, trans. James W. Leitch (Philadelphia: Fortress, 1963), 17–61.

ures and church councils. They paid little attention to how early Christian beliefs and practices informed, and were informed by, the reading and hearing of the scriptures. The programmatic division between the formation and interpretation of the Bible and the teachings of the fathers is particularly visible in the standard handbooks in the field, such as the magisterial *Patrologie* of Roman Catholic scholar Berthold Altaner, which ran through several editions from the interwar period to the 1970s. In the first edition of the work, Altaner's 1931 revision of Gerhard Rauschen's *Patrologie*,[4] the title of the first chapter is telling: "Between the Bible and the Writings of the Fathers," as if the two were separate entities that had relatively little to do with each other.[5] At the heart of each section is a list of the respective father's teaching on dogmatic topics such as Trinitarian doctrine, Christology, the Eucharist, and orders of ministry.[6] Although Altaner lists a number of works of patristic biblical interpretation, as well as New Testament apocrypha, the only explicit attention he gives to the subject concerns the catechetical schools of Alexandria and Caesarea, which he characterizes as practicing a philosophically speculative, allegorical method of interpretation, and the Antiochene school of exegesis, with its more strictly scientific, historical-grammatical method of interpretation.[7] Otherwise, biblical interpretation appears only when the material absolutely demands it, such as in Origen's foregrounded exegetical method, discrete biblical commentaries by particular writers,[8] and the Bible translations of Origen and Jerome.[9] Yet even in these sections the teachings of the respective writers are still presented in lists of dogmatic loci with no reference to how they involve the authors' constant interaction with the Bible.[10] In the editions that followed World War II,[11] the same format remains, even as new topics related to the Bible began to appear, such as a section on canon development in 1950. The overall thrust of Altaner's handbook is to see a teleological progress in pa-

4. Gerhard Rauschen, *Patrologie: Die Schriften der Kirchenväter und ihr Lehrgehalt*, 10th and 11th eds., rev. Berthold Altaner (Freiburg: Herder, 1931).

5. Ibid., ix.

6. One explicitly biblical topic, fulfillment of prophecy, does appear in second- and third-century literature such as in that of Ignatius of Antioch; e.g., ibid., 63.

7. Ibid., 114, 194.

8. Ibid., 258f, 292.

9. Ibid., 122, 305.

10. E.g., ibid., 139.

11. Berthold Altaner, *Patrologie: Leben, Schriften und Lehre der Kirchenväter*, 2nd rev. ed., Herders theologische Grundrisse (Freiburg: Herder, 1950), 157–59.

tristic literature toward a proper theological science that stands on its own.[12]

While it is difficult to avoid the material evidence that the early Christian theologians were constantly reading, translating, and commenting on the scriptures, most twentieth-century textbooks tend to present their work as though the apostolic deposit of faith is a fixed given that requires no interpretation, and they imply that early Christian beliefs and practices are, for all intents and purposes, the discrete products of the mind of the fathers. The phenomenon is not limited to Roman Catholic scholarship. The Protestant Reinhold Seeberg's four-volume *Lehrbuch der Dogmengeschichte*, with editions from 1895 to 1954, contains little to nothing on scripture and biblical interpretation, except to note when certain figures weighed in on whether scripture is authoritative.[13] In English-language scholarship, the massive *Patrology* of Johannes Quasten (also a German Roman Catholic scholar) adopts a similar perspective. In the first volume of the work, published in 1950, Quasten wrote, "The twentieth century [thus far] has been predominantly concerned with the history of ideas, concepts, and terms in Christian literature, and the doctrine of the various ecclesiastical authors."[14] Accordingly, the first volume of Quasten's *Patrology* gives little attention to the Bible and biblical interpretation, and the series as a whole largely mirrors Altaner in the structure of its presentation.[15] In a sense J. N. D. Kelly's much-used *Early Christian Doctrines* (1958–77) represents the final installment of the old way of thinking, being a study in the development of dogma in the mold of Altaner and the early Quasten.

Yet, because Quasten chose to offer summaries of many of the fathers' works and to present excerpts of many passages verbatim, in effect he showcased the fathers' engagement with scripture in ways that supersede the intended format. When the third volume appeared in 1963, even more attention to the Bible and its interpretation was evident: Quasten notes, for example,

12. "Die apologetische und antihäretische Literatur des 2. Jh stellte die erste Etappe auf dem Wege zur Ausbildung einer theologischen Wissenschaft dar: Das Gesetz geistigen Lebens und Wachstums drängte weiter zu einem *systematischen* und möglichst umgassenden Ausbau der Theology, die damit zum Range einer Wissenschaft erhoben werden sollte"; ibid., 157.

13. Reinhold Seeberg, *Lehrbuch der Dogmengeschichte*, 2 vols. (Erlangen: A. Deichert, 1895–98). For an overview of Seeberg's prolific career, see Traugott Jähnichen, "Seeberg, Reinhold," in *Biographisch-Bibliographisches Kirchenlexikon* (Bautz: Herzberg, 1995), 9:1307–10.

14. Johannes Quasten, *Patrology* (Utrecht: Spectrum, 1950–86), 1:5.

15. A three-page section on Irenaeus's treatment of the Bible (ibid., 1:306–8) is an exception. Quasten gives passing attention to the biblical canon, which is otherwise taken for granted.

Gregory of Nyssa's argument that scripture must be "the guide of reason" and "the criterion of truth" when one makes use of philosophy and other secular learning[16] and Basil's appeal to the educational value of scripture in *Ad adolescentes*.[17] Fifteen years later, in the final, 1978 edition of Altaner's *Patrologie*, we find four pages of new bibliography, in very fine print, on the canon, inspiration, and role of the Bible; the principles of exegesis; texts and translations of the Bible; and commentaries, catena, and the history of interpretation.[18]

By the 1970s patristic exegesis had clearly made itself felt within the received tradition of *dogmengeschichtliche* scholarship, and the deeply biblical character of patristic literature now commanded the attention of many scholars. In a very real sense, the transition from the older history-of-doctrines method to the study of early Christian biblical interpretation as the most basic method of patristic theology is the product of the patristic sources themselves, in conjunction with related developments in the field of biblical studies. As scholars began to edit and translate patristic texts anew, beginning in earnest in the 1950s, these publications naturally included many works that focused on scripture either explicitly or implicitly. Yet it took another twenty or thirty years for the import of patristic exegesis to command the attention of scholars to a broad extent.

In the intervening decades of the 1950s and '60s, the proceedings of the Oxford Patristics Conference saw a steady increase in papers on the Bible in the early church. The German *Reallexikon für Antike und Christentum* (1950–) likewise produced important articles on biblical interpretation, and the Texte und Untersuchungen monograph series offered similar titles, thanks in part to the leadership of Kurt Aland, who was at that time collecting patristic witnesses for inclusion in the textual apparatus of the Greek New Testament. The same period saw a handful of seminal studies. In 1957 Robert Grant published his landmark *The Letter and the Spirit*, a sympathetic though not uncritical study of Origen's allegorical interpretation of scripture within the long tradition of pagan and Christian Greek allegorization. Grant concluded that, for all its failings, Origen's allegorization, by moving from the letter to the spirit of the text, served well "to translate the gospels, as least in part, into terms

16. Ibid., 3:284.

17. Ibid., 3:214.

18. Altaner, *Patrologie: Leben, Schriften und Lehre der Kirchenväter*, 8th ed., with Alfred Stuiber (Freiburg: Herder, 1978), 20–24.

meaningful in their own environment."[19] In the same period Jean Daniélou and others were pioneering the study of patristic exegesis in France. Henri de Lubac published his major study *Exégèse médiéval: Les quatre sens de l'Écriture* in 1959. Although the work is oriented toward the fourfold sense of scripture in Western medieval thought, as the title indicates, the book served to reintroduce many European readers to the hermeneutics of Origen and the mainstream patristic practice of spiritual exegesis. Although there was some reaction against works such as these that cast a scornful eye on patristic exegetical methods, often in the name of defending a modernist notion of "history,"[20] the study of early biblical interpretation advanced in noticeable ways nevertheless.

With the foundations laid of new critical editions and a number of seminal monographs and reference articles, the study of patristic exegesis began to hit its stride in the 1970s and 1980s. The 1970s saw the publication of the *Cambridge History of the Bible* (1970–), a number of monographs on patristic exegesis in Patristische Texte und Studien, the birth of the index Biblia Patristica (1975–), and the (still relatively brief) bibliography *Exegesis Patrum* by Hermann Josef Sieben (1983). Angelo Di Bernadino's *Dizionario patristico e di antichità cristiane* (1983; ET 1992)[21] presented several articles on patristic exegesis by Manlio Simonetti, who had recently authored *Profilo storico dell'esegesi patristica* (1981; English translation 1994).[22] In English the work of Rowan Greer, initially on the patristic exegesis of Hebrews (1973), provided a guide for many. Greer characteristically argued that in the early church "exegesis and theology were largely indistinguishable."[23] Two important works in the 1990s represent the sort of full-scale attention to patristic exegesis that the new generation of scholars now takes for granted. Frances Young's *Biblical Exegesis and the Formation of Christian Culture* (1997) highlights several

19. Robert M. Grant, *The Letter and the Spirit* (London: SPCK, 1957), 104.

20. On which see Young, "Interpretation of Scripture," in Harvey and Hunter, *Oxford Handbook of Early Christian Studies*, 846–64.

21. Angelo di Bernardino, ed., *Dizionario patristico e di antichità cristiane*, 2 vols. (Rome: Institutum patristicum Augustianum, 1983–84); Adrian Walford, trans., *Encyclopedia of the Early Church*, foreword and bibliographic amendments by W. H. C. Frend (Cambridge: James Clarke, 1992).

22. Manlio Simonetti, *Profilo storico dell'esegesi patristica* (Rome: Istituto Patristico Augustinianum, 1981); Simonetti, *Biblical Interpretation in the Early Church: An Historical Introduction to Patristic Exegesis*, trans. John A. Hughes (Edinburgh: T. and T. Clark, 1994).

23. Rowan A. Greer, *The Captain of Our Salvation: A Study in the Patristic Exegesis of Hebrews*, Beiträge zur Geschichte der biblischen Exegese 15 (Tübingen: Mohr, 1973); see also James L. Kugel and Rowan A. Greer, *Early Biblical Interpretation*, ed. Wayne A. Meeks, Library of Early Christianity (Philadelphia: Westminster Press, 1986).

ways in which early Christian exegesis emulated classical methods of composition and interpretation. Although the connection was not unknown, Young's book opened the eyes of many readers to the extent to which patristic biblical interpreters, especially from the third century onward, made extensive use of the tools of Hellenistic rhetoric and literary theory in their own work, and it argued that the Christian scriptures came to occupy the central cultural place that had previously been held by the Greek and Latin classics.[24] Elizabeth Clark's 1999 *Reading Renunciation* further broadened our perspective on early biblical interpretation by examining the ascetical values that patristic exegetes brought to the texts they read and how those values influenced the interpretive results. A self-described work of reception history, or "asceticized *Wirkungsgeschichte*," Clark's book argues, against the formalistic study of early interpretation, that "the moral, religious, and social values" of patristic exegetes deeply informed their interpretation of biblical texts that relate to ascetical theory and practice.[25]

In the present generation of English-speaking scholars working on patristic theology, the fathers' deep engagement with scripture is more generally recognized. In R. P. C. Hanson's *Search for the Christian Doctrine of God* (1988), which set the stage for the present discussion, biblical references pepper the work, and Hanson offers a long section near the end of the book that takes up many of the key texts in the trinitarian debates and outlines various approaches to their interpretation. John Behr's *The Way to Nicaea* (2001) brings to the fore even more clearly the way in which pre-Nicene theologians constantly worked within, and sought to define, the apostolic tradition of the scriptures.[26] In his 2004 study *Nicaea and Its Legacy*, Lewis Ayres devotes sev-

24. Young, *Biblical Exegesis and the Formation of Christian Culture* (Cambridge: Cambridge University Press, 1997).

25. Elizabeth A. Clark, *Reading Renunciation: Asceticism and Scripture in Early Christianity* (Princeton: Princeton University Press, 1999), 4, 13. Other seminal works in English from the last twenty years include Douglas Burton-Christie, *The Word in the Desert: Scripture and the Quest for Holiness in Early Christian Monasticism* (New York: Oxford University Press, 1993); Harry Y. Gamble, *Books and Readers in the Early Church: A History of Early Christian Texts* (New Haven: Yale University Press, 1995); and Paul M. Blowers, ed. and trans., *The Bible in Greek Christian Antiquity*, Bible through the Ages 1 (Notre Dame, Ind.: University of Notre Dame Press, 1997).

26. R. P. C. Hanson, *The Search for the Christian Doctrine of God: The Arian Controversy 318–381* (Edinburgh: T. and T. Clark, 1988), 543–64; Lewis Ayres, *Nicaea and Its Legacy: An Approach to Fourth-Century Trinitarian Theology* (Oxford: Oxford University Press, 2004); John Behr, *Formation of Christian Theology*, vol. 2, *The Nicene Faith* (New York: SVS, 2004). Behr's attention to patristic exegesis takes on a lower key in *The Nicene Faith*, which offers a more purely dogmatic analysis. See also the im-

eral sections in the third part of the work to the theological and spiritual use of scripture in pro-Nicene theology. And more recently, Christopher Beeley's *The Unity of Christ* (2012) reexamines the tradition of patristic Christology by concentrating on how various theologians interpreted the *communicatio idiomatum*, or the cross-predication of divine and human attributes of Christ, found in scripture. Each of these studies offers a welcome step toward a fuller appreciation of the biblical dimension of patristic trinitarian theology.

Patristic Trinitarian Theology and the Bible

That biblical exegesis played a decisive role in the development of early trinitarian theology is the fundamental presupposition of this book. The major dogmatic endeavors of the fourth and fifth centuries were concerned above all with establishing the correct interpretation of key biblical passages, to the point that theologians often structured their treatises around the exegesis of particular biblical texts. If it was once possible to focus on the development of doctrinal formulae per se, for today's scholars a serviceable history of the trinitarian controversy must give serious attention to patterns of doctrinal exegesis.

Since the second century, Christian theologians pursued their thinking on the Trinity through direct engagement with scriptural texts. If we consider Tertullian's *Against Praxeas* and Origen's *First Principles*, for example—both seminal texts in the respective Latin and Greek traditions of trinitarian theology—we discover that they are each de facto extended works of biblical interpretation. Much of what made these works so influential is that they identified key biblical texts and established a range of exegetical possibilities that set the course for trinitarian thinking in the centuries that followed. As later patristic authors addressed themselves to these well-established biblical passages, often carefully studying their forebears' exegesis, they also followed their predecessors in producing theological treatises that were sustained works of biblical interpretation. Many of the trinitarian works of Athanasius, Gregory of Nazianzus, and Augustine, for example, show a close engagement with scripture on page after page.[27]

Yet the use of scripture in these works was not always straightforward.

portant essay by Michel René Barnes, "The Fourth Century as Trinitarian Canon," in *Christian Origins: Theology, Rhetoric, and Community*, ed. Lewis Ayres (New York: Routledge, 1998), 47–67.

27. This is particularly true of Athanasius's *C. Ar.*, Gregory of Nazianzus's third and fourth *Theological Orations*, and Augustine's *Tract. in Jn.* and *Trin.*

The fathers' biblical interpretation could sometimes be problematic even by ancient standards. The confusion that could result in the high-patristic period is perhaps most evident in the pro-Nicene exegesis of Proverbs 8:22, a passage that became a flashpoint of controversy in the fourth-century debates. Prior to the Arian crisis, influential teachers of trinitarian doctrine such as Tertullian and Origen interpreted Wisdom's statement that God "created me as a beginning of his ways for his works" as referring to Christ's precosmic generation from God the Father,[28] an interpretation that reflected the plain sense of the text and its surrounding context. Apart from the word "created," which came to have a technical significance for Athanasius and his associates that it did not have beforehand, Proverbs 8 speaks rather clearly of Wisdom's life with God apart from the world, or "before the hills," as the text has it. But, for the modalist theologian Marcellus of Ancyra, who could not allow that Christ had ever existed as a preincarnate entity of any kind, Proverbs 8:22 refers not to Christ's generation from the Father before all worlds, but to his incarnation in the flesh—that is, his "creation" as Jesus of Nazareth. Marcellus influenced Athanasius's exegesis of this passage, and from the mid-fourth century onward, almost all pro-Nicene theologians adhered to this reading, against the plain sense of the text and its interpretation by earlier authorities. Yet there were some exceptions. Hilary of Poitiers advocates for both senses of the passage, the economic interpretation of the pro-Nicenes and the precosmic interpretation of the older tradition, which had been carried forward into the fourth century by the Eusebians, whom Athanasius considered enemies.[29] Hilary's interpretation not only acknowledges both sides of the question, but it leads him to develop one of the first accounts of divine infinity in the pro-

28. Tertullian, *Adv. Prax.* 6; Origen, *De Prin.* 1.2.1–2. For the interpretation of Proverbs 8:22 in the patristic era, see M. van Parys, "Exégèse et théologie trinitaire (Prov. 8:22 chez les Pères cappadociens)," *Irenikon* 43 (1970): 362–79; Anthony Meredith, "Proverbes, VIII:22 chez Origène, Athanase, Basile et Grégoire de Nysse," in *Politique et théologie chez Athanase d'Alexandrie*, ed. Charles Kannengiesser (Paris: Éditions Beauchesne, 1974): 349–57; and Maurice Dowling, "Proverbs 8:22–31 in the Christology of the Early Fathers," *Perichoresis* 8, no. 1 (2010): 47–65.

29. See Beeley, *The Unity of Christ: Continuity and Conflict in Patristic Tradition* (New Haven: Yale University Press, 2012), especially 201–3, for more on this point. As Beeley shows, both Gregory of Nyssa and Gregory of Nazianzen were to various degrees constrained by prior pro-Nicene attempts to exegete Proverbs 8:22, and their own exegesis reflects the sometimes convoluted nature of pro-Nicene exegesis. For an examination of Athanasius's attempt to make sense of the conundrum, see Charles Kannengiesser, "Lady Wisdom's Final Call: The Patristic Recovery of Proverbs 8," in *Nova doctrina vetusque: Essays on Early Christianity in Honor of Fredric W. Schlatter, S.J.*, ed. Douglas Kries and Catherine Brown Tkacz (New York: Peter Lang, 1999).

Nicene tradition, a move that may have influenced Gregory of Nyssa and that certainly had implications for the course of pro-Nicene trinitarian thought.[30]

Most patristic exegesis, however, was not so disruptive of the received tradition. One of the most consistent practices in early trinitarian exegesis was to establish a hermeneutical framework on the basis of certain major texts, which then informed how other, disputed ones were read. Athanasius's use of the prologue to John's Gospel is a premier example of this approach. Like many other patristic exegetes, Athanasius consistently uses John 1:1–14, which he takes as proof of the Son's eternal generation, to guide his exegesis of other controversial passages.[31] When his Arian opponents pointed to Christ's exaltation in Philippians 2:9–10 as evidence that the Son must be inferior to God the Father in substance,[32] Athanasius turns to John 1:14 for support in his counter-interpretation: since Christ is the Word made flesh (Jn 1:14),[33] Philippians 2 need not refer to the exaltation of his divinity, but can easily be taken as referring to his flesh. He points out that, in the text of Philippians, Christ's exaltation occurs after the incarnation: it "was not said before the Word became flesh that it might be plain that 'humbled' and 'exalted' are spoken of his human nature."[34] John's prologue thus helps Athanasius to establish a framework for interpreting other passages about Christ, particularly those under dispute at the time. These two examples illustrate the variety of ways that pro-Nicene theologians managed the relationship between scripture and trinitarian doctrine. The multitude of approaches even among the orthodox fathers is one of the main factors that invite further study.[35]

A final aspect of patristic trinitarian exegesis concerns the larger goals

30. See Mark Weedman, "The Polemical Context of Gregory of Nyssa's Doctrine of Divine Infinity," *Journal of Early Christian Studies* 18, no. 1 (2010): 81–104.

31. James D. Ernest, *The Bible in Athanasius of Alexandria*, Bible in Ancient Christianity 2 (Boston: Brill, 2004), 154. Athanasius is an important witness to this point precisely because he is so overt and deliberate in his attempt to find the scope of scripture. For an overview, see Anatolios, *Retrieving Nicaea*, 108–26. Still useful is T. E. Pollard, *Johannine Christology and the Early Church* (Cambridge: Cambridge University Press, 1970.

32. *CA* I.44.

33. *CA* I.41; NPNF 330.

34. Ibid.

35. For a detailed examination of another biblical passage, see Michel René Barnes, *The Power of God: Dunamis in Gregory of Nyssa's Trinitarian Theology* (Washington, D.C.: The Catholic University of America Press, 2001), which shows how the exegesis of 1 Cor 1:24 in the second and third centuries influenced the trinitarian controversy in the fourth century.

of the interpretive enterprise. For most theologians of this period, the ultimate purpose of biblical exegesis was spiritual in nature. Following a method pioneered by Origen, pro-Nicene theologians and others aimed to read, interpret, and teach the scriptures in a way that produced spiritual growth in Christ. Augustine's major work *The Trinity* illustrates this method beautifully. As Augustine explains at the outset, the entire work depends on the correct interpretation of the scriptures about Christ and consequently about the Trinity as a whole.[36] The work opens with an account of orthodox Christological hermeneutics, a method of reading all biblical statements about Christ as applying to the divine Son of God, either apart from the incarnation or within it, just as Gregory Nazianzen and Cyril of Alexandria had articulated previously.[37] Interpreted in this way, the scriptures provide both the Christian understanding of the Trinity, doctrinally speaking, as well as the spiritual participation in the Trinity that will be fulfilled only in the eschaton, when believers will know the Father, Son, and Holy Spirit face to face. By allowing themselves to be formed by God's self-communication in the language of scripture, Christians are thus enabled to move from the earthly concepts and images, which typically mislead on account of sin, to the transcendent God to which they properly refer.[38] This process of interpretation produces both faith and spiritual purification. Within this framework and to these ends, the rest of Augustine's work addresses many of the controversial scriptural passages that had arisen in the previous trinitarian controversy.[39]

As these brief remarks indicate, the course of patristic trinitarian exegesis was both more central and more complex than is often recognized. A great deal more work remains to be done, from the treatment of specific biblical passages to the broader relationships among exegesis, trinitarian speculation, and Christian faith and practice.

36. Augustine, *Trin.* 1.1–4.

37. Augustine, *Trin.* 1.14, 22, 28; 2.2, 4; see also Augustine, *doctr.* 1; Beeley, *Unity of Christ*, 241–46.

38. Augustine, *Trin.* 1.2.

39. Ibid., 1.4. On the polemical context of *De Trinitate* 1, see Michel René Barnes, "Exegesis and Polemic in Augustine's *De Trinitate* I," *Augustinian Studies* 30, no. 1 (1999): 43–59. Also illuminating is Barnes's "The Visible Christ and the Invisible Trinity: Mt. 5:8 in Augustine's Trinitarian Theology of 400," *Modern Theology* 19, no. 3 (2003): 329–55.

Biblical Studies

The field of biblical studies has also shown increased interest in how Christians in the first several centuries of the church interpreted the Bible, and many have noted the changes that are occurring in both research and pedagogical methods.[40] While historical criticism remains the dominant method of study, scholars have begun approaching the biblical text in a variety of new ways, some of which include increased attention to early Christian biblical interpretation and theology.

Historical Criticism of the Bible

Historical criticism—or what some scholars now prefer to call simply "historically grounded" study—aims to establish the original ancient meaning of biblical texts. The original or historical meaning of the Bible is normally identified with the original author(s)' intention in writing or editing the text and/or how the original audience would have understood it. As a collection of submethods or disciplines, historical criticism makes use of text criticism and philology, which help to establish the original wording and lexical meaning of texts; form criticism and redaction criticism, which aid in identifying possible sources used and the editorial or authorial tendencies of a text; the tools of literary criticism, both modern and postmodern; archeology; and social-scientific analysis, among others.[41] Historical critics typically eschew interpretations that synthesize large parts of the Bible, choosing instead to focus on individual authors and texts independent of one another, and they tend to emphasize the vast difference between the ancient contexts of the Bible and those of modern interpreters. As many have noted, the overriding aim of historical-critical scholarship is to arrive at the singular meaning of the text wherever possible, however much scholars may debate what that one meaning is. Related concerns include assessing the historical factuality of events related in the Bible and reconstructing alternative views of Christian origins from those presented in the New Testament, often drawing on noncanonical documents, some of which have been discov-

40. For a helpful recent overview of the field, see Megan Bishop Moore and Milton C. Moreland, "Historical Criticism," in *The Oxford Encyclopedia of Biblical Interpretation*, ed. Steven L. McKenzie, 2 vols. (New York: Oxford University Press, 2014).

41. Dale Martin, *Pedagogy of the Bible: An Analysis and Proposal* (Louisville: Westminster John Knox Press, 2008), 9.

ered only in the last century, such as the trove of Gnostic texts found at Nag Hammadi in 1945 and the Dead Sea Scrolls discovered between 1946 and 1956.

The Limitations of Historical Criticism

For all of its strengths, the limitations of historical criticism have increasingly attracted the attention not only of theologians, clergy, and scholars outside the field, but also that of trained biblical scholars who practice historical criticism professionally. Perhaps the most glaring limitation is one that was self-imposed at the outset of historical criticism in the nineteenth century: the sharp distinction between historical (sometimes called "scholarly") interpretation and "theological," ecclesiastical, or devotional meanings ascribed to the biblical text. With some notable exceptions,[42] scholars have often been so concerned to strip away the accretions of later theologians and church bodies that they have de facto rejected any attempt to read the biblical texts with theological or doctrinal questions in mind. Consequently, the biblical text came to be seen as solely a historical artifact whose theological or religious elements were systematically excluded from serious study. While most would agree that nineteenth- and twentieth-century scholars were right to insist that the interpretation of the Bible should be subject to historical inquiry and human reason, there is a growing consensus that they erred in claiming that those processes are mutually exclusive with theological and devotional meanings. Robert Grant spoke for many in his comment nearly sixty years ago that there will inevitably be "an indissoluble mixture of theology and history" in a religion that speaks of God's working in history, a mixture that theologians such as Origen (Grant's immediate subject) labored diligently to interpret.[43]

In its simplest form, the claim that the original historical meaning of a biblical text does not refer to God or has nothing to say about God, who is the subject of theology, not only ignores the character of the texts but is also impossible to justify on the grounds of the established science of historical biblical scholarship. The historical critic is not in a position to assess the truth of beliefs that derive from the theological content of the Bible. Conversely,

42. E.g., the "lux mundi" project by a collection of English scholars and the work of German scholar Gerhard von Rad: see Charles Gore, ed., *Lux Mundi: A Series of Studies in the Religion of the Incarnation*, 4th ed. (London: J. Murray, 1890); Gerhard von Rad, trans. and commentary, *Das erste Buch Mose: Das Alte Testament deutsch 2–4* (Göttingen: Vandenhoeck and Ruprecht, 1953).

43. Grant, *Letter and the Spirit*, 114.

to hold that the theological formulations and the devotional experiences and practices of the Bible's readers have nothing to do with the original historical meaning of the text risks misunderstanding those formulations and practices, as well. This is not to claim, in reverse, that later theological beliefs and practices have an equal claim to being "biblical"—they are not immune to critical study just because they are churchly or theological—but it is false on both historical and purely rational grounds to claim that such beliefs cannot possibly represent authentic, original biblical meaning.

A related problem is the confusion of two different senses of the word "history." As New Testament scholar Dale Martin notes,[44] while most Christians and many biblical interpreters would want to maintain that the significance of the biblical text, and of Christianity itself, in large part consists in its relation to "historical" events, above all the history of Israel and the life, death, and resurrection of Jesus Christ, what that claim means can differ significantly. It can mean that the people of Israel and the career of Jesus are things that existed or events that happened in the past, but it can also mean that they are things that can be adequately understood by the methods of modern historical scholarship, and that is another matter entirely. There are many aspects of human life even in our own time that most people would say the historian is not in a position to explain in any exhaustive sense. To claim that the true, or even the original, meaning of the biblical text can be provided by the historian, apart from any other sort of knowledge, is far-fetched in this sense, as well. In short, the theological claims that define Christianity, most of which are represented fairly straightforwardly in the pages of scripture, "can neither be confirmed nor denied by modern historiographical methods," however helpful those methods might be for contributing to a fuller understanding of such claims.[45]

Analogously, difficulties arise as well from the way in which some historical critics manage the distinction between humanly generated meaning and the notion that the Bible is divinely inspired and conveys the word of God.

44. Martin, *Pedagogy of the Bible*, 41–42.

45. Ibid., 42. In Martin's judgment, to insist that historical criticism is indispensable for understanding the Bible properly is a form of "modernist imperialism" (44). Martin arguably goes too far in associating the claims of modern historiographical research with all historical knowledge—e.g., in his claim that "historical criticism ... is not necessary for confirming or understanding, Christianly, the foundational events of Christianity." Some of the types of judgment that historical critics make *are* involved in Christian beliefs about God and Christ. As the church fathers maintained, the knowledge of God comes *through* the earthly means of language, bodies, mental cognition, and judgment—including much of what we would call history—not apart from them.

The assumption that human and divine fields of meaning are mutually exclusive cannot be established on the basis of the biblical text or the parameters of rational inquiry. When we consider the mainstream traditions of biblical interpretation that derive from Origen or Augustine, who argued that the biblical text was *both* humanly generated in very particular and earthy historical circumstances *and* divinely inspired, the historian is simply not in a position to judge one way or the other.

Without denying the veracity of certain historical-critical interpretations, the exclusion of theological and devotional meanings from proper biblical interpretation has proven to be both intellectually false and exclusive of whole swathes of responsible and quite sophisticated biblical interpretation, including much of Christian history prior to the advent of modern historical criticism. Among those readers who have been excluded from proper interpretation have been women, minorities, and other communities that look very different from the scholarly leadership of most Anglo-European academies until fairly recently.

Further limitations derive from the epistemological construction of historical criticism. The most serious liability here is the implicit avowal of historical positivism and objectivism—the belief that there is a fact or meaning "out there," like a sort of object, that the scholar will be able to discover and verify, either self-evidently or against some other external standard. The major problem with this approach is that it pretends that the interpreter him- or herself is outside of the phenomena being investigated rather than being a participant in the construction of the realities that she or he is trying to understand. (This is not to deny objective reality, but to deny that human beings are in a position to define and evaluate that reality without the conditions of knowledge impinging on the data and vice versa.) Historical positivism in turn allows the scholar to claim with great certainty that he or she has discovered *the* true meaning of the text and to insist that any who disagree are simply wrong. Moreover, the assumption that the primary or true meaning of a text exists only in its original situation is not self-evident, either. Positivist critics tend to exempt themselves from examining their existential condition and their cultural and personal biases, which might color the results of interpretation,[46]

46. The recognition that this is a potential problem in biblical scholarship has helped fuel the rise of a number of different interpretative frameworks that begin from the historical situation of the reader. For two very different examples, see Elizabeth Clark, *History, Theory, Text: Historians and the Linguistic Turn*

while the wholesale dismissal of readers and audiences in other times and places impoverishes the enterprise. The parallels between this sort of stance and the power wielded by colonial authorities have not been lost on the readers of some modern biblical scholarship.

Four Recent Proposals

To be sure, the strengths of at least a modified form of historical criticism remain, and the method continues to anchor most disciplined biblical scholarship. Nevertheless, the recognition of problems such as these has spurred a number of biblical scholars to explore new approaches to reading the Bible. Here we look briefly at four assessments and proposals from a variety of biblical scholars.

(1) Following the developments in philosophical hermeneutics in the twentieth century and reaching as far back as Plato, German Old Testament scholar Manfred Oeming examines a broad range of methods currently used to study the Bible, from high-modern historical criticism to varieties of literary criticism and theory, archeological studies, feminist exegesis, liberation theology, and psychological exegesis.[47] Oeming evaluates the strengths and weaknesses of each method in light of a circle (or square) of communication that includes authors and readers. Communication and meaning-making run dynamically in both directions around the circle between authors and readers, by means of texts and subject matter. The circle is meant to illustrate the fact that interpreters are part of a process of interpretation and meaning-making together with the author, text, and subject matter, not outside of or apart from them.

Integral to Oeming's argument is the observation that each method has strengths and blind spots. Similar to the medieval fourfold sense of scripture, multiple approaches are therefore needed to interpret the Bible in any full sense.[48] For Oeming, the choice of method should depend on the particular text at hand, the context of the interpreter, and the purpose of the interpretation. Speaking from within the field of academic biblical study, Oeming warns that interpreters must "relativize our passion for objectivity" by think-

(Cambridge, Mass.: Harvard University Press, 2004), and Janice Capel Anderson and Stephen D. Moore, eds., *Mark and Method: New Approaches in Biblical Studies*, 2nd ed. (Minneapolis: Fortress, 2008).

47. Manfred Oeming, *Contemporary Biblical Hermeneutics: An Introduction*, trans. Joachim F. Vette (Aldershot: Ashgate, 2006).

48. Ibid., 141, 143.

ing less of bulletproof explanations, as if biblical interpretation were a natural science, and more of "subjectively coloured and complex *understanding* that can be measured only to a degree and only with great difficulty."[49] By emphasizing that the true location of biblical studies is in the humanities, scholars are reminded that it is impossible to define precisely the methods of interpretation, let alone to use them mechanically.[50] On the one hand, Oeming stresses that interpreters must bear in mind the persistent distinction between the original sense of the text and its later reception, and the original sense must retain priority in the academic study of the Bible. Yet, on the other hand, he urges that historical criticism remain open to insights from other quarters, remember that it does not have a monopoly on interpretation, and adapt itself accordingly. By practicing interpretation in this way, he believes, scholars may help to rebuild some of the reputation of biblical exegesis.[51]

(2) Canadian-British New Testament scholar Markus Bockmuehl has issued a proposal for the future of New Testament study that represents much of the agenda of reception history, which we discuss further later.[52] Bockmuehl likewise urges scholars to recognize that the reader is involved in the work of interpretation, even deeply so, yet draws our attention more directly to the concrete traditions of interpretation in which readers find themselves. For Bockmuehl, the biblical text is not a purely passive instrument awaiting the work of the reader upon it, but, in the language of literary critic Umberto Eco, it has an *intentio operis*, a purposeful meaning, and even an existential aim that guide a range of possible meanings. He regards the Christian scriptures primarily as a word of address, a proclamation that confronts the reader with the gospel about which it speaks. Bockmuehl is not denying that texts require active readers in order to convey meaning, but he is maintaining that the Bible, when read with a modicum of responsibility and accuracy, does indeed have

49. Ibid., 146, italics in original.

50. Ibid., 147.

51. Ibid., 144; see also Werner G. Jeanrond, *Text und Interpretation als Kategorien Theologischen Denkens*, Hermeneutische Untersuchungen zur Theologie 23 (Tübingen: Mohr Siebeck, 1986); Anthony C. Thiselton, *New Horizons in Hermeneutics* (Grand Rapids: Zondervan 1992); and Sandra M. Schneiders, *The Revelatory Text: Interpreting the New Testament as Sacred Scripture*, 2nd ed. (Collegeville, Minn.: Liturgical Press 1999).

52. Markus N. A. Bockmuehl, *Seeing the Word: Refocusing New Testament Study*, Studies in Theological Interpretation (Grand Rapids, Mich.: Baker Academic, 2006). See also the review "Seeing the Word: Refocusing New Testament Study," by C. Kavin Rowe, in *Pro Ecclesia* 18, no. 1 (2009): 111–15.

a particular (if complex) message that makes a demand on the life of readers, whether or not they choose to respond to that demand. The New Testament, moreover, presumes a certain kind of reader—namely, a Christian believer who has undergone "a religious, moral, and intellectual *conversion* to the gospel of which the documents speak."[53]

Accordingly, the Bible is so "intertwined with its own tradition of hearing and heeding, interpretation and performance" that good interpretation involves a confluence between the implied reader of the text and the history of its effects, including the present-day actual reader. This continuity of text, interpretation, and meaning in history gives the living memory of the apostles and the immediately succeeding generations a functional importance as "a vital historical index" of the range of possible meanings of authentic apostolic faith, which the Bible seeks to convey.[54] Hence, the reception and interpretation of scripture in the context of the memory of the apostles in the early church is a necessary part of proper biblical interpretation.

(3) American New Testament scholar Dale Martin offers yet another proposal for refining the way the Bible is studied and, especially, how it should be taught in theological schools and seminaries.[55] Martin affirms several of the limitations of historical criticism noted— above all, the overreach of historical study into claims about theological meaning and the classical truths of the Christian faith. In response, he proposes a curriculum that teaches historical criticism as one among other ways of reading, but with no privileged position among the rest. Yet the heart of Martin's proposal is to advocate for renewed *theological* knowledge and skills that readers can bring to the work of interpretation, beginning with a theology of the scriptures before specific methods of interpretation are taught.[56] For Martin, the surest way to acquire a sound foundation in theology is to study premodern biblical interpretation, which was not arbitrary, as is sometimes thought, but rather "the product of the employment of skills learned in important socialization" in Christian communities.[57] The aim is not to replicate premodern exegesis, but to learn basic theological and exegetical principles from skilled interpreters and to let their

53. Bockmuehl, *Seeing the Word*, 70.

54. Ibid., 188.

55. Martin, *Pedagogy of the Bible*.

56. Ibid., 101–2.

57. Ibid., 47.

works inspire the Christian imagination of today's readers, enabling us also to reassess our own contemporary interpretive assumptions while connecting today's interpreters with Christian readers of the past.[58] For Martin, what interpreters of the Bible need most of all is "theological sophistication."[59]

(4) Another trend in recent scholarship bears mentioning because it correlates study of the Bible with study of the early church in direct ways. A number of scholars have begun to attend to the ways in which the very text of the New Testament bears the marks of the theological and practical interests of early Christian communities, including, eventually, the highly networked, international "great church" of which Irenaeus and other church fathers speak.[60] The fundamental insight here is that the redaction, collection, and selection of biblical texts was intimately tied up with the ongoing theological concerns and practical life of early Christian communities. From this perspective it makes even more sense to study the Bible in close connection with early Christian theology and biblical interpretation.

Reception History

The trends described thus far have mainly been internal to each discipline. However, one recent movement has begun to demonstrate the possibilities of a convergence between the two in more obvious ways. Building on twentieth-century developments in literary theory and the philosophy of history, the hermeneutical practice known as "reception history" approaches the task of biblical exegesis by attending to the history of its interpretation, often drawing heavily on patristic resources.

The study of the reception history of the Bible arose in part from the reaction against historical positivism by philosopher Hans-Georg Gadamer, who

58. Ibid., 49.

59. Ibid., 91.

60. The literature in this area is of widely varied types; see, e.g., Bart D. Ehrman, *The Orthodox Corruption of Scripture: The Effect of Early Christological Controversies on the Text of the New Testament* (New York: Oxford University Press, 1993); Paul Ricouer, "The Canon between the Text and the Community," in *Philosophical Hermeneutics and Biblical Exegesis*, ed. Petr Pokorny and Jan Roskovec, Wissenschaftliche Untersuchungen zum Neuen Testament 153 (Tubingen: Mohr, 2002), 7–26; and Ched Spellman, *Toward a Canon-Conscious Reading of the Bible: Exploring the History and Hermeneutic of the Canon* (Sheffield: Sheffield Phoenix Press, 2014). This type of study is to be distinguished from the method of "canonical criticism" advocated by Brevard S. Childs, *Introduction to the Old Testament as Scripture* (London: SCM, 1979), and other works.

decried the claims to scientific objectivity in much modern interpretation.[61] Gadamer stressed that interpreters do not stand above history, able to describe it as an object, but that they exist within history, are a product of it, and are formed by it: "history does not belong to us; we belong to it."[62] Contrary to the near-canonical claim of modern scholarship, Gadamer argued that the temporal distance between ancient texts and modern interpreters is not a fundamental problem to be overcome, as historical critics have long maintained, so much as "a positive and productive condition enabling understanding. It is not a yawning abyss but is filled with the continuity of custom and tradition, in the light of which everything handed down presents itself to us."[63] To imagine that the modern interpreter stands at the far side of a vast chasm of difference equipped with powerful tools that will help him or her to reconstruct the strange conditions on the other side is, in Gadamer's view, a naïve assumption of modern historicism. Indeed, one may fairly ask, if the ancient past is so unequivocally strange to us, how would we know that? How could we interpret anything at all in Christian antiquity if there were not some points of continuity and connection that provide linguistic anchors and standards of comparison by which we are able to translate the things that we do not understand? How, indeed, would we know them *to be strange* if there were not a more fundamental point of similarity? In this regard Gadamer's work finds a parallel in Ludwig Wittgenstein's argument against modernist epistemologies beginning with Descartes. In his posthumous work *On Certainty*, Wittgenstein seeks to demonstrate that a fundamental layer of trust and certainty necessarily precedes doubt and questioning and that, without this broader framework of certainty, doubting would not even be possible.[64] For those engaged in biblical interpretation, the likes of Gadamer and Wittgenstein showed that the epistemological positivism implied in much biblical historical criticism is unfounded.

Gadamer's work set the backdrop for the development of reception history

61. See Christopher Rowland and Ian Boxall, "Reception Criticism and Theory," in *The Oxford Encyclopedia of Biblical Interpretation*, ed. Steven L. McKenzie (Oxford: Oxford University Press, 2013), 206–15.

62. Hans-Georg Gadamer, *Truth and Method*, trans. Joel Weinsheimer and Donald G. Marshall, 2nd rev. ed. (New York: Crossroad, 1989), 276.

63. Ibid., 297.

64. E.g., Ludwig Wittgenstein, *On Certainty*, ed. G. E. M. Anscombe and G. H. von Wright, trans. Denis Paul and G. E. M. Anscombe (Oxford: Blackwell, 1969), §337: "The game of doubting itself presupposes certainty"; see also §§115, 125, 163, 341.

as a formal academic discipline. German literary critic Hans-Robert Jauss then transposed Gadamer's insights into the practice of literary criticism, particularly in his 1967 essay "Literary History as a Challenge to Literary Theory."[65] Jauss concentrated his attention on the question of how a historically located text can have universal relevance, or, in the case of the Bible, how an ancient text can have an influence on modern readers. Over against theories that see texts as absolute, either in their historical contexts or simply as self-contained artifacts, Jauss argues that we can assess the aesthetic value of a text not by searching for the author's intention or for some universal aesthetic standard. Instead, he says, we must consider the "active reception" of the text, by which he means the ways that readers react to and appropriate texts within their own contexts and expectations.[66] While it may sound as though Jauss is advocating a sort of subjective response that assigns the task of meaning-making solely to the reader, regardless of the author's intention or the text's historical context, he stresses, on the contrary, that the reader always approaches a text within a "transsubjective horizon of understanding,"[67] which includes not only other texts by the same author but also texts of both similar and differing genres. Interpretation thus always takes place within a well-established set of expectations and a very full context. Because each text carries with it an entire history that includes not only the circumstances of its production but also its reception by other readers, the thorough interpreter is obligated to assess the circumstances of that history.[68] And because other texts and the various influences on the interpretive process are now overtly acknowledged, their involvement in interpretation can be assessed and further investigated, making reception history, in a sense, more objective than modernist historical criticism can claim to be. As a result of these and similar developments in literary criticism, the notion that the reader's preconceptions and the history of interpretation affect the result of interpretation is commonplace in many circles.

The reception history, or reception criticism, of the Bible includes a wide variety of readers and interpreters, whether ecclesiastical, academic, or non-

65. Hans-Robert Jauss, "Literary History as a Challenge to Literary Theory," in *Theory and History of Literature*, vol. 2, *Toward an Aesthetic of Reception*, trans. Timothy Bahti (Minneapolis: University of Minnesota Press, 1982), 3–45.

66. Ibid., 19.

67. Ibid., 23.

68. Ibid., 22.

academic, or in media other than writing. (The related notion of *Wirkungsgeschichte*, "the history of effects," typically focuses on the influence of the biblical text in other times and places rather than on the text itself as illuminated by later readings.) Reception critics believe not only that they are free to consult the interpretations of other interpreters in the past and present, but that good interpretation must take into account the historical traditions that connect us to the scriptures, however consciously or unconsciously we may be aware of them at first. While many Christian readers find reception history amenable to explicit theologies of tradition, reception history as a method does not formally entail a particular view about the relationship between tradition and scripture. By more directly incorporating the reader and the history of interpretation in the work of biblical interpretation, reception critics argue, we stand to make better historical readings of texts, because a fuller scope of human activity and context is now in view. Reception criticism is thus not so much a distinct method of scholarship as it is a dynamic process in which interpretation takes place, potentially involving a range of literary, historical, theological, and performative modes. Yet its focus on the participation of interpreters in the act of interpretation does contrast with the presumed nonparticipatory objectivity of much historical criticism. The inclusion in this volume of several essays that attend to reception history is meant to demonstrate the possibilities of this approach for both biblical and patristic studies.

The Present Volume

This book is intended to represent the sort of broad, cross-disciplinary biblical interpretation that our respective fields have come to value in recent years. One of our operating assumptions is that scholarship on the Bible and other early Christian texts has too often languished from resistance to work outside of the confines of a particular discipline. Our aim is to allow scholars from each discipline to converse with each other about common texts in order to produce the sort of broad readings that will further the work of interpretation. This book, which began as a multi-year consultation on the Bible and early Christian theology in the Society of Biblical Literature, is intended to open new vistas and raise new questions rather than to offer single, definitive interpretations once and for all. By modeling cutting-edge biblical and historical-theological scholarship we provide concrete examples of the possibilities inherent in this type of dialogue.

This is an opportune conversation to have for several reasons. Not only do the two fields dovetail in their common interest in early Christian biblical interpretation, but, as many of us have long believed, they have much to learn from one another. Just as patristics scholars are giving more attention to the foundational role of scripture in the development of early Christianity, biblical scholars are becoming more interested in the role that the history of early biblical interpretation and theology can play in the task of contemporary biblical exegesis. Biblical scholars can benefit from studying patristic patterns of exegesis, as well as the methods with which scholars of early Christianity understand the interplay between theology and exegesis in patristic-era sources. Similarly, patristic scholars can benefit from the ways in which biblical scholars seek to establish the meaning of biblical texts in their own historical location and identity. By becoming better able to assess whether patristic authors have interpreted the biblical text well, scholars will be in a better position to evaluate both the history of biblical exegesis and the development of Christian theology.

Our decision to focus on questions of trinitarian doctrine is likewise intended to open up a range of substantive and methodological insights. We focus on trinitarian doctrine not only because it lies at the heart of Christian theology and church life, but because it illustrates so well the complex relationship between the Bible and theological development in the early church. Current scholars are increasingly aware that pro-Nicene doctrines of God did not progress inexorably to the supposed anchor point of Christ's consubstantiality with God the Father or to the fabled definition of "one nature, three persons," which was once believed to represent the logical crux of all orthodox trinitarian theology. Recent studies have shown, instead, that pro-Nicene thought ran in multiple and sometimes circuitous channels; that key elements of what eventually became trinitarian orthodoxy, particularly the work of the Cappadocians, drew significantly from streams that were originally *anti*-Nicene; and that the goals of orthodox theology were often very different from these and other formulae that later scholars and churchmen attributed to the fathers and the early councils.[69] Patristic trinitarian doctrine was not a grand effort to define the categories of

69. The scholarly literature on this point is substantial and growing; see the key works listed in nn. 26–27.

ousia and hypostasis, or any other metaphysical construct, let alone to establish the veracity of the creed of Nicaea, as it has often been imagined. Rather, what unites the orthodox theologians of the patristic period is their attempt to make sense of the biblical text within the lived practice of the catholic faith and vice versa.

These essays by leading scholars in each field are concerned with the use of the biblical text in the development of trinitarian theology and with the historical-critical reading of trinitarian doctrine in the biblical texts. The first set of essays considers trinitarian theology in the Old and New Testaments at large. In his essay "Scholarship on the Old Testament Roots of Trinitarian Theology: Blind Spots and Blurred Vision," Bogdan Bucur uses reception history in order to reinterpret the Genesis theophanies, which were a standard source of trinitarian doctrine in the early church. As a new entrée into the study of trinitarian theology in the Old Testament, Bucur's chapter identifies a variety of early Christian approaches to biblical theophanies in exegetical, doctrinal, hymnographic, and iconographic productions of Genesis 18. An essay by Larry Hurtado, "Observations on the 'Monotheism' Affirmed in the New Testament," then identifies key features of the mutation of ancient Jewish monotheism into the early Christian belief that Jesus is both distinguished from God ("the Father") and yet also intimately linked with God in belief and devotional practice.

A second set of essays considers trinitarian questions in relation to the Gospel of John. In the first piece, "Trinitarian Theology and the Fourth Gospel," Harold Attridge argues that the basic building blocks of what later came to be regarded as trinitarian orthodoxy are indeed present, if often implicitly, in the Fourth Gospel, as seen particularly in the narrative strategies of the final form of the text. Paul Anderson similarly examines proto-trinitarian elements in "The Johannine Riddles and Their Place in the Development of Trinitarian Theology." Anderson concentrates on the evangelist's dialectical thinking, the agency of Jesus as the Son sent from the Father, and the literary-rhetorical devices of the narrator. Moving into the patristic period, Marianne Meye Thompson's "The Gospel of John and Early Trinitarian Thought: The Unity of God in John, Irenaeus, and Tertullian," analyzes the relationship between the Fourth Gospel's presentation of the Father, Son, and Holy Spirit and that of second-century writers Irenaeus and Tertullian. Thompson has in view both explicit and implicit judgments about the Father, Son, and Spirit, their relationship to one another, and the unity of God. What follows are two essays that consider the role of John's Gospel in early trinitarian theology. Mark Edwards's "The Johannine Prologue before Origen" examines the textual variants of John 1:13 and 1:14 in order to reconsider the translation of "Logos" and the meaning of the terms "begotten," "made," and "created" in early trinitarian development and in the Latin Vulgate and later English Bibles. Second, Mark DelCogliano's essay "Basil of Caesarea on John 1:1 as an Affirmation of Pro-Nicene Trinitarian Doctrine" explores several details of Basil's use of the Gospel of John to develop his pro-Nicene trinitarian doctrine. DelCogliano argues that Basil's interpretation of John 1:1 is a unique, and somewhat remarkable, synthesis of the earlier interpretations of Origen and other exegetical traditions.

A third major unit covers trinitarian themes in Paul's writings. In a general study on "Paul and the Trinity," Stephen Fowl argues that a pro-Nicene interpretation of Paul succeeds as a way of adjudicating perceived tensions between God's singularity and the Christological maximalism of Paul's letters. Fowl thus offers an alternative to a fairly common view among biblical scholars that the Trinity of later Christian metaphysics is incompatible with Paul's ideas about God and Jesus Christ. Adela Yarbro Collins's "Paul and His Legacy to Trinitarian Theology" next offers a detailed study of Paul's language about God, Christ, and the Spirit within the context of Second Temple Judaism and relevant Greek and Roman texts and in the aftermath of Paul's work in the deutero-Pauline epistles and several patristic authors. Three final essays concentrate on the patristic reception of Paul. Jennifer Strawbridge's "The Image and Unity of God: The Role of Colossians 1 in Theological Controversy" examines the interpretation of Colossians 1:15–20, the most frequently cited Pauline text in pre-Nicene theology. Strawbridge shows how patristic writers from Irenaeus through the Arian controversy drew on Colossians 1 to counter problematic notions of either a divided Christ (human and divine) or a divided God (Father and Son), and she highlights the complex hermeneutical moves required to achieve this end. In a second broad, comparative study, Christopher Beeley's "The Spirit and the Letter: 2 Corinthians 3:6 in Fourth-Century Greek Exegesis" traces the legacy of Origen's spiritual exegesis among major fourth-century theologians by concentrating on the varying interpretations of Paul's famous statement that "the letter kills, but the Spirit gives life." Finally, Mark Weedman's essay "Augustine's Move from a Johannine to a Pauline Trinitarian Theology" draws our attention to an important, but typically unrecognized, shift in the development of Augustine's trinitarian theology. Weedman shows that, by changing his focus from John's Gospel to the writings of Paul in his thinking about the Trinity, Augustine moved from an earlier emphasis on the Logos as revealer of God to the notion of Christ incarnate as the mediator of redemption.

Each of these essays illuminates an important aspect of the biblical teaching on the Trinity and its interpretation in early Christian theology. We hope that the conversation offered here will contribute to the ongoing work of biblical and patristics scholars and to the study of early Christian biblical interpretation at large.

PART I

TRINITARIAN THEOLOGY IN THE OLD AND NEW TESTAMENTS

Bogdan G. Bucur

1. SCHOLARSHIP ON THE OLD TESTAMENT ROOTS OF TRINITARIAN THEOLOGY

Blind Spots and Blurred Vision

Introduction

In what follows, I offer two critical observations on scholarly treatments of the emergence of Trinitarian theology in early Christianity. I discuss, first, the hypothesis that the early Christian appropriation of the Old Testament, especially of biblical theophanies, led, in a first stage, to the formation of "binitarian monotheism," followed later by the full-blown Trinitarianism that would constitute the classic position of the church. It seems to me that this account is emblematic for the type of problems associated with the entire project of giving a scholarly account of early Trinitarian doctrine. The second part of the essay will examine some of the biblical texts that have played an important role in the articulation of early Trinitarian theology—namely, Genesis 18, Isaiah 6, and Habakkuk 3:2 (LXX). My thesis is that the exegetical, doctrinal, hymnographic, and iconographic productions that illustrate the reception history of these texts offer a variety of exegetical approaches, which, however, are not adequately distinguished by the current scholarly concepts.

Is Binitarian Monotheism a First Step toward Trinitarian Theology?

Scholars of early Christianity such as Gilles Quispel, Jarl Fossum, Alan Segal, Larry Hurtado, Daniel Boyarin, and Richard Bauckham often note that Christian worship and theological reflection in the early centuries are characterized by a "binitarian" pattern.[1] Although the terms vary in scholarship—"relative dualism," "binitarian dualism," "complementary dualism," "Jewish 'two-power' traditions," "heterodox Jewish binitarianism," or, more recently, "dyadic devotional pattern"—the point is to conceptualize the early Christian worship of Jesus as Lord and God within the context of continued exclusive devotion to the Lord God of Israel. The defining mark of the emerging Jesus movement would be that, while similar to the "two-power" theology characteristic of the prerabbinic or nonrabbinic forms of Judaism (e.g., Philo's language of Logos as "second God"; the memrā-theology of the Targums), it views the "second power," the Logos, as having "become flesh and lived among us" (Jn 1:14) and being set forth to be worshipped as "Lord and God" (Jn 20:28) in a cultic setting.

But "binitarian"/"binitarianism" is an older coinage. In an 1898 encyclopedia article on Christology, Friedrich Loofs first used "binitarischer Monotheismus" to designate an early stage of Christian reflection at which the heavenly reality of Christ was thought of not in terms of a preexistent λόγος, but rather as a πνεῦμα whose distinction from God begins only at the indwelling of the man Jesus.

As such, *binitarianism* is associated with *Geistchristologie*—another favorite Loofsian term, designating the inability to account theologically for a distinction between Pneuma and Logos. Loofs's concept of "binitarianism" entered Adolf von Harnack's *Lehrbuch der Dogmengeschichte*, starting with the fourth edition, in 1909. Since then, a large group of early Christian writers have been diagnosed with *Geistchristologie* and binitarianism, and the combination of the two is generally viewed as a sort of growing pains in the maturation of early Trinitarian theology.

The discussion of the pre-Nicene Trinitarian deficiency and the problems it raises for classical definitions of faith is a much older one, however, already

1. For a more extensive account, see Bogdan G. Bucur, "'Early Christian Binitarianism': From Religious Phenomenon to Polemical Insult to Scholarly Concept," *Modern Theology* 27 (2011): 102–20.

in full swing in the seventeenth century. I have in mind a treatise published in 1700, bearing the title *Platonism Unveiled, or an Essay Concerning the Notions and Opinions of Plato and Some Ancient and Modern Divines, His Followers, in Relation to the Logos, or Word, in Particular, and the Doctrine of the Trinity in General.* The author, Matthieu Souverain (1656–1700), who was a master of many languages and well versed in both patristic and rabbinic literature, argued that the scriptural references to the second and third persons of the Trinity were initially meant in reference to God's *Shekinah*. That early Christians misunderstood this circumlocution for God himself is only due to the growing influence of Greek thought over their theology—hence, Souverain's stated intention of unveiling the source of "the doctrine of Trinity in general": Platonism! One step back from Souverain's sophisticated discourse and it becomes abundantly clear that the same ideas were put forth by Unitarian theologians at war with the early church's "absurd," "monstrous," "heathen," "horrible" fabrication—the doctrine of the Trinity. This sort of anti-Trinitarian controversy literature found that the pure tradition of the apostles had been corrupted by "Platonism" and often points to Justin Martyr as a prime example of the phenomenon. This is not without irony, since the mantra of scholarship in the past century has been that Justin is not a good enough Trinitarian!

It is clear that in the original (Loofsian) setting, *Geistchristologie* and "binitarianism" are not objective descriptors of an early Christian phenomenon, but notions carrying significant theological freight. Less obvious—or at least less discussed—are the theological assumptions that undergird the more recent use of "binitarian" and "binitarianism." It is true that Loofs and his followers write about the early church's attempts at altering an originally *low* view of Jesus of Nazareth by positing his preexistence in terms of "spirit" and, later, by articulating a Logos doctrine of Hellenic import, while the more recent scholars mentioned previously are concerned with the emergence of a very early *high* Christology. Nevertheless, we are dealing in both cases with scholarly descriptions of a first stage in the development that led, eventually, to full Trinitarian theology. It is significant in this respect that Segal authored an essay entitled, "'Two Powers in Heaven' and Early Christian Trinitarian Thinking," and that Hurtado quotes approvingly Darryl Hannah's view that the *Ascension of Isaiah* reflects "a primitive effort at what later became Trinitarian doctrine" and himself speaks of "the struggle to work out doctrinal formulations that could express in some coherent way this peculiar view of God as 'one' and yet somehow comprising 'the Father' and Jesus, *thereafter also including the Spirit as the third 'Person' of the Trinity.*'"[2] It seems, then, that the characterization of earliest Christian devotion as binitarian or dyadic—a form of "two powers in heaven"—includes the anticipation of a later "triadic" stage—let's call it "three powers in heaven"—that is identified with the classical Christian Trinitarian doctrine.

Both the two-step evolutionary process leading from a binitarian to a Trinitarian pattern of worship and the assumed theoretical framework for thinking God as Trinity are problematic. Let me start with the latter and appeal to the witness of Gregory of Nazianzus, the champion of classic Trinitarian theology. Addressing those who possess a theology of the divine Son but refuse to grant the same status to the Spirit, Gregory writes (*Orat.* 31.13–14):

> Though ... you are in revolt from the Spirit, you worship the Son. What right have you, to accuse us of tritheism—are you not ditheists (τί φατε τοῖς τριθεΐταις ἡμῖν ... ὑμεῖς δὲ οὐ διθεῖται)? ... If you do revere the Son ... we shall put a question to you: What defense would you make, were you charged with ditheism? ... The very arguments you can use to rebut the accusation will suffice for us against the charge of tritheism.

It is obvious that "ditheism" is used here as a rhetorical put-down of his adversaries. Their accusation—adding a third term to the divinity amounts to "tritheism"—applies to their own addition of the Son to the "one God" of scripture, and they know full well that such a charge is refuted by stating that the distinction of the hypostases does not preclude the fundamental oneness of the divinity. They are, indeed, "ditheists"—that is, they believe in distinct "powers," which happen to be two—and Gregory's accusation corresponds to the rabbinic charge against those who worship "two powers in heaven" and thereby also to the scholarly notion of "binitarianism." By contrast, Gregory's own theology is not "tritheistic" according to the same logic, since it does not count several powers but, as he states repeatedly, "the one single Godhead and Power." In short, the Christian worship of God as Trinity, at least as defended

2. Alan F. Segal, "'Two Powers in Heaven' and Early Christian Trinitarian Thinking," in *The Trinity: An Interdisciplinarry Symposium on the Trinity*, ed. Stephen Davis, Daniel Kendall, and Gerald O'Collins (Oxford: Oxford University Press, 1999), 73–95, and Larry W. Hurtado, *Lord Jesus Christ: Devotion to Jesus in Earliest Christianity* (Grand Rapids: Eerdmans, 2003), 600, 651 (emphasis added).

by Nazianzen, *is not triadic*. This is why it is problematic to state that the binitarian pattern of worship characteristic of earliest Christianity constitutes "a primitive effort at what later became Trinitarian doctrine."

Some hesitation about the notion that the first-century worship of Jesus "at the right hand of God" (Heb 1:3; 8:1; 10:12; Rom 8:34; Acts 7:55–56; 1 Pt 3:22; Mk 16:19 / Mt 26:64 / Lk 22:69) can be described as "binitarian" or "dyadic" is also warranted. For early Christians the Holy Spirit is not so much a "third power in heaven" as the very condition for the possibility of a confession of Jesus as Lord. We are all indebted to Hurtado for his insistence on the factor of "religious experience" as the medium and catalyst of the fusion between Jewish monotheism and early Christian worship of Jesus. It is this "religious experience," usually called "being in the Spirit" (Rv 1:10) or being "filled with the Spirit," that makes possible "binitarian monotheism"—the worship of Jesus—and that is retained by Trinitarian formulas of faith. Thus, Paul states that the earliest and fundamental proclamation of Christological monotheism —"Jesus is Lord"—was a confession made ἐν πνεύματι ἁγίῳ (1 Cor 12:3); similarly, before stating that Stephen saw the Son of Man standing at the right hand of God and that he prayed to him (Acts 7:59–60, "Lord Jesus, receive my spirit ... Lord, do not hold this sin against them"), the author of Acts describes Stephen as "filled with the Holy Spirit," ὑπάρχων πλήρης πνεύματος ἁγίου (Acts 7:55–56). In the book of Revelation the indicators of divine status (the divine Name, the divine throne, the fact of receiving worship) point to God and, associated to God, the Son or Lamb, with no third entity enthroned and worshipped together with the Father and the Son. The Spirit is described in angelomorphic fashion ("the seven holy spirits before the throne"), indissolubly linked to the worshiped second person ("seven horns of the Lamb," "seven eyes of the Lord," "seven stars in the Lord's hand"). If we describe this as "binitarianism," we overlook the text's claim that John the Divine received his "binitarian" revelation ἐν πνεύματι on a Sunday, presumably in the course of worship.

A possible objection may be raised on the basis of some early Christian texts that seem perfect examples of "three powers in heaven" theology. In *Ascension of Isaiah* (8.18; 9.27–40), for example, after an explicit reference to "Father," "Son," and "Spirit" the visionary seems to worship each of the three distinctly and then reports on God receiving the worship of the angel identified as "my Lord" (e.g., Christ) and "the angel of the Holy Spirit." Very similar passages occur in Irenaeus (*Epid.* 10) and Origen (*princ.* 1.3.4.). Yet, even in these passages, the angelomorphic Spirit is first and foremost "the angel of the Holy Spirit *who has spoken in you* and also in the other righteous" (*Asc. Isa.* 9.36), and, for Origen, the ground of all theognosy. In other words, the Spirit is the guide, the enabler, and the interpreter of the prophetic and visionary experience of worshipping Jesus alongside God.

An unexpected witness to similar views can be found at the very heart of Justin Martyr's theology (*Dial.* 61.1), although scholars have time and again been labeled it "binitarian":

> I shall now show you the Scriptures that God has begotten of himself as a Beginning before all creatures. The Holy Spirit indicates this power by various titles, sometimes *the Glory of the Lord*, at other times *Son*, or *Wisdom*, or *Angel*, or *God*, or *Lord*, or *Word*. He even called himself *Commander-in-chief* when he appeared in human guise to Joshua, the son of Nun. Indeed, he can justly lay claim to all these titles from the fact that he performs the Father's will and that he was begotten by an act of the Father's will.

Scholars who find in this passage a strong confession of Justin's all-encompassing Logos theory, which precludes the articulation of a robust pneumatology and thus a fully Trinitarian theology, overlook or minimize the fact that the identification of the second power as such is a function of the Holy Spirit: the Glory, the Lord, Son, or Logos is proclaimed as such by the Holy Spirit (ὑπὸ τοῦ πνεύματος τοῦ ἁγίου καλεῖται).

Let me return to my question: is binitarian monotheism the first step to Christian Trinitarian theology? In my opinion, "binitarianism" is less an early Christian phenomenon than it is a scholarly phenomenon: a term that alerts us to a built-in blind spot in the academic approach to sacred texts. From a methodological perspective, the problem arises from the discontinuity between the implied readers of much of early Christian literature and the actual readers in academia. The texts that exemplify early Christian binitarianism typically claim to be rooted in a pneumatic religious experience that the readers are exhorted to emulate beginning with the very act of reading. Indeed, early Christians understood their sacred texts as divine revelation, dispensed pedagogically by heavenly agents to be appropriated mystagogically by the community of initiates. The scholarly reading of these texts is by definition one that maintains a critical distance to the text. We approach these texts not through liturgical mediation and not with the expectation that they should continually transform and perfect us as members of a worshipping community; we approach them rather through the mediation of critical scholarship (critical editions, academically annotated translations, historical and exegetical studies), within the framework of an academic guild that does not venerate the texts it studies as guides to the God worshiped by their ancient authors. Here also, it is the perspective that creates the phenomenon: when the mystagogical approach of early Christian texts is set aside—a matter of professional necessity in academia—the ancient writers are often found to lack explicit references to the Holy Spirit and are thus labeled "binitarian."

From Theophany to Trinitarian Symbolism: Three Test Cases

Genesis 18, Isaiah 6, and Habbakuk 3:2 (LXX) are biblical texts whose history of interpretation is intertwined, in early Christianity, with the articulation of Trinitarian theology. Even though the reception history of these verses is certainly not an untrodden path in scholarship, I think that the current scholarly concepts fail to distinguish properly between the various types of exegesis proposed along the centuries. This failure is especially obvious in the case of the earliest and most enduring Christian exegesis of Old Testament theophanies.

Genesis 18: The Lord and His Two Angels

Early Christian exegetes generally see in the three visitors the Son of God and his two angelic assistants. Their main interpretive move echoes the famous Johannine affirmation "before Abraham was, I am … Abraham rejoiced that he would see my day; he saw it and was glad" (Jn 8:53, 56), and consists in the identification of "the Lord" of Genesis 18 with "the Lord" of Christian worship—the angelomorphic Son of God. This interpretation is exemplified by major writers of the second and third centuries, such as Justin Martyr, Irenaeus of Lyon, Tertullian, and Origen, who deployed it as a valuable weapon in a variety of polemical (anti-Jewish, antidualistic, antimodalistic) contexts. This Christological reading of the Mamre theophany remains normative for later authors, such as Eusebius of Caesarea, Athanasius of Alexandria, and some of his Arian adversaries: Novatian, Hilary of Poitiers, the *Apostolic Constitutions*, Theodoret of Cyrus, and John Chrysostom. The convergence of so many theologically diverse sources on the Christological interpretation of Genesis 18 suggests that we are dealing here with a venerable and widespread tradition.[3]

The early centuries also know of an alternative exegetical tradition. Even though Origen speaks of the three visitors as the Logos and his angels, for him this received tradition is merely a springboard for deeper theological speculation. This strand of interpretation, later exemplified by Evagrius and Ambrose, is interested in the spiritual significance of all details of the account: the time of the apparition (Abraham receiving God at "noon" indicates the resplendent light of the intelligence and purity of heart; Lot, by contrast, receives the angels "in the evening"), the number of visitors (three for Abraham, two for Lot), the location of the vision ("outside the tent" signifies withdrawal from carnal thoughts), and the type of bread served to the visitors (Abraham provides the "mystical" bread made of finer flour than Lot).

It is this tradition that gives rise to a Trinitarian reorientation of the interpretation of Genesis 18. The three visitors and three measures of flour suggest to Origen and his many theological heirs that Genesis 18 intends to communicate something about the mystery of the Trinity. The idea that "Abraham saw three, but worshipped only one," which becomes an oft-recurring formula by the end of the fourth century, can, however, mean different things to different writers. Hilary of Poitiers, for instance, argues that, even though three men are present, the eyes of faith direct Abraham to worship only *one of the three*, inasmuch as he was able to discern in him the mystery of the incarnation to come; Ambrose, by contrast, although sometimes espousing the traditional (Christological) view, pivots toward a Trinitarian interpretation of the formula: at Mamre, Abraham "saw the Trinity in figure."

With Cyril of Alexandria and Augustine, the earlier Christological interpretation of Genesis 18 seems indeed to have been abandoned in favor of a Trinitarian reading. (This exegetical move is motivated, in the case of Augus-

3. For a more detailed account and complete references, see Bucur, "The Early Christian Reception History of Genesis 18: From Theophany to Trinitarian Symbolism," *Journal of Early Christian Studies* 23 (2015): 245–72.

tine, by his dissatisfaction with the subordinationist vulnerability of the Christological interpretation of theophanies and further complicated by his revolutionary proposal to speak of theophanies such as Abraham's three visitors as *created* manifestations of the Trinity.) At any rate, by the time of Maximus the Confessor, the Trinitarian interpretation has acquired normative status.

The shift from a Christological to a Trinitarian interpretation of Genesis 18 can also be observed in hymnography and iconography. Not surprisingly for these more conservative areas of Christian reflection, the change occurs significantly later. Romanos the Melodist, for instance, writing in the first half of the sixth century, still views the Mamre theophany as a Christophany. It is only later that the Trinitarian exegesis of Genesis 18, which had become widespread from the fifth century onward, is enshrined as canonical by being taken up in the hymns of the Sunday Midnight Office, ascribed to the ninth-century writer Metrophanes of Smyrna. Through this hymnography, spread over a huge area and recited on a weekly basis for over a millennium, devout Christians were taught that God appeared to Abraham "in human form," revealing "in figure" the pure doctrine of the three-hypostatic godhead.

As for the iconographic exegesis of Genesis 18, the majority of mosaics, icons, and manuscript illuminations depict a central figure, more important than the other two, and explicitly or implicitly identify it as Jesus Christ. Around the turn of the millennium, icons of Abraham's hospitality begin to be labeled "The Holy Trinity," even though the central figure is clearly marked as Jesus Christ. Finally, around the middle of the second millennium and especially with Rublev's famous "Trinity," the transition from Christological to Trinitarian signification was complete. It is significant, however, that this icon, painted for the Trinity-Sergius monastery, was mounted on the iconostasis as the first icon to the right of the royal doors—that is, it was displayed as an icon of Christ!

Isaiah 6: The Lord and the Two Seraphim

Two broad avenues for the exegesis of Isaiah 6 can be distinguished. The first one is a reading of the theophany as a "Christophany," characteristic of the widespread early Christian identification of the Logos-to-be-incarnate as subject of all Old Testament theophanies. This is the earliest Christian interpretation of Isaiah 6 and, judging from its presence in hymnography and iconography, the more popular one. The second reading, with roots in second-century Alexandria, discerns in the three characters of the narrative—the enthroned Lord and the two seraphim—a symbolic image of the Holy Trinity.[4]

The Gospel of John identifies the *kyrios* in Isaiah's vision with the *kyrios* of Christian worship: "[Isaiah] saw his glory" (Jn 12:41; recall Isaiah: "I saw the Lord ... the house was full of his glory"), just as "we have seen his glory" (Jn 1:14). Moreover, in the book of Revelation the "holy, holy, holy" sung by heavenly creatures is also addressed to the Lamb (Rv 4:6–9; 5:8–14). This Christological interpretation is echoed by prominent writers of the pre-Nicene era such as Justin Martyr, Irenaeus of Lyon, and Clement of Alexandria and in later centuries in the writings of Cyril of Jerusalem, Eusebius of Caesarea, Jerome, John Chrysostom, Pseudo-Asterius the Sophist, and the Pseudo-Macarian Homilies.

A different reading started to spread in the opening decades of the second century. In the *Martyrdom and Ascension of Isaiah*, the prophet gazes upon a triad composed of "the glorious one" or "the Father of the Lord," whose glory it is impossible to behold, and his two attendants, the Lord Jesus and the angel of the Holy Spirit (*Asc. Isa.* 10.2–6). Obviously, the "Father" corresponds to the enthroned Lord in Isaiah 6:1, while the angelomorphic Son and Spirit, referred to earlier (*Mar.Asc.Isa.* 9) as "the angel of the Logos" and "the angel of the Holy Spirit," correspond to the two seraphim. Irenaeus (*Epid.* 10) will appropriate this imagery, but apply a significant theological corrective: the two cherubim/seraphim are no longer identified with, but subordinated to, the Son and the Spirit. Origen (*princ.* 1.3.4; *Hom. Isa.* 1.2), by contrast, will invoke the authority of a "Hebrew teacher" in support of his identification of the two seraphim with the Son and the Spirit. Even though he had himself translated Origen's homilies on Isaiah into Latin, Jerome would later criticize this exegesis as heretical because of its subordinationistic connotations.

The fourth century will consecrate the Trinitarian interpretation of Isaiah 6. Following Origen's lead ("the seraphim ... guard the mystery of the Trinity"), but leaving behind any trace of subordinationism, Gregory of Nyssa, Basil of Caesarea, and Gregory of Nazianzus take the threefold cry of the seraphim (and perhaps the triadic structure of the vision—God and two seraphim) as in some way suggesting or adumbrating the mystery of the Trini-

4. For a more detailed account and complete references, see Bucur, "*I Saw the Lord*: Observations on the Early Christian Reception of Isaiah 6," *Pro Ecclesia* 23 (2014): 309–30.

ty. Their point is that the seraphs are *distinct* from the Persons of the Trinity, uttering their thrice-holy song as angelic powers, subordinated to the Father, Son, and Holy Spirit. Gregory of Nazianzus makes it clear that the single object of worship, the "God" addressed by the angelic hymn, is Father, Son, and Spirit.

The Trinitarian exegesis of Isaiah 6, together with its antisubordinationist connotations, is continued and refined by Cyril of Alexandria and Theodoret of Cyrus. Although theological adversaries, their exegesis of Isaiah 6 is identical: both take the triple exclamation "holy, holy holy" as a reference to the Trinity, while the singular "Lord Sabaoth" points to the oneness of the divine nature.

The anti-Eunomian polemics brought to the fore a distinct emphasis on the paradox that Isaiah 6 is both an overwhelming visionary experience and an experience in which the ultimate reality of God is not exhausted. Basil of Caesarea, for instance, is at pains to show that even as the prophet was allowed a contemplation of the divine *glory*, God's *ousia* remained utterly inaccessible to him. Similarly, John Chrysostom explains that the throne-vision is not a vision of the divine *ousia*, but a matter of "condescension" (*sunkatabasis*).

The angelic hymn "holy, holy, holy is the Lord Sabaoth!" in Isaiah 6 proved an indispensable building block for liturgical compositions. The older exegesis of "holy, holy, holy" was, in Syria-Palestine, Christological. The Trinitarian readings of Isaiah 6 eventually find liturgical expression in the Eucharistic prayer of Serapion of Thmuis, the Liturgy of St. Mark, and the *Apostolic Constitutions* (with a subordinationist tendency: God the Father is worshipped by all ranks of heavenly powers, culminating with the worship offered by the Son and Spirit) and by the Byzantine Liturgy of John Chrysostom, where worship is given by the angels, culminating with the cherubim/seraphim, to God as Trinity.

Hymnography also displays a shift from the Christological to the Trinitarian interpretation of Isaiah 6. Romanos the Melodist, for instance, reads the text Christologically, as do some of the Byzantine festal hymns. A hymn of Palm Sunday Matins, for instance, exhorts its hearers to "*look on the one whom Isaiah saw*, who has come for our sake in flesh!" By contrast, the hymns of the Sunday Midnight Office, composed in the ninth century by Metrophanes of Smyrna, popularized a Trinitarian reading of Isaiah 6.

The iconography of Isaiah 6, however, seems to have never moved beyond the Christological interpretation of Isaiah 6, in conjunction with the older hymns of the church, which are also Christological.

Habakkuk 3:2 (LXX)

The Septuagint version of Habakkuk 3:2 ("Lord, I have heard report of you, and was afraid: I considered your works, and was amazed: you will be known between the two living creatures") is significantly different from its correspondent in the Masoretic text ("O LORD, I have heard of your renown, and I stand in awe, O LORD, of your work. In our own time revive it; in our own time make it known; in wrath may you remember mercy"). In Latin-speaking Christianity, despite the Vulgate's option for the Hebrew version of Habakkuk 3:2, the Old Itala, which followed the LXX (*in medio duorum animalium innotesceris*), remained popular. One of the main reasons for this type of conservatism is the ongoing liturgical use of Habakkuk 3 ("the prayer of Habakkuk") as part of the so-called biblical odes, a series of biblical hymns that became part of the Daily Office of both Eastern and Western Christianity.[5]

Scholars have discussed at length the difficulties of the Hebrew text, offering various and conflicting reconstructions of the pre-Masoretic text and analyzing the puzzling divergences between the Greek and the Hebrew. It is now generally assumed that the translators had in front of them a Hebrew Vorlage slightly different from that of the Masoretic Text, which they understood and vocalized in a peculiar manner. In any case, the occurrence of the "two living beings" in the LXX version is not so much a matter of philology as of theology: the translator made an interpretative choice under the inevitable influence of the imagery of Exodus 25 (God's appearance between the two cherubim) and Isaiah 6 (God's appearance between the two seraphim). For Christian exegetes, the connection of Habakkuk with Isaiah and Ezekiel was natural: the (two) *ζῷα* of Habakkuk 3:2 quite naturally suggested a relation with the two cherubim on the mercy-seat (Ex 25:22; Nm 7:89), the two seraphim of Isaiah 6:3, and the four *ζῷα* in Ezekiel 1 (reinterpreted in light of Revelation 4).

The most widespread interpretation of Habakkuk 3:2 LXX is Christologi-

5. For a more detailed account and complete references, see Bucur, "Vision, Exegesis, and Theology in the Reception History of Hab 3:2 (LXX)," in *"What Does the Scripture Say?": Studies in the Function of Scripture in Early Judaism and Christianity*, vol. 2, *The Letters and Liturgical Traditions*, ed. Craig A. Evans and H. Daniel Zacharias (London and New York: T. and T. Clark International, 2011), 134–46.

cal. It occurs in Tertullian (God known between the two living beings is Christ between Moses and Elijah, at the Transfiguration), Cyril of Alexandria, and Symeon the New Theologian, and in Latin, *The Gospel of Ps.-Mt.*14 (the newborn Jesus between the ox and the ass), Hesychius of Jerusalem (Christ crucified between the two thieves), Cyril of Jerusalem (Christ between his earthly life and his life after the resurrection), Eusebius of Caesarea (Christ between the human and the divine natures). There is then also Christ between the Old Testament and New Testament (Cyril of Alexandria, Augustine, and Jerome) and Christ between the present life and future life (Theodoret). Augustine and Jerome rehearse all these interpretations.

Origen set forth a highly speculative version of this Christological reading. In his *Commentary on Romans* (3.8.2–8), he combines Habakkuk 3:2 with Exodus 25:22 ("There I will meet with you, and from above the ἱλαστήριον, from between the two cherubim that are on the ark of the covenant") and Romans 3:25 (God set Christ forth as the ἱλαστήριον), and proposed the following exegesis: (1) The two living beings in Habakkuk 3:2 are the two cherubim between which God makes himself known in theophany above the mercy-seat; (2) The mercy seat (ἱλαστήριον) is the human soul of Jesus, in whom the Word and Spirit dwell perpetually, and it covers the ark, which represents Jesus' flesh; (3) The statement in Habakkuk 3:2 ("God will be known between the two living beings") applies "to any saint who is a servant of God: God does not become known from any other place … except from that propitiatory, which we have expounded above" (Hb 3.8.8)—in other words, the locus of theognosy is Jesus, in whom dwell the Spirit and the Logos.

The Christological reading of Habakkuk 3:2 was cemented by its liturgical use in connection with the celebration of the resurrection and by its iconography. "Habakkuk's vision" is found in manuscripts of Gregory of Nazianzus's orations, as an illustration of *Orat.* 45.1:

> I will stand upon my watch and mount upon the rock" [Hb 2:1], says the venerable Habakkuk.… Well, I have taken my stand, and looked forth; and behold a man riding on the clouds and he is very high, and his countenance is like the countenance of an angel, and his vesture is like the brightness of piercing lightning [Hb 3:4]; and he lifts his hand toward the East, and cries with a piercing voice.… "Today salvation has come to the visible and to the invisible world. Christ is risen from the dead, rise all with Him!"

This very popular text, echoed by John Damascene's Canon of the Resurrection, interprets Habakkuk's vision as a vision of the risen Christ, hyperluminous and angelic in appearance. In a famous manuscript illumination (*Codex Taphou* 14), the two angels flanking Jesus indicate that Habakkuk 3:2 has been "filtered" through the Gospel of Peter, where "two men in great brightness" descend into the tomb and reascend with the risen Christ in their midst (Pt 9:35–10:40). In other cases (as in the fifth-century mosaic at the Latomos monastery in Thessaloniki and its fourteenth-century copy, the Poganovo icon) the vision of Habakkuk, merged with that of Ezekiel, becomes a throne-vision, with Christ seated on the merkabah, gazed upon by the two prophets.

So much for the Christological interpretation of Habakkuk 3:2. The "Trinitarian turn" we have by now come to expect of theophanic texts does, indeed, occur; and it does so, perhaps unsurprisingly, in Origen. *De principiis* (1.3.4), a text I have already mentioned in passing, uses Habakkuk 3:2 in conjunction with Isaiah 6 and explains:

> My Hebrew master also used to say that those two seraphim in Isaiah, which are described as having each six wings, and calling to one another, and saying, "Holy, holy, holy, is the Lord God of hosts" [Is 6:1] were to be understood of the only-begotten Son of God and of the Holy Spirit. And we think that that expression also which occurs in the hymn of Habakkuk ... ought to be understood of Christ and of the Holy Spirit. For all knowledge of the Father is obtained by revelation of the Son through the Holy Spirit, so that both of these beings which, according to the prophet, are called either "living things" or "lives," exist as the ground of the knowledge of God the Father.

As far as I am aware, Origen's Trinitarian interpretation of Habakkuk 3:2 has remained an isolated phenomenon. This is not without irony, given the rich reception of his work on Isaiah 6, which occurs in same passage of *princ.* 1.3.4. If Habakkuk 3:2 is not found among the theophanies to which the hymns of the Sunday Midnight Office gives a Trinitarian interpretation, it is perhaps because Metrophanes of Smyrna could not draw upon any predecessors.

What Kind of Exegesis? Inadequacy of Scholarly Categories

It seems clear that two broad exegetical avenues can be distinguished in the Christian reception of Genesis 18, Isaiah 6, and Habakkuk 3:2 LXX. The first one is a reading of these biblical theophanies as "Christophanies," characteristic of the widespread early Christian identification of the Logos-to-be-incarnate as subject of all Old Testament theophanies. This is the earliest Christian interpretation of the texts under discussion and, judging from its adoption by later hymnography and iconography, also the more popular one. The second reading, with roots in second-century Alexandria, discerns in the three characters—the three visitors of Abraham, Isaiah's enthroned Lord, and the two seraphim and Habakkuk's vision of the Lord between two living beings—a symbolic image of the Trinity.

My concern here is mainly with the straightforward identification of the Septuagint *kyrios* with the New Testament's *kyrios* Jesus. To call this reading "Christological," although correct, only provides a category for understanding *that* the text was read with a specific doctrinal aim in sight, but no grasp of *how* the text came to be read in that way. The current scholarly concepts fail to adequately grasp the distinctiveness of this exegesis and they thereby obscure the importance of the earliest and most enduring Christian exegesis of Old Testament theophanies. This is not a trivial issue: without recognizing the phenomenon and crafting an appropriate concept to designate it (assuming the risk, of course, as with all scholarly concepts, of obscuring certain other elements), we fail to grasp an important factor in the development of early Christian theology.

In his almost exhaustive treatment of the Mamre theophany, Bunge writes, "This typological level of meaning, according to which an Old Testament event is understood as the type (image, figure, sketch) of the New Testament fulfillment, is, in our case [Genesis 18] Christological and Trinitarian."[6] For him, "typological" accounts for the exegetical linking of the three men with the tri-hypostatic Christian God, but also for the exegetical linking of the "Lord" in the Genesis account with the "Lord" Jesus.[7] Lars Thunberg also views the

6. Gabriel Bunge, *The Rublev Trinity: The Icon of the Trinity by the Monk-Painter Andrei Rublev* (Crestwood, N.Y.: St. Vladimir's Seminary Press, 2007), 45.

7. Bunge, *Rublev Trinity*, 47: Abraham's three visitors can be interpreted as "a type of the Trinity,"

Christological interpretation of Genesis 18 as "mainly of a *typological* character," "based on a *typological* exegesis."[8]

Writing about Eusebius's exegetical method in the *Commentary on Isaiah,*[9] Michael Hollerich uses the problematic terms "allegory" and "typology" and the no-less-(in)famous distinction between Antioch ("typological") and Alexandria ("allegorical")—although the latter is helpfully nuanced, thanks to some insights gleaned from Jacques Guillet.[10] In the end, Eusebius appears situated more or less in between the two alternative camps. Left out of the account—because the chosen conceptual lenses create a blind spot—is precisely Eusebius's interpretation of Isaiah 6 as Christophany. Studies of the iconography of Isaiah 6 exhibit the same problem. "Christ himself is depicted in the illustration, showing the Christian belief in the *prefiguring* nature of this Old Testament vision," writes Glenn Peers. "In this vision shared by both prophet and viewer, the viewer is made superior by his or her knowledge of *the event's typological significance* since Christ is depicted enthroned as the Lord of the Old Covenant."[11]

As the survey of our three test cases shows, the exegesis of theophanies dominant in exegetical and doctrinal writings of the first four centuries (and dominant for an even longer time in hymnography and iconography) does not speak of Christ as somehow "foreshadowed" or "signified" by the characters and events recorded in the texts. In the case of a type-antitype relation, one would expect the exegete to acknowledge a nonallegorical, non-Christological level of the text and then posit a second Christological level as "fulfillment" of the Old Testament type. For the vast majority of early Christian writers, however, a non-Christological reality in the Mamre theophany or the vision of Isaiah simply does not exist: the central character of those narratives *is* Christ, and

---

in which case "on the typological level, we have ... a representation of the Holy Trinity"; ibid., 51: "If the Lord, who appeared to Abraham, may also be understood as the Logos in his hidden presence, so can the threefold number of the visitors be equally interpreted as a reference to the threeness of the persons."

8. Lars Thunberg, "Early Christian Interpretation of the *Three Angels* in Gen. 18," *Studia Patristica 7 / Text und Untersuchen* 92 (1966): 565, 569 (emphasis mine).

9. Michael J. Hollerich, *Eusebius of Caesarea's Commentary on Isaiah: Christian Exegesis in the Age of Constantine*, Oxford Early Christian Studies (Oxford: Clarendon, 1999), esp. 94–102.

10. See Hollerich, *Eusebius of Caesarea's Commentary on Isaiah*, 94n107, 98–99; Jacques Guillet, "Les *exégèses* d'Aléxandrie et d'Antioche: Conflit ou malentendu?," *Recherches de science religieuse* 34 (1947): 257–302.

11. Glenn Peers, "Angelophany and Art after Iconoclasm," *Deltion tes Christianikes Archaiologikes Hetaireias* 26 (2005): 339b, 340a.

the "Lord" of Christian worship is straightforwardly *identified* with the Old Testament "Lord."

It is one thing to say that the threeness of Abraham's visitors offers an image of the modes of spiritual perception; it is another to say that Abraham's three visitors set forth an image of the Holy Trinity; and it is quite another matter to say that Abraham encountered the word of God in a theophany that anticipates the incarnation of the Word. Similarly, it is one thing to say that the three characters in Isaiah 6 (the enthroned Lord and the two seraphim) provide an image of Philo's triad (ὁ ὤν—θεός—κύριος) or of the Christian Holy Trinity; it is another to say that the anthropomorphism of Isaiah 6 "foreshadows" the incarnation; and it another altogether to affirm that Isaiah encountered the Word of God in a theophany that also points to the Logos-to-be-made-man. There is need for better distinctions that would sharpen our focus.

A first distinction should be drawn between interpretations in which the connection between sign and signified does not presuppose and require a link between Old and New Testament and interpretations for which such a link is fundamental. It is this distinction that older scholarship (most famously Jean Daniélou) tried to bring out through a sharp opposition between "allegory" and "typology." Even if most scholars today reject the opposition between the terms "typology" and "allegory" as historically unfounded, and therefore misleading, and prefer to view typological exegesis as a species of allegory, it is clear that the underlying distinction is real and must be expressed somehow.[12]

More important, however, is another distinction, drawn between the interpretation of Genesis 18, Isaiah 6, and Habakkuk 3:2 as "foreshadowing" the incarnation or presenting a symbolic image of the Trinity and the interpretation of Old Testament theophanies as Christophanies. In the latter case, everything turns on the strong claim to a real encounter or real "presence"; in the former, the divine presence is not an epiphanic self-evidence, but rather a "weaker" symbolic presence, a matter of exegetical and theological convention.

12. An excellent essay on this problem, Peter Martens, "Revisiting the Allegory/Typology Distinction: The Case of Origen," *Journal of Early Christian Studies* 16 (2008): 283–317, concludes with the following recommendation: "first, that we discontinue using 'typology' and 'allegory' as labels for better and worse forms of nonliteral exegesis respectively; second, that we find alternative labels for these two forms of nonliteral interpretation; and third, that we develop a conversation around the criteria for successful nonliteral scriptural interpretation" (316).

Terms such as "typological" and "allegorical" do not account satisfactorily for the Christological interpretation of Genesis 18, Isaiah 6, and Habakkuk 3:2 LXX because they do not capture the epiphanic dimension of the text as read by many early Christian exegetes. Scholarship has rarely seized upon this aspect. In a book published in 1965, which met with undeserved neglect, A. T. Hanson pointed out the distinction between "real presence" and "typology" and argued that the former is typical of New Testament authors.[13] His views were echoed four decades later by Charles Gieschen's essay on *"the real presence of the Son before Christ" in* pre-Nicene writers.[14] Alexander Schmemann made very similar observations about liturgical symbolism.[15] Today, Larry Hurtado provides the clearest distinction among three exegetical approaches to the Old Testament characteristic of "second-century proto-orthodox Christians" (e.g., Justin Martyr): first, "proof texts" drawn from the prophets; second, "a wider 'typological' reading of the Old Testament as filled with figures and events that foreshadow Jesus"; and, third, "the interpretation of Old Testament accounts of theophanies as manifestations of the pre-incarnate Son of God."[16]

Given the ideological freight of terms like "symbolic," "typological," and "epiphanic"—to say nothing of "real presence"!—it might be more profitable to find a new conceptual tool. I have argued elsewhere that the exegesis of biblical theophanies in Byzantine hymnography often follows the logic of "re-

13. Anthony Tyrrell Hanson, *Jesus Christ in the Old Testament* (London: SPCK, 1965).

14. Charles Gieschen, *"The Real Presence of the Son Before Christ: Revisiting an Old Approach to Old Testament Christology," Concordia Theological Quarterly 68 (2004): 103–26.*

15. Alexander Schmemann speaks of a shift from one type of symbolization to another: in his words, from *symbol* to *symbolism*, from "ontological/real/eschatological symbol" to "illustrative symbolism." In the older type of symbolization, "the empirical (or 'visible') and the spiritual ('invisible') are united not *logically* (this 'stands for' that), nor *analogically* (this 'illustrates' that), nor yet *by cause and effect* (this 'means' or 'generates' that), but *epiphanically*. One reality *manifests* and *communicates* the other, but ... only to the degree to which the symbol itself is a participant in the spiritual reality and is able or called upon to embody it." By contrast, "illustrative symbolism" is the sign of something that does not exist logically, but only by convention, just as there is no real water in the chemical symbol H_2O; see Schmemann, "Symbol and Symbolism in the Byzantine Liturgy: Liturgical Symbols and Their Theological Interpretation," in *Liturgy and Tradition*, ed. Thomas Fisch (Crestwood, N.Y.: St. Vladimir's Seminary Press, 1990), 115–28; compare Schmemann, *The Eucharist: Sacrament of the Kingdom*, trans. Paul Kachur (Crestwood, N.Y.: St. Vladimir's Seminary Press, 1983), 38–39; see also Schmemann, *For the Life of the World* (Crestwood, N.Y.: St. Vladimir's Seminary Press, 1973), 141: "In the early tradition, ... the relationship between the sign in the symbol (A) and that it 'signifies' (B) is neither a merely semantic one (A *means* B), not causal (A *is the cause of* B), nor representative (A *represents* B). We called this relationship *epiphany*."

16. Hurtado, *Lord Jesus Christ*, 565–66.

written Bible" literature.[17] This term, coined by Geza Vermes in 1961, has since been used by scholars dealing mainly with Second Temple pseudepigrapha. In the above-mentioned articles on Genesis 18, Isaiah 6, and Hab 3:2, LXX, I argued that the Christological and "epiphanic" readings of Genesis 18, Isaiah 6, and Habakkuk 3:2 LXX documented previously could be viewed as a form of "rewritten Bible." Indeed, numerous early Christian texts (and images) identify the central character in Isaiah 6— "the Lord"—as Jesus Christ in the same way that the Wisdom of Solomon identifies the heavenly agent at work in the Exodus events as Lady Wisdom and the book of Jubilees has Moses receive the Law from the Angel of the Presence.

Nevertheless, I have changed my mind on this point.[18] It is quite clear that, if it is to retain any explanatory power, "rewritten Bible" must refer to the production of actual *texts*—"narratives following a sequential, chronological order," which "cover a substantial portion of Scripture," according to a widespread definition of the genre.[19] For Christian readers of the Old Testament, however, the rewriting in question is a metaphor for interpretation, since the Christologically rewritten Old Testament episodes do not constitute a new *text*, but offer new *readings* of the existing ones. There are, of course, similarities between "rewritten Bible" and early Christian exegesis, just as there are similarities between "rewritten Bible" and rabbinic midrash—yet, the latter is not considered "rewritten Bible."[20] If patristic "Christophanic exegesis" (the

17. Bucur, "The Mountain of the Lord: Sinai, Zion, and Eden in Byzantine Hymnographic Exegesis," in *Symbola caelestis: Le symbolisme liturgique et paraliturgique dans le monde chrétien*, ed. B. Lourié and A. Orlov (Piscataway, N.J.: Gorgias, 2009), 129–72, esp. 162–68.

18. See Bucur, "Christophanic Exegesis and the Problem of Symbolization: Daniel 3 (the Fiery Furnace) as a Test Case," *Journal of Theological Interpretation* 10 (2016): 227–44.

19. Philip S. Alexander, "Retelling the Old Testament," in *It Is Written: Scripture Citing Scripture: Essays in Honour of Barnabas Lindars*, ed. D. A. Carson and H. G. M. Williamson (Cambridge: Cambridge University Press, 1988), 116, 117.

20. This is evident for classical midrash: "*Unlike rabbinic midrash*, [in 'rewritten Bible' literature] the actual words of Scripture do not remain highlighted within the body of the text, either in the form of lemmata, or by the use of citation-formulae"; Alexander, "Retelling the Old Testament," 116. It is true, as Steven D. Fraade observes ("Rewritten Bible and Rabbinic Midrash as Commentary," in *Current Trends in the Study of Midrash*, ed. Carol Bakhos (Leiden: Brill, 2006), 62) that midrash "may be viewed as containing aspects of 'rewritten Bible' beneath its formal structure of scriptural commentary" (e.g., expansive paraphrase, filling in scriptural gaps, removing discomforting details, identifying anonymous with named persons and places). Nevertheless, the distinction between midrash and rewritten Bible remains true even of *Pirqe de-Rabbi Eliezer*, despite the latter's many similarities with *Jubilees* or the *Liber Antiquitatum Biblicarum*; see Rachel Adelman, *The Return of the Repressed: Pirqe De-Rabbi Eliezer and the Pseudepigrapha* (Leiden: Brill, 2009), 5–19; Adelman, "Can We Apply the Term 'Rewritten Bible' to

term I would myself propose) is accepted as a form of "rewritten Bible," the same would apply to *midrash*. In this case, however, it would become necessary to find yet another, more specific term to designate the kind of literature for which Vermes coined the term "rewritten Bible" in the first place: "a narrative that follows Scripture but includes a substantial amount of supplements and interpretative developments."[21] This erosion of the descriptive power of the concept derives from its metaphorization; the root problem is to have allowed "rewritten" to stand for "interpreted."

Conclusions

In the first part of my essay I have criticized the scholarly notion of early Christian "binitarian monotheism" as a first stage of development toward Trinitarian theology. The problems I noted are, first, the lack of acknowledgment of the significant theological freight that "Binitarianismus" has been carrying since the days of Loofs and Harnack and, second, the lack of acknowledgment of the inevitable distortion that occurs when texts are uprooted from their original performative and mystagogical contexts, flattened into mere letters on paper, and studied in a library. The second part of my essay has offered a survey of the history of interpretation of Genesis 18, Isaiah 6, and Habakkuk 3:2 LXX—three texts that have played a crucial role in the articulation of early Trinitarian theology—and a critique of what I regard as the inadequate conceptual equipment available to scholars who are reflecting on this topic today. Neither "allegory" nor "typology" nor "rewritten Bible" are adequate descriptors of what I would simply (?) call "Christophanic exegesis."

My "airing of grievances" in these pages is not meant to disparage the contributions of the scholars I am criticizing—many of them true giants from decades past or giants among us. Ultimately, the "blurred vision" and "blind spots" to which I point in both sections of this essay are inherent to the project of giving a scholarly account of early Trinitarian doctrine. The relevant affirmations occur in texts claiming to narrate a transformational religious experience and aiming at refashioning their readers/hearers through the very act of

Midrash? The Case of Pirqe de-Rabbi Eliezer," in *Rewritten Bible after Fifty Years: Texts, Terms, or Techniques?: A Last Dialogue with Geza Vermes*, ed. J. Zsengellér (Leiden and Boston: Brill, 2014), 295–317.

21. Geza Vermes, *Scripture and Tradition in Judaism: Haggadic Studies* (Leiden: Brill, 1961), 326.

reading/hearing. By contrast, ours is a self-correcting scholarly analysis, deliberately detached from the liturgical-mystagogical context of the sacred texts and aimed at approximating a dispassionate account of how the ancients' handling biblical texts led to the formation of the Trinitarian doctrine. My intention, then, is simply to push the discussion forward by raising some questions and presenting my own difficulties with the subject matter, in the hope of provoking a discussion that will help me understand a little bit more and a little bit better.

Larry W. Hurtado

2. OBSERVATIONS ON THE "MONOTHEISM" AFFIRMED IN THE NEW TESTAMENT

In a book first published in 1988, I used the phrase "ancient Jewish monotheism" in the title to designate the crucial religio-historical context in which to situate and appreciate historically the intense Jesus-devotion that erupted so early and so quickly in the first century C.E.[1] I also proposed that the effects of this intense Jesus-devotion comprised the emergence of a novel innovation or "mutation" in ancient Jewish monotheism that I characterized as a "binitarian" devotional pattern in which Jesus was both distinguished from God ("the Father") and yet linked with God in a unique manner in beliefs and devotional practices.[2] Subsequently, in a number of publications I have sought to clarify and articulate my views further, also engaging with the work of other participants in the discussion of these important matters.[3] In this presentation I

1. Hurtado, *One God, One Lord: Early Christian Devotion and Ancient Jewish Monotheism*, 2nd ed. (1988; repr. Edinburgh: T. and T. Clark, 1998; 3rd ed. with new Epilogue, London: Bloomsbury T. and T. Clark, 2015). Paul Rainbow captured this aspect of the book in the title of his review-essay, "Jewish Monotheism as the Matrix for New Testament Christology: A Review Article," *Novum Testamentum* 33 (1991): 78–91.

2. See esp. Hurtado, *One God, One Lord*, chap. 5, "The Early Christian Mutation," 93–124.

3. On ancient Jewish monotheism, see Hurtado, "First Century Jewish Monotheism," *Journal for the Study of the New Testament* 71 (1998): 3–26, republished in my book *How on Earth Did Jesus Become a God? Historical Questions about Earliest Devotion to Jesus* (Grand Rapids, Mich.: Eerdmans, 2005), 111–33, which I cite here; "Monotheism, Principal Angels, and the Background of Christology," in *Oxford Handbook to the Dead Sea Scrolls*, ed. J. J. Collins and T. H. Lim (Oxford: Oxford University Press,

seek to continue the discussion by underscoring some key features of this early Christian "mutation" in ancient Jewish monotheism as they are reflected in some texts of earliest Christianity.

The Terminology Question

Before we turn to this matter, it is necessary to consider briefly recent questions about the suitability of the term "monotheism" to describe ancient Jewish and Christian religion. In a recent essay, I have dealt with this matter more fully, with particular reference to Second Temple Jewish tradition, and so I will be brief here.[4]

The problem is that the dictionary definition of "monotheism" typically requires the denial of the existence of any more than one deity, and it is not always clear that ancient Jews and Christians were concerned to do this.[5] Over the last couple of decades, several scholars have noted this and have urged that "monotheism" is not a suitable term in describing ancient Jewish and Christian religious stances.[6] As I noted in my 1988 book, *One God, One Lord: Ancient Jewish Monotheism and Early Christian Devotion,* "Jewish belief in the uniqueness of God was able to accommodate surprising kinds of reverence for

2010), 546–64; "Monotheism," in *The Eerdmans Dictionary of Early Judaism*, ed. J. J. Collins and Daniel Harlow (Grand Rapids, Mich.: Eerdmans, 2011), 961–64; and especially "'Ancient Jewish Monotheism' in the Hellenistic and Roman Periods," *Journal of Ancient Judaism* 4 (2013): 379–400. On early Jesus-devotion, see Hurtado, *At the Origins of Christian Worship: The Context and Character of Earliest Christian Devotion* (1999; repr. Grand Rapids, Mich.: Eerdmans, 2000), esp. 63–97; *Lord Jesus Christ: Devotion to Jesus in Earliest Christianity* (Grand Rapids, Mich., and Cambridge: Eerdmans, 2003); and *How on Earth Did Jesus Become a God?* I have engaged work of other scholars in the discussion in the preface to the second edition of *One God, One Lord*, vii–xxii, and more fully in the epilogue to the third edition (London: Bloomsbury T. and T. Clark, 2015), 135–88; and in *How on Earth Did Jesus Become a God?*, 13–30.

4. Hurtado, "'Ancient Jewish Monotheism' in the Hellenistic and Roman Periods."

5. As an example of the sort of popular definition that one finds in dictionaries, note the following: "Monotheism: The doctrine or belief that there is only one God"; http://www.thefreedictionary.com/monotheism; last accessed July 15, 2015.

6. E.g., Peter Hayman, "Monotheism—A Misused Word in Jewish Studies?," *Journal of Jewish Studies* 42 (1991): 1–13; Paula Fredriksen, "Mandatory Retirement: Ideas in the Study of Christian Origins Whose Time Has Come to Go," *Studies in Religion–Sciences Religieuses* 35 (2006): 231–46; also published in *Israel's God and Rebecca's Children: Christology and Community in Early Judaism and Christianity*, ed. David B. Capes, A. D. DeConick, H. K. Bond, and T. A. Miller (Waco: Baylor University Press, 2007), 25–38; Michael S. Heiser, "Monotheism, Polytheism, Monolatry, or Henotheism? Toward an Assessment of Divine Plurality in the Hebrew Bible," *Bulletin for Biblical Research* 18 (2008): 1–30.

and interest in other heavenly figures."[7] These include angelic beings, whom ancient Jews sometimes referred to as "gods" and "sons of God" (Heb. *elim* or *beney elohim*), as reflected in Old Testament and Second Temple Jewish texts.[8] As well, ancient Jews and Christians sometimes appear to acknowledge the existence of beings worshipped as gods by "pagans," or at least do not clearly deny their existence, insisting, however, that the biblical deity is superior to them (e.g., Ex 15:11, 18:11; Ps 86:8, 135:5; 1 Cor 8:5, from many instances in biblical and extra-canonical writings).

As noted by the scholars I have mentioned, it can be misleading to ascribe monotheism *simpliciter* to ancient Jewish and Christian traditions if the modern and simple definition of the term is applied. That is why, in several publications beginning with my 1988 volume, I have repeatedly urged that in any usage of the term "monotheism" the specific meaning *should be derived inductively from relevant evidence* and that we should distinguish different kinds of ancient monotheistic belief and practice (none of them tightly conforming to the modern dictionary definition of monotheism).[9]

To underscore the point, for ancient Jews, and ancient Christians, as well, the primary concern was not to deny the *existence* of other divine beings, but instead to avoid/refuse offering *worship* to any being other than the one biblical God. Moreover, ancient Jewish texts often go further than simply urging Jews to practice this exclusivity in worship and ascribe a universal domain and unique significance to the biblical God, sometimes even portraying the worship of other gods by Gentiles as at best misguided and at worst as the grossest sin (e.g., Jub 15:30–32; Ws 13–15). We see this stance reflected also by Paul in 1 Corinthians 10:14–22, where he forbids participation in the worship of Roman-era deities, calling it "idolatry" (v. 14), and referring to the pagan gods as "demons" (vv. 20–21), likely drawing upon a similar characterization of pagan deities in

7. Hurtado, *One God, One Lord*, 8.

8. Heiser, "The Divine Council in Late Canonical and Non-Canonical Second Temple Jewish Literature" (Ph.D. diss., University of Wisconsin-Madison, 2004); see also Michael Mach, *Entwicklungsstadien des jüdischen Engelglaubens in vorrabinischer Zeit*, Texte und Studien zum Antiken Judentum 34 (Tübingen: J. C. B. Mohr, 1992), who shows increased interest in various angelic/heavenly beings in second-temple Judaism.

9. See Hurtado, *One God, One Lord*, e.g., 129n1, where I briefly note differences between so-called "pagan monotheism" and the religious stance advocated in ancient Jewish texts. At that point, I proposed that "monotheism" be reserved for the latter stance. I have come to think now that it is better to use the appropriate modifier to identify the particular religious outlook of texts and groups: e.g., "pagan monotheism," "ancient Jewish monotheism," "early Christian monotheism."

Deuteronomy 32:17. That is, the "monotheism" of devout ancient Jews and Christians was expressed primarily in their *cultic exclusivity*.

The Early Christian Mutation

In earliest Christianity, I propose that we see the emergence of a distinctive variant form of this ancient Jewish monotheism, to which I now turn. In previous publications I have characterized this as a novel mutation or innovation, which appeared initially within circles of the Jesus movement when it was still within the first-century Jewish religious matrix. This mutation thereafter quickly developed as a new and distinguishable form of monotheistic piety in which God and Jesus were uniquely linked in belief and devotional practice. By referring to this development as a "mutation," I intend no pejorative connotation. I simply mean that there is both a recognizable organic connection to the parent religious tradition (in this case, Second Temple Judaism) and an equally recognizable element of innovation that distinguishes what we may call "early Christian monotheism." My own focus here and in previous discussions is on the earliest observable expressions of this stance as we see them in the New Testament. As I have discussed matters more fully in previous publications, I will confine myself here to a few basic points, focusing on some illustrative texts.[10]

One God, One Lord

First, I trust that it will not be controversial to begin by noting that earliest Christian religious discourse and practice reflect the exclusivist stance of "ancient Jewish monotheism," rejecting the worship of the many deities of the first-century religious setting in favor of the one deity of biblical tradition.[11] Note, for example, how (in what is likely the earliest Christian text extant) Paul describes the religious reorientation of his Thessalonian readers. They "turned to God [τὸν θεόν] from the idols, to serve a true and living God, and to await his Son from heaven, whom he raised from the dead, Jesus who de-

10. E.g., Hurtado, *One God, One Lord*, 93–124; "The Binitarian Shape of Early Christian Worship," in *The Jewish Roots of Christological Monotheism*, ed. Carey C. Newman, James R. Davila, and Gladys S. Lewis, Supplements to the Journal for the Study of Judaism 63 (Leiden: Brill, 1999), 187–214; and *At the Origins of Christian Worship*, 63–97.

11. I draw here upon my discussion in *God in New Testament Theology*, esp. 27–31.

livers us from the coming wrath" (1 Thes 1:9–10). The typical Jewish disdain for pagan deities and the worship of them is evident in this statement. They are mere "idols" (εἴδωλα), the derisive term taken from Jewish religious discourse of the time, and the Thessalonian believers have now turned away from (ἐπεστρέψατε) these unworthy beings to serve (δουλούειν) "a true and living God."[12] It is obvious that we have here an unhesitating expression of the religious exclusivity that marked ancient Jewish monotheism. As with proselyte conversion to Judaism of the time, so in becoming a member of the ecclesial groups established by Paul, pagans were expected to renounce their former deities and commit themselves to an exclusive devotion to the one biblical deity. Moreover, as I have emphasized concerning ancient Judaism, so in these early Christian groups this exclusivity was expressed most blatantly and firmly in worship practice.

In the context of this sharp distinction between the error of reverencing the many deities of the Roman religious environment and a proper devotion to the one God, it is all the more interesting to note the place of Jesus in the new religious orientation of Paul's converts.[13] Jesus is referred to here as God's (unique) Son (as indicated by the definite article: τὸν υἱὸν αὐτοῦ), whom God has raised from death, and who now is the divinely designated deliverer from eschatological "wrath." In short, Jesus here is clearly the unique agent of the one true God and the one whom believers look to and await for their promised salvation.[14] On the one hand, Jesus is certainly defined with reference to God's actions (especially God's resurrection of him) and purposes (eschatological salvation) and so is in some real sense subordinate to and distinguishable from this God. On the other hand, we can say that Jesus is centrally integral to Paul's religious discourse here and to the religious reorientation of Paul's converts, bearing a unique significance and role in executing God's salvation—that is, in Paul's view Jesus is to feature crucially in their faith stance, in a manner for which we have no analogy in Jewish traditions of the time.

Indeed, we see this striking and unique duality, or what we might call a

12. The word δουλουειν here carries the cultic connotation it has in some Old Testament contexts—e.g., Ex 23:33; Ps 2:11; 1 Sm 12:20; 2 Chr 30:8, where it designates an exclusive worship and obedience. Compare Paul's reference to the Galatian believers as having served "things/beings that by nature are not gods" (Gal 4:8–9) prior to their conversion.

13. See also my discussion in *God in New Testament Theology*, 49–71, esp. 59–64.

14. C. A. Wanamaker, "Christ as a Divine Agent in Paul," *Journal of Theological Studies* 39 (1986): 517–28.

"dyadic pattern," involving God and Jesus from the opening words of this epistle, where Paul refers to the Thessalonian church as "in God the Father and the Lord Jesus Christ" (1:1), the religious position of these believers now identified with reference both to God and Jesus.[15] As a more extended illustration, note the prayer-wish in 1 Thessalonians 3:11–13, where Paul appeals both to God and Jesus to enable a reunion with his addressees and then specifically invokes "the Lord" (who must be Jesus here) to cause them to flourish in love and holiness, in anticipation of their being presented before God at the *parousia* of "our Lord Jesus with all his saints."[16] At various other points in this epistle, we have reflections of this same strong linkage of God and Jesus, such as Paul's reference in 5:9–10 to God's designation of believers for "salvation through our Lord Jesus Christ," whose redemptive death and risen life comprise the basis for their hope. Notice also how Paul exhorts his readers to "give thanks in everything, for this is God's will for you in Christ Jesus" (1 Thess 5:18).

Paul's most extended discussion of the religious stance of Christian believers in the larger Roman religious environment, however, is in 1 Corinthians 8–10. Here, too, we have the same intense distinction between the vain worship of the pagan deities and the valid worship of the one God. This distinction is apparent from the outset of this discussion in 8:1, where Paul refers to sacrifices to the pagan deities as "offerings to idols" (εἰδωλόθυτα), using similarly derisive language again in 8:4, where he dismisses pagan deities as idols and affirms that there is only one God (οὐδεὶς θεὸς εἰ μὴ εἷς). We see this same viewpoint in vv. 5–6, where Paul contrasts the pagan polytheistic outlook with the exclusivist stance that believers should affirm. Derisively referring to "so-called gods" and to the "many gods and many lords," Paul then declares (v. 6),

15. In a number of previous publications, I referred to a "binitarian" shape to earliest Christian devotion, meaning by this term only an inclusion of Jesus with God, not as a second deity but as the unique agent of God, with Jesus' divine status defined consistently with reference to God. Unfortunately, however, some scholars have wrongly supposed that my use of "binitarian" involved (or allowed) imputing to New Testament texts doctrinal concepts from later Trinitarian debates. So, I resort here to referring simply to a "duality" or "dyadic pattern" in early Christian discourse and devotion, as described previously. Some have referred to the phenomena as comprising a Christological monotheism, as, e.g., Richard J. Bauckham, *God Crucified: Monotheism and Christology in the New Testament* (Carlisle: Paternoster, 1998), chap. 2, "Christological Monotheism in the New Testament," 25–42; and in the title of the volume from the 1998 conference in St. Andrews: Newman, Davila, and Lewis, *Jewish Roots of Christological Monotheism*.

16. In 1 Thes 5:1–6, we have Paul's further exhortation to believers to live in anticipation of Jesus' *parousia*.

But for us there is one God, the Father, from whom (are) all things, and we (are) for him [καὶ ἡμεῖς εἰς αὐτόν], and one Lord, Jesus Christ, through whom (are) all things, and we (are) through him [καὶ ἡμεῖς δι' αὐτοῦ].

It is widely (but not universally) recognized that Paul's statement here draws upon and adapts the traditional Jewish confession of God's uniqueness, the *Shema'* (derived from Dt 6:4), with motifs that also reflect Hellenistic Jewish discourse about God (e.g., the use of the several Greek prepositions that likely stem from Greek philosophical tradition).[17] But the most striking thing about Paul's statement is the line about Jesus in 1 Cor 8:6b.[18] Paul includes here the affirmation of Jesus' unique and universal role as an equally central component of the religious stance that he commends, reflecting a conspicuous duality of God and Jesus similar to that which we noted in the several texts examined in 1 Thessalonians. It is especially noteworthy here that Paul portrays "all things" (τὰ πάντα) with reference both to God and to Jesus, ascribing a universal scope to both. Yet, again, this duality is one in which Jesus is functionally subordinate to "God the Father," all things and believers *from* God and *for* God, and all things and believers *through* Jesus, who here, as typically in the texts considered earlier, is represented as the unique agent of divine purposes. Nevertheless, this programmatic linkage of Jesus with God is with-

17. Erik Peterson, *Εις Θεος*, Forschungen zur Religion und Literatur des Alten und Neuen Testaments 23 (Göttingen: Vandenhoeck and Ruprecht, 1926), 219–40, suggested that Paul's language here is influenced by the *Shema'*, and this view has been taken up subsequently by others; see, e.g., Anthony Thiselton, *The First Epistle to the Corinthians*, New International Greek Testament Commentary (Grand Rapids, Mich.: Eerdmans, 2000), 635–38; Raymond F. Collins, *First Corinthians*, Sacra Pagina (Collegeville, Minn.: Liturgical Press, 1999), 315–18; Hans Conzelmann, *1 Corinthians: Hermeneia Commentary* (Philadelphia: Fortress, 1975), 142–45; Charles H. Giblin, "Three Monotheistic Texts in Paul," *Catholic Biblical Quarterly* 37 (1975): 528–47 (esp. 529–37). Oddly, Birger Gerhardsson, "The Shema' in Early Christianity," *The Four Gospels 1992: Festschrift Frans Neirynck*, ed. F. van Segbroeck et al. (Leuven: Leuven University Press, 1992), 275–93, makes no mention of 1 Cor 8:4–6.

18. On whether in 1 Cor 8:6b Paul incorporates Jesus into the confession of God in the *Shema'* or couples an assertion about Jesus to it, compare opinions discussed by James D. G. Dunn, *Did the First Christians Worship Jesus? The New Testament Evidence* (London: SPCK, 2010), 107–10. James McGrath prefers the latter option: *The Only True God: Early Christian Monotheism in Its Jewish Context* (Champaign: University of Illinois Press, 2009), 38–44. In any event, McGrath certainly errs in claiming that such a coupling of Jesus with God was "not in fact unparalleled in Jewish literature" (40). In point of fact, he provides no true analogy or precedent, and I know of none. However one construes 1 Cor 8:6, it is a novel and even astonishing statement in the way that Jesus is so closely linked with God. Compare the recent in-depth study by Erik Waaler, *The Shema and the First Commandment in First Corinthians*, Wissenschaftliche Untersuchungen zum Neuen Testament, series 2, vol. 253 (Tübingen: Mohr Siebeck, 2008), who concludes decisively that "in 1 Cor 8:6 Paul divided the *Shema* in two" and "reinterpreted" and "expanded" the traditional Jewish confession to accommodate Jesus (433).

out precedent or analogy in Second Temple Jewish tradition and is certainly remarkable.[19] Indeed, we can even note that this inclusion of Jesus into early Christian devotional discourse and practice is the probable reason that God is so often referred to as "Father" in early Christian texts, as is the case in 1 Corinthians 8:6. "Father" both reflects the paradigmatic relationship of God to Jesus and serves to distinguish clearly "God" from the divine "Lord" Jesus.

There is, however, no hint in any Pauline text that this subordination reflects any hesitation or reserve about what Jesus' significance should be in belief and devotional life.[20] Instead, it is impressive how Paul boldly refers to Jesus in statements where he might simply have referred to God. For example, in 1 Corinthians 10:14–22, Paul counterposes "the worship of idols [εἰδωλολατρία]" against participation/fellowship in the blood and body of Christ (vv. 14–16), urging that "you cannot drink the cup of the Lord and the cup of demons; you cannot partake of the table of the Lord and the table of demons" (v. 21), and warning against provoking "the Lord" to jealousy (v. 22). Although the idea of divine jealousy stems from Old Testament references to *Yahweh*'s response to idolatry (e.g., Ex 20:5, 34:14; Dt 5:8–9; and esp. Dt 32:15–21), in the passage before us "the Lord" must obviously be the risen Jesus, whose table, bread, and cup comprise the Christian sacred meal.[21] The broad effect of Paul's statements here is certainly to make Jesus centrally integral in Christian worship and to identify Christian worship as much with reference to Jesus as to God.

Likewise, notice how in the opening lines of 1 Corinthians Paul so easily combines references to the Corinthian believers as "the church of God" and as "sanctified in Christ Jesus" and then even designates Christians simply as "all those everywhere who call upon the name of our Lord Jesus Christ, (who is) their Lord and ours" (1:2). As is well recognized among exegetes, the verb ἐπικαλέω (in middle voice form) used with reference to a deity typically connotes an act of worship.[22] Indeed, the full phrase that Paul uses here is

19. I demonstrated this most fully in my 1988 book, *One God, One Lord.*

20. Paul was no first-century Unitarian reacting against what he saw as exaggerated Christological claims.

21. So, e.g., Thiselton, *First Epistle to the Corinthians*, 778, and see Raymond F. Collins, *First Corinthians*, 381, for references to divine jealousy in Old Testament and post-biblical Jewish texts.

22. See, e.g., Thiselton, *First Epistle to the Corinthians*, 78–80, who cites examples of the verb used in pagan texts (Plato, *Timaeus* 27c; Epictetus, *Dissertations* 2.7.12), in addition to the more commonly recognized Old Testament uses.

specifically a remarkable adaptation of a familiar Old Testament formula, to "call upon the name of the Lord," that designates offering worship (typically sacrifice) to *Yahweh* (e.g., Gn 12:8, 13:4, 21:33, 26:25; Ps 99:6, 105:1; Joel 2:32 [Heb 3:5]). But Paul's remarkable use of the phrase explicitly makes Jesus the recipient of this action.[23] As Conzelmann noted, we have here "a technical expression for 'Christians'" by reference to a ritual action that is reflected in other New Testament texts as well (Acts 9:14, 21, 22:16; 2 Tm 2:22).[24] It is also one of the most obvious instances of Paul's application to Jesus of what David Capes called "Yahweh texts."[25]

In Romans 10:9–13, we get another reference to this ritual invocation/confession of Jesus as a common feature of gathered worship. Moreover, in v. 13, Paul's obvious (indeed, remarkable) use of the statement from Joel, "whoever calls upon the name of the Lord will be saved," shows that he sees the ritual acclamation of Jesus in terms of the Old Testament expression. The acclamation of Jesus is now the proper way in which to "call upon the name of the Lord." That is, the worship of God must now be done with reference to Jesus, and the acclamation of Jesus is now integral (even requisite) to the proper worship of God.[26]

Furthermore, this close linkage of Jesus and God is by no means peculiar to Paul but, instead, is reflected rather broadly across the New Testament. To cite a text from a very different provenance, consider, for example, the Johannine statement, "This is eternal life, that they may know you, the only true God, and Jesus Christ whom you have sent" (Jn 17:4). Note here that salvific

23. Note also how in Acts 9:14 Saul is pictured as persecuting Jewish believers, referred to simply as "all who call upon your name" (Ananias addressing the risen Jesus who has appeared to him in a vision). For further discussion of the verb, see, e.g., K. L. Schmidt, "επικαλεω," *Theological Dictionary of the New Testament*, ed. Gerhard Kittel (Grand Rapids, Mich.: Eerdmans, 1964–76), 3:496–500; compare W. Kirchschläger, "επικαλεω," *Exegetical Dictionary of the New Testament,* ed. Horst Balz and Gerhard Schneider (Grand Rapids, Mich.: Zondervan, 1990–93), 2:28–29, who emphasizes the confessional nature of the act and seems to me to ignore the cultic connotation. For more on the Old Testament background of the phrase and the cultic action it connotes and the New Testament instances of the phrase, see Carl J. Davis, *The Name and Way of the Lord: Old Testament Themes; New Testament Christology*, Supplement series 129 (Sheffield: Sheffield Academic Press, 1996), 103–40.

24. Conzelmann, *1 Corinthians*, 23.

25. Capes, *Old Testament Yahweh Texts in Paul's Christology*, Wissenschaftliche Untersuchungen zum Neuen Testament, series 2, vol. 47 (Tübingen: J. C. B. Mohr, 1992), esp. 116–23.

26. A point emphasized by C. Kavin Rowe, "Romans 10:13: What Is the Name of the Lord?" *Horizons in Biblical Theology* 22 (2000): 135–73.

knowledge involves both God and Jesus. It is all the more significant that this statement is part of John 17, the priestly prayer of Jesus, which is typically taken as the passage that most likely reflects the theological outlook of the author.[27] This duality of God and Jesus in v. 4 is echoed all through the prayer. But it is a "shaped" duality, by which I mean that Jesus' divine status is consistently defined with reference to God (the Father), with Jesus represented as the unique agent of, and subordinate to, the Father.[28] For example, God has given the Son "authority over all flesh to grant eternal life to all whom you [God] have given to him" (v. 2). Jesus claims to have made God's name known to those given to him by God (v. 6), and affirms, "All mine are yours, and yours are mine" (v. 10). Indeed, the prayer presents Jesus and the Father as in some real sense "one" (vv. 11, 22). Nevertheless, Jesus repeatedly affirms here that he has been sent by God (vv. 3, 18, 23) and that his glory is conferred by God (vv. 5, 22, 24). In short, the passage presents Jesus as both integral to the knowledge of God and "one" with God, sharing in divine glory, and yet also as a distinguishable figure, "the Son" who was sent forth by God (the Father). Indeed, this remarkable presentation of Jesus as linked with and yet also distinct from God (the Father) appears right from the opening words of John, where the author declares that "the Word" was both "with God" and "was God" (1:1).[29]

In Mark 12:29 we have the only explicit quotation of the *Shema'* in the New Testament in the response of Jesus to the scribe's question about the greatest commandment. But we also have a rather obvious allusion in another scene where a man asks Jesus how to obtain eternal life in Mark 10:17–22 (parallels in Mt 19:16–22; Lk 18:18–23), and Jesus responds, "Why do you call me good? No one is good but God alone [εἰ μὴ εἷς ὁ θεός]" (v. 18).[30] In both of

27. For proposals on the origin of John 17, compare, e.g., Raymond E. Brown, *The Gospel according to John (xiii–xxi)* (Garden City, N.Y.: Doubleday, 1970), 744–51, and Rudolf Schnackenburg, *The Gospel according to St. John*, vol. 3, *Commentary on Chapters 13–21* (New York: Crossroad, 1982), 197–202.

28. Paul N. Anderson, *The Christology of the Fourth Gospel*, Wissenschaftliche Untersuchungen zum Neuen Testament series 2, vol. 78 (Tübingen: J. C. B. Mohr, 1996); Jan-A. Bühner, *Der Gesandte und sein Weg im 4. Evangelium: Die kultur- und religionsgeschichtlichen Grundlagen der johanneischen Sendungschristologie so wie ihre traditionsgeschichtliche Entwicklung*, Wissenschaftliche Untersuchungen zum Neuen Testament series 2, vol. 2 (Tübingen: J.C.B. Mohr, 1977); Rudolf Schnackenburg, "'Der Vater, der mich gesandt hat': Zur johaneischen Christologie," in *Anfänge der Christologie: Festschrift für Ferdinand Hahn zum 65. Geburtstag*, ed. Cilliers Breytenbach and Henning Paulsen (Göttingen: Vandenhoeck and Ruprecht, 1991), 275–91.

29. That is, each affirmation in John 1:1–2 is intended to be read in connection with the other.

30. The Matthew passage has slightly different wording: "Why do you ask me about the good?

these references to the *Shema'*, Jesus is presented as a pious and humble Jew, affirming God's uniqueness and, in the second scene especially, demurring from flattery and self-exaltation. In the larger context of each of the gospels, however, it is clear that this in no way was regarded as in tension with the affirmation of Jesus' unique significance—for example, as "Son of God," Messiah, and exalted "Lord."[31] Instead, these monotheistic statements simply reflect the typical stance of earliest Christian circles: that with all their reverence of Jesus, they really were loyal adherents of the one God and aligned themselves with what they took as the biblical tradition, but their loyalty to this tradition modified in light of God's new revelatory act in Jesus.[32]

I consider one additional New Testament writing to illustrate further this close association of Jesus with God. Over thirty years ago Richard Bauckham drew attention to the noteworthy way that the author of Revelation both strongly affirms an exclusivist worship-stance and yet also approves of Jesus being a joint recipient of worship with the one God.[33] The prophet John rejects as idolatry and religious "fornication" the offerings to the pagan deities (Rv 2:14, 9:20–21), condemns as blasphemy the worship of "the beast" (13:1–4), and, conspicuously, reflects a prohibition against worshipping God's angels (19:10, 22:8–9), insisting that only the one biblical deity is to be worshipped (19:10, 22:8–9). Yet his portrayal of heavenly worship in Revelation 4–5 (which John must intend as ideal and paradigmatic) culminates in a scene where the heavenly courtiers (the four "living creatures" and the twenty-four "elders") sing "a new song" acclaiming "the Lamb" as worthy of their praise on

There is one who is good [εἷς ἐστιν ὁ ἀγαθός]." I cannot engage here questions about what this variation may have represented for the author of Matthew.

31. E.g., Mk 8:34–9:1 makes one's commitment to Jesus the determining factor in eschatological judgment, and in Mk 14:62–64 Jesus declares that he is to be given the unique status as God's vizier.

32. In Jas 2:19 we have another allusion to the *Shema'*: "You believe that God is one. You do well. The demons also believe (this) and they fear." But the allusion does not contribute much to our desire to map out early Christian beliefs.

33. Bauckham, "The Worship of Jesus in Apocalyptic Christianity," *New Testament Studies* 27 (1981): 322–41. See also his revised and expanded discussion: Bauckham, "The Worship of Jesus," in *The Climax of Prophecy: Studies on the Book of Revelation* (Edinburgh: T. and T. Clark, 1993), 118–49. Bauckham's seminal observations were taken up for more extended investigation by Loren T. Stuckenbruck, *Angel Veneration and Christology*, Wissenschaftliche Untersuchungen zum Neuen Testament, series 2, vol. 70 (Tübingen: J. C. B. Mohr, 1995), who referred to a "refusal tradition" in a number of ancient Jewish and Christian texts reflected in scenes where a human attempts to offer worship to an angel, who then refuses this and directs the human to worship God. In Rv 19:10 and 22:8–9, we have this tradition affirmed by John.

account of his redemptive death (5:9–10), this praise then echoed by an innumerable host of heavenly beings (5:11–12). Then, climatically, John depicts worship directed "to him who sits on the throne and to the Lamb" given by "every creature in heaven and on earth and under the earth and in the sea" (5:13–14). It is difficult to avoid the conclusion that the author intends to depict true/heavenly/ideal worship as inclusive of Jesus "the Lamb" along with God.

Nevertheless, Revelation also reflects the sort of structured duality noted in the other New Testament texts previously examined. John's book records "the revelation of Jesus Christ, which God gave him to show his servants what must soon take place" (1:1). John's greeting to readers (1:4–6) invokes grace and peace from God ("the one who is and who was and who is to come"), from "the seven spirits," and from "Jesus Christ."[34] This greeting is followed by a doxology that seems to be directed to Jesus, but note also here that Jesus' redemptive work constitutes believers as "a kingdom, priests to his God and Father" (v. 6). Likewise, the august and glorious Jesus who appears to John (1:9–20) and dictates messages to the seven churches refers to having received "authority from my Father" so that he can give to faithful believers "authority over the nations" (2:26–28). In Revelation 21:22–23, "the Lord God the Almighty, and the Lamb" together comprise the temple of the new Jerusalem, and "the glory of God is its light, and its lamp is the Lamb," and then in 22:1 the author refers to "the throne of God and of the Lamb," linking them in rule as well as in worship.

This structured/shaped duality of God and Jesus in the discourse and religious practices reflected in the New Testament could be illustrated further, but I trust that the texts considered here will suffice to demonstrate the extraordinary linkage of Jesus with God in the distinctive religious stance that I have labeled "early Christian monotheism."

The Spirit

Although the most distinctive feature of the discourse about God in the New Testament is the prominence of references to Jesus, references to the divine Spirit certainly comprise another salient feature of this discourse.[35] Of

34. Granted, we have here what seems more a triadic-shaped statement, the "seven spirits" likely a curious way of referring to the divine Spirit, who also is mentioned as the co-source of the messages to the churches (Rv 2:7, 11, 17, 29, 3:6, 13, 22).

35. Further discussion in Hurtado, *God in New Testament Theology*, 73–94, where I also cite a num-

course, the Old Testament and Second Temple Jewish texts refer to the divine Spirit, but there is a far greater frequency of references in the New Testament.[36] Compare, for example, the roughly seventy-five references to the Spirit in the Old Testament (Hebrew *Tanach*) with some 275 in the New Testament. When one takes into account the far greater size of the Old Testament, the frequency of references to the Spirit in the New Testament is all the more impressive. Likewise, although the divine Spirit is certainly a part of the religious discourse attested in extra-canonical Jewish texts, there is a considerably greater frequency of references to the Spirit in the New Testament. For instance, compare the twenty-seven references to the Spirit in Paul's epistle to the Romans, or the fifty-eight references in Acts, with the total of thirty-five references identified by Sekki in the whole body of nonbiblical Hebrew texts from Qumran.[37]

Moreover, the New Testament references often portray actions that seem to give the Spirit an intensely personal quality, probably more so than in Old Testament or ancient Jewish texts. So, for example, the Spirit "drove" Jesus into the wilderness (Mk 1:12; compare "led" in Mt. 4:1/Lk 4:1), and Paul refers to the Spirit interceding for believers (Rom 8:26–27) and witnessing to believers about their filial status with God (Rom 8:14–16). To cite other examples of this, in Acts the Spirit alerts Peter to the arrival of visitors from Cornelius (10:19), directs the church in Antioch to send forth Barnabas and Saul (13:2–4), guides the Jerusalem council to a decision about Gentile converts (15:28), at one point forbids Paul to missionize in Asia (16:6), and at another point warns Paul (via prophetic oracles) of trouble ahead in Jerusalem (21:11).

But perhaps the most striking feature of New Testament references to the Spirit of God is the repeated connection made with Jesus. There is certainly no similar linkage of the divine Spirit with any figure other than God in biblical and Jewish tradition of the time.[38] This linkage includes such statements

ber of other publications. Most recently, see John R. Levison, *Filled with the Spirit* (Grand Rapids, Mich.: Eerdmans, 2009), esp. 225–421, for his discussion of New Testament texts.

36. See, e.g., Robert P. Menzies, *The Development of Early Christian Pneumatology with Special Reference to Luke-Acts, Journal for the Study of the New Testament*, Supplements 54 (Sheffield: Sheffield Academic Press, 1991), esp. 52–112, and Levison, *Filled with the Spirit*, 109–221, for discussions of Second Temple Jewish evidence.

37. Arthur Everett Sekki, *The Meaning of Ruah at Qumran*, Society of Biblical Literature Dissertation Series 110 (Atlanta: Scholars Press, 1989), 71.

38. Max Turner, "The Spirit of Christ and Christology," in *Christ the Lord: Studies Presented to*

as Paul's declaration that the Spirit prompts the confession "Jesus is Lord" (1 Cor 12:3), where Paul seems to make this an identifying distinction between God's Spirit and the spiritual forces connected with the "idols." Likewise, in 1 John 4:1–3, we have a similar and even more explicit statement: "By this you know the Spirit of God: every spirit that confesses that Jesus Christ has come in the flesh is from God, and every spirit that does not confess Jesus is not from God" (NRSV).

Still more arresting are New Testament statements that interweave references to the Spirit and Jesus. Consider, for example, Paul's discussion of Christian empowerment for life in Romans 8 and his combination of stating that believers are "in Christ Jesus" (8:1) with a summons to live "according to the Spirit" and to set their minds on the Spirit (8:4–6). In the same immediate context, Paul declares that believers are "in the Spirit" and indwelt by the Spirit of God (8:9) and that they have "the Spirit of Christ" and that "Christ is in you" (8:10), all of these phrases likely complementary descriptions of the same boon given to believers. Similarly, in Galatians 4:6, Paul writes that "God has sent the Spirit of his Son into our hearts."

In what is the most extended discourse about the Spirit in the New Testament, John 14–16, the Spirit is given the distinctive sobriquet "the *Paraklētos*" (ὁ παράκλητος), indicative of what is to be the Spirit's role as advocate of Jesus sent by God in Jesus' name (14:25) and consequent on Jesus departure and glorification (14:15–17, 16:7). As Jesus' advocate, the Spirit will teach and remind believers about Jesus (14:25–26) and testify to them about Jesus (15:26), guiding them "into all truth" (about Jesus), glorifying Jesus (to believers) and declaring his significance (16:12–15).

In sum, the greater frequency of references to the divine Spirit, the frequent depiction of the Spirit in personalized terms, and the strong linkage of God's Spirit to Jesus combine to make the representation and place of Spirit in the New Testament distinctive in the context of Second Temple Judaism. But, though the Spirit features prominently in the "God-discourse" reflected in the

---

Donald Guthrie, ed. H. H. Rowdon (Leicester: InterVarsity, 1982), 168–90; and "The Spirit of Christ and 'Divine' Christology," in *Jesus of Nazareth, Lord and Christ*, ed. Joel B. Green and Max Turner (Grand Rapids, Mich.: Eerdmans, 1994), 413–36; Mehrdad Fatehi, *The Spirit's Relation to the Risen Lord in Paul: An Examination of Its Christological Implications*, Wissenschaftliche Untersuchungen zum Neuen Testament, series 2, vol. 128 (Tübingen: Mohr Siebeck, 2000); and Gordon D. Fee, *Pauline Christology* (Peabody, Mass.: Hendrickson, 2007), esp. 586–93.

New Testament, it is noteworthy that the Spirit is not portrayed as a recipient of cultic devotion, which, instead, is typically offered to God and to the risen/glorified Jesus. Although what became mainstream Christianity subsequently affirmed the propriety of including the Spirit as recipient of worship (as reflected in the developed form of the "Nicene Creed"), perhaps the closest that we get to this in the New Testament is in Paul's famous benediction at the end of 2 Corinthians, "The grace of our Lord Jesus Christ, the love of God and the communion of the Holy Spirit be with all of you" (13:13), or the triadic baptismal formula in Matthew 28:19.[39]

A Triadic-Shaped Discourse

Nevertheless, although the New Testament devotional/worship pattern has what we might term a "dyadic shape"—devotion directed to God and to Jesus—it is appropriate to characterize the discourse about God in the New Testament as having a certain "triadic shape," with God (the Father), Jesus, and the Spirit featuring regularly.[40] Of course, we should not ascribe the later-developed doctrine of the Trinity to New Testament writers (not because they rejected such a doctrine, but because the philosophical questions and categories taken up later had not arisen among them in their time). But it is clear that the theological developments that led to the doctrine of the Trinity were to some significant degree prompted and even made unavoidable by the dyadic devotional pattern and the triadic shape of discourse about God that we see amply attested in the New Testament texts.

> That is, the N[ew] T[estament] writings vigorously affirm the "one God" stance inherited from the Jewish matrix of earliest Christian faith, but also (and with at least equal vigor) affirm especially the non-negotiable significance of Jesus in belief and devotional practice, and further, frequently refer to the divine Spirit as the mode or agency by

39. The affirmation of the legitimacy of including the Spirit as explicitly corecipient of worship was added in the later, enlarged form of the Nicene Creed, the "Nicene-Constantinopolitan Creed" (usually linked to the second Ecumenical Council of 381 C.E.). The added material includes the statement that the Spirit "with the Father and the Son together is worshipped and glorified"; see Philip Schaff, *The Creeds of Chistendom* (1931; repr. Grand Rapids, Mich.: Baker, 1977), 1:24–29. Curiously, in standard histories of the early Christian Trinitarian controversies there are only limited discussions of the question about worshipping the Spirit; see, for example, Adolph von Harnack, *History of Dogma*, trans. Neil Buchanan (1900; repr. New York: Dover, 1961), 4:108–37, and, more recently, Hanson, *Search for the Christian Doctrine of God*, 738–90.

40. See Hurtado, *God in New Testament Theology*, 99–110, "The Triadic Shape of God-Discourse in the NT."

which "God" and Jesus are made present and real to believers. So, the question of how to harmonize these affirmations, particularly how to posit "one God" genuinely and yet also recognize Jesus as somehow really sharing in divine glory, could not be avoided by Christians in the second and third centuries C.E.[41]

Corollaries of Early Christian Monotheism

In the final part of this discussion, I briefly consider two matters that may serve as examples of corollaries of the monotheistic stance affirmed in the New Testament. Each of these illustrates for us how early Christian monotheism was not simply a matter of belief and a pattern of devotional practice; there were wider implications.

The first and perhaps the earliest illustration is reflected in Romans 3:27–31, where Paul uses the traditional affirmation of the one God (εἴπερ εἷς ὁ θεός) as a premise with strong soteriological and practical consequences for the basis on which Jewish and Gentile believers should relate to one another.[42] Here, one God means one basis for putting people right with God, which is faith (in Christ), whether they be Jews or Gentiles.[43] "There is no distinction" (Rom 3:22), for "all have sinned" and so stand dependent on the redemptive provision of the one God.

This line of thought, which we might refer to as a distinctive "monotheistic soteriology," is reflected also in Romans 10:1–13, except that in this passage the emphasis is placed on the one Lord Jesus and the universal dimensions of his redemptive significance. Here Paul declares that "Christ is the end-purpose or goal [τέλος] of the Law for righteousness to everyone who believes (in him)" (v. 4).[44] Then, after a rather creative appropriation of texts from Leviticus and

41. Ibid., 100—that is, this question could not be avoided by Christians in the so-called "proto-orthodox" circles.

42. See a fuller discussion of this passage in, for instance, Robert Jewett, *Romans: A Critical Commentary*, Hermeneia (Minneapolis: Fortress, 2007), 299–302; Paul-Gerhard Klumbies, "Der Eine Gott des Paulus—Röm 3:21–31 als Brennpunkt paulinischer Theologie," *Zeitschrift für die Neutestamentliche Wissenschaft und die Kunde der Älteren Kirche* 85 (1994): 192–206; and Giblin, "Three Monotheistic Texts," 543–45. On Paul's monotheistic stance more broadly, see Wolfgang Schrage, *Unterwegs zur Einzigkeit und Einheit Gottes: Zum "Monotheismus" des Paulus und seiner alttestamentlich-frühjudischen Tradition* (Neukirchen-Vluyn: Neukirchener Verlag, 2002).

43. I emphasize that "faith" in Paul is not some abstract principle. Even when stated in absolute form, as in Rom 3:30–31, "faith" always means trusting in God, and this side of Jesus' *parousia* appearance that always means trusting in him as God's final provision for salvation.

44. I take this frequently commented-on statement as primarily reflecting Paul's view of Jesus' eschatological significance vis-a-vis the Torah. He supersedes Torah in securing eschatological salvation,

Deuteronomy (vv. 5–8), Paul posits as the appropriate responses the acclamation of and faith in Jesus as the risen Lord, and he cites the scriptural assurance that "no one who believes in him will be made ashamed" (v. 11, citing Is 28:16). This leads to Paul's proclamation that "there is no distinction between Jew and Greek; the same Lord is Lord of all and generous to all who call upon him" (v. 12), which means that "everyone who calls upon the name of the Lord shall be saved" (v. 13). Essentially, in this passage Paul declares that the universality of the one God is expressed now in the finality and universality of Jesus as the one Lord upon whom all may (indeed, must!) call for salvation.[45]

In Galatians 3:19–22, we see yet another instance where Paul invokes a monotheistic statement in the course of making a case for the universal salvific relevance of the faith in Jesus. These statements form part of Paul's larger discussion of the relationship of Torah and faith in Christ in 3:1–4:6. In 3:6–18, Paul lays out an intricate argument that the promise to Abraham is fulfilled not through Torah but through Christ. This prompts the question in 3:19, "Why then the Law?," to which Paul answers that Torah was a provisional measure with a limited purpose. Reflective of this relative inferiority of Torah, says Paul, it was delivered by angels and through "a mediator" who must obviously be Moses. Then comes the key statement, "But/so the mediator is not of one; but God is one" (v. 20).[46] That is, Moses was mediator of a revelation given to him by angels, this plurality (of angels) contrasting with the oneness of God, whose promises Paul has made primary in the preceding discussion. The logic seems to be that the oneness of God must issue in a revelation that directly corresponds to God's promise, and Paul's obvious claim is that this revelation has come in Christ, the fulfillment of the promise thus available to all who trust in him (v. 22).

In Revelation, we have another but different practical expression of early Christian monotheism, in this case in what we might term the "sociopolitical sphere." Although there is no explicit statement of or direct allusion to the *Shema'* in Revelation, as we have noted earlier it is undeniable that the author held an exclusivist monotheistic stance. Indicative of the author's strictness is

but also brings to reality the ultimate purpose of Torah in making righteousness available to all; e.g., Jewett, *Romans*, 619–20.

45. See also discussion by Rowe, "Romans 10:13," esp. 146–50.

46. I follow here the analysis by Giblin, "Three Monotheistic Texts," 537–43, esp. 540–41, on how to understand v. 20.

his sharp criticism of those in the churches of Pergamum and Thyatira who promoted what he regarded as a dangerously lax attitude about "food sacrificed to idols" (2:14–15, 20–23). To be sure, as we have observed earlier, Revelation portrays the true and proper worship of God as inclusive of "the Lamb," seeing no conflict with his exclusivist stance in this "dyadic" devotional pattern nor any weakening of his negative attitude toward the worship of other deities.

But the author's sharply negative view about giving worship to other deities extends also specifically to a condemnation of "the Beast" (Revelation 13), which is commonly taken as the author's term for what he regards as the (increasingly) monstrous and blasphemous demands and claims of the Roman imperial rulers.[47] In 14:9–12, an angel warns earth's inhabitants not to worship "the Beast" or accept his mark, for the penalty of doing so will be the wrath of God. The seat of the Beast's rule is "Babylon" (also used in 1 Pt 5:13), a term emblematic of the rapacious and adversarial nature that the author ascribes to this regime. In Revelation 18 the author depicts a future angelic celebration of the downfall of "Babylon," citing the many sins of this evil city and concluding with the charge that "in her was found the blood of prophets and saints, and of all who have been slain upon the earth" (18:24).

This is clearly a political and economic regime of international dimensions, but the author's critique is not really based on what we would regard as a "political" or "economic" premise. Instead, the author's primary line of attack is against the (rising?) religious claims and demands of "the Beast" and the regime that he leads. The readiness of kings and merchants to ally themselves with "Babylon" must mean that there were advantages to be shared. But for this author, first and foremost, allegiance to "the Beast" and his regime constitutes idolatry.

47. It appears that under the Flavians (and thereafter), the religious claims of the sitting/living emperor escalated, from being the designated "son" of the deified (dead) emperor (his immediate predecessor) to being himself divine and so to be given cultic reverence; see, e.g., Paul Keresztes, "The Imperial Roman Government and the Christian Church," in *From Nero to the Severi: Aufstieg und Niedergang der römischen Welt*, series 2, vol. 23, part 1, 247–315 (Berlin: De Gruyter, 1980); Kenneth Scott, *The Imperial Cult under the Flavians* (1936; repr. New York: Arno, 1975); and Steven J. Friesen, *Imperial Cults and the Apocalypse of John: Reading Revelation in the Ruins* (New York: Oxford University Press, 2001).

Conclusion

I conclude simply by underscoring the main points in the preceding discussion. The first of these points is terminological. Although it is dubious to ascribe the "monotheism" of the modern dictionaries to ancient Jews and Christians, nevertheless, it is clear that ancient Jews (and Christians, at least as reflected in the New Testament) typically took a stance that involved rejecting the worship of the many deities of the religious environment in favor of an exclusive worship of the one deity of biblical tradition and that this comprised a distinctive religious posture in the ancient Roman setting. I propose that the cultic exclusivity typical of ancient Judaism may be referred to as "ancient Jewish monotheism." I emphasize that this is not "monotheism" as defined later, but "ancient Jewish monotheism," which was expressed most clearly in a cultic exclusivity.

Moreover, the New Testament reflects a further distinctive feature central to the religious stance it promotes, which involves the inclusion of the risen/exalted Jesus uniquely as a co-recipient of cultic devotion along with the one God. Yet Jesus is not represented as a second deity; instead, he is designated by God as the unique agent of divine purposes and as the rightful corecipient of devotion. In obedience to God, therefore, the proper worship of the one God must now include the exalted Jesus. To avoid confusion, this dyadic pattern of devotion can be designated "early Christian monotheism." It comprises a distinctive mutation or innovation in the "ancient Jewish monotheism" in which it first appeared. This innovation reflects and shares the cultic exclusivity of the Jewish matrix from which it historically derived but has this distinctive "dyadic shape," making "early Christian monotheism" a further distinguishable kind of religious posture and practice.

This distinctive stance also served as the basis for engaging questions beyond whether to worship other deities. Paul argues from a "one God" premise that there must be one basis of salvation for Jews and Gentiles—this in support of his Gentile mission. In Revelation, we see how the cultic exclusivity of the author makes it impossible to accept the rising claims and demands of the Roman imperial system, leading to the stark alternatives of acquiescence or martyrdom that are held out in this text.

In sum, there is a distinctive kind of monotheism affirmed in the New Testament, and it clearly had profound significance in what we regard as the religious sphere and in other spheres of life, as well.

PART 2

JOHN AND THE TRINITY

Harold W. Attridge

3. TRINITARIAN THEOLOGY AND THE FOURTH GOSPEL

The path from the experience of the first followers of Jesus to the Trinitarian theology of the fourth century is a long and complex one, often traced by historians of doctrine.[1] The Gospel According to John played an important role in the shaping of that path. This essay will not attempt to retrace that

1. In general, see Cilliers Breytenbach and Henning Paulsen, eds., *Anfänge der Christologie: Festschrift für Ferdinand Hahn zum 65. Geburtstag* (Göttingen: Vandenhoeck and Ruprecht, 1991); Joel B. Green and M. Turner, eds., *Jesus of Nazareth: Lord and Christ; Essays on the Historical Jesus and New Testament Christology* (Grand Rapids: Eerdmans, 1994); Hurst and Wright, *Glory of Christ in the New Testament*; and Martin Hengel, *Studies in Early Christology* (Edinburgh: Clark, 1995). For discussion of Johannine Christology, see, e.g., T. E. Pollard, *Johannine Christology and the Early Church*; Jerome Neyrey, *An Ideology of Revolt: John's Christology in Social-Science Perspective* (Philadelphia: Fortress, 1988); Udo Schnelle, *Antidocetic Christology in the Gospel of John*, trans. Linda M. Maloney (Minneapolis: Fortress, 1992), English translation of *Antidoketische Christologie im Johannesevangelium*, Forschungen zur Religion und Literatur des Alten und Neuen Testament 144 (Göttingen: Vandenhoeck and Ruprecht, 1987); Maarten J. J. Menken, "The Christology of the Fourth Gospel: A Survey of Recent Research," in *From Jesus to John: Essays on Jesus and New Testament Christology in Honour of Marinus de Jonge*, ed. Martinus de Boer, Supplements to the *Journal for the Study of Judaism* 84 (Sheffield: Sheffield Academic Press, 1993): 292–320; William R. G. Loader, *The Christology of the Fourth Gospel: Structure and Issues*, 2nd ed., Beiträge zur biblischen Exegese und Theologie 23 (Frankfurt: Peter Lang, 1992); C. K. Barrett, "The Father is Greater Than I" (John 14:28): Subordinationist Christology in the New Testament," in *Neues Testament und Kirche, für Rudolf Schnackenburg*, ed. J. Gnilka (Freiburg, Basel, and Vienna: Herder, 1974), 144–59; repr. in Barrett, *Essays on John* (Philadelphia: Westminster Press, 1982), 19–36; M. E. Boismard, *Moses or Jesus: An Essay in Johannine Christology* (Minneapolis: Fortress; Leuven: Peeters, 1993); Paul Anderson, *Christology of the Fourth Gospel*; and Hans Weder, "*Deus Incarnatus*: On the Hermeneutics of Christology in the Johannine Writings," in *Exploring the Gospel of John: In Honor of D. Moody Smith*, ed. R. Alan Culpepper and C. Clifton Black (Louisville: Westminster/John Knox, 1996), 327–45.

history, but will simply outline what I take to be the critical elements of the Fourth Gospel that might contribute to current reflection on the Trinity.

Before I lay out those elements, it might be useful to sketch the main lines of my own approach to the gospel. Like many Johannine scholars of recent years, I have been less concerned with the process by which the gospel came to be, its literary prehistory, than with the shape of the text in more or less its canonical form.[2] It may at some point be of interest to reflect on the possible trajectory that produced the text, but that has not been the major focus of my work and will not be my focus of this essay.[3]

Second, while I am intrigued by what we might say about the social history of the Johannine community—that is, with the possible historical background to the gospel and especially its polemics[4]—I am more concerned with the ways in which the narrative works to engage and challenge its possible readers. Particularly relevant to our task is what I take to be a fundamental literary and conceptual characteristic of the gospel: its regular use of tensive symbols and unexpected twists of plot or character to engage and provoke. We shall no doubt return to that feature of the work.

The basic building blocks of a Trinitarian theology are, sure enough, in the text. The Father and the Son figure throughout the work, and the relationship between them is obviously of great concern to the evangelist. The Holy Spirit plays more of a cameo role as the promised Paraclete,[5] the Spirit of Truth. How

2. For examples of my approach, see Harold W. Attridge, *Essays on John and Hebrews*, Wissenschaftliche Untersuchungen zum Neuen Testament 264 (Tübingen: Mohr Siebeck, 2010).

3. For a recent commentary dedicated to the issue, see Urban C. von Wahlde, *The Earliest Version of John's Gospel: Recovering the Gospel of Signs* (Wilmington: Glazier, 1989), and his recent commentary, *The Gospel and Letters of John*, 3 vols., Eerdmans Critical Commentary (Grand Rapids, Mich.: Eerdmans, 2010).

4. See J. Louis Martyn, *History and Theology in the Fourth Gospel*, rev. ed. (Nashville: Abingdon, 1979), and, with different methodological tools, Neyrey, *Ideology of Revolt*, and Neyrey, *The Gospel of John in Cultural and Rhetorical Perspective* (Grand Rapids, Mich.: Eerdmanns 2009).

5. The literature on the Spirit/Paraclete is vast. Among important earlier treatments, see Hans Windsich, *The Spirit-Paraclete in the Fourth Gospel*, trans. James W. Cox, Facet Books Biblical Series 20 (Philadelphia: Fortress, 1968); Raymond E. Brown, "The Paraclete in the Fourth Gospel," *New Testament Studies* 13 (1967): 113–32; Otto Betz, *Der Paraklet: Fürsprecher Im Häretischen Spätjudentum, Im Johannes-Evangelium und in Neugefundenen Gnostischen Schriften*, Arbeiten zur Geschichte des Spätjudentums und Urchristentums 2 (Leiden: Brill, 1963). More recently, see Anthony Casurella, *The Johannine Paraclete in the Church Fathers: A Study in the History of Exegesis*, Beiträge zur Geschichte der biblischen Exegese 25 (Tübingen: Mohr, 1983); Eskil Franck, *Revelation Taught: The Paraclete in the Gospel of John*, Coniectanea Biblica, New Testament Series 14 (Lund: Gleerup, 1985); Christian Dietzfelbinger, "Paraklet und theologischer Anspruch im Johannesevangelium," *Zeitschrift für Theologie und Kirche* 82,

that Spirit relates to Father and Son is not a question addressed with anything like the detailed passion that surrounds the Father-Son relationship, but there is some effort to delineate the relationship, as we shall see in due course.

It would first be useful to review what the gospel says about Father and Son. The prologue is an appropriate place to begin, since it functions much like the hypothesis of a Greek drama, giving the audience a clue about what to expect in the story that follows.[6] But given the complexity of the prologue and its relationship to the subsequent narrative, it is best to hold it in abeyance and turn initially to the narrative. That story has two well-known and tensive foci. One is the affirmation that there is a unity between Father and Son. Jesus says so explicitly when he claims that the "Father and I are one" (Jn 10:30). That unity can, of course, be understood in several ways, as an ontological unity, or as a unity of will, purpose, or mission. The other focal point is the affirmation that "the Father is greater than I" (Jn 14:28), but exactly how that difference is to be understood remains an open question. Does the difference point to the simple fact of relationship between source and offspring who are on the same ontological level, or does it point to a difference in kind between creator and creature?

The tension and the ambiguity will remain, despite all our best efforts to resolve them, but in various subtle ways, the gospel seems to push in a direc-

no. 4 (1985): 389–408; Gary M. Burge, *The Anointed Community: The Holy Spirit in the Johannine Tradition* (Grand Rapids: Eerdmans, 1987); M. P. Wilson, "St. John, the Trinity and the Language of the Spirit," *Scottish Journal of Theology* 41, no. 4 (1988): 471–83; John Breck, *Spirit of Truth: The Holy Spirit in Johannine Tradition*, vol. 1, *The Origins of Johannine Pneumatology* (Crestwood, N.Y.: St. Vladimir's Seminary Press, 1991); Thomas B. Slater, "The Paraclete as Advocate in the Community of the Fourth Gospel," *Ashland Theological Journal* 20 (1991): 101–8; James Swetnam, SJ, "Bestowal of the Spirit in the Fourth Gospel," *Biblica* 74, no. 4 (1993): 556–76; Stephen S. Smalley, "'The Paraclete': Pneumatology in the Johannine Gospel and Apocalypse," in *Exploring the Gospel of John: In Honor of D. Moody Smith*, ed. R. Alan Culpepper and C. Clifton Black (Louisville: Westminster John Knox Press, 1996), 289–300; Benedict Viviano, OP, "The Spirit in John's Gospel: A Hegelian Perspective," *Freiburger Zeitschrift für Philosophie und Theologie* 43 (1996): 368–87; Cornelis Bennema, *The Power of Saving Wisdom: An Investigation of Spirit and Wisdom in Relation to the Soteriology of the Fourth Gospel*, Wissenschaftliche Untersuchungen zum Neuen Testament 2, no. 148 (Tübingen: Mohr Siebeck, 2002); Bennema, "The Giving of the Spirit in John's Gospel: A New Proposal?" *Evangelical Quarterly* 74 (2002): 195–214; Lochlan Shelfer, "The Legal Precision of the Term 'παράκλητος,'" *Journal for the Study of the New Testament* 32, no. 2 (2009): 131–50; Gitte Buch-Hansen, *"It Is the Spirit That Gives Life": A Stoic Understanding of Pneuma in John's Gospel*, Beihefte zur Zeitschrift für die neutestamentliche Wissenschaft 173 (Berlin: De Gruyter, 2010).

6. On dramatic elements in the gospel, see most recently George Parsenios, *Rhetoric and Drama in the Johannine Lawsuit Motif*, Wissenschaftliche Untersuchungen zum Neuen Testament 258 (Mohr Siebeck: Tübingen, 2010).

tion that defines the unity of Father and Son as much more than the unity of a prophet with the will of the deity who speaks through him.[7]

Two examples of this tendency are the defensive dialogue between Jesus and his interlocutors in chapter 5 and the appropriation by Jesus of the self-identification by God found in the Old Testament.

Consider first chapter 5, where the healing of the cripple at the Pool of Bethesda, or Bethzatha, in Jerusalem occasions a challenge to Jesus. Here a redaction of some earlier source seems likely, since there are two issues that trouble Jesus' opponents. One is that he healed on the Sabbath, a type of complaint that we find several times in the Synoptic Gospels. The other issue is that he is making a claim to be "equal to God." It thus seems likely that a traditional controversy story has been reworked into a discussion about a theological point, although the remnants of the original remain, displaced to chapter 7.[8]

The defense by Jesus is interesting and interestingly ironic. Readers might be initially tempted to say that the charge against him, that he makes himself equal to God and is therefore a blasphemer, is erroneous. If one understands Jesus to be a very special prophet, one with God in will and mission, but nothing else, one might react to the charge in this way and start rooting for Jesus to show those opponents why they are wrong. And some of what Jesus says in his defense could be construed as an argument in that direction. He is simply like an apprentice, the child of the Father, doing what the Father authorizes. He is, that is, like Elijah and Elisha, who can heal and raise the dead back to life because they are endowed with divine power and authorized from on high to use it.

But the image of the childlike apprentice learning from the Father is a two-edged sword. It suggests subordination, to be sure, and therefore a refutation of the charge that Jesus makes himself equal to the Father. At the same time it suggests a relationship between Son and Father that is more than that of prophet and authorizing God. The way Jesus frames his "apprenticeship,"

7. That elements of a "prophetic" Christology underlie the gospel is undeniable; see Wayne A. Meeks, *The Prophet-King: Moses Traditions and the Johannine Christology*, Supplements to Novum Testamentum 14 (Leiden: Brill, 1967); M. Eugene Boring, "The Influence of Christian Prophecy on the Johannine Portrayal of the Paraclete and Jesus," *New Testament Studies* 25 (1978–79): 113–23; Adele Reinhartz, "Jesus as Prophet: Predictive Prolepses in the Fourth Gospel," *Journal for the Study of the New Testament* 36 (1989): 3–16.

8. On this point, see Attridge, "Thematic Development and Source Elaboration in John 7," *Catholic Biblical Quarterly* 42 (1980): 160–70.

that he simply has done what he has always seen the Father doing, not only healing but raising the dead to life, suggests that the apprenticeship has a transcendent, eternal quality. These are not ordinary, mundane relationships or experiences. For Jesus to have had the experience he claims, he must share the world of the Father and must see things from the Father's perspective. He is, it would seem, to use language that John does not use, on the other side of the boundary that marks the Creator from the created.

Hence, the defense that Jesus mounts against the charge that he makes himself equal to God ironically affirms the substance of the charge, but not its corollary, that the claim implies blasphemy. To claim that Jesus is one with the Father precisely as eternal Son is not blasphemy, says the evangelist, but simply the Truth.[9]

A second element of the gospel that makes a strong claim about the relationship of Father and Son is the set of predicateless "I am" statements that surface at critical moments. Jesus' discourse in the gospel is peppered with two kinds of "I am" predications. Some claim "I am X," where X is some image or symbol that reveals an aspect of the reality that is Jesus: Light, Way, Truth, Life, Resurrection.[10] The multiplicity of ways of imaging Jesus may have its own significance for defining his relationship to ultimate reality, but the second type of "I am" predication is even clearer. The phrase *ego eimi*, in and of itself, is not a pointer to a theological claim. It can simply be an expression, like "c'est moi" or "it is I," or, more colloquially, "it's me," in a situation where the speaker is identifying himself.[11] But when Jesus, in the midst of a heated debate with his opponents in chapter 8, says that "before Abraham was, I am," more is at stake than an ordinary speech act of self-identification. How to characterize the claim is debatable. Jesus is at least claiming a transtemporal or transhistorical existence. And he is doing so with the language that the God of Israel used to reveal himself to Moses on Mt. Horeb (Ex 3:13).

Using the language of being to define the reality of God has precedents in philosophically informed circles of the day, in the writings of Philo and

9. For further discussion of the complexities of chapter 5, see Attridge, "Argumentation in John 5," in *Rhetorical Argumentation in Biblical Texts: Essays from the Lund 2000 Conference*, ed. Anders Eriksson, Thomas H. Olbricht, and Walter Übelacker, Emory Studies in Early Christianity 8 (Harrisburg, Pa.: Trinity Press International, 2002), 188–99.

10. Of the many studies of these sayings, see Craig Koester, *Symbolism in the Fourth Gospel: Meaning, Mystery, Community*, 2nd ed. (1995; repr. Minneapolis: Fortress, 2003).

11. See Mk 6:50.

Plutarch, especially the latter's *On the E at Delphi*, which finally interprets the mysterious glyph on Apollo's temple as an instruction to the worshipper about what he should say to God in prayer, the simple affirmation that "Thou art."[12]

Jesus' argumentative claim in chapter 8 to divine status parallels and re-emphasizes the claim made more subtly in chapter 5. Jesus is part of the reality of God's very self.

The allusion to the divine name in Jesus' locution of chapter 8 in turn evokes one of the reverential ways in which pious Jews referred to God without pronouncing his holy name. He is simply *haShem*, the Name. A further play on that motif occurs at the end of the Last Supper discourses, where Jesus offers a final prayer in which he tells the Father that he has revealed his name to the disciples and prays that they may be one. That pericope has a riddling quality to it,[13] since it does not define what the revealed name is. This is one of those texts in the gospel that challenge the reader to return to the story, to reread it and answer the question, "So, what is that name?" Various answers are possible, from "I am" to "Jesus" to "love one another as I have loved you" to simply "love." However we answer the question, we find our way to the Father, through the One who is one with him.[14]

It is not clear how much the evangelist himself is playing on the conceit of Jesus as, in some sense, the name of the Father, but it is clear that at least one perceptive reader of the Fourth Gospel in the second century did precisely that and did so in a way that gets the point of John's general Christological affirmation. I refer to the *Gospel of Truth*, a meditation on the truth of Christian proclamation from a Valentinian point of view, composed sometime in the mid- to late second century. That homily offers an interpretation of the claim that the Son is the name of the Father that builds on early Jewish-Christian name theology filtered through a philosophical lens. That lens, combining elements of Plato and Aristotle, suggests that there is a natural relationship between the name or the signifier and the named or signified when the name accurately conveys

12. Plutarch, *On the E at Delphi* 20, ed., trans. Frank Cole Babbitt, LCL 306.

13. For others who have worried about the "riddling" character of the gospel, see Tom Thatcher, *The Riddles of Jesus in John: A Study in Tradition and Folklore*, Society of Biblical Literature Monograph Series 53 (Atlanta: Society of Biblical Literature, 2000).

14. For an argument that the name is the key to Johannine Christology, see Jarl Fossum, "In the Beginning Was the Name: Onomatology as the Key to Johannine Christology," in *The Image of the Invisible God: Essays on the Influence of Jewish Mysticism on Early Christology* (Freiburg: Universitätsverlag and Vandenhoeck and Ruprecht, 1995), 117–33.

the "essence" or "ousia" of the signified. The homily claims that that is just what Jesus, the name of the Father, does.

The *Gospel of Truth* obviously extends and deepens the name theology hinted at in the Fourth Gospel, but it does so in a way that conforms to the fundamental thrust of the gospel. The Jesus who reveals the name of the Father to his disciples can affect them profoundly because of his intimate knowledge of who the Father is.

A claim about that intimacy between Father and Son concludes the prologue, and that now deserves our attention. Enormous amounts of ink have been spilled on the prologue's eighteen verses, and it is not necessary to review the extensive scholarship in detail here,[15] but a few points are worth recalling as we explore possible Trinitarian theology in John.

The prologue, which, as noted, functions as a kind of literary hypothesis before the beginning of the Johannine drama, gives the reader or hearer of gospel clues essential to understanding the story that follows. The central affirmation is that what we encounter in the man of flesh and blood, Jesus, is nothing less than the very word of God, which is itself divine (Jn 1:1). But surrounding that affirmation are multiple ambiguities, which fueled the Trinitarian and Christological controversies of later centuries.

Efforts to trace the background of the affirmations of the prologue tend to mitigate, but never eliminate, some of these ambiguities. Hellenistic Jewish speculation, like that found in Philo of Alexandria and the Wisdom of Solomon, provides the closest parallels. There older sapiential traditions were combined with Greek philosophical notions, which themselves had a complex heritage, to describe the relationship of God to the world in general and to a particular part of it, Israel and its scriptures. Philo's Logos, which could be named a "Second God,"[16] bridged the gap between Creator and creation

15. For some treatments particularly relevant to this essay, see Robert Kysar, "Christology and Controversy: The Contributions of the Prologue of the Gospel of John to New Testament Christology and Their Historical Setting," *Currents in Theology and Mission* 5, no. 6 (1978): 348–64; Craig A. Evans, *Word and Glory: On the Exegetical and Theological Background of John's Prologue*, Journal for the Study of the New Testament Supplement Series 89 (Sheffield: Sheffield Academic Press, 1993); William S. Kurz, "The Johannine Word as Revealing the Father: A Christian Credal Actualization," *Perspectives in Religious Studies* 28 (2001): 67–84; and Siegert, "Der Logos, 'älterer Sohn' des Schöpfers und 'zweiter Gott': Philons Logos und der Johannesprolog," in *Kontexte des Johannesevangeliums: Das vierte Evangelium in religions- und traditionsgeschichtlicher Perspektive*, ed. Jörg Frey and Udo Schnelle, Wissenschaftliche Untersuchungen zum Neuen Testament 175 (Tübingen: Mohr Siebeck, 2004), 277–94.

16. For a general religio-historical perspective, see Ernst Käsemann, "The Structure and Purpose

by combining a Platonic world of ideas with a Stoic immanent rational force. That Logos was made available to humankind not only through the rational principles embedded in nature, but through their expression in Torah, which the Jewish sapiential tradition had long affirmed was where wisdom had pitched her tent. Much of what Philo says about the Logos can be transferred to the Jesus of the Fourth Gospel, who is contrasted at the end of the prologue to Moses and the grace and truth that the Torah brought.

The final designation of Jesus in the prologue may neatly encapsulate the claim, whatever the original reading of v. 18. If the text calls Jesus the "Unique (or 'only begotten') God," the implications for the status of Jesus are clear, but the claim to divine status of the Logos was already made in the first verse of the prologue. If "God" is not the original reading, but is merely an "orthodox corruption" of scripture,[17] importing a later theological judgment into the text, the analysis suggested here is not substantially affected. In fact, the language of Sonship is just as suitable for the kind of affirmation that the prologue is making and, by the way, is paralleled in Philo's reflections on his Logos. The language of Sonship, based upon a divine "begetting" involving a primordial divine principle, preserves both the sense of intimate relationship guaranteeing reliable revelation and a sense of subordination. This combination matches the tensive foci of the gospel's reflection on the relationship of Son and Father.

In summary thus far, although it may be building on earlier formulations that frame the significance of Jesus primarily in prophetic terms, the Fourth Gospel clearly attributes to him a much higher status, intimately bound up with God the Father. If not "Trinitarian," the gospel is at least decidedly "bina-

---

of the Prologue to John's Gospel," in *New Testament Questions of Today* (London: SCM, 1969), 138–67; Carsten Colpe, "Von der Logoslehre des Philo zu der des Clemens von Alexandrien," in *Kerygma und Logos: Beiträge zu den geistesgeschichtlichen Beziehungen zwischen Antike und Christentum; FS für Carl Andresen zum 70. Geburtstag*, ed. A. M. Ritter (Göttingen: Vandenhoeck and Ruprecht, 1979), 89–107; reprinted in Colpe, *Der Siegel der Propheten: Historische Beziehungen zwischen Judentum, Judenchristentum, Heidentum und frühen Islam* (Berlin: Institut Kirche und Judentum, 1990), 141–64; for a comparison of John and Philo, see John Painter, "Rereading Genesis in the Prologue of John," in *Neotestamentica et Philonica: Studies in Honor of Peder Borgen*, ed. David E. Aune, Torrey Seland, and Jarl Henning Ulrichsen, Supplements to Novum Testamentum 106 (Leiden and Boston: Brill, 2003), 179–201; Attridge, "Philo and John: Two Riffs on one Logos," *Studia Philonica Anuual* 17 (2005): 103–17; and Jutta Leonhardt-Balzer, "Der Logos und die Schöpfung: Streiflichter bei Philo (Op 20–25) und im Johannesprolog (John 1:1–18)," in Frey and Schnelle, *Kontexte*, 295–320.

17. On the text critical issue, see D. A. Fennema, "John 1:18: 'God the Only Son,'" *New Testament Studies* 31, no. 1 (1985–86): 124–35; Gerard Pendrick, "Monogenes," *New Testament Studies* 41, no. 4 (1995): 587–600; and Ehrman, *Orthodox Corruption of Scripture.*

tarian." While this stance has its roots in Judaism, its insistent articulation by the evangelist and his community may well have been involved in the "expulsion from the Synagogue" often "prophesied" in the gospel, whatever lies behind that language.[18]

But what of the third person of the Trinity? Are there any grounds for seeing this gospel according equal status to someone or something else? The crucial texts for answering that question are the passages on the Paraclete in the Last Supper discourses. These are a set of parallel comments in chapters 14 and 16, which overlap considerably, though each has some distinctive elements. This is one point at which theories of the compositional development of the gospel might be invoked, since many scholars have suggested that chapters 15–17 are a secondary layer, perhaps coming from the same hand or workshop. The major reason for maintaining this possibility is the fact that these chapters seem to break the smooth transition between the end of the postprandial discourse in chapter 14 and the movement to the garden where Jesus is arrested in chapter 18. George Parsenios, however, has suggested that the chapters instead exemplify a common device of ancient drama, the "delayed exit," a move that enables a protagonist on the point of death to deliver a final set of remarks before moving offstage.[19] Whatever the overall relationship between chapters 15–17 and their literary context, we should treat the two passages on the Paraclete, first for what they each affirm about the figure, and then for the possible relationship between them. There are tensions within each of these chapters that merit attention and may be significant for our inquiry.

The first appearance of the Paraclete is at John 14:16, where Jesus, in return for the disciples' obedience to his commandments, promises to ask the Father for "another Paraclete" to be with the disciples forever. The identity of the "other" promised Paraclete is given two verses later when Jesus says that he will not leave his disciples orphans but would come to them himself. So

18. See Wayne A. Meeks, "The Man from Heaven in Johannine Sectarianism," *Journal of Biblical Literature* 91, no. 1 (1972): 44–72, reprinted in *Interpretations of the Fourth Gospel*, ed. John Ashton (London: SPCK; Philadelphia: Fortress, 1986), 141–73; Meeks, "Breaking Away: Three New Testament Pictures of Christianity's Separation from the Jewish Communities," in *"To See Ourselves as Others See Us": Christians, Jews, "Others" in Late Antiquity*, ed. Jacob Neusner and Ernest S. Frerichs (Chico, Calif.: Scholars, 1985), 93–115. For a recent alternative analysis of the relationship between the gospel and "the Jews," see Raimo Hakola, *John, the Jews and Jewishness* (Leiden: Brill, 2005).

19. See Parsenios, *Departure and Consolation: The Johannine Farewell Discourses in Light of Greco-Roman Literature*, Supplements to Novum Testamentum 117 (Leiden: Brill, 2005).

the Paraclete is another Jesus, and Jesus is what a Paraclete should be, one who advises and advocates for those to whose side he is called. Before the promise not to abandon the disciples, Jesus also offers a hint about the character of the Paraclete, saying (v. 17) that he is the "spirit of truth."

The end of this pericope on the Paraclete, vv. 25–26, providing a kind of bookend to the whole discussion, continues in a similar vein. The Paraclete is now defined as "The Holy Spirit" (v. 26). Sent by the Father, he will teach and remind the disciples about what Jesus said, an allusion to the theme of "remembrance" prominent in the gospel.[20]

Most of what is said about the Paraclete in John 14:15–26 comports with what would be familiar from the other accounts in the New Testament about the Holy Spirit, although those accounts add other interesting details about the Spirit's activity. It is he who speaks through the words of scripture (Heb 3:7), inspires hope (Gal 5:5), dwells within disciples individually and collectively (1 Cor 3:16; 6:19), giving expression to their deepest fears and longings (Rom 8:26), makes itself known in ecstatic worship phenomena (1 Cor 12 and 14), and provides the fruits of a virtuous life (Gal 5:22). These affirmations about the Holy Spirit are clearly rooted in ancient biblical expressions about the Spirit of Yahweh manifest in the life of Israel, as Luke reminds us in his account of Pentecost (Acts 2:4, 17–18). They may also reflect understandings of the divine spirit at home in the eschatological writings of Jewish sectarians, but those roots and antecedents do not quite prepare us for the connection made in these verses between Jesus and the Spirit.

Another point, however, is remarkable. Although vv. 16–18 are not completely explicit, they seem to suggest very strongly that the Paraclete, the Spirit of Truth, while other than Jesus, is in some sense Jesus himself. That suggestion is supported by what follows, the material framed by the somewhat conventional affirmations about the Paraclete/Spirit at the beginning and end of the pericope.

Verses 20–24 are quite explicit on the complexity of the spiritual presence that will abide in the disciples who keep the commands of Jesus. After promising his return, Jesus further promises (v. 20) that "in that day" the disciples would know that he is in his Father and they are in Jesus and Jesus in them. If Jesus is in the Father and they are in him, logic suggests that they are in the Fa-

20. Compare Jn 2:17, 22; 12:16; 15:20; 16:4.

ther, as well. That point is made explicit several verses later (v. 23), where Jesus reiterates his promise. If anyone loves him and keeps his word, the Father will love him and Jesus and the Father will come and make their abode (*monên*) with them. This verse, providing a realized interpretation of the eschatological promise of a heavenly *monê* (14:2–4), is hardly surprising in light of the affirmation of intimate union between Father and Son already explored. What is significant for our purpose is the way in which the affirmation seems to reinforce and interpret the promise of the presence of the Paraclete. That promise ultimately consists of the presence of Jesus and his Father with the disciples.

The second passage on the Paraclete, 16:7–15, begins on the positive note that Jesus' departure, a cause for sadness, is necessary for the coming of the Paraclete, now to be sent by Jesus himself and not, as in chapter 14, by the Father at the request of Jesus (v. 17). A new set of functions is attributed to the Paraclete, focusing on the theme of examination (*elegxei*) of the world for "sin, righteousness, and judgment" (v. 8). Jesus promises that the Paraclete, again defined as the "Spirit of Truth," will have a second function, "to "lead you in all truth," telling the disciples things that they could not bear while Jesus was with them (v. 12). In doing so, it will simply convey what it hears from Jesus, to whom the Father has entrusted all things (vv. 13–15).

The description of the first function of the Paraclete sounds a note not present in chapter 14. It might also have its roots in traditional affirmations about how the divine spirit can examine the depths of human and divine reality (1 Cor 2:10), but it also ties in with the theme of judgment that pervades the gospel. The passage may, in fact, resolve a tension in the theme of judgment, between the affirmations that Jesus came to judge and those that he does not himself judge.[21] One way of resolving that tension is to think of judgment as something that happens as each individual chooses to react to the claims of Jesus. But how will that work when Jesus himself is gone? The Paraclete provides an answer; it will happen as individuals after Jesus' departure confront the Spirit in the community of his disciples.

The description of the second function accorded to the Paraclete in chap-

21. The significance of forensic motifs in the gospel has long been noted; see, e.g., Josef Blank, *Krisis: Untersuchungen zur johanneischen Christologie und Eschatologie* (Freiburg im Breisgau: Lambertus Verlag, 1964); A. E. Harvey, *Jesus on Trial* (Atlanta: John Knox, 1976); and, most recently, Parsenios, *Rhetoric and Drama in the Johannine Lawsuit Motif*, Wissenschaftliche Untersuchungen zum Neuen Testament series 1, vol. 258 (Tübingen: Mohr Siebeck, 2010).

ter 16 recalls the promise in chapter 14 that it would "teach and remind." Also, in its insistence that the Spirit simply conveys what Jesus teaches and that teaching simply consists in what Jesus learned from the Father, this promise reinforces the sense of intimate unity between Father, Son, and Spirit that was at the heart of the earlier passage. There is, however, something new added in the description of this promised teacher. The emphasis in the previous chapter was on remembrance. Teaching consisted in remembrance of the past. Here the view is prospective. The Spirit will teach what Jesus did not because the disciples could not bear it. The presence of the Spirit can introduce genuine novelty, but that novelty will always cohere with what Jesus taught at the Father's command.

The passages on the Paraclete, therefore, make complex theological claims. These claims go beyond what other early Christians were wont to say about the Spirit of God active in their lives. The Paraclete/Spirit is the presence of Jesus and the Father in the life of the community; it extends and reinforces the ministry of Jesus, but it also expands it, in total conformity, of course, with the will of Father and Son.

The attention of Christian theologians for the first several centuries was on the relationship of Father and Son, particularly as they explored the implications of the Logos metaphor for defining the Son. Theologians who were also serious readers of the Fourth Gospel, such as Origen, could treat the spirit as at best an instrument of Father and Son, a creature, perhaps the first of all creatures, but a creature nonetheless.[22] Such a reading of the gospel's account of the Paraclete cannot be easily disproven. Yet those theologians of the fourth century who developed the framework of what came to be orthodox Trinitarian theology were not introducing totally new perspectives into a discussion begun by the Fourth Gospel. In its insistence, especially in John 14, on the intimacy of the relationship of Father, Son, and Spirit, the gospel moves beyond, even while it systematizes traditional early Christians affirmations about the Spirit. In its insistence on the subordination of Son and Spirit to the Father, especially in chapter 16, it may compromise that intimacy, but no more so than does its recognition that the Father, the one who "sent" the Son, is

22. See Attridge, "Heracleon and John: Reassessment of an Early Christian Hermeneutical Debate," in *Biblical Interpretation, History, Context, and Reality*, ed. Christine Helmer and Taylor G. Petrey, Society of Biblical Literature Symposium 26 (Leiden and Boston: Brill, 2005), 57–72.

greater than the Son. In the gospel's insistence that the Spirit, though subordinate, functions both to reinforce what Jesus taught and to teach what Jesus could not, it establishes the presence of the Spirit as a distinct element in the divine economy.

The Gospel of John, in other words, has all the makings of a Trinitarian theology, even if it remains implicit.

Paul N. Anderson

4. THE JOHANNINE RIDDLES AND THEIR PLACE IN THE DEVELOPMENT OF TRINITARIAN THEOLOGY

Not only is the Fourth Gospel the source of some of the greatest theological debates in the modern era (namely, the divorcing of the Jesus of history from the Christ of faith, the expunging of John from canons of historicity, and its resultant exclusion from Jesus research for the first three quests for Jesus), but it was also the source of most of the greatest theological controversies over at least three centuries in the patristic era. In his treatment of the Christological debates during that period, Philip Jenkins describes the aftermath of the Second Ecumenical Council held at Constantinople in 381 C.E.

In the 380s, St. Gregory of Nyssa was astounded at the spread of theological discourse to every Constantinople shopkeeper:

> Every part of the city is filled with such talk; the alleys, the crossroads, the squares, the avenues. It comes from those who sell clothes, moneychangers, grocers. If you ask a moneychanger what the exchange rate is, he will reply with a dissertation on the Begotten and Unbegotten. If you enquire about the quality and the price of bread, the baker will reply: "The Father is greatest and the Son subject to him." When you ask at the baths whether the water is ready, the manager will declare that "the Son came forth from nothing."[1]

1. Philip Jenkins, *Jesus Wars: How Four Patriarchs, Three Queens, and Two Emperors Decided What Christians Would Believe for the Next 1,500 Years* (New York: HarperCollins, 2010), 34.

Indeed, in this terse description of theological strife that had come to dominate even conversations in the marketplace, Johannine contributions to debates over the ontological origin and nature of the Son and the Father-Son relationship are apparent. While it would be anachronistic to impose later Trinitarian language and Greek metaphysical constructs upon the theology and language of the Johannine Gospel, it certainly provided the raw data contributing to later debates *and* their resolutions. The questions are how that might have been so, and how a historical-critical understanding of the origins and character of John's theological riddles might contribute to a fuller historical, biblical, and theological appreciation of the development of Christian theology—enhancing its meaning for modern believers.[2]

Patristic Approaches to John's Christological and Theological Riddles

As early as the letters of Ignatius, God the Father, Jesus Christ, and the Holy Spirit (*Letter to the Ephesians* 9:2) are associated together, building on the threefold associations in the New Testament (Mt 28:19; Lk 10:21; Eph 1:17; 1 Pt 1:2). In the early third century, Origen refers to the Son's relation to the Father as being of one essence (*homoousios*) on the basis of the Johannine prologue, and while he maintains three *hupostases* (persons) of the same essence, he seeks to preserve the Son's dependence on the Father—also based on John's Father-Son relationship. A century later, Arius affirms the created origin of Jesus over and against his preexistent divinity. In arguing the Son was of "like essence" with the Father (*homoiousios*), Arius was willing to preserve a monotheistic Godhead at the expense of the divine status of the Son. One might argue

2. While several important works on the Trinity and the Gospel of John have been produced in recent years, few have directly explored the epistemological origins of John's theological tensions and riddles; see Andreas J. Köstenberger and Scott R. Swain, *Father, Son, and Spirit: The Trinity and John's Gospel* (Downers Grove, Ill.: Intervarsity, 2008), and Royce Gordon Gruenler, *The Trinity in the Gospel of John: A Thematic Commentary on the Fourth Gospel* (Grand Rapids: Baker, 1986). However, see also Anderson, *The Christology of the Fourth Gospel: Its Unity and Disunity in the Light of John 6*, Wissenschaftliche Untersuchungen zum Neuen Testament, series 2, volume 78 (Tübingen: Mohr Siebeck, 1996, 3rd printing, with a new introduction and epilogue, Eugene, Ore.: Cascade, 2010), and Anderson, "On Guessing Points and Naming Stars—The Epistemological Origins of John's Christological Tensions," in *The Gospel of St. John and Christian Theology*, ed. Richard Bauckham and Carl Mosser (Grand Rapids: Eerdmans, 2007), 311–45 (arguments developed more fully elsewhere will simply be summarized and referenced in this essay).

that the first of the seven ecumenical councils (Nicaea, 325 C.E.) restored the Johannine tension that Arius had diminished in his subordinated Christology, and this was reaffirmed at Constantinople (381 C.E.) with the doctrine of the dual nature of the Son.[3] Likewise, the next three councils affirmed further Johannine contributions on the Holy Spirit, the Father-Son relationship, and the dual nature of the Son.[4]

More specifically, as Emperor Constantine called together the 318 bishops from all over the Roman Empire, they addressed the Johannine tension by adding the phrase "that is from the substance of the Father, God from God, light from light, true God from true God, begotten not made, consubstantial" with the Father. As Arius and others had been teaching that there was a time when the Son was not, and that as Jesus had said "the Father is greater than I" (drawing on the Gospel of John), this created an international theological crisis that had to be addressed. Note, however, the Johannine contributions also to the rebuttal of Arius: (a) Christ and the Father are "one" (i.e., of one essence—*ousia* in Greek; of one substance—*substantia* in Latin); (b) Christ is "God from God, light from light, true God from true God" (drawing on the Johannine prologue); (c) Christ is "begotten, not made," also drawing on John 1:1–2; and (d) there was never a time when he was not (also from Jn 1:1–2). Of course, material from other Christological passages in the New Testament were also formative here (especially Col 1:15–20 and Heb 1:1–4), as well as references to the Father, the Son, and the Holy Spirit (Mt 28:19; 1 Jn 5:7–8—later mss.),[5] but the theological polarities of the Fourth Gospel played major roles in the formation of the Christian doctrines of the Father, the Son, and the Holy Spirit, and in doing so restored tensions that had been disregarded otherwise. In the discussions accompanying the second and third councils (Con-

3. T. E. Pollard, *Johannine Christology and the Early Church*; Maurice Wiles, *The Spiritual Gospel: The Interpretation of the Fourth Gospel in the Early Church* (Cambridge: Cambridge University Press, 1960); Charles E. Hill, *The Johannine Corpus in the Early Church* (Oxford: Oxford University Press, 2004); J. N. Rowe, "Origen's Subordinationism as Illustrated in His Commentary on St. John's Gospel," *Studia Patristica* 11, no. 2 (1972): 222–28; and Richard A. Norris Jr., *The Christological Controversy* (Philadelphia: Fortress, 1980).

4. Anthony Casurella, *Johannine Paraclete in the Church Fathers*; Stanley M. Burgess, *The Holy Spirit: Eastern Christian Traditions* (Peabody, Mass.: Hendrickson, 1989); and William G. Rusch, *The Trinitarian Controversy* (Philadelphia: Fortress, 1980).

5. Later manuscripts replaced the three witnesses of the Spirit, the water, and the blood—emphasizing the human suffering of Jesus on the cross (cf. Jn 19:34–35) with the Father, the Son and the Holy Spirit—reflecting later Trinitarian understandings.

stantinople 381 C.E.; Ephesus 431 C.E.), emphases on the *flesh* of Jesus (from Jn 1:14) were also drawn into play and finally confirmed in the Chalcedonian Definition in 451 C.E.

Further, a variety of dialectical developments on the ground contributed to the development of Christian doctrine, and these grounded factors cannot be overlooked. As debates between Arius and Athanasius (and their followers) developed after the First Ecumenical Council, the Arian position began to get the upper hand, and Athanasius was exiled at least five times for holding what eventually became reestablished as the orthodox Christological view at the Council of Constantinople (381 C.E.). Here the equal divinity of the Father, the Son, and the Holy Spirit were emphasized by Emperor Theodosius, as the Holy Spirit's proceeding from the Father (rooted in Jn 14:16, 26; 15:26) was asserted: "Who proceeds from the Father, who with the Father and the Son together is worshiped and glorified, who spoke by the prophets." With the human and divine natures of Christ also affirmed, the question, of course, orbited around *how* this was so, and the Council of Ephesus (431 C.E.) condemned Nestorius and his followers regarding the separation of the human and divine natures of Christ, while the Council of Chalcedon (451 C.E.) condemned Eutychus and the Monophysites regarding the view that Jesus' humanity and divinity were fused into a single unity. Given that the Gospel of John describes the Holy Spirit being sent from the Son as well as the Father, however, the Western Church added "and the Son" (*filioque*—rooted also in Jn 15:26; 16:7) at the Council of Toledo (589 C.E.), and this move posed one of several issues contributing to the separation of Eastern Orthodoxy and Roman Catholicism in 1054 C.E.

Most fascinating about the Fourth Gospel, however, is not simply that it played a key role in the theological and Trinitarian debates ranging from the second through the fifth centuries of the Common Era, but that it often was used by leading figures on *both sides* of many of these debates. As T. E. Pollard reminds us, as illustrated in the dialogue between F. C. Conybeare and Alfred Loisy, not only was the Fourth Gospel essential to Athanasius's confuting of Arius, but in Loisy's terms, "if Arius had not the Fourth Gospel to draw texts from, Arius would not have needed confuting."[6] Therefore, the most fascinating feature of the Fourth Gospel is its theological, historical, and literary

6. Pollard, *Johannine Christology and the Early Church*, 3.

riddles, which account also for the fact that John is the most disagreed-upon book of the Bible—in terms of its origin, composition, and meaning—in the modern era.[7] In addition to the interests of patristic interpreters, however, modern scholarship has also been fascinated with Johannine theological polarities, which have led to a variety of literary-critical approaches to their origins and character.

John's Theological Tensions and Modern Approaches to Their Character and Origins

Most striking within John's theological content is the fact of its presentation with a high degree of dialectical tension. While these tensions also can be found in John's other themes (such as whether or not the Son judges, the embellished and existentialized signs of Jesus, John's present and future eschatology, universal and particular soteriology, determinism and free will for the believer, prescriptive and reflective dualism, anti- and pro-Jewish/Judean themes, embellished and deconstructed sacramentology, and petrified and dynamic ecclesiology), the dialectical presentation of Christological, theological, and pneumatological themes in John gave rise most directly to Trinitarian debates, from Tertullian through the post-Chalcedonian period.

Rather than account for these tensions metaphysically and ontologically, however, modern scholars have largely sought to understand them first in historical-critical and literary-critical terms. Modern scholars ask, "Did particular religious ideas in the New Testament have their origin in contemporary religions or differing literary sources?" Likewise, "How was a Johannine feature understood and regarded by its original authors and audiences, and how is that similar to or different from later understandings in the development of Christian theology?" As answers are posed to these and other epistemically oriented questions, new "theological-critical" insights and possibilities emerge. In the light of such insights, earlier theological (both orthodox

7. In Anderson, *The Riddles of the Fourth Gospel: An Introduction to John* (Minneapolis: Fortress, 2011), I limit myself to laying out thirty-six sets of problems, or riddles (a dozen in each category: theological tensions, historical problems, literary aporias), which are then accounted for in terms of their origin, character, and development—leading, then, to interpretation. In chapter 7 I outline what are arguably the primary epistemological origins of each of these riddles, leading into the final three chapters involving meaningful interpretation.

and heretical) discussions are illumined in ways that may lead to new possibilities in the integration of biblical, historical, and theological analyses.

Consider first, however, some of the leading theological tensions within the Fourth Gospel.[8]

Is Jesus Human, Divine, or Both?

The question of Jesus' humanity and divinity is more pronounced in John than any other single writing in the New Testament. Jesus is referred to as the Word and as God, who was with God from the beginning—the very source of creation (Jn 1:1–2, 18), and yet the Word also became human flesh (1:14), and water and blood flowed forth from his side (19:34). The Johannine community attests having beheld his divine glory, and yet the eyewitness attests to having witnessed his fleshly humanity. Consider further these features of the divine and human Jesus as the Christ.

On one hand, Jesus' divinity is pronounced in John:

• The glory of Jesus is testified to from the beginning of the gospel (1:14c; 11:4; 14:13; 17:1) and his glorification is emphasized extensively (1:51; 3:14; 6:62; 8:28; 12:23, 34; 13:1).

• Jesus is equated with God in John 1:1–2 and 18 (in the earliest texts) and is called "my Lord and my God" by Thomas in John 20:28. Likewise, the "I AM" of Exodus 3:14 is used to point to Jesus in John 8:58—an obviously blasphemous claim (see v. 59)—and Jesus' appearance on the lake is presented as a theophany (an appearance of God, 6:20).

• Further, the divine certainty and sway of Jesus are featured (1:47–51; 2:24–25; 4:17–19; 5:41–42; 6:64; 13:1–3); Jesus knows full well what he will do and what is going to happen to him (6:6; 13:1, 3; 16:19, 30; 18:4; 19:28); his adversaries cannot arrest him unless his time has arrived (7:30; 8:20); and people experience themselves as being "known by the Divine" in their encounters with Jesus (1:48; 4:19, 39; 5:6; 9:38; 10:4, 14, 27; 20:16; 21:7).

• Jesus is thus presented as God striding over the earth in John.

On the other hand, Jesus' humanity is also unmistakable in John:

8. The previously mentioned theological tensions, as well as those listed hereafter, are outlined and discussed more fully in Anderson, *Riddles of the Fourth Gospel,* 25–43.

• The incarnational "flesh" of Jesus is emphasized in John (1:14a; 6:51, 53–56), and his humanity is acknowledged by others (1:45; 10:33; 18:5–7).

• His human-family references are clear (1:45; 2:1–12; 6:42; 19:19; 25–27), and not even his brothers believed in him (7:5).

• Out of his side flow physical blood and water (19:34), and Thomas is allowed to touch Jesus' flesh wounds with his finger and hand (20:27). Further, Jesus weeps at Lazarus's tomb (11:35); his heart is deeply troubled (11:33; 12:27; 13:21); he groans (11:33, 38); on the cross he thirsts (19:28); and he loves his own unto the end (11:3, 5, 36; 13:1, 23, 34; 14:21; 15:9, 10, 12; 19:26; 20:2; 21:7, 20).

• The fleshly, pathos-filled Jesus is also a reality in the Johannine text.

How have modern scholars addressed John's Christological tensions? As a means of accounting for the humanity and divinity of Jesus in John, Rudolf Bultmann and other diachronic theorists have inferred a set of source-critical dialogues between earlier sources and the evangelist. Whereas the evangelist's Christology was incarnational and low, according to Bultmann, he purportedly made use of a proto-Gnostic Revelation-Sayings source, which he diminished and co-opted within his narrative. Conversely, Ernst Käsemann dealt with the tensions by denying the fleshly humanity of Jesus in John, but such an approach totally overlooks John's antidocetic thrust and its clear presentation of the fleshly suffering of Jesus.[9] C. K. Barrett argues that we have here a dialectical thinker who looked at something from one side and then another, holding truth together in tension.[10] Raymond Brown noted that as the Johannine tradition developed, it engaged a variety of groups and audiences internal and external to the Johannine community. Some of these (Samaritans with a high Christology)[11] pushed John's Christology higher—leading to tensions with Jewish monotheism, while Gentile converts to Christianity struggled to accept a suffering and human Son of God. These issues, of course, engage the Son's relation to the Father.

9. Rudolf Bultmann, *The Gospel of John: A Commentary*, trans. G. R. Beasley-Murray, R. W. N. Hoare, and J. K. Riches, Johannine Monograph Series 1 (1971; repr. Eugene, Ore.: Wipf and Stock, 2014); Ernst Käsemann, *The Testament of Jesus: A Study of the Gospel of John in the Light of Chapter 17*, trans. G. Krodel, Johannine Monograph Series 6 (1968; repr. Eugene, Ore.: Wipf and Stock, 2017).

10. C. K. Barrett, "The Dialectical Theology of St John," in *New Testament Essays*, edited by C. K. Barrett (London: SCM, 1972), 49–69.

11. Wayne A. Meeks, *The Prophet-King*, Johannine Monograph Series 5 (1967; repr. Eugene, Ore.: Wipf and Stock, 2017).

The Son's Relation to the Father—Subordinate, Egalitarian, or Neither?

A most perplexing feature of the Father-Son relationship in John is the fact that it is hard to know whether John's is a theocentric Christology or a Christocentric Theology.[12] In revealing the Father's love to the world, God is made known by the flesh-becoming Word. Therefore, the Son comes to make the Father known. Then again, the primary activity of the Father in John is the sending of the Son. Were it not for the "having-sent-me" work of the Father in John, the role of the Father would be diminished by half, if not more. Consider these tensions between the Father and the Son in John.

On one hand, the Father and Son appear to share an egalitarian relationship:

- The Son is equal to the Father (Jn 1:18; 5:18; 10:29–30, 33, 38; 12:41; 14:10–11; 16:32; 17:5, 11, 21); "I and the Father are one," declares John's Jesus.
- The Father loves the Son and has placed all things in his hands (3:35; 5:20; 13:3; 16:15); the Son works just as the Father does (on the Sabbath, 5:17); the Father shows the Son all that he is doing and gives him the power to raise the dead (5:19–20, 25–26); all who honor the Son honor the Father (5:23), and the Father glorifies the Son (8:54; 17:1). To know the Father is to know the Son, and to know the Son is to know the Father (8:19; 14:7; 17:1); to hate the Son is to hate the Father (15:23–24).
- The Son gives life to whomever he chooses (5:21), and the Father testifies on the Son's behalf (8:16; literally, note the voice from heaven in 12:28).
- In the Gospel of John the Son and the Father are one.

On the other hand, the Son's relation to the Father is presented as one of subordination:

- The Son is also subordinate to the Father (Jn 5:19, 30; 7:16; 8:16, 28; 12:49; 14:10, 28) and declares, "The Father is greater than I."
- Jesus honors and glorifies the Father (8:49; 17:1) and does whatever the Father commands; he testifies to what he has seen and heard from the Father

12. See Marianne Meye Thompson's treatment of the issue: *The God of the Gospel of John* (Grand Rapids: Eerdmans, 2001), as well as Anderson, "The Having-Sent-Me Father: Aspects of Agency, Encounter, and Irony in the Johannine Father-Son relationship," *Semeia* 85 (1999): 33–57.

(3:32; 5:19, 36; 8:26–28, 40; 10:18, 32; 12:49–50; 14:31; 15:15) as one sent from the Father (5:23, 36–37; 6:44, 57; 8:16, 18, 26, 42; 10:36; 12:49; 14:24; 17:21, 25; 20:21).

• The living Father has entrusted life to the Son (5:26), and the Son lives because of the Father (6:57).

• In John, the Son can do nothing except what the Father commands.

Modern scholars have approached the ambivalent Father-Son relationship in John in a variety of ways. Bultmann argued that we have here a Gnostic Redeemer-Myth, which was thought to have originated in the worship community of John the Baptist, whose followers became followers of Jesus. Given that the Revealer descends from heaven and returns to the Father as a means of carrying out his divine commission, Bultmann assumed that this was still part of a hypothetical sayings source, typified by the worship material of the Johannine prologue. Another approach, argued by Ernst Haenchen and others, assumed there were multiple Christologies underlying the Fourth Gospel—one egalitarian and the other subordinationist. Still another approach, developed by Peder Borgen and others, infers a Jewish agency schema, rooted in Deuteronomy 18:15–22, wherein the agent is in all ways like the one who has sent him.[13] In that sense Jesus and the Father are one precisely because the Son does nothing except what the Father tells him to do. Indeed, John's presentation of the Father-Son relationship displays twenty-four ways in which Jesus as the Christ fulfills the Deuteronomy 18 passage in Septuagintal Greek.[14] Because his words come true, Jesus is indeed the one Moses predicted would be sent by God, and this is why the words and deeds of Jesus as the Son are to be regarded as those of his "having-sent-me" Father.

Does the Holy Spirit Proceed from the Father, the Son, or Both?

The role of the Holy Spirit in John is presented as being commissioned by the Father and the Son. While two passages in John 14 present Jesus as de-

13. Bultmann, *Gospel of John*; Ernst Haenchen, *John: A Commentary on the Gospel of John*, ed. Ulrich Busse, trans. R. W. Funk, Hermeneia, 2 vols. (Philadelphia: Fortress, 1984); Peder Borgen, "God's Agent in the Fourth Gospel," in *The Interpretation of John*, ed. John Ashton, 2nd ed. (Oxford: Clarendon, 2007), 83–96.

14. Anderson, "Having-Sent-Me Father," 33–57, in Anderson, *Christology* (2010), lxxiv–lxxviii.

claring that the Father will send the Spirit, two passages in John 15–16 present Jesus as promising to send the Holy Spirit to his disciples. The Spirit proceeds from the Father, as does the Son, and yet the Spirit is the second advocate (Jesus' being the first advocate, 1 Jn 2:1), and he will teach believers all things and will disclose the truth of Jesus' teachings to later generations in ongoing ways. While John baptizes with water, Jesus baptizes with the Holy Spirit (Jn 1:33). He whom the Father has sent gives the Spirit without measure (3:34), and in his post-resurrection appearance to the disciples, Jesus breathes on them and bestows the Holy Spirit upon them (20:22).

On one hand, the Holy Spirit proceeds from and is sent by the Father:

- Jesus declares that he will ask the Father to send the Holy Spirit (14:16), and he also declares that the Father will send the Holy Spirit in his name (14:26).
- As the Son proceeds from the Father, so does the Spirit (15:26; 16:28–27, 30).
- The Father sends the Spirit in the Gospel of John.

On the other hand, the Holy Spirit will be sent by the Son, making his teachings known:

- Jesus also declares that he will send the Spirit from the Father (15:26), and he promises to send the *Paraklētos* after he departs (16:7).
- The Holy Spirit is the Spirit of Jesus as the Christ, who reminds believers of Jesus' teachings and who makes his will known (14:26; 16:13–14), testifying on Jesus' behalf (15:26).
- The Son sends the Spirit in John.

Unlike patristic discussions, the question of who sends the Spirit, or whether the Spirit proceeds from the Father or the Son, or both, has not been as significant a problem for modern interpreters. However, if John 15–17 reflects a later addition, the emphasis on the Father's sending the Spirit would be part of the earlier material (in my view, being finalized around 80–85 C.E.), while the later material (added around 100 C.E. after the death of the Beloved Disciple) contains the emphases that the Son is the one who sends the Spirit.[15]

15. A full theory of Johannine composition is laid out in Anderson, "On 'Seamless Robes' and 'Leftover Fragments': A Theory of Johannine Composition; Structure, Composition, and Authorship

This also coheres with the view of 1 John 3:24 and 4:13—Jesus, in whom believers abide, sends them his Spirit as a source of guidance and empowerment, and he also is a *paraklētos* (1 Jn 2:1). Therefore, the movement to the Son as the sender of the Spirit may relate to the addressing of needs of Johannine believers caught in crises with the world, as the Epistles were arguably written by the final editor of the gospel in between its first and final editions.

John's Dialogical Autonomy and the Epistemological Origins of Its Theological Tensions

While the overall theories of several Johannine scholars, especially that of Rudolf Bultmann, merit discussion, readers will have to engage them elsewhere.[16] Nonetheless, an overall theory of John's composition based on the strongest of critical studies, in my judgment, includes the following elements.

The Dialogical Autonomy of the Fourth Gospel

First, John's narrative reflects an autonomous Jesus tradition developed alongside Mark, but as an alternative rendering of Jesus' ministry, reflecting the evangelist's perspective and ministry.[17] Second, rather than reflecting literary dialogues between alien sources, the evangelist, and the redactor (versus Bultmann), the Fourth Evangelist is a dialectical thinker, and many of John's theological tensions reflect the dialogue between perception and experience in the thinking of the evangelist (with Barrett).[18] Third, John's major literary riddles can be solved fairly simply with a modified form of Lindars's two-edition theory, seeing John 1:1–18 and chapters 6, 15–17, and 21 and eyewitness and Beloved Disciple references as added by an editor—plausibly after the death of the Beloved Disciple (Jn 21:24). Fourth, rather than infer a Gnos-

of John's Gospel," in *The Origins of John's Gospel*, ed. Stanley E. Porter and Hughson Ong (Leiden: E. J. Brill, 2015), 169–218.

16. See my treatments of Bultmann's diachronic theory of John's composition as a means of addressing John's theological, historical, and literary riddles (chaps. 4–7 of Anderson, *Christology of the Fourth Gospel*) and in my foreword to the recent JMS edition of Bultmann, *Gospel of John*, i–xxviii.

17. Paul N. Anderson, "Mark, John, and Answerability: Interfluentiality and Dialectic between the Second and Fourth Gospels" *Liber Annuus* 63 (2013): 197–245, and "Mark and John—the *Bi-Optic* Gospels," in *Jesus and the Johannine Tradition*, ed. Robert Fortna and Tom Thatcher (Philadelphia: Westminster/John Knox, 2001), 175–88.

18. Paul N. Anderson, "The Cognitive Origins of John's Christological Unity and Disunity," *Horizons in Biblical Theology: An International Dialogue* 17 (1995): 1–24.

tic Redeemer-Myth as the basis for the Johannine sending motif (versus Bultmann), more plausible is the inference of a prophet-like-Moses agency schema rooted in Deuteronomy 18:15–22.[19] Fifth, John's relations to other gospel traditions were more variegated than just one type; interfluence between John's tradition and the early Markan and later Matthean traditions is likely (with John's first edition augmenting Mark and John's later material harmonizing with Mark and the other gospels), and John's tradition was plausibly a source for Luke and possibly a resource for Q.[20] Sixth, John's dialectical situation involved engaging at least six or seven crises over seven decades: Judean-Galilean tensions and followers of the Baptist in a Palestinian setting (30–70 C.E.), Jewish leaders and the Roman imperial presence in a diaspora setting (70–85 C.E.), and docetizing and institutionalizing Christians within the early church (85–100 C.E.). These were accompanied by various dialogues with other gospel traditions spanning all three periods.[21] A seventh dialogical feature of John's narrative is that it is designed in such a way as to engage later audiences rhetorically—engaging them in an imaginary dialogue with the subject of the narrative, Jesus.[22]

While other factors contributed to John's historical and literary riddles, John's theological tensions have as their epistemological origin four primary sources: the dialectical thinking of the evangelist, the Jewish agency schema, the dialectical Johannine situation, and the literary-rhetorical devices employed by the narrator.[23] Within the larger overall theory of John's dialogical autonomy, understanding the roles each of these factors played within the development of the Johannine material facilitates a fuller understanding of the issues debated within the historical development of Trinitarian theology, and engaging the results of critical biblical scholarship is essential to understand-

19. Anderson, "Having-Sent-Me Father," 33–57.

20. Anderson, "Interfluential, Formative, and Dialectical—A Theory of John's Relation to the Synoptics," in *Für und Wider die Priorität des Johannesevangeliums: Symposion in Salzburg am 10. März 2000*, ed. Peter Hofrichter, Theologische Texte und Studien 9 (Hildesheim, Zürich, and New York: Georg Olms Verlag, 2002), 19–58.

21. Anderson, "Bakhtin's Dialogism and the Corrective Rhetoric of the Johannine Misunderstanding Dialogue: Exposing Seven Crises in the Johannine Situation," in *Bakhtin and Genre Theory in Biblical Studies*, ed. Roland Boer, Semeia Studies 63 (Atlanta: SBL, 2007), 133–59.

22. Anderson, "The *Sitz im Leben* of the Johannine Bread of Life Discourse and Its Evolving Context," in *Critical Readings of John 6*, ed. R. Alan Culpepper, Biblical Interpretation Series 22 (Leiden: Brill, 1997), 1–59.

23. Anderson, *Christology of the Fourth Gospel*, 252–65.

ing the content of orthodox Christian theology as well as its lesser alternatives. Epistemology is thus essential for understanding both philology and ontology when it comes to Trinitarian theology and its biblical antecedents.

Epistemological Origins of John's Theological Tensions

Given that highly diachronic approaches to John's composition as means of accounting for John's theological tensions fail to convince overall,[24] John's theological tensions are more likely explicable as emerging from several other dialogical factors.

1. The first epistemological source of John's theological tensions involves a *cognitive dialogue*: the dialectical thinking of the Johannine evangelist, who worked reflectively, synthesizing earlier perceptions and experiences with later ones. As Plato described thinking as "the soul's dialogue with herself" (*Theatetus* 189), first looking at things from one side and then another until one's understanding has reached its glory (*doxa*), this is precisely the way the Fourth Evangelist regarded many of his subjects. Therefore, it is misguided to infer disparate literary sources when tensions are found between John's high and low Christological motifs, as well as virtually every other theological motif. The evangelist thus operated in a both-and way instead of either-or dichotomies. Drawing in James Fowler's *Stages of Faith*, this phenomenon evidences Stage 5, Conjunctive Faith, representing matured reflection upon first-order encounters involving more distanced perspectives.[25] Plausibly, such a thinker had his own story of Jesus to tell, rather than repackaging a derivative rendering based on alien sources or even the Synoptics. Therefore, intratraditional reflection and intertraditional engagement go hand-in-hand within the developing Johannine memory of Jesus. At times polarities are held together in tension; at other times either reinforcing or contradistinctive emphases are made in dialogue with other traditions—especially the Markan. It is precisely because John's memory of Jesus coheres with and departs from Mark's presentation that we have here an

24. While an impressive attempt to discern three editions of John's composition, including the layered development of eleven theological themes, has been contributed by von Wahlde, *The Gospel and Letters of John*, 3 vols. (Grand Rapids: Eerdmans, 2010), the dialectical thinking of the evangelist is neglected as a plausible factor in the formation of John's theological tensions.

25. James F. Fowler, *Stages of Faith: The Psychology of Human Development and the Quest for Meaning* (New York: HarperCollins, 1981); see my cognitive-critical engagement in Anderson, *Christology of the Fourth Gospel*, 137–65, 252–65.

alternative Jesus tradition, likely reflecting an individuated memory of Jesus from day one. In that sense, John is different from Mark on purpose—*because of* its apostolic origination rather than discrediting it.

2. A second factor of John's theological tensions involves the *Jewish agency Christology* of the evangelist, based on the prophetic-agency schema (*shaliach*) of Deuteronomy 18:15–22. As the one who is sent from God deserves to be treated in all ways like the one who sent him, the egalitarian and subordinated features of the Father-Son relationship are presented in John as flipsides of the same coin—a Jewish agency schema. The Son is to be regarded as equal to the Father precisely because he does and says nothing on his own, but only what the Father commands. This motif is also presented strikingly in the Q tradition, as the mutuality of knowing between the Father and the Son in Matthew 11:27 and Luke 10:22 appears thoroughly Johannine. Connected with the preaching of Peter and the witness of Stephen (Acts 3:22; 7:37) but missing from later Christological hymns, this Mosaic-prophet motif is likely early in the development of gospel traditions rather than later—perhaps reflecting debates over Jesus's authorization among the Jewish leaders of his day. Therefore, John's showing that Jesus' proleptic words had indeed come true demonstrates the fulfillment of this scriptural typology (Jn 14:29; 16:4; 18:9, 32), calling for belief in his divine agency as the Son of the Father. The overall exhortation in John, of course, is to call for a response of faith to the divine initiative, which Jesus as the Son conveys and is.

3. A third epistemological source of John's theological tensions involves the evolving *dialectical situation of the Johannine tradition*, as its preachers, narrators, and editors sought to engage evolving audiences with the message of the Johannine story. As each of John's three phases experienced two largely sequential, yet somewhat overlapping crises, history and theology are operative in the development and crafting of John's story of Jesus. As a result, in engaging (a) Judean leaders and (b) followers of John the Baptist (Phase One), emphases upon Jesus' divine authorization and mission would have been acute. Following a move to a Gentile- mission setting (and there is no more suitable prospect than the traditional setting of Ephesus and Asia Minor—phases two and three), (c) dialogues with the local Jewish presence, (d) under the umbrella of emerging requirements of emperor laud under Domitian (81–96 C.E.), emphases upon Jesus as the Son of God became more strongly asserted. Here the I-Am language of the Johan-

nine Jesus evolved into an apologetic showing that he fulfilled the typological ideals of Israel; and as an anti-Domitian challenge to Roman imperialism, Thomas is presented as proclaiming Jesus as *Lord and God* (20:28—the same language Domitian required of his subjects). (e) The cross-cultural rendering of John's Jewish agency motif into a Hellenistic-friendly Logos hymn by the Johannine leaders bridged the gaps between Gentile and Jewish believers, although belief in a divine Jesus allowed some Gentile believers to minimize his fleshly existence, leading to docetizing tendencies—an issue addressed with intentionality in the later Johannine material. (f) As a correction to rising institutionalism in the late first-century situation, the Johannine emphasis upon the more primitive memory of Jesus' emphasis on the active role of the Holy Spirit in the lives of the faithful became an incisive ecclesial emphasis.

4. A fourth factor of John's theological tensions involves *the literary means* by which the conveyors of the Johannine message sought to engage later hearers and readers in imaginary dialogues with Jesus by means of crafting a dialogically engaging text. As misunderstanding is always rhetorical, here the narrator crafts the story as a means of creating a set of imaginary dialogues with the protagonist, Jesus, evoking a response of faith involving the divine initiative, which Jesus embodies and communicates. Rather than simply addressing one primary set of issues, such as portrayed in John 9 and the engaging of Jewish-Johannine relations, John 6 betrays several levels of engagement, inviting later audiences to receive the Bread that Jesus gives and is versus lesser alternatives—the way of life rather than the way of death (6:27).[26] Rather than desiring the food that perishes, later audiences are invited to seek the spiritual nourishment that Jesus' signs convey; rather than opposing one exegetical ploy with another, audiences are invited to receive what God eschatologically gives rather than seeking what Moses gave; rather than allow docetizing Gentile believers to escape the implications of the Way of the Cross, the Johannine Jesus is rendered as requiring the ingesting of his flesh-and-blood sacrificial act if one wishes to partake also of the gift of life he offers. Finally, Peter is present-

26. Note that John 6 evidences four or five crises in the Johannine situation, rather than a single dialogical concern reflected in John 9; see Anderson, *Sitz im Leben*, 24–58, over and against J. Louis Martyn, *History and Theology in the Fourth Gospel*, 3rd ed. (1968; repr. Louisville: Westminster John Knox, 2003). In addition to (a) tensions with Jewish leaders in local synagogues (with Martyn and others), also discernible within a two-level reading of John 6 are tensions related to (b) the local Roman presence, (c) docetizing tendencies, (d) emerging Petrine hierarchy within the later Johannine situation, and (e) the prevalent Synoptic valuation of Jesus' miracles.

ed as "returning the keys to Jesus" in his confession in John—challenging Diotrephes (3 Jn 9–10) and his kin—and affirming the life-giving word of Christ for the community of faith.

In addition to these sources of John's theological riddles, several other sources of John's historical and literary riddles are present.[27] Considering these particular factors, however, assists the interpreter in understanding more fully the content of John's theology as well as the history of its interpretation, from the patristic through the modern eras. At the heart of all four of these modes, however, is the synthesizing work of the evangelist, who wove these factors together into an engaging narrative whole.

Origins of John's Theological Tensions and Trinity-Discussion Implications

Given that the epistemological origins of John's primary theological tensions have been identified, an appreciation of their character in relation to Trinitarian theology deserves consideration, along with two other factors. First, many other theological tensions present themselves in John beyond the three outlined in this essay; these are simply some of the primary ones that led to Trinitarian discussions. Second, while each of the aforementioned four sources of John's theological tensions is arguable, this does not preclude other factors. Therefore, in addition to a primary source of each of John's theological tensions, a secondary source will also be explored, with a special focus on their Trinity-discussion implications.[28]

27. An analysis of the epistemological origins of all thirty-six of John's is in chap. 7 of Anderson, *Riddles of the Fourth Gospel*, 157–72. Contributing to John's historical riddles are: (a) an augmentive and corrective alternative to Mark (in John's first-edition material) and a complement to the Synoptics in John's final-edition material (esp. chaps. 6 and 21); (b) intratraditional dialogue, reflecting the cognitive dialectic of earlier perceptions and later understandings; (c) intertraditional dialogue, reflecting interfluentiality between the Johannine tradition and early Markan and later Matthean traditions; and (d) the dialogue between history as theology and theology as history. Contributing to John's literary riddles are: (a) the dialogue between orality and literacy in the Johannine narrative, whereby preaching units were rendered in written form and gathered alongside other material to comprise a larger narrative whole; (b) John's first edition, which poses an apologetic narrative affirming Jesus as the Jewish Messiah-Christ; (c) the continued preaching of the Beloved Disciple and the work of the Johannine Elder, which addressed emerging issues in the Johannine situation rhetorically; and (d) John's later material, which calls for unity and abiding in Christ and his community of faith; see Anderson, "Interfluential, Formative, and Dialectical."

28. For a list of primary and secondary origins of a dozen of John's theological tensions, see Anderson, *Christology of the Fourth Gospel*, lxxix–lxxxi.

- *The Humanity and Divinity* of Jesus:
  1. The Dialectical Thinking of the Evangelist—Perception/Experience Dialogues
  2. Dialectical Situation of Johannine Christianity

As outlined, Jesus is presented as both human and divine in John—more so than in any other part of the New Testament. Therefore, the dual nature of the Son, as a central feature of Trinitarian discussions, owes a great deal to the Fourth Gospel, and the primary factor in John's Christological tensions is *the dialectical thinking of the evangelist.* Here we observe first-order reflection on Jesus' identity and mission as the Messiah-Christ and Son of God. While there exists some rhetorical development of the Johannine narrative, employing the literary feature of anagnorisis (presenting knowing and discovery events) within the Johannine narrative, John's story of Jesus nonetheless reflects the memory of transformative encounters with the divine associated with the ministry of Jesus of Nazareth. These impressions came to be narrated in the form of Jewish and Hellenistic wonder-narratives, but comparative religions cannot account for epistemic origins of the distinctively Johannine rendering of Jesus' ministry. Transformative encounters associated with the presentation of the calling of the disciples (Jn 1), Jesus' signs (Jn 2, 4, 5, 6, 9, 11, 21), dialogues with Jesus (Jn 3, 4, 6, 7, 9, 11, 18, 20, 21), and other episodes suggest that some sort transformative knowing event lies behind the distinctive Johannine tradition from a cognitive-critical perspective.[29]

This first-order character of John's theological reflection accounts for several of its features. While the distinctive form of the Johannine I-Am sayings is not found in the Synoptics, none of John's nine metaphors is absent from the speech of the Synoptic Jesus. Therefore, we have in John the evangelist's paraphrastic rendering of Jesus' mission in terms rooted in historical memory but crafted to suit the teaching ministry of the evangelist.[30] Additionally, the absolute render-

29. Here James Loder's work is significant, as it provides a basis for considering originative differences between the pre-Markan and early Johannine traditions; Loder, *The Transforming Moment: Understanding Convictional Experiences* (New York, Harper and Row, 1981); see also my cognitive-critical engagement of Loder's work in *Christology of the Fourth Gospel,* 137–93, 252–65. For John's contributions to the historical quest for Jesus, see Anderson, *The Fourth Gospel and the Quest for Jesus: Modern Foundations Reconsidered,* Library of New Testament Studies 321 (London: T. and T. Clark, 2006).

30. Anderson, "The Origin and Development of the Johannine *Egō Eimi* Sayings in Cognitive-Critical Perspective." *Journal for the Study of the Historical Jesus* 9 (2011): 139–206.

ings of Jesus' I-Am sayings of Jesus are not exclusive to John; they are also found in the Synoptics, including allusions to the theophany of Moses before the burning bush in Exodus 3:14 (Mk 6:50; 12:26; 14:61–62). These associations, plausibly connected to the historical ministry of Jesus, given their independent attestation in the Synoptics and John, nonetheless took on new meanings within the developing Johannine tradition as encounters with the spirit of the risen Christ caused deepened reflection on the meaning of Jesus as the Messiah-Christ in post-resurrection consciousness. This is where the Johannine prologue emerged as a fitting communal confession—plausibly devised by the Johannine elder as a means of affirming the witness of the Beloved Disciple, designed to lead later audiences into experiential encounter as witnessed to in the Johannine narrative. It was thus added to the narrative as a means of engaging later audiences with its subject—seeking to evoke an experiential encounter to further dialectical experience and subsequent reflection. Therefore, the flesh and glory of Jesus emerged from the dialectical reflection between experience and perception of the evangelist; the both-and appreciation of that tension is furthered by means of the engagement-oriented character of the narrative's construction.

A secondary origin of the humanity and divinity of Jesus in John is the result of the tradition's development within *the dialectical Johannine situation of Johannine Christianity*, with high and low aspects indebted to early and late factors. In addition to early transformative encounters with Jesus and later rhetorical emphases upon his divinely commissioned status, the Johannine tradition also shows evidence of mundane memories of Jesus' pathos-imbued existence as well as later emphases on his suffering humanity. Thus, the history of the Johannine situation reflects challenges to Ebionite-type affirmations of Jesus' status as a prophet, but not as the Messiah-Christ or Son of God, and correctives to docetizing tendencies to embrace Jesus' divinity at the expense of his humanity. Therefore, emphases upon Jesus' divinity and humanity are both *early and late* within the emerging Johannine situation, and dialectically so.

Here Trinitarian discussions correctly rejected all-too-clever explanations of "how" the humanity and divinity of Jesus are to be envisioned—an appeal to mystery finally makes the best sense of the tensive character of Johannine Christology as well as its epistemological origins. Whether the Fourth Evangelist would have agreed with ontic and metaphysical interpretations of his dialectical reflections upon God's saving-revealing work, operative through the time-bound ministry of Jesus of Nazareth and the timeless work of the resurrected Lord, others will have to judge. It may well be that he would have affirmed such confessions, as John 20:31 reflects a pistic (faith-oriented) development in ways formulaic. John's narrative is thus crafted so as to facilitate belief in Jesus as "the Christ, the Son of God" in order that, believing, people might experience life in his name.[31] Then again, the contextual settings of patristic discussions are not the only settings to be considered; modern settings also pose contexts for interpreting these first-century texts, so the historical-critical scholar and the historical theologian must work together in understanding how first-century texts were interpreted over the next three or four centuries, noting both conjunctions and disjunctions between them.

- *The Father/Son Relationship in John*:
  1. John's Human-Divine Dialogue and Agency Schema
  2. Dialectical Situation of Johannine Christianity

The egalitarian and subordinated relation of the Son to the Father in John must be envisioned from the perspective of *the Jewish Agency Motif* as flipsides of the same coin. Therefore, we do not have two differing Christologies rooted in disparate literary sources; such is a modern fiction. Nor, according to some patristic inferences, is the Son's oneness with the Father to be sacrificed as a factor of his faithful obedience to the Father. Rather, the Son is to be equated with the Father identically because he is sent from the Father as his representative agent, fulfilling the prophet-like-Moses typology rooted in Deuteronomy 18:15–22. Further, Jesus confirms that he is the one predicted by Moses as his words come true, confirming his authentic agency as the mouthpiece of the divine Word. As this motif is echoed in the Q tradition and in the preaching of Peter and Stephen in Acts, it is likely rooted in the memory of early Jesus tradition, although its presentation in John reflects an understanding of ongoing revelation. The point of the Son's connectedness to the Father is to emphasize the divine origin of his mission and message. Therefore, humanity is exhorted to be open to the divine address—effected in the mission and message of Jesus as the Son of the Father—and humanity will be judged according to its responses by the divine source of the agent's commission.

31. Anderson, *Navigating the Living Waters of the Gospel of John: On Wading with Children and Swimming with Elephants*, Pendle Hill Pamphlet 352 (Wallingford, Pa.: Pendle Hill, 2000).

A second factor in the Father/Son relationship in John is *the dialectical Johannine situation*, wherein three chapters plausibly influenced the development of the motif. (a) Beginning with the ministry of Jesus of Nazareth, his challenge to the religious leaders in Jerusalem was likely met with disputes over his authorization to act and speak as he did. In emphasizing the basis for his ministry, it is not unlikely that the Galilean challenger of Judean institutions appealed to Mosaic agency as the source of his concerns. (b) In moving to a diaspora setting, new sets of engagements with Jewish leadership emerged within local synagogues claiming Mosaic authority in their interpretations of Torah. Here, Pharisaic insistence on adherence to the Law of Moses were met with appeals to Moses' having written about Jesus, whose authenticity is attested by his word having come true. Therefore, if one loves the Father, one will also lovingly receive the one sent by him—so the Johannine evangelist asserts. (c) As the Johannine narrative is embraced among Gentile believers, in addition to Jewish ones, the Jewish agency motif gets translated into Hellenistic-friendly terms—fitting especially well with understandings of the divine Logos as taught by the likes of Heraclitus and Philo. Perhaps influenced by the Christological hymns of Colossians 1:15–21 and Hebrews 1:1–4, this worship-confession was then added to a final edition of the Johannine narrative by the compiler, connecting the Son with the Father in preexistent and cosmos-effecting ways.[32]

It is especially the Johannine prologue that determined the patristic discussions of Jesus' divinity and humanity and his relation to the Father. The Word was *with* God, and the Word *was* God, so the Johannine evangel proclaims (Jn 1:1–2). Further, the Son's role in creation and preexistent oneness with the Father, reflecting a cross-cultural expansion of John's agency motif, contributed to heated theological discussions over the ensuing centuries. John's presentations of Jesus' will and that of his Father being in tension contributed to monothelite debates, just as John's tensive Christology contributed to adoptionistic, Apollinarian, and monophysite debates. What contributed most powerfully to the inference of distinctive persons regarding the Father and the Son is John's presentation of Jesus' relation to the Father and his representative mission. Therefore, it is precisely because of John's presentation of Je-

32. Anderson, "The Johannine *Logos*-Hymn: A Cross-Cultural Celebration of God's Creative-Redemptive Work," in *Creation Stories in Dialogue: The Bible, Science, and Folk Traditions*, Radboud Prestige Lecture Series by Alan Culpepper, ed. R. Alan Culpepper and Jan van der Watt, Biblical Interpretation Series 139 (Leiden: Brill, 2016), 219–42.

sus' agency as sent by the Father, carrying out his will and returning to the one who sent him, that Trinitarian discussions were forced to envision individuated faces and persons within a unitive Godhead. In that sense, the Jewish agency motif never really was excluded from Trinitarian discussions; it was simply modified and incorporated into the ensuing Neoplatonist discussions.

- *The Holy Spirit's Proceeding from the Father and also from the Son*:
  1. Dialectical Situation of Johannine Christianity
  2. The Dialectical Thinking of the Evangelist—Perception/ Experience Dialogues

The Holy Spirit's relation to the Father and the Son also is presented more clearly in John than in any other part of the New Testament, and like the presentation of the Father and Son as distinctive personae, the role of the Holy Spirit in the lives of believers is most extensively emphasized in John 14–17. The revelatory-empowering work of the Holy Spirit, however, is not distinctive to John; it is also emphasized by the Synoptic Jesus in Matthew 10:16–20, where the Spirit of the Father and the Holy Spirit (Mk 13:11; Lk 12:11–12) will guide believers and speak through them. Parallel to the Synoptics (Mt 3:11; Mk 1:8; Lk 3:16; 11:13) in the Gospel of John the Holy Spirit is emphasized as a gift from God, empowering believers as an indwelling manifestation of the divine presence (Jn 3:5–8, 34; 7:37–39). This theme goes back to Jesus tradition operative within all four gospels. Within the Johannine situation, though, the guiding and instructive work of the Holy Spirit becomes especially significant. Jesus is here remembered as promising the Holy Spirit as a *paraklētos*—an advocate, helper, and comforter—who will guide and instruct believers in their time of need (14:17, 26; 15:26; 16:7, 13). The Spirit of truth will bring to mind the teachings of Jesus and will lead them into all truth. Therefore, the mutuality of agency between the Father, the Son, and Holy Spirit cohere within these four chapters, culminating with Jesus' followers being one with him as he is with the Father—witnessing through the empowerment of the Holy Spirit in the world (17:21–26).

Within these chapters it is also easy to see how a monarchial view of the Trinity, as embraced within Eastern Orthodoxy, is arguable. Both the Son and the Spirit are sent by the Father, with the Spirit also proceeding from the Father (15:26). Such texts embolden the originative role and character of the Father. And yet, the Son's unity with the Father and the Son's sending of the Spirit moved the discussions at Constantinople, Ephesus, and Chalcedon further—leading to Western *filioque* affirmations a century or more later. Interestingly, the two passages where the Father sends the Spirit are in the first edition of John (14:16, 26), while the two passages where the Son will send the Spirit are in the later material (15:26; 16:7). Here we see evidence of development within the Johannine tradition and situation, likely a factor of the evolving needs of John's audience. As an apologetic to Jewish family and friends, asserting the Father's role in the sending of the Son and the Spirit would have been compelling. After all, as affirmed in Hebrew scripture, the Holy Spirit is the Spirit of God—at work in the world and in the lives of individuals. Within the later Johannine situation, however, as this Spirit-led community seeks to discern direction and guidance as to how to address the emerging needs of this dynamically changing set of communities, connecting leadings of the Spirit with the teaching and ministry of Jesus becomes an objective referent by which to judge subjective leadings. Therefore, the dialectical character of John's pneumatology is primarily ordered by *the developing needs of the emerging Johannine situation.*

A secondary contributor to the evangelist's stance on the place of the Holy Spirit as part of the divine being and operation, however, is the *cognitive dialectic between perception and experience within the reflection and thought of the evangelist.* Given that we probably have at least some firsthand memory of the words and works of Jesus as a resource for the preaching and teaching of the evangelist,[33] we likely have a continuity of revelatory openings—"Aha! experiences," as James Loder would describe them—within the post-resurrection consciousness of the Johannine evangelist and others among his associations. Therefore, while Jesus-tradition memory may have informed his asserting that the Father would send forth the Holy Spirit, just as he sent the Son (Jn 14), the emphasis appears to have shifted toward the discerning of spirits and an emphasis upon the words and works of Jesus as the measure for accountability in the later Johannine situation (Jn 15–16). Indeed, the testing of spirits is required in the Johannine situation (1 Jn 4:1), and an emphasis upon Christ as the *paraklētos* (1 Jn 2:1) before the Father informs the convic-

33. See the overlooked first-century clue to John's apostolic authorship in Anderson, *Christology of the Fourth Gospel*, 274–77.

tion that another advocate will be sent (Jn 14:16) who will convict people of the truth—both of sin and of righteousness—in the later Johannine situation (16:7–15). Therefore, from a cognitive-critical perspective, we also see a shift in the thinking of the evangelist, who comes more and more to associate the convincing/convicting work of the Holy Spirit with the normatizing work of Jesus as the Christ, because the Spirit is the one who clarifies and magnifies his work as the present and ongoing teacher within the community of believers.

Once more, implications for Trinitarian understandings are considerable here. While the patristic discussions moved toward ontic and metaphysical categories of being, the Johannine presentation of the Holy Spirit's work as sent by the Father and the Son, continuing the saving-revealing work of the Son on behalf of the Father's love for the world, reflects a more dynamic understanding of these realities. While the being and work of the Holy Spirit may finally remain a mystery, as does the dual nature of the Son, the work of God's Spirit on behalf of the Son furthers his redemptive mission of grace and truth in the world beloved by God (1:14, 17; 3:16). Of course, it is the Spirit of God that is here operative, and yet, the gift of the Spirit is precisely what Jesus as the Christ came to avail to the world, as a gift of the Father's love. Therefore, one can appreciate the patristic inference that the love of the Father for the world indeed has a name—it is the Holy Spirit—who continues the saving/revealing work of Jesus as the Christ in the world, full of grace and truth. Again, the Johannine presentation of these realities is less in terms of being and more in terms of agency and mission; and with that fact, many a Trinitarian analysis, from the patristic to the modern eras, would agree.

As a result of the previous analysis, it is clear that the church fathers and mothers were indeed seeking to address the Johannine theological riddles by means of the best analytical tools of their day, just as modern scholars have. Note, however, that one of the features observable is the restoring of dialectical tension that had been diminished or sidestepped by alternative proposals or that had been distorted speculatively in attempting to account for a particular feature in the biblical witness. Therefore, the orthodox syntheses tended to restore balance to understandings of John's theological, Christological, and pneumatological features. In the light of John's dialogical autonomy, though, would they have come up with the same elements of Trinitarian theology, or might they have come up with something different? Such a question, however, cannot be answered with any sort of certainty; it simply remains a mystery and a question. Perhaps, however, the structure of orthodox faith—as well as some lesser alternatives—might be altered if the pervasively dialogical character of John's presentation of the Father, the Son, and the Holy Spirit is to be taken seriously and faithfully within an epistemological appraisal of the biblical text.

Conclusion: Trinitarian Theology in Johannine Perspective

While it cannot be imagined that the fathers and mothers of the church would have viewed the Johannine riddles leading up to the construction of Trinitarian theology in the light of modern historical-critical analysis, or even that the Johannine evangelist and compiler would have thought in patristic terms, what can be explored is a renewed look at orthodox Trinitarian theology in Johannine perspective. Put otherwise, given that the church fathers and mothers were seeking to address John's riddles in the light of the best analytical tools of their day, what if contemporary theologians sought to address the elements of Trinitarian theology in the light of our having considered the Johannine riddles (their character and origin) using the best tools of the present day? In particular, what if an appreciation for the epistemological origins of the Johannine riddles themselves were to be applied to the ways in which one approached the doctrine of the Trinity in the modern era? Given that the source of orthodox theology has as its Johannine roots a living and dynamic set of factors, the question is how to restore the Johannine tensions to later understandings—moving living faith to orthodox creeds ... and back again.[34] And to do so implies not simply viewing John's narrative in Trinitarian perspective, but also viewing Trinitarian theology in Johannine perspective.

That being the case, what would happen if Trinitarian theology were viewed with a healthy sense of Johannine dialectical regard? Rather than including or excluding people from Christian communions on the bases of creedal or cultic measures, an invitation to Conjunctive Faith (Fowler's Stage-Five Faith) poses an alternative to dogmatism. After all, the light of Christ en-

34. In Anderson, "On Guessing Points," 344–45: "Implications: From Living Faith to Orthodox Creed ... and Back Again."

lightens all (1:9), and Jesus has many sheep "not of this fold" (10:16). Given the dynamic agency of the Son's relation to the Father and the Spirit's relation to both, the existential question is whether modern believers are open to being drawn into the communion of that agency whereby they become receptive and responsive to the divine initiative as Christ's witnesses and redemptive partners in the world—Jesus' friends (15:14–15). In reading Trinitarian theology contextually, it is vital to appreciate the syntheses within the trajectories of contemporary theses and antitheses—viewing conclusions in the light of the questions they were addressing. In addressing the needs of the world today, how might embracing the Father, Son, and the Holy Spirit further grace and truth and love in the world today—the very heart of Trinitarian theology? How might the central elements of Trinitarian theology be expressed today in ways that draw audiences compellingly into its subject (God's saving-revealing work, power, and presence) in ways that are biblically sound, rationally coherent, and experientially adequate? If the Johannine prologue points the way forward, perhaps the facilitating of transformational encounter may hold the key over resorting to propositional debates.

While it cannot be said that John's story of Jesus envisioned or articulated the fully developed components of Trinitarian theology, it cannot be denied that the role of this dialectical presentation of Jesus as the Christ was central to its development. As Trinitarian theology did not originate out of a vacuum in the patristic era, so its embrace in the modern era will best be facilitated by remaining in dialogue with the best of historical-critical inferences. If that happens, not only will Trinitarian theology be connected more effectively with its epistemological Johannine origins; it will more powerfully engage contemporary audiences in the modern era as well. After all, as the mission of the Father, the Son, and the Holy Spirit endeavors to convey grace and love to the world, the reception of that message involves knowing the truth, and all truth is liberating (8:32).

Marianne Meye Thompson

5. THE GOSPEL OF JOHN AND EARLY TRINITARIAN THOUGHT

The Unity of God in John, Irenaeus, and Tertullian

One of the issues dealt with in the Gospel of John is that of the unity of God. In what sense can Jesus, the Son of God, be considered "equal to God" and yet not be a second deity, independent of God? The question of God's unity confronted early Trinitarian thinkers as they faced challenges from Gnosticism, with its demotion of the Creator to the status of a secondary and inferior deity. Irenaeus especially deals with the question of God's unity, insisting that there is but one God, the Father, who created the world, and that this God is also the Father of the Son, the Lord Jesus Christ. Yet Irenaeus can also write, "The Father is God and the Son is God" (*Dem.* 47). It is not only the Gnostics who challenged the unity of God; Irenaeus's own formulations might seem to do so, as well. Tertullian confronts a different challenge in the figure of Praxeas, who, in order to preserve the *monarchy*, the one God, apparently identified Father, Son, and Spirit as one and the same. In his inimitable way, Tertullian insists on the distinction of the three while holding to their unity; the *economy* does not overthrow the *monarchy*.

I will begin this essay with a brief summary of how the Gospel of John speaks of God, the explicit or implicit judgments the gospel makes about Father, Son, and Spirit and their relationship to one another, and how John preserves God's unity. Obviously, it is difficult not to be influenced by the categories of later thought in even posing questions to John, but I hope that my brief summary will reflect a reading of John that takes seriously its first-century context. Second, I will suggest how two early Trinitarian thinkers, Irenaeus and Tertullian, made similar *judgments* about Father, Son, and Spirit, even when new introducing new *concepts* or imagery (to borrow David Yeago's phrasing).[1] It goes without saying that my discussion will be suggestive, rather than exhaustive, and that much will have to be left out, both of the discussion of the Gospel of John and of my sketch of these early thinkers.

The Only True God

With two (possibly three) important exceptions (1:1; 20:28; 1:18?), God refers, in John, to the one whom Jesus calls "my Father" or "the Father."[2] This Father is "the only true God" (17:3; compare 8:54), a designation that reflects the Jewish monotheistic matrix of early Christian belief. In John Jesus alone calls God "my Father." The absolute "Father" also alludes to God as the author and creator of all that is, a term for God found frequently, for example, in Josephus and Philo and other Hellenistic Jewish thinkers.[3] As the source and creator of life, God is, therefore, "greater than all" and has all authority.

John resonates with motifs from the biblical and Jewish traditions about God's creation of the world through his word or wisdom. Hence, in John, God is the "living Father" (6:57), the one who "has life in himself" (5:26). All things were made through the Word, the logos, which already has the attributes of wisdom and Torah (see here Gn 1, Ps 33, Prv 8, and Sir 24). God has no other intermediaries.

1. David Yeago, "The New Testament and Nicene Dogma: A Contribution to the Recovery of Theological Exegesis," *Pro Ecclesia* 3 (1994): 152–64.

2. Occurring about 120 times, "Father" is the most common designation of God. The generic *theos* ("god") occurs 108 times.

3. Philo, "The Father": *Spec.* 2.197; *Opif.* 74, 76; *Mut.* 29; "Father of all things, for he begat them," Cher. 49; "Father and Maker," *Opif.* 77; "Father and Maker of all," *Decal.* 51; Josephus: God is "father and source of the universe …creator of things human and divine," *Ant.* 7.380; "the Father of all," *Ant.*1.230; 2.152. Homer characterized Zeus as "Father of gods and human beings"; *Iliad*, 15.47.

The Son

While the gospel begins with a statement about the preexistent word of God (1:1, 14, 18), it then narrates the history of the Word made flesh: Jesus, who heals, teaches, debates, hungers, thirsts, bleeds, and dies. He is Israel's Messiah, whose role is to "gather together the children of God who are scattered abroad" (11:48–52). Not only is he the Messiah, the king of Israel, he is also the Savior of the world (4:42), a not particularly surprising designation, given the fact that he is the embodied word, the agent of creation of "all things."

In carrying out his messianic vocation, Jesus exercises the prerogatives of God. John's claim for Jesus is not that his work is like God's work, or furthers God's purposes, but that Jesus' work is in fact God's own work, because the Father has entrusted all things to the Son (3:35; 5:20; 6:37; 6:39; 10:29; 12:32; 15:15; 16:15; 17:10), particularly the power to confer life. The key verse here is John 5:26: "Just as the Father has life in himself, so he has granted the Son also to have life in himself." Such predications assume and are dependent upon the conviction that there is but one God, one source of life. The Son confers the Father's life, which the Son *has in himself*.[4] John thus predicates a remarkable status of the Son, one that is not made of any other creature or entity, either in John or in Jewish literature—namely, that there is one who has that which is unique to God (life in himself) and so is what God is (living, and eternally living). While the Son has what the Father has ("life in himself"), the Son has it because the Father "has granted" (or given, *edōken*) it to the Son.

The context for this argument in chapter 5 is the charge that Jesus has usurped the prerogatives of God and so has falsely exalted himself to equality with God, a charge leveled in biblical and Jewish literature, as well as Greek and Roman sources, against kings, emperors, and even philosophers for accepting veneration, usurping divine prerogatives or failing to acknowledge the supremacy of the one true God. The implicit charges in John are not only that Jesus claims that which is not rightfully his (equality with God), but that by setting himself up as God, Jesus sets himself *over against* God, as a *rival* to

4. "Just as the Father as Creator and Consummator possesses life, he has given that possession also to the Son, not merely as the executor of incidental assignments but in the absolute sense of sharing in the Father's power"; Herman Ridderbos, *The Gospel of John: A Theological Commentary* (Grand Rapids, Mich.: Eerdmans, 1997), 198.

God. Jesus' words are taken, in essence, as a declaration of independence and hence of arrogant disobedience.

But John argues that the Son always and only does what the Father does. While this is an argument for the Son's *dependence* on the Father, it is ultimately an argument for the *unity* of the Father and the Son. The Son does what the Father shows and tells him to do; the Son does what the Father does. The point of the argument in John 5 is "not to subordinate the Son but to safeguard monotheism";[5] indeed, John does not use the word *hypotassesthai* to describe the relationship of the Son to the Father (compare 1 Cor 15:28).

Because the unity of Father and Son is a unity of work and mission—that is, to give life, to preserve the flock of God in life—the rabbinic category of the *shaliach* has often been employed to explain their relationship.[6] The *shaliach* is authorized and sent to fulfill a task on behalf of the sender; hence, "the one who is sent is like the one who sent him."[7] But in my view this category cannot fully explain the permanent and intimate relationship of the Father and Son in John, the preexistent identity of the Word, the Son's possession of divine life "in himself," and the mutual indwelling of Father and Son as is expressed in statements such as "the Father is in me and I am in the Father." The Son is the Father's word, not simply the prophet to whom that word was given. The Son is never "decommissioned" or "deauthorized."

To put it differently, in the Gospel of John Jesus is a *representative* of God, but not only a representative; the Son is also the *representation* of the Father. If Jesus alone and always embodies the Father's will in word and deed, it is because of who he is: the Son who is loved from before the foundation of the world (17:24; compare 3:35; 5:20; 10:17; 17:22–26); the Son who shared God's glory before the world; the agent of the creation of the world, in whom there

5. So J. N. D. Kelly, in discussing Justin and the apologists' use of "second God" and "secondary Rank" to refer to the Logos; Kelly, *Early Christian Doctrines*, rev. ed. (New York: Harper and Row, 1960), 101.

6. So striking are the parallels between Johannine Christology and halakhic principles of agency that A. E. Harvey has concluded that "much of the language used of Jesus in the Fourth Gospel [is] drawn from juridical practice." According to Harvey, the Jewish conception of "agency" explains even the designation "Son of God" when it is recognized that a principal's son could be considered his supreme and natural agent; Harvey, "Christ as Agent," in *The Glory of Christ in the New Testament: Studies in Christology in Memory of George Bradford Caird*, ed. L. D. Hurst and N. T. Wright (Oxford: Clarendon, 1987), 241.

7. A common saying in the rabbis was "the one who is sent like the one who sent him" (*m. Ber.* 5:5; *b. B. Mes.* 96a; *b. Hag.* 10b; *b. Menah* 93b; *b. Nazir* 12b; *b. Qidd.* 42b, 43a; *Mek. Ex.* on Ex 12:3 and 6).

is life. Precisely because the Word, the Son, has that "life in himself" that is distinctive of God, the Word is therefore called *God* (1:1). It is the risen Jesus, who lives and returns to the presence of the Father from whom he came, and to the glory he had before the world was made, whom Thomas acknowledges as *My Lord and My God* (20:28).[8] But he is always the Word, the Son, and never the Father. His Father, in fact, is the one true God, from whom he has come and to whom he returns.

The Spirit

There is no explicit argument in John about how the Spirit relates to God, whether the Spirit acts in harmony with God, or whether the Spirit has usurped the prerogatives of God, as can be found with respect to the Son. This is not particularly surprising, since the Spirit who descends from heaven, who makes possible the birth from above so that one may see the kingdom of God, who may be called "holy," and who effects life, obviously is the Spirit of God, God's sanctifying and life-giving power at work. This Spirit descends from God and remains on Jesus; Jesus will baptize with the Spirit, but the Spirit will come only after Jesus departs.

The Spirit will come as the Paraclete. On analogy with the incarnation of the Word, after Jesus' death and resurrection the Spirit becomes manifest and present in the world and among the disciples as the Paraclete. The functions of the Paraclete overlap and continue both those of Jesus, who himself is obliquely referred to as Paraclete (14:16), and those of the Father. Both the Father and the Paraclete testify to Jesus (5:37; 8:18; 15:26–27) and glorify Jesus (5:44; 8:54; 12:23, 28; 13:31–32; 17:1, 5; 16:14); both will be with the disciples (14:23; 17:11, 15, 26; 14:27); and both will teach them (5:45; 14:26; 16:13). The Spirit reflects Jesus, because both the Son and the Spirit come from the Father. The Spirit, however, bears witness to and glorifies Jesus, and Jesus will send the Paraclete from the Father (15:26). There is an implicit parallelism between the statements about life and the Spirit: if Jesus has life in himself and confers it on others because the Father has given it to him, so Jesus has and may confer

8. Ignatius often refers to Christ as *theos*, but it is noteworthy how often he uses the possessive pronoun in such constructions. For example, "our God"; *Eph proem* 15:3; *Rom proem* 3:3, 9:5); "my God" (Rom 6:3).

the Spirit because "[God] gives the spirit without measure" (3:34). In turn, the Spirit makes possible the life given by the Father through the Son.

Irenaeus, Tertullian, and the Unity of God

At this point, I want to offer some brief remarks on Irenaeus and Tertullian and their own particular attempts to wrestle with the unity of God in their own contexts. First, Irenaeus.

We find in Irenaeus both increased attention to the identity of the Son and to the pressing problem of the unity of God; indeed, as we saw in the Gospel of John, the one implicates the other. And, as in the Gospel of John, while the role of the Spirit is also brought into focus, it is not addressed as directly and fully as the question of Father and Son is.

Irenaeus's anti-Gnostic writings sought to secure the unity of God and to locate the work of creation and salvation in that one God. Irenaeus speaks emphatically of the one God, the Father, as the source of all that is: "the only God, the only Lord, the only Creator, the only Father, alone containing all things, and Himself commanding all things into existence" (*Adv. Haer*. 2.1.1; *Dem. Ap. Pr*. 3, 5).

Irenaeus drew heavily on the opening verses of the Gospel of John to insist on the creation of all things through the Word (*Adv. Haer*. 3.11.1; compare Jn 1:1–3). Furthermore, in his exegesis of John 1:3–4, Irenaeus, following the punctuation found in many ancient fathers,[9] comments that when John writes, "what was made in him is life," he means that "all things were made *by* him, but *in* him was life." Irenaeus continues: "This, then, which is *in* Him, is more closely connected *with* Him than those things which were simply made *by* Him" (*Adv. Haer.* 1.8.5). As John would put it, not only is life uniquely given by the Father through the Son, but life is also that inherent property of the Father given to the Son.

Irenaeus's understanding of God's unity was graphically set forth in the image that the Word and Wisdom, Son and the Spirit, are the two hands of

9. "All things were made through him, and without him was nothing made. What has come to be in him was life, and the life was the light of all people" (contrast, e.g., the RSV, which reads, "Without him was nothing made that has been made. In him was life").

this Father (*Adv. Haer.* 4.20.1; 5.1.3; 5.6.1; 5.28.4; compare 4.7.4).[10] Because Son and Spirit are the Father's own hands, what the Son or the Spirit does is truly the work of the Father, and, conversely, the Father truly accomplishes his own work with these hands. God does not work with other hands, and he does not work without both hands. Thus elsewhere Irenaeus can articulate the way in which the Son and the Spirit are not only the means by which the Father works, but the ways in which the work of the one relates to the work of the other. For example, the Spirit leads people to the Word who leads them to the Father; without the Spirit one cannot behold the Word, and without the Son one cannot be drawn near to the Father (*Dem.* 75).

Finally, Irenaeus asserts the eternal presence of the Son and Spirit with the Father, perhaps not very surprisingly, since Son and Spirit are God's own Word and Wisdom, "the hands of the Father" (*Adv. Haer.* 4.20.1; *Dem.* 10.). While the Son has come at the appointed time and the Spirit descended in the time determined by the Father (*Adv.* 3.17.4), neither the Son nor the Spirit came into being at the time of their manifestation. As Irenaeus writes, "With him were always present the Word and Wisdom, the Son and the Spirit" (4.20.1; 4.20.3).

Tertullian's diatribe *Against Praxeas* explicates several passages in the Gospel of John ("I and the Father are one," 10:30; "If you have seen me, you have seen the Father," 14:9; and "I am in the Father and the Father is in me," 14:10; 17:21). In explicating John 10:30, "I and the Father are one," Tertullian argues that the Father and Son are one thing (*unum*; Greek, *hen*) but *not* one person (*unus*).[11] Elsewhere, Tertullian famously explains this reality as follows: "The ray is extended from the sun, it is still part of the whole; the sun will still be in the ray, because it is a ray of the sun" (*Apol.* 21). Even as a ray truly is "sun," one may distinguish between them, naming the one as "ray" and the other as "sun."

Taking such passages into account, Tertullian writes that "[we] believe that there is one only God, but under the following *economy* … that this one only God has also a Son, His word … who sent from heaven from the Father … the Holy Spirit, the Paraclete" (*Adv. Prax.* 2). The three are of one *substance*, but "the mystery of the economy … distributes the unity into Trinity,

10. Note also the similar but less developed use of the image in Theophilus, *Ad Autolycum* 2.18, who also speaks of the "trinity" of God, his Word and his Wisdom.

11. Hippolytus, *Against Noetus* 3; Tertullian, *Against Praxeas* 22; Cyril of Alexandria, *Gospel of John* 7.1, LF.

setting forth Father, Son and Spirit as three" (*Adv. Prax.* 2); hence, the "trinity." To secure the unity of God, however, Tertullian argues that even as a monarch may have thousands of servants without imperiling his single rule, so a monarch may have a son without imperiling his unity (*Adv. Prax.* 3). It is not the Trinity that destroys the unity of God; it is only the assertion that there is another creator, another power that rivals and stands over against this one power that does so.

The "mystery of the economy" is that "the Son and the Spirit, revealed in the economy as other than the Father, were at the same time inseparable with Him in his eternal being."[12]

Concluding Reflections

Irenaeus and Tertullian share with John the conviction of the unity and uniqueness of God. God is the Father, the ultimate source of all that is; the Son and Spirit come from the Father, and have always been with the Father. Irenaeus and Tertullian find appropriate imagery to emphasize both the distinction between Father and Son (and, to a lesser degree, Spirit) and the unity of the one God, following, but not merely repeating, the judgments found in the Gospel of John. According to John, the only true God is the Father, who gives his only Son a share of his glory and the powers of judgment and life. Even when exercising distinct divine prerogatives, the Son always expresses and carries out the will of his Father, because the Son is the Word who was with God in the beginning. Against the Gnostics, Irenaeus particularly emphasized that the Creator God is the Father of the Son, the Lord Jesus. The image of the Father's having two hands, Son and Spirit, expresses the unity of the one God. God's works may be made known through his hands, through his Son and Spirit; and these works are not alien works, but the very works of God. God has no other hands. Similarly, Tertullian's imagery—the ray from the sun, the roots and a tree, the river and its source—insures the unity of the one God: a ray will cease to be a ray if disconnected from the sun—yet distinguishes them, as well. Moreover, Tertullian's use of the terms "monarchy" and

12. J. N. D. Kelly, *Early Christian Doctrines*, 109–11; see Andrew McGowan, "God in Early Latin Theology: Tertullian and the Trinity," in *God in Early Christian Thought: Essays in Memory of Lloyd G. Patterson*, ed. Andrew McGowan, Brian E. Daley, and Timothy J. Gaden (Boston: Brill, 2009), 71.

"economy," "substance" and "persons," aims to preserve the unity of the one God while, at the same time, accounting for the language and reality of Father, Son, and Spirit.

But, as Tertullian repeatedly pointed out, the Son is not the Father. Going back to John, Jesus shares or has divine life and divine glory; he is the incarnation of the Word who was in the beginning; the Word is the agent of creation; and therefore John calls him God. But John does not call him Father. Similarly, Irenaeus can speak of the Spirit and Son as the hands of the Father—hence, truly part of God, truly God—but he also speaks of the "hands" of the *Father* as the means by which the Father works. Again, Irenaeus speaks of the one true God as the Father, the source of all, but proclaims that the "rule of faith" has three points of confession: God, the Father, his only Son, and the Spirit. Finally, Tertullian distinguishes substance and persons, and the three "persons" share one substance and, writes Tertullian, "God is the name for the substance, that is, the divinity" (*Adv. Hermog.* 3).

John has no Trinitarian or triadic formulas or benedictions, no explicit statements of God's triune. But John could say that the Father is God and the Son is God and the Spirit is God, but, equally, that the Son is not the Father or the Spirit; the Spirit is not the Father or the Son. John also happily formulates predications about the Son in what later theology would call "functional" terms. The Son has the Father's prerogatives and powers, and so does the Father's work. But it is clear that in John these functional categories are linked to other statements, statements that might be called "ontological." Thus the Word was with God "in the beginning" and, therefore, was God. One can say that John's functional statements are ways of doing ontology, although differently from the way later thinkers would approach their tasks; that John's functional statements express his ontological convictions; but also that the ontological convictions rise logically or inexorably out of the Johannine assertions that Jesus has and gives what only the Father has in himself—namely, life. By extension, the same applies to the Spirit who effects the new birth, the new life. It is John's functional and ontological "both/and"—that the work of God is done in the world by Son and Spirit, and that the Son and Spirit are always with God and come from God—that puts pressure on early Christian theologians to reformulate and articulate John's implicit convictions about Father, Son, and Spirit in their own terms and when faced with new questions.

Mark J. Edwards

6. THE JOHANNINE PROLOGUE BEFORE ORIGEN

The gospel ascribed to John has been the jewel of Trinitarian orthodoxy ever since Clement of Alexandria pronounced it the most spiritual of the four. This judgment, making a virtue of its departures from the other three, is corroborated by the paradoxical tradition that it is the latest, yet the only one to issue from the pen of an apostle. Both these claims have been impugned by the biblical scholarship of the last two centuries, which is also far from unanimous in finding any doctrine of the Trinity in the New Testament. The gospel, we are repeatedly informed, is not the work of any apostle, but a composition of the second century; it represents a docetic, or fleshless, Christ and was taken up by the hegemonic church of the second century to preempt any further use of it by the Gnostics. Those who accept this view that it is a spurious document, canonized to support a false theology, will find it hard to refrain from attributing variants in the Greek manuscripts of the gospel to pious tampering or, in Burgon's phrase, to "orthodox corruption."[1] No portion of the narrative is more open to suspicion than the prologue, where textual variation is both frequent and occasionally momentous, while the theological interest is acknowledged to be profound.

I shall not abuse the patience of the reader by reproducing a recent study

1. The expression "corruption by the orthodox" was used by R. W. Burgon, *The Causes of the Corruption of the Traditional Text of the Gospels* (1896; repr. New York: Cosimo, 2007), 211. The term has been made familiar to a new generation by Ehrman, *Orthodox Corruption of Scripture*.

in which I hope to have demonstrated that the choice between textual variants at John 1:18—the choice, that is, between "only god" and only-begotten Son"—is not determined by the theological premises of those who cite it in antiquity.[2] Nor have I anything to add to what I have said elsewhere on the application of the term *theos* to the Word at John 1:1, which I take, with Origen and a number of modern commentators, to be predicative rather than substantive.[3] On the translation of Logos as "Word," I shall have something to say in an epilogue; I shall begin, however, with some remarks on the currency of the Gospel in the early second century, and shall then proceed to discuss the reading of two contested verses, John 1:13 and John 1:13—all topics that appear to me to be handled with less care in recent scholarship than the complexity of the evidence demands.

"The Word Became Flesh": John 1:14

Since the mid-nineteenth century, it has commonly been assumed (and sometimes argued) that the gospel ascribed to John is a late composition, or at least that it was the last to achieve a place in the fourfold canon. The term "Johannophobia" has been coined to describe the supposed hostility of Catholic writers to a text that was initially patronized only by the Gnostics, and where parallels appear in Catholic writings of the early second century, they are put down to coincidence or to knowledge of a "Johannine tradition" cognate with the gospel. We need not rehearse here the whole of Charles Hill's skeptical review of the skeptic's case in *The Johannine Corpus in the Early Church*.[4] Since, however, the question has been raised again with regard to the earliest echoes of John 1:14—"the Word became flesh and tabernacled among us"—a brief re-

2. M. J. Edwards, "Orthodox Corruption? John 1:18," *Studia Patristica* 44 (2010): 201–7. Irenaeus has said, "*deum nemo vidit umquam nisi unigenitus filius,*" at *Against Heresies* 4.20.6; at 4.20.10, however, he reads "*unigenitus deus,*" and at 3.12.6 he paraphrases or misremembers the phrase as "*unigenitus filius dei*"; see Bernhard Mütschler, *Das Corpus Johanneum bei Irenäus von Lyon: Studien und Kommentar zum dritten Buch von Adversus Haereses*, Wissenschaftliche Untersuchungen zum Neuen Testament 189 (Tübingen: Mohr Siebeck, 2006), 237, for *unigenitus deus* at *Codex Claromontanus* 2.28.6, and on the assimilation at 3.11.5 to John 3:16. Epiphanius, *Panarion* 37.27.2, cites "*monogenês theos*" as the reading at *Against Heresies* 1.8.5. In Clement's *Excerpts from Theodotus* we find "*monogenês theos*" (6), then "*monogenês huios*" (7). The reading "*unigenitus filius*" is presupposed in Tertullian, *Against Praxeas* 7.2, while at 8.3 we find "*solus filius patrem novit.*"

3. See Edwards, *John through the Centuries* (Oxford: Blackwell, 2003).

4. Hill, *Johannine Corpus in the Early Church.*

view of the witnesses who were writing a generation or two generations before Irenaeus may help us to ascertain whether there are any reasons to doubt their familiarity with this verse that could not be pressed with equal force against the testimony of Irenaeus himself.

Ignatius of Antioch is, by common acclaim, a Catholic author, though, if we accept the traditional date for the letters that are commonly assigned to him, he also served, like many of his canonical predecessors, as a mine of Gnostic imagery.[5] The studies of Caroline Bammel and Charles Hill should leave no doubt that, whether or not he knew the Fourth Gospel as we possess it, Ignatius was acquainted with all the elements of the Johannine tradition.[6] But why should we doubt that he had perused the prologue to the gospel, at least, when at Ephesians 7:2 he speaks of Jesus Christ, the one doctor of the one church, as *en sarki genomenos theos*, "God having come to be in the flesh"? Christian Uhrig argues that there is no direct allusion to John 1:14 and that *genomenos* signifies not "having become," but merely "subsisting."[7] His evidence is the absence of any reference to becoming in the subsequent clause "in life true death," together with the implication of *Smyrnaeans* 4.2 that Christ became not flesh but man. Both arguments are fragile: it is not absurd to take "in life true death" to mean that in dying Christ became true life for us, and there is no reason to suppose that the notion of Christ's becoming flesh is excluded by the equally scriptural assertion at *Smyrnaeans* 4.2 that he became perfect man. If no reminiscence of John 1:14 were intended, the choice of the verb *gignesthai* to denote mere existence requires some explanation. This is not to deny that, like many after him, he claimed the right to give a new application to a Johannine phrase; for example, the title "logos" at *Magnesians* 8.2 is not applied, as in the Fourth Gospel, to any work of revelation that preceded the birth of Christ, but to his advent in the body as the palpable fruit of a plan matured in silence.[8] If, therefore, we

5. See Edwards, "Ignatius and the Second Century: An Answer to R. Hübner," *Zeitschrift für Antikes Christentum* 2 (1998): 214–26. The article to which this is a reply is R. Hübner, "Thesen zum Echtheit und Datierung der sieben Briefe des Ignatius von Antiochien," *Zeitschrift für Antikes Christentu* 1 (1997): 44–72.

6. C. P. Bammel, "Ignatian Problems," *Journal of Theological Studies* 33 (1982): 62–97; Hill, *Johannine Corpus in the Early Church*, 421–44.

7. Christian Uhrig, *"Und das Wort ist Fleisch geworden": Zur Rezeption von Joh 1:14a und zur Theologie der Fleischwerdung in der griechischen vornizänischen Patristik*. Münsterische Beiträge zur Theologie 63 (Münster: Aschendorff, 2004), 36–46.

8. See W. R. Schoedel, "Ignatius of Antioch A Commentary on the Letters," in *Hermeneia* (Philadelphia 1985), 120–22. It is therefore highly implausible to see in this passage a reference to ay gnistci the-

conclude that he is echoing John 1:14 at Ephesians 7:2, we have not yet determined whether he means that God became a man in the womb of Mary or that Mary's child became God in the course of an arduous life.

In the same passage Ignatius declares that Christ was first flesh, then spirit. When *2 Clement* 9.4 avers that the one Christ was first spirit, then became flesh, we may surmise that he is inverting this conceit.[9] If, then, there is no allusion to John 1:14 in Ignatius, one would need second sight to discover any trace of the verse in a text that depends upon him. The date of Justin Martyr's *First Apology* is more easily ascertained, and his acquaintance with the Fourth Gospel seems to me at least undeniable.[10] The participle *sarkôpoiêtheis*, hitherto unattested in Christian prose, appears at *1 Apology* 32.7–9, 32.10; *Trypho* 45.4, 84.1, 87.2, 100.2. Uhring notes that, in contrast to the prologue to the Fourth Gospel, Justin repeatedly couples the assumption of the flesh with the virgin birth, but this is what we should expect from a man who could tolerate no discrepancy in the "memoirs of the apostles." In our present state of knowledge, we cannot hope to say whether these memoirs reached him as separate narratives, as a digest resembling Tatian's *Diatessaron* or as a medley of traditions and texts now lost to us. Nor can we be sure whether the ecclesiastical doctrine that the Eucharist is the flesh and blood of the Word made flesh, which he cites at *1 Apology* 66.1, is an interpretation of John 6:53 in the light of the prologue to the Fourth Gospel.[11] The exegesis of John 6:53 was no more uniform in the early Christian world than it is today.

In Melito of Sardis, *On the Pasch* 70, 104, we read that the one who was enfleshed (*sarkôtheis*) in the virgin is now suspended on the cross. It is possible that he read the words "and we beheld his glory" at John 1:14b in conjunc-

---

ory of the procession of the Logos from silence before the creation of the universe. This point is already made by J. B. Lightfoot, *The Apostolic Fathers*, part 2, *Ignatius and Polycarp* (London: Macmillan, 1889), 2:126–27, whom T. D. Barnes professes to have refuted without quoting any of his arguments, in "The Date of Ignatius," *Expository Times* 120, no. 3 (2008): 125–26. Following R. Hübner and others, Barnes maintains that the letters ascribed to Ignatius are inauthentic, since *Magnesians* 8.3 is designed to confute a Valentinian cosmogony that had not been propounded before the martyrdom of the real Ignatius. Despite the admonitions of John Pearson, *Vindiciae Epistolarum S. Ignatii* (repr. Oxford: 1852), 397–415, all champions of this position have failed to note that in the Valentinian system of Ptolemaeus, Logos does not proceed directly from silence but from the offspring of silence, intellect, and truth.

9. See further Uhrig, *"Und das Wort ist Fleisch geworden,"* 53–57.

10. The best evidence, to my mind, is Justin Martyr's inadvertent conflation of Numbers 21:8 with John 3:19 at *First Apology* 60, where he asserts that Moses fashioned a cross to save the Israelites from a plague of serpents.

11. *Pace* Uhrig, *"Und das Wort ist Fleisch geworden,"* 91–92.

tion with John 12:27–32, where the glory for which Christ prays is his elevation on the cross. Again, this cannot be proved, and his own works afford no evidence that he embraced the common reading of John 1:13 as a reference to the virgin birth of Christ. He may be the first, as Uhrig observes,[12] to date the incarnation from the conception, not the birth. The Valentinian Ptolemaeus maintained with greater hardihood, according to Irenaeus, that, while Word become flesh is one of the Savior's titles (*Against Heresies* 1.8), all designations that he bears on earth pertain properly to the unfallen aeons (1.9.2), of which he has shown us only a fleeting image in his sojourn below.

We come now to Irenaeus of Lyons, who, as the first to promulgate a fourfold canon of the gospels, was undoubtedly acquainted with the prologue to that of John and cites John 1:14 repeatedly against those who deny the reality of Christ's flesh. Nevertheless, he frequently invokes the verse without quoting it and does not feel bound at all times by the words that he makes his own. At *Against Heresies* 3.16.6, he declares that the Word who is always present with us has become flesh for our salvation, and adds at 3.16.7 that he became incarnate in the fullness of time to vindicate all that had been foretold; direct quotation of the text to which he alludes, however, is postponed to 3.16.8. It is he, not the Fourth Evangelist, who infers from the incarnation of the Word that our own flesh is capable of salvation (5.14.1) and draws the corollary, against the Gnostics, that he could not have effected his goal by adopting flesh of a different nature (5.14.2).[13] It is his own eschatology, derived from Paul,[14] that

12. Ibid., 105.

13. Not all Gnostics found it impossible to celebrate the incarnation. The *Tripartite Tractate*—possibly, though not certainly, a late specimen—laments that humans fail to contemplate the Word become flesh, firstborn and beloved of the Father; *Nag Hammadi Codices* 1.5.113 and 125). It is not clear whether Clement of Alexandria or Theodotus is the one who urges, at *Excerpts from Theodotus* 19, that the assumption of flesh was the circumscription (*perigraphe*) of an eternal being who suffered no change of nature. It is certainly Clement who holds the object of the incarnation was to publish the truth (*Stromateis* 5.16.5) and exhibit a perfect synergy of practical and theoretical virtue (*Paedagogus* 1.9.4), surpassing the thieves and robbers who went before (*Strom.* 1.81.1, citing John 10:8). Fear turns to love at the advent of the Savior (*Paed.* 1.59.1), while body and soul are purified by participation in his heavenly flesh (*Paed.* 1.53.3 and 2.201; compare John 6:53). As in the Gospel of Truth, so in Clement, the incarnation bears fruit on the cross, writes Clement (5.72.3), and in both texts *gnosis* is its flower.

14. The term *apokatastasis* ("recapitulation") is derived from Ephesians 1:10, though Paul applies it only to the last day, not to the work of Christ on earth. While it is generally recognized that Irenaeus rediscovered Paul's understanding of Christ as the second Adam, it is not so often perceived that his anthropology is already stated *in nuce* at Ephesians 4:13–14, where the *nêpios*, or immature believer, is contrasted with the *teleios anêr*, the perfect man, whose fullness is realized in Christ.

leads him to represent the incarnation as a renewal of God's likeness in humanity and a renewal of the image in its perfection. When he writes that the prophets foretold the incarnate Word (3.19.2) or that we must not slight the afflictions to which the Word exposed himself by becoming flesh, he is saying more than the evangelist, perhaps more than the evangelist would have countenanced.[15] We do not read in the Fourth Gospel that the Son of God was enfleshed for our salvation (*Against Heresies* 1.10.1) or that the baptized are sealed with the name of the Son incarnate. If, as Uhrig contends, becoming man is not a synonym for becoming flesh in Ignatius, Irenaeus must have been the first to misunderstand him, since he uses these expressions interchangeably in successive sentences (3.19.1). When all agree that it would be misplaced pedantry to doubt that Irenaeus was familiar with the precise words of the gospel, it will surely require strong arguments to persuade us that Ignatius and Justin were ignorant of a text that, for all who have read them since, their own words irresistibly call to mind.[16]

Placing the Stop: John 1:1–4

The third verse of the prologue commences "through him all things came to be," and then we have a choice of punctuations, reading either "without him nothing came to be; what came to be in him was life" or "without him nothing came to be that came to be; in him was life." One might take the view that there can be no such thing as the true punctuation of this passage, since the first scribes would have had no symbol to mark a break between sentences; nevertheless, the dispute wags on, and it seems that one cannot take either side of it

15. At *Epideixis* 31 this argument is conflated with Philippians 2:6: by emptying himself to assume the flesh that had been abased by sin, he restored that flesh to glory and communion with God.

16. Similar ingenuities are practiced on John 1:14 by Catholic apologists of the generation after Irenaeus. Tertullian gloats that the docetists are confuted by the authoritative statement that the Word "took flesh" (*On the Flesh of Christ* 20.3); the fact that this is said of the Word and not of the Father proves, against the monarchians, that it was not the Father who suffered on the cross (Tertullian, *Against Praxeas* 21.3). At *Against Praxeas* 15.6, the words "we beheld his glory" (John 1:14b) are cited, in conjunction with John 1:18, to show that the Word is the revelation of an invisible Father who is therefore logically distinct. For Hippolytus the blessing of Judah at Genesis 49:9 presages the growth of the enfleshed Word in the womb (*Blessing of Jacob* 16) and his coming as prophet (*Antichrist* 8.1. Jacob's surreptitious receipt of his father's blessing prefigures the secret ministry of the word made flesh in the form of a slave (*Blessing* 8, citing Phil 2:8); God's presence in us is his presence in the Word who was made flesh among us (Hippolytus, *Contra Noetum* 4.2), assuming all that is ours apart from sin (17.2).

without being credited with a partiality for one of two opposing heresies. One must, in short, be a Gnostic or an Arian. According to Bruce Metzger, the majority of commentators now opine that the "Arian" reading, shunned or overlooked by many Catholics in the fourth century, is in fact the original one.[17]

> The majority of the committee was impressed by the consensus of ante-Nicene writers (orthodox and heretical alike) who took *ho gegonen* with what follows. When, however, in the fourth century Arians and the Macedonian heretics began to appeal to the passage to prove that the Holy Spirit is to be regarded as one of created things, orthodox writers preferred to take *ho gegonen* with the preceding sentence, thus removing the possibility of heretical usage of the passage.
>
> A minority of the committee held, however, that the reading "what came to be in him was life" was not original, but the product of a heretical intervention:
>
> It was natural for the Gnostics, who sought support from the Fourth Gospel for their doctrine of the Ogdoad, to take *ho gegonen* with the following sentence ("That which has been made in him was life"—whatever that may be supposed to mean).

In this second view the Gnostics were the architects of the consensus to which the first quotation alludes, for there can be no doubt as to the unanimity of Christian witnesses—orthodox and heretical alike, as Metzger says—before the Council of Nicaea in 325 C.E. Irenaeus refers to John 1:3 on at least three occasions.[18] At *Against Heresies* 3.8.2 we read, *nec quidquam ex his quae constituta et in subiectione sunt comparabitur Verbo dei per quem facta sunt omnia*—that is, "nor will anything among those that have been caused to exist and are in subjection bear comparison with the Word of God through whom all things have been created." A direct quotation follows at 3.8.3: *Omnia per eum facta sunt, et sine eo factum est nihil* ("through him all things have been made, and without him nothing has been made"). At 3.11.2 he repeats that all things were made by the Word who was with the Father in the beginning. The translation of *egeneto* as *factum est* will furnish some concluding observations for this essay; the conjunction of the masculine pronoun *quem* with the neuter antecedent *Verbum* is a calculated solecism, enabling the transla-

17. Bruce Metzger, *A Textual Commentary on the Greek New Testament* (London: United Bible Societies, 1975), 195. The book is written on behalf of the editorial committee of the United Bible Societies' Greek New Testament.

18. See further Mütschler, *Das Corpus Johanneum bei Irenäus von Lyon*, 145–51, 264–73. For the full apparatus, see W. R. Sanday and C. H. Turner, *Novum Testamentum sancti Irenaei episcopi lugdunensis* (Oxford: Clarendon Press, 1923), 76.

tor to maintain the personal character of the Word. It is also an indication of his date, since it was only after Nicaea that Verbum superseded *sermo*, a masculine noun, as the standard equivalent to Logos. A translator of the second century could have matched the gender of the relative pronoun with that of its antecedent, at the same time achieving a closer correspondence to the Greek.

While we may frown at his choice of vocabulary, we have no reason to suspect that the translator abbreviates any of the prooftexts that he finds in Irenaeus. Since he never carries his citation of John 1:3 beyond the affirmation that nothing was made except through the Word, it seems most likely that Irenaeus himself would have broken the sentence here, allotting the subsequent words (*ho egeneto*) to a new period: "what came to be in him was life." If that is so, his punctuation of John 1:3 agrees with that of the Naassenes, an early group of Gnostics, who, according to Hippolytus of Rome, adopted the reading "without him not one thing [*oude hen*] came to be, and what came to be in him was life" (*Refutation* 5.8.5). In a second quotation from the Naassenes, *oude hen* is replaced by *ouden* (nothing), and it is possible that *oude hen* is a false transcription, foreshadowing Hippolytus's passage of arms with Basilides in book 7. On the other hand, this reading is attested or implied in numerous passages of Clement of Alexandria (*Paedagogus* 1.7.60.2, 1.11.97.3, 3.4.33.3; *Stromateis* 6.7.58.1, 6.11.95.1, 6.15.125.2, 6.16.141.7, 6.16.145.5, 6.17.153.4), though at *Stromateis* 1.9.45.5 he appears to favour *ouden*. We do no injustice to the early fathers if we impute to them an occasional inconsistency in the use of texts that they often cite from memory; at the same time, we must remember that when we follow a version both the editor and the typesetter stand between us and the manuscript and that editors themselves are often parsing the vagaries of a single scribe.

Again, it seems clear enough that the heretics known to Hippolytus made *ho egeneto* at John 1:3 the beginning of a new period, "what came to be in him was life." At *Refutation* 5.16.2 we are told that the Peratae, following this punctuation, understood the text as a reference to Eve. Clement of Alexandria, who adopts or assumes the same punctuation at *Paedagogus* 1.6.27.1, 1.9.79.3, and *Strom.* 5.14.103.1, ascribes it also to a distinguished representative of the Valentinian school at *Excerpts from Theodotus* 19.2. Citing Ptolemaeus at *Panarion* 33.3.6, Epiphanius of Salamis confirms that the Valentinian reading coincided with that of Irenaeus: "without him nothing came to be."

Tertullian, quoting John 1:3 exactly at *Against Praxeas* 21.1, has *sine eo factum est nihil*, "without him nothing was made." He speaks of Christ at 2.1 as the only Son of God (*unicus filius dei*), without whom (sine quo) nothing was made. At 7.3, this becomes *sine qua*, because Christ is identified with the Wisdom of God at Proverbs 8:22. At 12.5 *sermo dei* (speech of God) is the antecedent to *per quem omnia facta sunt at sine quo factum est nihil* ("through whom all things were made and without whom nothing was made"). At 19.3 we meet the variation *sine eo nihil factum*. Similar quotations or allusions at *Against Hermogenes* 18.3, 20.4, 45.1, and *On the Resurrection of the Dead* 5.3 leave no doubt that in Tertullian's text of John 1:3 the periods were divided after "him": "without him nothing was made."

It is therefore true that heterodox and orthodox witnesses before Nicaea were undivided in their punctuation of John 1:3; as consensus rarely proceeds from schism, we can only think it strange that this unanimous reading should have been set aside by a minority of scholars on the supposition that it originated with the Gnostics. It is strange again that the argument should be founded on speculation as to what the Gnostic might have said, when we know well enough what they did say, and the evidence also shows that their conjectures, however invidious, did not induce their Catholic adversaries to propose any emendation of the text. It lies beyond the scope of the present essay to trace the source of the punctuation that gained currency after Nicaea; but if we cannot demonstrate that partisans of any cause were engaged in willful corruption of the text before the fourth century, we should not be too quick to assume that any theological interest was consulted in the subsequent transmission or redaction of this verse.

The One and the Many: John 1:13

In all the best Greek manuscripts, we are told, John 1:13 reads, "who were born not of blood, nor of the will of the flesh, but of God." The antecedent "as many as received him" is supplied by John 1:12, and the verse, thus read, looks forward to Christ's pronouncement at John 3:5 that those who would enter the kingdom must be born not only of water but of the Spirit. The variant "*who was born,*" which can only refer to Christ, has been rejected in modern editions and translations, whether Catholic or Protestant, and the prevalence of this reading in the earliest Christian writers is alleged by Metzger to be of little consequence, as the majority of our ante-Nicene tradents wrote in Latin.[19]

Is this true? The reading "who was born, not of the will of the flesh" is espoused by Irenaeus at *Against Heresies* 3.16.2, 3.19.2, and 5.1.3[20]—all Latin texts to us, as Metzger says, but only because the Greek original has been lost. We have seen that as a rule there is no reason to doubt the veracity of the translator, and in this case he finds a Greek ally in the *Epistle of the Apostles*, which avers at 13 (14) that the Word was not born of the will of the flesh when he took his flesh from Mary, while at 14 (25) the Word is made to say this of himself.[21] The same reading is endorsed or implied by Hippolytus at *Refutation* 6.9.2 and 6.9.5. We can hardly be surprised to find the same reading in Tertullian, *On the Flesh of Christ* 19.2 and 19.3, though we have some reason to wonder why Bart Ehrman should surmise that Tertullian falsified the text to rebut the Valentinian reading "who *were* born," because this was their warrant for styling themselves "pneumatics."[22] Tertullian, as we see, concurs with his Greek-speaking predecessors and would seem to be accepting the only reading known to him. It was certainly not a reading that he found entirely propitious to his own cause, since he intimates at *Flesh of Christ* 19.3 that it might be thought to furnish a proof text for docetists who denied that Christ had come in solid flesh. Against them he can urge that, though not born of the will of the flesh, Christ was born of its substance; had his dealings with the text been as tendentious as Ehrman supposes, however, he could have outflanked the docetists by embracing the other variant of the text. This, since it refers to all pneumatics, cannot be understood to deny the reality of the fleshly envelope, though it can be taken (and surely should be taken) to mean that the flesh is not the whole man. If Ehrman replies that, since this reading played into the hands of the Valentinians, it was even more abhorrent to Tertullian than its rival, we must ask him to explain how a Catholic could avoid shipwreck when the textual tradition offered him no middle way between Scylla and Charybdis.

19. Metzger, *Textual Commentary*, 196, citing Irenaeus and Origen as Latin texts. On 197 he appends a list of distinguished scholars who have preferred the singular form.

20. For full apparatus, see Sanday and Turner, *Novum Testamentum S. Irenaei*, 77.

21. See Uhrig, *"Und das Wort ist Fleisch geworden,"* 62–63. The extant text of the epistle is an Ethiopic translation from Greek or Coptic, and the date remains uncertain.

22. Ehrman, *Orthodox Corruption of Scripture*, 27 see note 1.

Tertullian in fact affords the only evidence that the Valentinians read the text as modern editors do. Since, however, we have no orthodoxy testimony to the reading "who were born," it would not be absurd to maintain that the church is indebted to these dissidents for the restoration of John 1:13 to its primitive form. The alternative hypothesis—that the text was corrupted by the Valentinians—is unlikely to commend itself to scholars until some motive can be offered for the collusion of the orthodox in a maneuver that robbed the Fourth Gospel of its one clear reference to the virgin birth.

Epilogue: On the Perfidy of Translators

It ought, then, to be clear that the theological allegiance of an author cannot be divined from his choice of a variant in the Greek text of the prologue to the Fourth Gospel. I shall argue in this brief epilogue that scholars might be best employed not in efforts to trace the imponderable sources of "corruption" in the text, but in examining the consequences of error, deformations, and ambiguities—some tendentious, some unavoidable—in the conversion of the Greek to other tongues.

Facio, the most common Latin verb for "I do" or "I make," has *facere* for its infinitive, which marks it as a verb of the third conjugation. The participle *factus* ("having been made") is formed according to common principles, and the perfect passive indicative *factus sum*, "I was made," presents no difficulties to the translator. But *factus sum* is also the perfect passive indicative of another verb, *fio*, "I become," whose infinitive, *fieri*, is passive in form but active in meaning; no participle being formed from the root of this verb, it borrows its perfect indicative from *facio*, but once again conferring an active meaning on a passive form so that *factus sum* now admits of a second translation, "I have become." In the sense "I have made," *factus sum* would render the Greek verb *epoiêthên*, while in the sense "I become," it corresponds to *egenomên*. When, therefore, the Greek of the prologue to the Fourth Gospel declares that "all things came to be (*panta egeneto*) through him," the inevitable equivalent in Latin is "*omnia per ipsum facta sunt*." In the King James version of 1611, as in many of its successors, what purports to be a rendering from the Greek is in fact a direct crib for the Latin: "all things were made through him."

This is not, we may add in passing, the sole intrusion of the Latin Vulgate into accepted English renderings from the New Testament. But for its incorrigible presence in the minds of seventeenth-century translators who used Latin in daily intercourse with the learned overseas, we should not be accustomed to "Word" as the equivalent of Logos in the opening verse of the gospel,[23] and translators of Acts might not be so inclined to impute to Paul the untenable claim that he had seen an altar to "*the* unknown God."[24] The translation of *pais theou* as "child of God" at Acts 4:27 may have been suggested by the *puer dei* of the Vulgate, though we cannot say in this case that the precedent was compelling, since *puer dei* was also the rendering of *pais theou* at Acts 4:25, where the referent is not Christ but David, and "servant" has therefore been preferred in English versions of both the Latin and the Greek.[25] It must surely have been the memory of the Latin *cultor dei* that induced Tyndale and his Protestant successors to render *theosebês* at John 9:31 as "worshipper of God,"[26] rather than as "servant of God" or godfearer"; we can only wonder why they eschewed the closer approximations to the Greek that were adopted by translators of the Vulgate who perceived that *cultor dei* is not an expression native to Latin but a calque.[27]

23. See Desiderius Erasmus, *Annotations on the New Testament: The Gospels; Facsimile of the Final Latin Text (1535) with All Earlier Variants (1516, 1519, 1522, and 1527)*, ed. Anne Reeve (London: Duckworth, 1986), 218–21.

24. That is, *ignoto deo* at Acts 17:23 is ambiguous, whereas the Greek original, since it lacks the definite article, ought to signify "to an unknown god." Paul himself assumes, of course, that it has a particular referent, but this may be a rhetorical improvisation on the wording of a real altar. Ancient sources (Pausanias 1.1.4 and 5.14.8; Diogenes Laertius 1.110) speak only of "altars" to unknown or anonymous "gods," but, while this entails that there was more than one altar, it does not entail that every one of these was dedicated to a plurality of gods. See further Kirsopp Lake, "The Unknown God," in *The Beginnings of Christianity*, ed. Kenneth Foakes Jackson and Kirsopp Lake (London: Macmillan, 1933), 5:240–46.

25. Compare Is 4:2.1, with Jackson and Lake, *Beginnings of Christianity*, 3:46–47. The translation *puer* may already have been known to Constantine, since in the Greek text of his *Oration to the Saints*, chap. 9, the repeated locution *pais theou* prepares the audience for his messianic reading of Virgil's Fourth Eclogue in chaps. 18–21.

26. See *Tyndale's New Testament*, ed. Priscilla Martin (Ware, Hertfordshire: Wordsworth, 2002), 174.

27. The Anglo-Saxon has "gif hwa is Gode gecoren" (apparently meaning, "he who is elect of God"). The Douai-Rheims version is, "if a man be a server of God." The *Sainte Bible* of 1707 (278) gives "si quelqu'un est serviteur de dieu," and the same translation satisfies Joseph Joubert, *Dictionnaire françois et latin* (Lyon: L. and H. Declaustre, 1710), 1137, as well as Prudentius, *Cathemerinon* 6.125, in Prudentius, *Cathemerinon liber*, ed., trans. Maurice Lavarenne (Paris: Belles Lettres, 1943). We are, however, reliably informed that in Toronto *cultor dei* can mean only "worshipper of god": T. D. Barnes, "Review: Constantine and Christendom; The Oration to the Saints; The Greek and Latin Accounts of the Discovery of the Cross; The Edict of Constantine to Pope Silvester," *Journal of Theological Studies* 55 (2004): 355.

It cannot be proved in any of these instances that the discord between the Latin and the Greek impaired the Western understanding of the New Testament. On the other hand, the rendering of *egeneto* as *facta sunt* at John 1:3, less willful than the substitution of *verbum* for *logos*, was of much greater import in determining the course of a theological controversy. If *facta sunt* is read as a derivative of *facio*, the distinction between the Logos and all that comes into being through it is that the Logos is not made. One consequence was that a certain punctuation—*sine ipso factum est nihil quod factum est*—was forced on those who wished to maintain the belief in a coeternal Trinity, since it would be possible to apply the verb *egeneto* to the Spirit without impairing his divinity, but not to speak of him as being made. Another consequence was that Latin readers were predisposed to regard the doctrine that the Son is among the things "made" as the hallmark of Arian theology. It was indeed impossible to reconcile this tenet with that clause in the Nicene Creed of 325 that declares that the Son is "begotten, not made" (*gennêthenta*, ou *poiêthenta*);[28] Arius, himself, however, could have endorsed both members of this clause sincerely enough—and more sincerely than some of his reputedly orthodox precursors—since he never denied the begetting of the Son and never, in any extant statement of his opinions, used the verb *poiein* to name the act by which the First Person of the Trinity brought the Second into being.

Whenever a Latin Christian undertakes to prove that the Son is not one of the *facta*, of things that are made, he traduces those whom he calls "Arians." It is true that Athanasius set the precedent and that the Latin Catholics echoed him in failing to differentiate between the "making" of the Son, which was disavowed by all parties to the council of 325, and the "creation" of Wisdom at Proverbs 8:22, which was accepted not only by Arius, but by some who signed the creed, as a legitimate description of the process that was also called "begetting." Athanasius, inverting a distinction employed by Platonists in reading the *Timaeus*, had contrasted the eternal generation of the Son, the only being who was *gennêton* or begotten of the Father, with the contingency of supervenient beings, the *genêta*, which are the products of his own and the Father's will. He had also treated *genêton* as a synonym both for *poiêthen* ("made") and for *ktiston* ("created"), alleging that the latter term was also pro-

28. Socrates, *Ecclesiastical History* 1.8.29; Theodoret, *Ecclesiastical History* 4.3.10.

scribed in the anathemas to the Nicene Creed.[29] As we have seen, *genêton* and *poiêthen*, formed from the verbs that mean "to become" and "to make, had already been conflated by the infamous poverty of the Latin tongue. When Ambrose of Milan goes on to identify the *factum* with the *creatum*, he is certainly not following the Athanasian reading of the anathemas, and he might have escaped this solecism had he been more aware of the ambiguity in the term *factum*, since it is evident that *facio* and *fio* are not coterminous in meaning. It is easier to assume that what is created is also "made" than to prove that it must be created in order to "become."[30]

Few translators, it seems, are able to bear the syntactic harshness that would be entailed by a literal reproduction of Arius's teaching on the origin of the Logos. An otherwise scholarly version of his letter to Eusebius of Nicomedia foists upon him the claim that the Son was "[made] from nothing."[31] When one of the most austere of recent studies introduces the term "created," we see the equivalent of a scribal improvisation, though in this case no position that he might have disowned has been ascribed to Arius. Scribal improvisations are the meat and drink of scholarship; the vagaries of translation may attract censure, but do not give birth to monographs, perhaps because—four hundred years and more since the King James Version—we are still too apt to think that when we read the New Testament in the Greek original we are reading only the Greek.

29. See further Maurice F. Wiles, "A Textual Variant in the Creed of the Council of Nicaea," *Studia Patristica* 26 (1993): 428–33.

30. See further Mark J. Edwards, "How to Refute an Arian: Ambrose and Augustine," in *Le "De Trinitate" de Saint Augustin: Exégèse, logique et noétique*, ed. Emmanuel Bermon and Gerard O'Daly (Paris: Institut des Études Augustiniennes, 2012), 29–42.

31. E. R. Hardy, *Christology of the Later Fathers* (Philadelphia: Westminster, 1954), 330, translating Epiphanius, *Panarion* 69.7. Rusch, *Trinitarian Controversy*, 30, refrains from interpolation.

Mark DelCogliano

7. BASIL OF CAESAREA ON JOHN 1:1 AS AN AFFIRMATION OF PRO-NICENE TRINITARIAN DOCTRINE

> In the beginning was the Word, and the Word was with God, and the Word was God.
>
> —John 1:1

The fathers of the church recognized that the Gospel of John offered a unique perspective on Christ. They saw John as building upon the other gospels and indeed going beyond them. For example, Irenaeus notes that the author of John begins his gospel with the Son's generation from the Father, while the other evangelists begin theirs only with the human origins of Jesus.[1] Clement of Alexandria describes the author of John as impelled by the Spirit to go beyond the "physical facts" recorded in the other gospels to write a "spiritual gospel."[2] Origen calls the gospels the first-fruits of the scriptures and the Gospel of John the first-fruits of the gospels.[3] What Origen seems to mean here is that John affords us the deepest insight into Christ. For Origen, the unique character of John with respect to the other gospels is due, at least in part, to the prologue. According to Origen (and similarly to Irenaeus), the other gos-

1. Irenaeus, *Adv. Haer.* 3.11.8
2. Eusebius, *Hist. eccl.* 6.14.7.
3. Origen, *Jo.* 1.20–21, 23.

pels begin with the human origins of Jesus (as in Matthew and Luke), or even with the preaching of Jesus (as in Mark). Only John speaks of the Word in the beginning with God. And so, for Origen "none of those [other gospels] manifested his divinity as fully as John."[4]

Writing more than a century after Origen, Basil of Caesarea adopts his view of the Gospel of John:

> Matthew explained the Son's begetting according to the flesh, as he himself said: *The book of the generation of Jesus Christ, the son of David* [Mt 1:1]. And Mark made the preaching of John the beginning of the gospel, saying: *The beginning of the gospel of Jesus Christ, as is written in Isaiah the prophet: a voice of one crying out* [Mk 1:1]. Luke for his part also approached the theology by going through the corporeal origins. The evangelist John was the last to write. Because of what the others did, he needed to raise his mind above every sensory thing and time (which is concomitant to such things). Or rather he had to be lifted up in the power of the Spirit and be brought near the one who is beyond all things, all but bearing witness that *even if we have known Christ according to the flesh, but now we know him thus no longer* [2 Cor 5:16]. Since he apprehended the beginning itself and left behind all corporeal and temporal notions as lower than his theology, his preaching surpasses that of the other evangelists on account of the nobility of his knowledge. According to him, the beginning was not from Mary, nor from the times mentioned in the other gospels. What, then, was it? *In the beginning was the Word, and the Word was with God, and the Word was God* [Jn 1:1].[5]

According to Basil, while the other gospels speak of the divine economy, God's actions in the world through Christ, John provides theology, an account of God in himself. And for Basil, the first words of the prologue are also the most important for understanding the eternal Word that the Gospel of John reveals: *In the beginning was the Word, and the Word was with God,*

4. Origen, *Jo.* 1.22.

5. Basil of Caesarea, *Contra Eunomium* (= *C.E.*) 2.15; see also *Homilia in illud: In principio erat Verbum* (=*Verb.*) 1 [CPG 2860]: "Every statement of the gospels is nobler than the other teachings transmitted by the Spirit. For in the latter he spoke to us through his servants the prophets, whereas in the gospels the Master conversed with us in his own person. Now among his preachers of the gospel, the most resounding is John, the son of thunder [Mk 3:17], whose utterances overwhelmed every ear and bedazzled every mind." All translations from *C.E.* are taken from Mark DelCogliano and Andrew Radde-Gallwitz, *St. Basil of Caesarea: Against Eunomius*, The Fathers of the Church 122 (Washington, D.C.: The Catholic University of America Press, 2011), which is based on the edition of Bernard Sesboüé, Georges-Matthieu de Durand, and Louis Doutreleau, *Basile de Césarée: Contre Eunome suivi de Eunome Apologie*, Sources Chrétiennes 299 and 305 (Paris: Cerf, 1982–83). All translations of *Verb.* (PG 31.471–83) are taken from DelCogliano, *St. Basil the Great: On Christian Doctrine and Practice*, Popular Patristics 47 (Yonkers, N.Y.: St. Vladimir's Seminary Press, 2012).

and the Word was God [Jn 1:1]. Basil remarks that these words are so profound that even non-Christians marvel at them and insert them into their treatises.[6] In this essay I examine Basil's interpretation of this verse that he considered so important, to demonstrate how a fourth-century theologian and exegete used the Gospel of John to develop a Trinitarian theology. Basil's interpretation of John 1:1 is in fact quite unique. While he drew upon earlier interpretations of John 1:1 (particularly Origen's), he went far beyond what his predecessors said about the verse, producing a remarkable synthesis of the prior exegetical tradition and his own innovative views.

Basil saw John 1:1 as an affirmation of the pro-Nicene doctrine of the Trinity.[7] Or rather, he saw in John 1:1 a refutation of a number of mistaken ideas about the relationship between the Father and the Son held by his opponents. He deals with this verse at length twice, once in his treatise *Against Eunomius* from the mid-360s and again in a homily specifically on John 1:1 from the mid-370s, and more briefly on numerous occasions.[8] In the anti-Eunomian treatise his interpretation of John 1:1 is aimed at refuting the Heteroousian theology of Eunomius.[9] This is also the goal in the homily, but here John 1:1 is also interpreted in an anti-modalist way to refute the theology of Marcellus of Ancyra.[10] This method of argumentation is entirely consistent with his approach

6. Basil of Caesarea, *Verb.* 1: "I know that many of those who are external to the word of truth and take pride in worldly wisdom also marveled at these words and even dared to insert them into their own treatises. After all, the devil is a thief, and what is ours he divulges to his own mouthpieces!" One non-Christian who esteemed the prologue of John and quoted it is the philosopher Amelius, a leading member of the school of Plotinus; see Eusebius, *Praep. ev.*11.19.1. Compare Eusebius, *Praep. ev.* 11.17–18, and Augustine, *Conf.* 7.9.13–14.

7. I adopt the usage of "pro-Nicene" from Ayres, *Nicaea and Its Legacy*, 236–40.

8. Basil of Caesarea, *C.E.* 2.14–15 and *Verb.* There is a brief summary of the homily in Volker Henning Drecoll, *Die Entwicklung der Trinitätslehre des Basilius von Cäsarea: Sein Weg vom Homöusianer zum Neonizäner*, Forschungen zur Kirchen und Dogmengeschichte 66 (Göttingen: Vandenhoeck and Ruprecht, 1996), 165–67. The same interpretation of John 1:1 is given more succinctly in Basil of Caesarea's homilies *In sanctum martyrem Mamantem* (=*Mam.*) 4 [CPG 2868], *Adversus eos qui per calumniam dicunt dici a nobis deos tres* (= *Trin.*) 4 [CPG 2914], and *Contra Sabellianos, et Arium, et Anomoeos* (= *Sab.*) 1 [CPG 2869], as well as in the treatise *De Spiritu sancto* (= *Spir.*) 6.14.

9. On Eunomius and Heteroousian theology, see Thomas A. Kopecek, *A History of Neo-Arianism*, Patristic Monograph Series 8 (Cambridge, Mass.: Philadelphia Patristic Foundation, 1979); Richard Paul Vaggione, *Eunomius of Cyzicus and the Nicene Revolution* (Oxford: Oxford University Press, 2000); Michel R. Barnes, *Power of God*, 173–219; Radde-Gallwitz, *Basil of Caesarea, Gregory of Nyssa, and the Transformation of Divine Simplicity* (Oxford: Oxford University Press, 2009), 87–112; and DelCogliano, *Basil of Caesarea's Anti-Eunomian Theory of Names: Christian Theology and Late-Antique Philosophy in the Fourth-Century Trinitarian Controversy*, Supplements to Vigiliae Christianae 103 (Leiden: Brill, 2010), 1–134.

10. On Marcellus's theology, see Ayres, *Nicaea and Its Legacy*, 62–69; R. P. C. Hanson, *Search for*

elsewhere in his corpus. Neither appealing to authoritative creedal statements nor employing technical terms like the Nicene *homoousios*, Basil aims to demonstrate that his opponents' theology contradicts scripture.[11] And so, in John 1:1 Basil found a kind of encapsulation of his understanding of the relationship between the Father and the Son that directly refuted the positions of its key opponents on opposite ends of the theological spectrum. Rarely in the history of ecclesiastical debates has a theologian used a single verse of scripture with such versatility.[12]

More specifically, Basil finds in John 1:1 an affirmation of four pro-Nicene doctrines about the relationship between the Father and the Son. The first three are anti-Heteroousian. The first affirmation is the eternity of the Word, which implies the Son's coeternity with the Father. Like most non-Nicene theologians, Eunomius held that if the Son had been begotten from the Father, it implied that the Father preexisted the Son.[13] Hence they are not coeternal. The second affirmation is that the birth of the Son from the Father takes place without any passion (πάθος)—that is, without suffering and change. Eunomius deemphasized Father-and-Son language because he maintained that these terms connoted passion, suggesting that the Father's begetting of the Son was somehow corporeal.[14] This, of course, goes against the idea of divine incorporeality, and it led Eunomius to favor the names "Unbegotten" and

the Christian Doctrine of God, 217–35; Klaus Seibt, *Die Theologie des Markell von Ankyra*, Arbeiten zur Kirchengeschichte 59 (Berlin: De Gruyter, 1994); Markus Vinzent, *Markell von Ankyra: Die Fragmente [und] Der Brief an Julius von Rom*, Supplements to Vigiliae Christianae 39 (Leiden: Brill, 1997); and Joseph T. Lienhard, *Contra Marcellum: Marcellus of Ancyra and Fourth-Century Theology* (Washington, D.C.: The Catholic University of America Press, 1999), 49–68.

11. See Jean Bernardi, *La prédication des pères cappadociens*, Publications de la Faculté des lettres et sciences humaines de l'Université de Montpellier 30 (Paris: Presses universitaires de France, 1968), 87.

12. Stephen M. Hildebrand, *The Trinitarian Theology of Basil of Caesarea: A Synthesis of Greek Thought and Biblical Truth* (Washington D.C.: The Catholic University of America Press, 2007), 161, considers John 1:1 "important for Basil" but "not at the center of his thought." In contrast, Drecoll, *Die Entwicklung*, considers that it has a "fundamental" and "extraordinary" importance (88 and 89) for Basil and lies "at the foundation of his Christology" (165). On Basil's use of John more generally, see Jean Gribomont, "La tradition johannique chez Saint Basile," in *Saint Basile Évangile et Église: Melanges* (Bégrolles-en-Mauges: Abbaye de Bellefontaine, 1984), 1:209–28. Gribomont notes (220–21) that John 1:1 is the Johannine verse Basil cited the most in his corpus (fifteen times) and that one cannot overestimate its importance to Basil. Gribomont also briefly sketches his anti-Heteroousian and anti-Marcellan interpretation of this verse (221–22). On Basil's use of John 1:1 in *C.E.*, see Drecoll, *Die Entwicklung*, 85–92, and Sesboüé, *Saint Basile et la Trinité: Un acte théologique au IVe siècle* (Paris: Desclée, 1998), 163–65.

13. See Eunomius, *Apol.*12. There is an English translation of Eunomius's *Apologia*, together with an edition of the Greek text, in Vaggione, *The Extant Works* (Oxford: Oxford University Press, 1987).

14. See Eunomius, *Apol.*16–17.

"Begotten" in preference to "Father" and "Son" and to interpret begetting as an act analogous to creating (which Eunomius considered inherently lacking the taint of passion). In contrast, Basil maintains that the divine begetting, which for him is something distinct from creating, can and must be understood as not involving any passion.[15] The third is the Son's essential likeness to the Father. According to Eunomius's theory of names, those names uniquely applied to God revealed substance, and thus Eunomius argued that the "unbegotten" Father and the "begotten" Son were two different substances.[16] Hence they did not share a single divine substance and were essentially unlike each other. The fourth and last is anti-Marcellan: that the Father and Son are distinct in number, or to use later terminology, two distinct persons. While similarly to Eunomius Marcellus downplayed Father-and-Son language, preferring to speak of God and his Word, in contrast to Eunomius he stressed the unity of God to such an extent that the distinct existence of the Word was compromised. Hence, through his interpretation of John 1:1 Basil presents his Trinitarian theology as the middle way between the extremes of the Heteroousian theology of Eunomius and the modalism of Marcellus.[17]

1. All theologians in the fourth century agreed that the Son had been begotten from the Father. They disagreed over what this meant and what it implied. Most non-Nicene theologians held that if the Son had been begotten from the Father, it implied that the Father preexisted the Son. Basil claims that Eunomians encapsulated their beliefs in catch phrases such as, "If he was begotten, he was not" (εἰ ἐγεννήθη, οὐκ ἦν), "Before his begetting, he was not" (πρὸ τοῦ γεννηθῆναι, οὐκ ἦν), and, "He received his subsistence from nothing" (ἐξ οὐκ ὄντων τὴν ὑπόστασιν ἔλαβε).[18] These phrases are reminiscent of sayings attributed to Arius: "There was a point when he did not exist" (ἦν ποτε ὅτε οὐκ ἦν) and, "He did not exist before he was begotten" (οὐκ ἦν πρὶν γένηται). In fact, these two statements had been anathematized in the original Nicene Creed of 325. While Eunomius himself did not use any of these formulas, he did say, "The substance of the Son was begotten but did not exist before its own constitution."[19]

15. See Basil of Caesarea, *C.E.* 2.5–6 and 2.22–24.
16. See DelCogliano, *Theory of Names*, 25–48.
17. The same tactic is found in Basil of Caesarea, *Ep.* 69.2, 210.4, 226.4, and *Sab.*
18. Basil of Caesarea, *Verb.* 1.
19. Eunomius, *Apol.* 12.

Basil believed that Eunomius meant the same thing as Arius—namely, that first the Father was alone and only afterward brought the Son into existence, such that they were not coeternal.[20] It is in this context that Basil appeals to John 1:1 to prove their coeternity.

Basil places great weight on the opening words, *In the beginning* (ἐν ἀρχῇ). He first seeks to determine what sort of beginning this is. He notes that most beginnings are merely relative to something else:

Do not let anyone deceive you through the multivalence of the term. For in this life there are many beginnings of many things, but there is one beginning for all things that is beyond them all. *The beginning of the good way* [Prv 16:7], the proverb says. But the beginning of the way is the first movement by which we begin our journey, and you can find something before this first movement. Also: *The fear of the Lord is the beginning of wisdom* [Prv 9:10; Ps 110:10]. But something else also precedes this beginning, namely, the preliminary instruction that is the beginning of the acquisition of the arts. So then, the fear of the Lord is a preliminary step to wisdom. But there is even something prior to this beginning, namely, the state of the soul that is not yet wise and has still to acquire the fear of God.... And indeed the point is the beginning of the line, the line is the beginning of the surface, and the surface is the beginning of the body. And the letters are the beginnings of a word when they are put together.[21]

So in every case these beginnings are the beginnings of something else, and each is relative. All such beginnings are not absolute, since something precedes them. But there is an absolute beginning, as Basil says: "For in this life there are many beginnings of many things, but there is one beginning for all things that is beyond them all."[22] Here Basil does not mean the creation of time and the physical, visible world, as recounted in Genesis, but the beginning of the spiritual universe.[23] When the human mind strives to imagine something "before" this absolute beginning, it fails:

The beginning is certainly not like this [i.e., a relative beginning]. For it is linked with nothing, bound to nothing, considered along with nothing, but rather utterly free, autonomous, unbound from relation to another, insurmountable to the mind. It is impossible to transcend it in thought. It is impossible to discover anything beyond it. For if you strive to pass beyond *the beginning* with your intellect's imagination, you will find that it has raced ahead of you, waiting for your thoughts to catch up to it. Allow

20. Basil of Caesarea, *C.E.* 2.11–14; *Verb.* 1.

21. Basil of Caesarea, *Verb.* 1.

22. Ibid.

23. Ibid.; *Hex.* 1.5–6.

your intellect to go as far as it wishes and reach for the heights. Then after countless wanderings and much stumbling around, you will find that it returns to itself again because it could not make *the beginning* lower than itself. Accordingly, *the beginning* is always beyond and greater than what can be conceived.[24]

There is nothing "before" this absolute beginning: there is only the timeless present of eternity. And so, if we were to paraphrase John 1:1 according to Basil's interpretation, it would go something like this: "At the absolute beginning was the Word."

Basil next turns to the significance of the word "was" (ἦν). While he recognizes that this verb normally implies a temporal existence that begins and ends, he argues that in John 1:1 it does not:

Nor is it possible for them [i.e., Eunomius and his Heteroousian allies] to use reason to go beyond "*was*" to "when he was not." For the conceptualization "that he was not" is the denial of "*was*." … Furthermore, "*was*" is coextensive with the insurpassibility of this [absolute] beginning. For "*was*" does not suggest temporal existence, as is the case for: *There was a man in the land of Uz* [Job 1:1], and: *There was a man from Armathaim* [1 Sm 1:1], and: *The earth was invisible* [Gn 1:2]. In another book the evangelist himself showed us the meaning of "*was*" in this sense when he said: *I am the one who is and who was, the Almighty* [Rv 1:8]. The one *who was* is just like the one *who is*: both are eternal and non-temporal alike. Saying that the one who *was in the beginning* [Jn 1:1] was not does not preserve the notion of beginning and does not connect the existence of the Only-Begotten to it. For something prior to the beginning is inconceivable and the being of God the Word is inseparable from this beginning. Hence as far back as you wish to run by the busy curiosity of your mind, you are unable to transcend "*was*" and use reasoning to go beyond it.[25]

For if the Word was at the absolute beginning, if the Word already existed at the absolute beginning, then there never was a point at which the Word did not exist. The Father's begetting of the Son cannot be regarded as a kind of temporal event for which there is a before and after. Rather, it is something

24. Basil of Caesarea, *Verb.* 2. See also *C.E.* 2.14: "It is impossible to conceptualize something prior to a beginning. After all, a beginning would not still be a beginning if it were to have something anterior to it.… If 'beginning' is one of those things said relative to another, such as is the case for *the beginning of wisdom* [Sir 1:14] and *the beginning of a good way* [Prv 16:7] and *in the beginning God made* [Gn 1:1], then it would perhaps be possible to use reflection to go beyond the begetting of what subsists from this kind of beginning. But since the meaning of 'beginning' here, being absolute and non-relative, reveals the supreme nature, how isn't it utterly ridiculous when he contrives things anterior to this beginning or attempts to use reasoning to go beyond it?" See also Basil of Caesarea, *Mam.* 4.

25. Basil of Caesarea, *C.E.* 2.14.

that belongs to the timeless present of eternity. Accordingly, the Arian slogans "there was a point when he did not exist" and "he did not exist before he was begotten" are wrong because they assume that the Son's birth was a kind of temporal event with a before and after. The terms "when" and "before" are meaningless in eternity. Since the Word already existed at the absolute beginning, the human mind cannot imagine a point "before" this, "when" the Word did not exist.[26] And so, this is how Basil used the first words of John 1:1, *In the beginning was the Word*, to show that the Word must be eternal, coeternal with the Father.[27]

2. Basil also argues that the Father's begetting of the Son was without passion on the basis of the name "Word" (Logos), in John 1:1:

Our mind now seeks who it was that was *in the beginning*. He says: *the Word*. What kind of word? The word of human beings? The word of the angels? After all, the Apostle intimated that the angels have their own language when he said: *If I should speak in the languages of men or angels* [1 Cor 13:1]. But "word" has a twofold meaning. The first is the word expressed with the voice (ὁ διὰ τῆς φωνῆς προφερόμενος), which perishes after it is produced in the air. The second is the internal word (ὁ ἐνδιάθετος) which sub-

26. Basil of Caesarea, *Verb.* 2: "*In the beginning was the Word.* What a marvel! How all these words are linked with one another and accorded equal honor! *He was* is equivalent in meaning to *in the beginning.* Where is the blasphemer? Where is the tongue that fights against Christ? I mean, the tongue that says, "There was a point when he was not." Listen to the gospel: *In the beginning he was.* If he was in the beginning, at what point was he not? Shall I groan at their impiety or loathe their stupidity? "But before his begetting, he was not." Do you really know when he was begotten, such that you can apply the word "before" to that time? For the term "before" is temporal, placing one thing before another in terms of how old it is. How is it logical that the maker of time has a begetting that is subject to temporal designations? *In the beginning he was.* Unless you discard *he was*, you will leave no opening for their wicked blasphemy to slip in. For just as sailors mock the waves whenever they find themselves rocked between two anchors, so too, when this wicked tumult is stirred up by the vehement spirits of wickedness and violently shakes the faith of the many, you for your part can laugh at it, if you have your soul harbored in the secure port of these words."

27. See also Basil of Caesarea, *C.E.* 2.17: "'But if he was,' says Eunomius, 'then he has not been begotten.' So let us answer that it is because he was begotten that he was. He does not have unbegotten being, but he always is and co-exists with the Father, from whom he has the cause of his existence. So, then, when was he brought into being by the Father? From whatever point the Father exists. Eunomius says that the Father is from eternity. So the Son is also from eternity, being connected in a begotten way to the unbegottenness of the Father. To prove to them that we are not responsible for this argument, we will cite the very words of the Holy Spirit. So, then, let us take the line from the gospel: *In the beginning was the Word* [Jn 1:1] and the line from the Psalm spoken in the person of the Father: *From the womb before the daybreak I have begotten you* [Ps 109:3]. When we combine both of these, we can say both that he was and that he has been begotten. The phrase *I have begotten* signifies the cause from which he has the origin of his being. The phrase *he was* signifies his non-temporal existence even before the ages." See also Basil of Caesarea, *Mam.* 4, *Spir.* 6.14, and *Trin.* 4.

sists in our hearts, the mental word (ὁ ἐννοηματικός). But the other is the articulated word (ὁ τεχνικὸς λόγος).... Why *Word*? So that it may be understood that it proceeds from the intellect. Why *Word*? Because he was begotten without passion ... he said *Word* so that he could communicate to you the Father's passionless begetting.... After all, our word, as something begotten of the intellect, is also begotten without passion. For it is neither severed nor divided from the intellect, nor does it flow out from and leave the intellect. On the contrary, while the whole of the intellect remains in its proper state, it brings the word into existence, whole and complete. And the word that comes forth contains within itself all the power of the intellect that has begotten it. So then, take as much as is pious from the term "word" for the theology of the Only-Begotten.[28]

First, Basil seeks to identify what sort of logos existed at the absolute beginning. He draws upon the well-known Stoic distinction between the expressed logos, or the spoken word, and the internal logos, or the thought in the mind.[29] The spoken word expresses the thought in the mind. So why is the Son called "the Logos" here? Basil says that it is to teach that the Son is begotten from the Father as a spoken word proceeds from the intellect. Just as the human intellect gives birth to a spoken word without any passion, suffering, or change in the mind, so too the Father gives birth to the Son. If John 1:1 had said, "In the beginning was the Son," Basil grants that it would be permissible to think of the Father's begetting of the Son as involving time, passion, and suffering. But the use of the term "Logos" precludes those associations, since a spoken word proceeds from the mind timelessly and without change.[30] Therefore, the fact that the Son is called "the Logos" in John 1:1 is of great importance for Basil when it comes to understanding the manner of the Father's begetting of the Son.

3. The same name is also used by Basil to argue for his third affirmation, that the Son is essentially like the Father:

Why *Word*? Because he is the image of his begetter, showing in himself the whole of the begetter, not divided from him in any way and existing perfect in himself, just as our word also reflects the whole of our thought. For what we express in words is that which we think in our heart, and that which is spoken is a reflection of the thought

28. Basil of Caesarea, *Verb.* 3.

29. See Hans Friedrich August von Arnim, *Stoicorum veterum fragmenta* (hereafter *SVF*), 4 vols (Leipzig: Teubner, 1903–1905), 2:223.

30. Basil of Caesarea, *Verb.* 3: "Now if he had said, 'In the beginning was the Son,' the notion of passion would have been introduced along with the designation 'Son.' For in our case, that which is begotten is begotten in time and begotten with passion. For this reason, in anticipation he said *Word*, preemptively correcting inappropriate suppositions so that your soul could be kept unharmed."

in the heart. For *out of the abundance of the heart* [Mt 12:34; Lk 6:45] the word is expressed. Indeed, our heart is like a fountain and the expressed word is like a stream flowing from this fountain. So then, the outflow is like the initial upsurge, and when something appears, it is similar what it was when hidden.[31]

Here Basil again draws upon the distinction between the internal, mental thought and the spoken word that expresses that thought. The content of what we express in spoken words reflects the content of the thoughts in our mind. According to Basil, there is a one-to-one correspondence between the interior logos and the expressed logos. So too it is with the Father's begetting of the Son. As the Logos, the Son is expressed by the Father and corresponds fully to what the Father is. As the word that comes from the human mind contains within itself all the power of that mind, so too the Son, as the Logos, comes from the Father with all the Father's power. And so, based on the name *Word* in John 1:1, Basil argues that the Son is essentially like the Father.

Basil sums up the anti-Heteroousian interpretation of John 1:1 at the conclusion of the passage just cited, where he singles out the Gospel of John:

According to him [i.e., John], the beginning was not from Mary, nor from the times mentioned in the other gospels. What, then, was it? *In the beginning was the Word, and the Word was with God, and the Word was God* [Jn 1:1]. The Son's existence from eternity. His begetting without passion. His connaturality with the Father. The majesty of his nature. All these points he covers in a few words. By including the phrase "*was*" he guides us back to the beginning. It is as if he is putting a muzzle on the mouths of the blasphemers who say that "he was not" and circumventing in advance any chinks whereby such sophisms may enter.[32]

John 1:1 affirms the Son's coeternity with the Father, the passionlessness of the Father's begetting of the Son, and the Son's essential likeness to the Father—the last here expressed as his "connaturality with the Father" and his nature being majestic, just as the Father's. Basil suggests as well that the evangelist chose to begin his gospel with these words proleptically to silence Arians and Heteroousians, foreseeing future heresies.

In fact, Basil saw the theological affirmations of John 1:1 repeated in the next verse and elsewhere in the Gospel of John. With regard to the last clause of John 1:1 and John 1:2, Basil writes, "*The Word was God. This one was in the*

31. Ibid.

32. Basil of Caesarea, *C.E.* 2.15.

beginning with God. Once again, in a few words he sums up his whole theology, which the Evangelist handed on to us about the Only-Begotten."[33] And so, the first verse is, as it were, a statement of the leitmotif of the gospel, as Basil goes on to explain:

Then, after sketching by his theology a kind of outline, a clear one, of the nature of the Only-Begotten,[34] he alludes to this with the following phrase as if speaking to those who already know: *He was in the beginning with God* [Jn 1:2]. Here once again by including the phrase "*was*" he connects the begetting of the Only-Begotten to the eternity of the Father. There's more: *He was life, and the life was the light of humanity* [Jn 1:4]. And: *he was the true light* [Jn 1:9]. Despite the fact that all these passages that include phrases indicative of eternity thereby confirm this account, Eunomius has rejected all the testimonies of the Spirit and does not seem to have heard the one crying out to us over and over again that he *was*. For he says: "he was begotten when he was not. When he was not, he was adventitiously begotten later on."[35] But if, as you claim, this begetting was not in the beginning, could there be a more conspicuous fight against the sayings of the gospels in which we believe?[36]

Not only does Eunomius blatantly, according to Basil, contradict the gospels, but Basil also advocates using John 1:1 (and John 1:2, too) in a kind of antirrhetic manner, to protect oneself and one's orthodoxy from the onslaughts of heretical teaching:

Please save these few words, imprinting them like a seal upon your memory. They will be for you an impregnable wall against the attacks of those who plot against you. They are the secure bulwark of souls against those who assault them. If anyone should come to you and say, "When he was not, he was begotten. For if he was, how could he be begotten?," repulse this blasphemy against the glory of the Only-Begotten as nothing less than a statement of the demons. Return to the words of the gospel and remain there: *In the beginning was the Word, and the Word was with God, and the Word was God. This one was in the beginning with God.* Say *he was* four times and you will quash their "he was not."[37]

And so, Basil proposes using John 1:1 just as the desert monks used verses of scripture in an antirrhetic manner to ward off attacks of the demons and tempting thoughts. Not only does Basil view the battle against heresy on par

33. Basil of Caesarea, *Verb.* 4.

34. That is, in Jn 1:1.

35. This is a paraphrase of Eunomius, not a citation.

36. Basil of Caesarea, *C.E.* 2.15.

37. Basil of Caesarea, *Verb.* 4.

with the spiritual battle, but he also clearly views heretics, and particularly Eunomius, as nothing less than a kind of demonic agent of the devil.[38]

4. The final affirmation that Basil makes based on John 1:1 is directed against the modalism of Marcellus. Marcellus had taught that God is an absolute unity who merely operates in different modes, as Father, as Son, as Spirit. God's Logos was not separate from God, but remained firmly in God. In contrast, Basil maintains that the Father and Son are distinct in number and in *hypostasis*. He sees the following words of John 1:1 as proof as this: *And the Word was with God.*

Marvel at the accuracy of each term! He did not say, "The Word was in God," but rather *with God*, so that he could communicate the distinctness of his subsistence (τὸ ἰδιάζον τῆς ὑποστάσεως). He did not say "in God," lest he give a pretext for a conflation of his subsistence [with the Father's]. For the wicked blasphemers who attempt to mix them all together claim that Father and Son and Holy Spirit are a single subject and apply different designations to the one reality [i.e., modalists like Marcellus]. This impiety is wicked and should be avoided no less than that of those who blaspheme that the Son of God is unlike the God and Father according to substance [i.e., Eunomians].[39]

For Basil the important term here is the preposition *with* (πρός). The fact that the Word is with God shows that there are two distinct *hypostases*. If John 1:1 had said that the Word was "in" God, then it would lend support to the Marcellan position that Father and Son are really one individual existent. But the wording of John 1:1 proves that they are distinct in number and in *hypostasis*. Simple attention to the grammar of John 1:1, therefore, reveals how inconsistent Marcellan theology is with the scriptures.

In his interpretation of John 1:1 Basil drew upon previous exegetical traditions, even as he synthesized them in a unique and remarkable way. Just as he adopted Origen's view of the Gospel of John in relation to the other gospels, so too he was influenced by the Alexandrian's extensive discussion of John 1:1.[40] First of all, Basil followed Origen in investigating the precise meaning of "beginning" (ἀρχή) as used in John 1:1. In his typically exhaustive manner, Origen discerned six different senses of the word not found in John 1:1: the change that belongs to a way and length, the beginning of creation, the material cause,

38. Basil considered Eunomius a liar in whom the devil spoke: see *C.E.* 1.3, 1.9, and 1.16.

39. Basil of Caesarea, *Verb.* 4.

40. In Origen's *Commentary on the Gospel of John*, most of book 1 and the beginning of book 2 is devoted to Jn 1:1–2.

the formal cause, the elements of something, and the final cause.[41] Then Origen suggested, tentatively, that the "beginning" of John 1:1 referred to Christ as the efficient cause ("by which") of creation.[42] And so, while Basil sought to determine the meaning of "beginning" in John 1:1 as Origen did, he does not adopt Origen's interpretation. Basil simplifies much of Origen's analysis by categorizing most of the "beginnings" the Alexandrian discussed as relative, as opposed to absolute. Yet he does borrow two of Origen's examples, Proverbs 16:7 (*the beginning of a good way*) and the letters as the beginning of words, as examples of relative beginnings.[43] Origen did not identify the "beginning" of John 1:1 as the absolute beginning as Basil later did.

But Basil follows Origen more closely when it comes to understanding the word "was." Origen contrasted how the Word "was" (ἦν) with how the Word "came to be" (ἐγένετο) in the prophets: while the latter implies the Word is adventitious, the former suggests coeternity with the Father. Origen wrote:

> And the same verb, "was," is predicated of the Word when he "was in the beginning" and when he "was with God." He is neither separated from the beginning nor does he depart from the Father. And again, he does not come to be "in the beginning" from not being "in the beginning," nor does he pass from not being "with God" to coming to be "with God," for before all time and eternity "the Word was in the beginning" and "the Word was with God."[44]

Hence Basil's interpretation of "was" as denoting eternity is probably a direct borrowing from Origen. Unlike Origen, however, Basil presents his interpretation of "was" with great rhetorical force by contrasting it with Arian expressions like, "There was a point when he was not."

Origen also devoted many pages to investigating the title given to the Son, "Word," little of which had an impact on Basil.[45] In fact, Origen explicitly denied that the Son was named "Word," understood as an expression uttered by the Father, because this would eliminate his distinct, independent existence.[46] Of course, Basil does not identify the Son as an uttered expression,

41. Origen, *Jo.* 1.91–108.

42. Origen, *Jo.* 1.109–23.

43. Origen, *Jo.* 91, 94, and 106.

44. Origen, *Jo.* 2.9; trans. Ronald E. Heine, in *Origen: Commentary on the Gospel according to John, Books 1–10*, Fathers of the Church 80 (Washington, D.C.: The Catholic University of America Press, 1989), 97.

45. Origen, *Jo.* 1.125–288.

46. Origen, *Jo.* 1.151–52.

but makes great use of this idea by way of analogy, as we saw, to explain the passionless manner of the Father's begetting of the Son and his essential likeness to the Father. Yet Origen did something similar in his interpretation of Psalm 44:2: "My heart has uttered a good word," which he discussed in his investigation of the meaning of "Word" in John 1:1.[47] Origen interpreted God's heart as "his intellectual and purposeful power concerning the universe" and the Word he uttered as "the expression of those matters in that heart."[48] Furthermore, because the Word is the expression of the Father's intellect and power, he is called "the image of God."[49] And so, the seeds for Basil's interpretation of "Word" in John 1:1, as suggesting the Son's essential likeness to the Father, are present, but Basil takes Origen in a direction that the Alexandrian was perhaps not prepared to travel.

Therefore, Basil has drawn upon Origen in a critical, selective, and creative manner in his anti-Heteroousian affirmations.[50] Origen factors most of all in the first affirmation about the coeternity of the Father and Son, though there is also some precedent in Origen for the third affirmation about their essential likeness. It should be noted too that Basil's view of John 1:2 as summarizing and reinforcing the teaching of John 1:1 is also taken from Origen.[51]

Origen's interpretation, of course, influenced others in the early fourth century prior to Basil, especially what we might call his view on the eternal "was" of the opening verses of John. Alexander of Alexandria and his successor Athanasius employ John 1:1 as a kind of scriptural refutation of the "Arian" phrase, "There was a point when he was not"—that is, when the Son did not yet exist.[52] Hence they affirm the coeternity of Father and Son using John 1:1 against their opponents' denial of this Nicene tenet. In fact, Athanasius adds to the scriptural argument by citing Revelation 1:8 (or 1:4) as a parallel text that makes the same point: *Who is and who was and who is to come.* "Who could take eternity," writes Athanasius, "away from the one *who is and who*

47. Origen, *Jo.* 1.280–87.

48. Origen, *Jo.* 1.282; trans. Heine, *Origen*, 92.

49. Origen, *Jo.* 1.283.

50. I have discussed Basil's multifarious use of Origen in DelCogliano, "Tradition and Polemic in Basil of Caesarea's Homily on the Theophany," *Vigiliae Christianae* 66 (2012): 30–55.

51. Origen, *Jo.* 2.34–35 and 64–69.

52. Alexander, *Urkunde* 4b.12 and 14.19, in Hans-Georg Opitz, *Athanasius Werke*, vol. III, part 1, *Urkunden zur Geschichte des arianischen Streites 318–28*, 1–2, Lieferung (Berlin and Leipzig: De Gruyter, 1934–35); Athanasius, *Orationes contra Arianos* 1.11, 2.32; *De sententia Dionysii* 2.

was?"[53] Basil also cited Revelation 1:8 as communicating the eternal "was," and it is very probable that he borrowed this from Athanasius, since Origen does not see Revelation 1:8 as a cross-reference to John 1:1. So Basil's use of Origen in his first affirmation has been colored by Athanasius, though we can be sure that for the most part Basil used Origen directly.[54]

The pre-Basilian roots of the second affirmation are harder to trace. The Homoiousian Basil of Ancyra twice connects John 1:1 with the Father's begetting of the Son without passion.[55] The Ancyran views John 1:1 as a restatement of Proverbs 8:22, perhaps the most hotly contested verse in the fourth century: *He created me the beginning of his ways.*[56] The Johannine *in the beginning* corresponds to the latter part of the verse, whereas *And the Word was God* corresponds to *He created me.*[57] Basil of Ancyra conceptualized God's creating as an inherently passionless activity (as many in the fourth century did) and, assimilating divine begetting to divine creating (again, as many in the fourth century did), used this concept to understand how the Father begot the Son without passion.[58] And so, since the Ancyran interprets John 1:1 through the lens of his interpretation of Wisdom's creation in Proverbs 8:22, one can see why he thinks that John 1:1 affirms the Father's begetting of the Son without passion. It hardly needs saying that Basil of Caesarea's use of John 1:1 to affirm the passionless begetting owes nothing to his Ancyran namesake, though the fact that the Ancyran connected John 1:1 with the passionless begetting does raise the intriguing question of whether he planted a seed in the Caesarean's mind.[59]

Basil's fourth affirmation is a development of Eusebius of Caesarea's

53. *Orationes contra Arianos* 1.11.6; Karin Metzler and Kyriakos Savvidis, eds., *Athanasius Werke*, vol. 1, part 1. *Die dogmatischen Schriften*, 1–2, Lieferung (Berlin and New York: De Gruyter, 1998–2000), 120.

54. On the influence of Athanasius's interpretation of John 1:1 on Basil, see Drecoll, *Die Entwicklung*, 124.

55. Epiphanius, *Pan.* 73.8.2, 73.11.6. The latter also connects John 1:1 with the Son's eternity.

56. See Manlio Simonetti, "Sull' interpretazione patristica di Proverbi 8:22," in *Studi sull' Arianesimo* (Rome: Editrice Studium, 1965), 9–87.

57. Epiphanius, *Pan.* 73.8.2. Basil identifies many other correspondences between Proverbs 8 and New Testament passages.

58. Epiphanius, *Pan.* 73.3.4–4.3.

59. The influence of the Homoiousians on Basil has been well documented; see, e.g., Jeffrey N. Steenson, "Basil of Ancyra and the Course of Nicene Orthodoxy" (Ph.D. diss., Oxford University, 1983); see also Ayres, *Nicaea and Its Legacy*, 188–89, 237–38, and DelCogliano, "The Influence of Athanasius and the Homoiousians on Basil of Caesarea's Decentralization of 'Unbegotten,'" *Journal of Early Christian Studies* 19 (2011): 197–233.

anti-Marcellan use of John 1:1. Eusebius had noted that this verse stated that the Logos was *with* (πρός) God, not "in" (ἐν) God, much as Basil himself would later do.[60] For Eusebius, the preposition signified that the Logos was not an accident in God's substance, such that the Son as the Word belonged to the Father as a quality rather having independent existence. The "with" also indicated for Eusebius that the Son was not separated from the Father, but that they were together and coexisting. Hence, Eusebius sees, *And the Word was with God*, as undermining Marcellus's conflation of the Father and Son and indicating instead that the Father and Son were distinct yet inseparable. Basil's anti-Marcellan use of the same part of the verse is more focused, but there can be little doubt that he was influenced by the precedent set by Eusebius.[61]

In merely two out of the three clauses of John 1:1, then, Basil finds ways to disprove mistaken notions about the relationship between the Father and the Son that had wide currency in the fourth century. He drew upon the groundwork of earlier exegetes, expanding upon and honing what they had said to produce a unique synthesis of their insights and his own. He extracted from John 1:1 a range of meaning that has rarely been matched in the history of interpretation. In his corpus Basil's demonstration and affirmation of these four pro-Nicene doctrines about the Trinity were of course not limited to arguments based upon John 1:1. But Basil found in John 1:1 a kind of encapsulation of his theology of the relationship between the Father and the Son that directly contradicted the positions of his various opponents. His interpretation may seem pedantic to us, or to invest the few words of John 1:1 with too much significance, or even to read into John 1:1 a meaning that is not really there. Indeed, his interpretation might be judged inadequate based upon modern exegetical standards. But in fact many modern interpreters of John 1:1 have detected a significance in this verse reminiscent of what Basil saw in it, despite the differences in methodology.[62]

Nonetheless, it is upon the sort of exegesis in which Basil engaged that the pro-Nicene doctrine of the Trinity is based. Patristic interpreters availed

60. Eusebius, *Ecclesiastica theologia* 2.14.4–5 and 2.14.13–14.

61. For another instance of Basil's indebtedness to Eusebius, see DelCogliano, "Basil of Caesarea on Proverbs 8:22 and the Sources of Pro-Nicene Theology," *Journal of Theological Studies* n.s. 59 (2008): 183–90.

62. E.g., Udo Schnelle, *Antidocetic Christology*, 213; Köstenberger and Swain, *Father, Son and Spirit*, 48–51; and Martin Hengel, "Prologue of the Gospel of John," 265–94. These bibliographical references are by no means exhaustive.

themselves of the exegetical resources of their culture—namely, the Greco-Roman grammatical reading techniques in which all educated elites had been trained since boyhood.[63] While such techniques were often preoccupied with minutiae to an extent tedious to moderns, at the same time these same techniques enable patristic interpreters to read the scriptures (both Old and New Testaments together) as a literarily unified work that narrated a single story of salvation history that begins with creation and culminates in Jesus Christ, who continues to be present in the church through the Spirit.[64] Basil typifies the use of these grammatical reading techniques in his exegesis of John 1:1. By squeezing every ounce of meaning from this verse, he was able to marshal it as a succinct and profound statement of the correct understanding of the relationship between the Father and the Son in refutation of his theological opponents. Basil's interpretation of John 1:1 therefore remains an outstanding testimony to his skill as both a theologian and an exegete.

63. On the teaching of grammarians, see Quintilian, *Institutio oratoria* 1.4–9; H. I. Marrou, *A History of Education in Antiquity* (Madison: University of Wisconsin Press, 1956), 160–85 and 274–91; and Irvine, *Making of Textual Culture.* On the Christian appropriation of grammatical reading techniques, see Bernhardt Neuschafer, *Origenes als Philologe*, 2 vols. (Basel: Friedrich Reinhardt, 1987), and Young, *Biblical Exegesis and the Formation of Christian Culture.*

64. See Kugel and Greer, *Early Biblical Interpretation*, 155–76, and John J. O'Keefe and J. J. Reno, *Sanctified Vision: An Introduction to Early Christian Interpretation of the Bible* (Baltimore: The Johns Hopkins University Press, 2005), 24–44.

PART 3

PAUL AND THE TRINITY

Stephen E. Fowl

8. PAUL AND THE TRINITY

I take the presence of a collection of essays such as this one to be a very good sign. On the one hand, the presence of biblical scholars in such a volume reflects an increasing openness to bringing theological concerns and judgments to bear on sophisticated exegetical discussions. On the other hand, the work of the constructive and historical theologians represented here displays a form of disciplined attention to biblical texts that I as a biblical scholar find admirable.[1]

Moreover, the willingness of biblical scholars and historical and constructive theologians to engage in such discussions is enhanced by the fact that scholars are much more open to recognizing the probability that Paul and the rest of the New Testament writers operated with what might be called an "extremely high Christology." This is in contrast to an older History of Religions view that Jesus' status was gradually ratcheted upward so that at some point long after the New Testament period Jesus came to be thought of as truly divine. Such views have been powerfully countered by the work of Richard Bauckham and Larry Hurtado, among others.[2] Although Hurtado's and

1. At its best, of course, this has always been true of theology. See David Yeago's comment, "One has only to look at the sermons, commentaries and treatises of the Fathers, Aquinas, or Luther to see how seriously they took, for example, the Trinitarian and Christological doctrines as analyses of the logic of the scriptural discourse, formal descriptions of the apprehension of God *in the* texts, which then serve as guides to a faithful and attentive reading *of* the texts"; Yeago, "The New Testament and Nicene Dogma: A Contribution to the Recovery of Theological Exegesis," in *The Theological Interpretation of Scripture: Classic and Contemporary Readings*, ed. Stephen Fowl (Oxford: Blackwell, 1997), 87.

2. Bauckham, *God Crucified*, and *Jesus and the God of Israel: God Crucified and Other Studies on*

Bauckham's works have generated a variety of critical responses,[3] it is perfectly reputable, if contestable, to argue that Paul operated with what George Lindbeck called a "Christological maximalism," ascribing every possible importance to Jesus.[4]

Not surprisingly, this has led to more writing on such topics as "Paul's Trinitarianism" and the "Trinitarian implications of Paul's writings." In working through this writing it became clear to me that there are a lot of interesting things going on under the general rubric of Paul and the Trinity. Given this state of affairs it seems appropriate also to begin to become a bit more self-critical and self-reflective about what we might mean when we talk about Paul's Trinitarianism or other such things. As far as I can tell, no contemporary scholar argues the historically implausible case that Paul operated with a Nicene account of the Trinity. Thus, when people talk about Paul's Trinitarianism, they do not mean that.

One can find more careful ways of framing the matter in some recent works on Paul that have chapters entitled, "Paul's View of God and Its Trinitarian Implications" and "The Church—Paul's Trinitarian Ecclesiology."[5] This is clearer and more accurate in that it points to the fact that Paul's language about God, his assertions about Christ, and his arguments about the Spirit can be unpacked in ways that are consistent with a pro-Nicene position without requiring the untenable claim that Paul held a pro-Nicene position on these matters. Although this is clearly true, it masks the fact that many of the contra-Nicene positions commonly labeled as "Arian" were founded on Pauline passages about God and Pauline assertions about Christ. I am thinking in particular of Philippians 2:9–11; 1 Corinthians 15:20–28, and Colossians 1:15. The point is that both pro- and anti-Nicene theologians made ready recourse to Paul. If one is to say that there are Trinitarian implications to Paul's view of God, then one must say that there are Arian implications, too.

the New Testament's Christology of Divine Identity (Grand Rapids: Eerdmans, 2009); Hurtado, *Lord Jesus Christ.*

3. See, for example, Andrew Chester, *Messiah and Exaltation: Jewish Messianic and Visionary Traditions and New Testament Christology* (Tübingen: J. C. B. Mohr, 2007); McGrath, *Only True God*; and Chris Tilling, *Paul's Divine Christology* (Tübingen: Mohr Siebeck, 2012).

4. George A. Lindbeck, *The Nature of Doctrine: Religion and Theology in a Postliberal Age* (Louisville: Westminster John Knox Press, 2009), 94.

5. The first comes from Thiselton, *The Living Paul* (Downers Grove, Ill.: IVP, 2009). The second is from James D. G. Dunn, *Jesus, Paul and the Gospels* (Grand Rapids: Eerdmans, 2011).

A further way of understanding Paul's Trinitarianism is to note that pro- and anti-Nicene disputes are in large part disputes over how best to interpret scripture theologically within a framework regulated by the rule of faith. In this respect, to speak of Paul's Trinitarianism or the Trinitarian implications of Paul's views is not so much to say something about Paul as to situate the Pauline interpreter on one particular side of a debate. For my part, I believe this is the correct side of the debate. Moreover, to have Pauline scholars stand on that side of the debate is important in that it helps to undermine a popular view that there is a significant and unfortunate gap between the lively, vibrant, and life-giving God found in Paul's letters and the static, unmoving Trinitarian God of Greek metaphysics.[6] For anyone who has had to sit through such sermons on Trinity Sunday, this is a welcome advance.

At the same time, it is equally clear that later patristic interpreters offered interpretations of relevant Pauline texts in support of pro-Nicene positions that are very different from the interpretations a Pauline scholar might offer of the same texts. Indeed, most Pauline scholars would seek to drive a wedge between Paul and his later patristic interpreters. For example, Paul's patristic interpreters seem deeply focused on clarifying the manner of the Son's generation from the Father.[7] This is an interest that Paul himself does not seem to share.

One response typical of Pauline scholars when faced with this fact is simply to treat patristic interpretation as a form of hermeneutical error, reflecting the baleful imposition of Greek metaphysics onto Paul. If one is to speak about Paul's Trinitarianism, this judgment must be countered.

The first thing to note is that although Paul and his writings do not straightforwardly resolve questions about the Son's generation, Paul, and not Greek philosophy, has to bear a great deal of responsibility for getting this question on the theological agenda. Paul has an unwavering devotion and commitment to one God of Israel: "There is no God but one" (1Cor 8:4, 6; 15:28; Eph 4:4–6).[8] At the same time, Paul boldly identifies Jesus Christ using language that in early Judaism seems to be reserved for God alone (e.g., Phil 2:9–11). Moreover, Paul and his churches were passionately and compre-

6. One can find a readable and incisive antidote for such misperceptions in David Yeago's "New Testament and Nicene Dogma."

7. See the examples in Ayres, *Nicea and Its Legacy*, 31–62.

8. Even if contemporary scholars are not disposed to treat Ephesians as Pauline, it is clear that patristic writers did.

hensively devoted to Christ, a devotion that reflects the Christological maximalism noted previously. Further, when Paul speaks of the relationship between Christ and believers, he describes it in terms that most closely match the ways in which the Old Testament speaks of Yahweh's relationship to Israel.[9] Paul does all of this without any sense of contradiction of his commitment to the one God of Israel and without any sense of being idolatrous. At the very least these specific commitments, practices, and devotion suggest that there is a tension that needs to be resolved. Paul is not obviously concerned about how to combine his unwavering commitment to the one God of Israel with his maximalist assertions about and devotion to Christ. As a result, he does not offer any straightforward resolution. Thus, the later debates about the Son's generation can be seen as attempts to work out a problem that Paul (but not only Paul) sets on the theological agenda without ever resolving.

The issue then for those who want to speak about Paul's Trinitarianism must focus on describing the nature and shape of the continuities between Paul and his later pro-Nicene interpreters. Of course, such continuities are constructed. They do not simply emerge on their own. If they did, there would have been no dispute between pro- and anti-Nicene parties. Each side attempted to construct a set of continuities between Paul as they understood him and their contemporary debates about the Son's generation from the Father. Even if such continuities were implicitly assumed, rather than explicitly discussed, one should be able to offer a construction that would make such continuities explicit. Such a comprehensive description lies well beyond the scope of an essay like this and well beyond the competence of Pauline and patristic scholars working in isolation. Nevertheless, one step in this process would be to describe the theological and ecclesiological pressures that seem to shape and are shaped by Paul's claims about the one God, Jesus Christ, and the Spirit. This may help us understand the underlying logic behind Paul's claims and thereby aid in establishing and accounting for the lines of continuity between Paul and Nicene doctrine. In the following I will offer a representative, but by no means exhaustive, survey of these theological and ecclesiological concerns and some of the ways they seem to shape and are shaped by Paul's convictions about God, Christ, and the Spirit. Thus, this essay is really offered as a step in a particular direction but by no means the whole path.

9. I owe these latter two observations to Chris Tilling, *Paul's Divine Christology*.

At the outset I should offer a word of warning: I will make recourse periodically to Ephesians. I do not have a great stake in the arguments about the authorship of Ephesians. If you do, perhaps you will grant that for the points I want to make here, Ephesians sometimes offers the most succinct formulation. I believe that everything in this essay based on Ephesians could also be justified from undisputed letters; it would just take longer.

For Paul, one of his chief theological and ecclesiological foci concerns the relationships between Jews and Gentiles in Christ. One sees this most clearly in Romans and Galatians. One central struggle for Paul and his churches is not whether Gentiles can be joined to these local manifestations of redeemed Israel, which the Pauline churches represent, but under what conditions they should be admitted. Do Gentiles who join themselves to this body of Jews committed to treating Jesus as the crucified and resurrected Messiah of Israel also need to become Jews? Paul's answer to this is "no." How do Paul and, for example, the Galatians know that Gentiles turning to Christ do not need to supplement their faith with such things as circumcision and dietary restrictions? In Galatians 3:1–5 the answer is clear. The Galatian Gentile Christians have received the Spirit independently of observance of the Law. This, of course, parallels the arguments given by Peter in Acts 10–15. The Spirit is both supplied by God, not generated by humans or any other agent (3:4) and is an unequivocal sign of God's acceptance of the Galatian believers (compare Eph 1:13). Further, Paul argues that reception of the Spirit by faith in Christ establishes the appropriate connection between believers and Abraham and his heirs. From Paul's perspective, this decisively answers the question about whether the Gentiles who are joined to the body of Christ need to be circumcised and adopt other practices associated with the Law.

For this part of Paul's argument to work, both he and the Galatians must believe that there is no significant difference between God's will and work and the Spirit's. The Spirit must be a complete and sufficient witness to the will and good pleasure of God (a point made for other purposes in Romans 8:26–28).[10] If there were some such difference it would reopen the claim that Torah observance was needed to supplement the Galatians' faith in Christ. Of course, the

10. The scripture 1 Cor 2:6–13 offers a parallel argument about the close connection between the work of the Spirit and God. In this case, unless the Spirit is an absolutely reliable revealer of the God's wisdom, there is no reason to take it as wisdom at all.

assumption here of an indistinguishable connection between God's will and work and the Spirit's might invite a pro-Nicene theologian of the fourth century to develop further the relationship between Father, Son, and Spirit, but that is not Paul's concern. Instead, he is focused on the manner in which the Spirit is received—by faith, not by Torah observance (Gal 3:1–5)—and the implications of this assertion both for the ecclesial life of Jews and Gentiles in Christ and for how one understands God's work in giving the Torah.

Paul and other early Christians put a great deal of argumentative and theological weight onto the witness of the Spirit in determining how Gentiles are to be joined to the body of Christ. Not only does this require the assumption of some large but undetermined measure of unity between God and Spirit, it also directly raises a variety of theological questions about God. As Paul clearly saw, these questions retain their sharpness precisely to the extent that the early Christians see themselves in continuity with God's dealings with Israel. As Paul sees it, the righteousness of God is at stake here (compare Rom 1:16–17). Does God save Jews through Torah observance (broadly conceived) and save Gentiles through faith in Christ? Has God simply abandoned the everlasting covenants with Israel in favor of a new covenant offered to Christians? Can such a God be trusted? These are questions that Paul and some of his congregations faced in the light of what Ephesians 3:5 calls the "mystery of Christ" that has now been revealed to the apostles and prophets through the Spirit.

On the one hand, Paul is clear about the apocalyptic nature of his gospel. Christ bursts on the scene in a manner and with effects that nobody could have reasoned their way to in advance. The surprising and cataclysmic invasion of the cosmos by the Son of God changes everything.[11] There is no sense that Paul or anyone else could have reasoned their way to this gospel simply given a copy of the scriptures and sufficient time. Recognizing this can certainly act as a break upon overly presumptuous theological pronouncements. On the other hand, once this apocalyptic moment has happened, once "the mystery hidden for ages in God who created all things" has been revealed, it is no longer hidden. It is Paul's job both to serve God by proclaiming that gospel and "to make everyone see what is the plan of the mystery hidden from the ages in God"

11. J. Louis Martyn in particular has emphasized this aspect of Pauline thought; see Martyn, "Epistemology at the Turn of the Ages" and "Apocalyptic Antinomies," both in *Theological Issues in the Letters of Paul* (Edinburgh: T. and T. Clark, 1997), 89–110 and 111–23, respectively.

(Eph 3:7–9). I take it that one of the things entailed in making everyone "see" the plan of God is what Paul is up to in Romans, Galatians, and Philippians in particular. In this sense, the apocalyptic invasion of the cosmos in Christ does not short-circuit subsequent theological reasoning; it invites and requires it.

In this light, large sections of Romans and Galatians are devoted to making the case that God has only ever saved people through faith. This is why both epistles ultimately have a deep, though slightly different, stake in Abraham, showing retrospectively that God's action in Christ is continuous with and the fulfillment of God's intentions in calling Abraham. This is why both epistles offer an account of God's giving of the Torah. Even if the Law gets hijacked by Sin, the Law is still, holy, just, and good. Properly understood, the law reaches its telos in Christ, thus reinforcing the notion that God's intentions in giving the law are to bring life to all.

Although most of his Jewish contemporaries did not accept Paul's theological unpacking of God's dealings with Israel in the light of the apocalypse of Christ, there is a theological and ecclesiological need to offer such an account if these communities of Jews and Gentiles united in Christ are to persist as faithful witnesses to God's work in the world. Moreover, this seems to be the point behind Paul's vehement assertion of the singularity of the gospel at the beginning of Galatians and his affirmation at the beginning of Romans that the gospel reveals the righteousness of God. The integrity, the righteousness, and ultimately the singularity of God are at stake here.

Thus far, I have mentioned how Paul's particular theological and ecclesiological concerns over relationships between Jews and Gentiles in Christ shape and are shaped by his discussions of Spirit and God. It is only appropriate also to offer some comments on Paul's discussions of Christ. To do this I want to focus on Ephesians. I hope that I can show that the same logic that drives Paul's claims about the Spirit in Galatians will also drive his assertions about Christ in Ephesians. Thus, one can recognize that Paul's case presumes a strong sense of unity of will and action between Christ and God.

Ephesians begins with a well-known doxology praising the "God and father of our Lord Jesus Christ" for God's actions on behalf of believers (1:3–14). God is the subject of the main verb in this single sentence; God is the one who bestows all blessings on believers. In this passage, though, the entire pattern and scope of divine blessing of believers is done "in" Christ (1:3, 4, 6, 7, 10,

11, 12, 13) or "through" Christ (1:5). Although the abundance of prepositional phrases here may raise a number of questions for later theologians attempting to account for the Son's generation from the Father, it would appear that Paul's main interest is to assert that the plentitude of God's blessing of believers is inconceivable and inaccessible apart from Christ's person and work. Everything God does with and for believers happens in or through Christ. This indispensable and unsubstitutable centrality of Christ is reechoed in the architectural images of Ephesians 2:19–22.[12] Moreover, 3:11 seems to indicate that bringing blessing to humans through Christ was an eternally established plan of God. Further, Ephesians speaks of God's power in raising Christ, establishing Christ at God's right hand, and subjecting all things to Christ (see also 1:10, where all things are brought into their proper relationship to God through Christ and the echoes of Psalms 8:6 and 110:1). Just as Paul presents an intimate and inextricable bond between God's blessings and the person and work of Christ, he also asserts that believers' growth in God is a Christologically directed growth in Ephesians 3:13, and the end of that growth is called "the fullness of Christ." Further, there is the clear implication in 5:19–20 that Christ is worshipped as Lord and Christ's name is invoked in order to offer thanks to God. In addition, Richard Bauckham has argued that 4:4–5 connects Jesus and God through language reminiscent of Deuteronomy 6:4.[13]

Nevertheless, I think one must admit that even the maximalist assertions about Christ in Ephesians, taken on their own, can be interpreted in both pro- and anti-Nicene ways. Moreover, if we are interested in making historical claims about how Paul or the Ephesian Christians understood these claims, our best judgments will have to be that they did not really think in terms of whether and how the Son was generated or the precise nature of his divinity. Instead, I think we are directed in much the same ways as in Galatians 3. Paul's assertions in Ephesians are dependent upon the assumption that there is a fundamental, though unspecified unity between God's will and work and Christ's. For believers, to be filled in Christ is to have the maximum amount

12. This is conceptually similar to Paul's case in Romans and Galatians that in and through Christ, and only in and through Christ, believers are welcomed or adopted into the most intimate of relationships with God. Neither circumcision nor Torah observance is able to bring believers into such a relationship with God.

13. See Bauckham, "Biblical Theology and Problems of Monotheism," in *Jesus and the God of Israel*, 102n04. This occurs in a larger discussion of 1 Cor 8:6.

of fullness (Eph 1:23). There is no need to supplement one's faith in Christ with anything else in order to be in proper relationship with God. There is nothing higher, closer, or more intimate in one's connection to God than the bonds forged in and through Christ. It is these latter convictions and the manner of life that arises in the light of those convictions that form Paul's central concerns in Ephesians. In this respect Chris Tilling is right to remind us that Paul's assertions about Christ are primarily directed and governed by the types of relationships he seeks to establish and nurture between Christ and his congregations.[14] These concerns are, for the most part, different from those pro- and anti- Nicene theologians who later read Paul's writings with a different set of interests.

Given these differing interests, what is one to say? It is too simple and facile to argue that because Paul was not, for example, concerned to articulate the manner of the Son's generation from the Father that such a concern is simply an imposition on the text. Alternatively, if one insists on calling it an imposition on the text, it is no more of an imposition than any other sort of interpretive interest. As I have tried to show, pro-Nicene readings of Paul are a way of resolving a tension that Paul's writings (among others') set on the agenda of subsequent generations of Christians. As long as one is careful about what one imputes to the consciousness of the apostle, pursuing a pro-Nicene set of interests with regard to Paul's letters would seem to be as legitimate as any number of modern critical practices that bring concerns to bear on Paul's letters that Paul himself would not have imagined. This would be particularly true for Christians, who by virtue of their convictions about the role of scripture in God's drama of salvation may be required to engage scripture with interests and concerns that may differ from those of scripture's human authors in order to live and worship faithfully before scripture's divine author. Instead of wandering down the hermeneutical blind alley of investigating what may and may not be "impositions" on texts, it may be better to shift the focus of our inquiry. It might be more fruitful to ask whether both pro-Nicene readings of Paul and an interpretation of Paul's assertions about God, Christ, and Spirit, which are focused more on Paul's own theological and ecclesiological con-

14. Chris Tilling, "Ephesians and Divine-Christology," in *The Spirit and Christ in the New Testament and Christian Theology: Essays in Honour of Max Turner*, ed. I. Howard Marshall, Cornelis Bennema, and Volker Rabens (Grand Rapids: Eerdmans, 2012).

cerns, can be comprehended within a single set of regulative Christian convictions and practices. The aim here would not be to show that the claims are identical; they clearly are not. Instead, the aim would be to discern whether there is some sort of common logic or theological grammar that allows one to speak of continuities between Paul's writings and the interpretations of Paul's writings common to pro-Nicene theologians.

I take it that in *The Nature of Doctrine* George Lindbeck presents a skeletal version of this logic or grammar. He argues that both Paul and pro-Nicene theologians observe a common set of regulative principles: (1) monotheism; (2) a principle of historical particularity of Jesus (i.e., he was a specific person who lived and died at a particular point in time); and (3) a principle of Christological maximalism.[15] Paul's writings observe principle 1 in a fairly straightforward way. In what I have said previously, it seems clear that Paul does recognize a sort of Christological maximalism, although that maximalism is primarily asserted relative to things like circumcision, Torah observance, and any other set of practices early Christians might have advocated in order to enhance or deepen their connection to God.[16] Finally, although the historical particularity of Jesus may have been a concern for pro-Nicene theologians, Pauline scholars will no doubt note that Paul does not display much interest in the historical particularities of Jesus' life. Nevertheless, both in his interpretation of scripture and in his discussions of the Law and of God's righteousness in saving Jews and Gentiles in Christ, Paul displays a passionate commitment to the historical particularities of God's dealings with Israel. Within that commitment Paul situates the historically specific claim that God's dealing with Israel reach their apocalyptic climax and eschatologically find their telos in the life, death, and resurrection of Jesus Christ, and only in Jesus Christ. In these respects, it appears that Paul does display a commitment to all of these "regulative principles." Although there must be more said in this regard, it does possibly establish continuities between Paul's writings and the interpretation of Paul by later theologians. To quote Lindbeck at length here:

> With the possible exception of Arianism, it seems almost self-evident that what ultimately became Catholic orthodoxy was a cognitively less dissonant adjustment to the joint pressure of these rules than any of the rejected heresies. It can thus be argued

15. George Lindbeck, *The Nature of Doctrine* (Philadelphia: Fortress, 1984), 93–95.
16. In this case, I am thinking primarily of the practices addressed in Col 2:16–19.

that the Nicene and Chalcedonian formulations were among the few, and perhaps the only, possible outcomes of the process of adjusting Christian discourse to the world of late classical antiquity in a manner conformable to the regulative principles that were already at work in the earliest strata of the tradition.[17]

If Lindbeck is correct in this, then we have a fuller and more coherent way of speaking of Paul's Trinitarianism. In this light, to speak of Paul's Trinitarianism is to assert that pro-Nicene Trinitarian doctrine is the best way of adjudicating the tensions between, for example, Paul's unwavering commitment to God's singularity and his Christological maximalism in the light of theological and ecclesial pressures different from those Paul faced.[18]

One can presume, then, that all subsequent Trinitarian formulations would have to show that they, too, can adequately observe the regulative principles arising out of Paul's writing and the subsequent faithful interpretations of Paul reflected in pro-Nicene readings, even as they seek to respond to their own theological and ecclesial pressures. It is equally important to recognize that there are no hard-and-fast formulae for assuring that one observes these regulative principles in any particular context. Instead, such matters will always be subject to discussion, debate, and argument. As Alasdair MacIntyre has observed, it is precisely in this way that traditions such as Christianity can live faithfully in the present while maintaining continuity with what is best in its past.[19]

17. Lindbeck, *Nature of Doctrine*, 95.

18. See Neil Richardson, *Paul's Language about God* (Sheffield: Sheffield Academic Press, 1994), 315.

19. Alasdair MacIntyre, *After Virtue*, 3rd ed. (Notre Dame, Ind.: University of Notre Dame Press, 2007), 222–25.

Adela Yarbro Collins

9. PAUL AND HIS LEGACY TO TRINITARIAN THEOLOGY

I will begin in what follows with a discussion of the historical Paul's language about God, Christ, and the Spirit. Focus on the historical Paul limits the discussion to the seven undisputed letters. For a historical reading of Paul, it seems appropriate to read the language in question in the context of Second Temple Jewish texts and, as appropriate, the Greek and Roman texts roughly contemporary to Paul.

The Historical Paul and the Trinity

Paul wrote far more frequently of God and Christ in the same context than he wrote about God, Christ, and the Spirit as a threesome. When the word "God" is qualified, it is most often as "Father." God is occasionally spoken of as the Father of Christ but more often as "our Father." Paul also speaks of God as the Creator. He does so in connection with the "new creation" as well as with the original creation.

Paul referred simply to "Jesus" more than a dozen times. He used the lone epithet "Christ," however, more than 150 times. This epithet, Χριστός, is equivalent to the Hebrew term *mashiach* and means "anointed one." Although Paul appears to use the epithet as a proper name in his letters, it is highly likely that he explained its meaning and significance to the Gentiles who made up the communities he founded. He must have explained to them that Jesus is the

Messiah, the anointed one of the God of Israel, and that this designation entails a position of authority. In fact, most of what Paul says about Christ and the communities' relation to him can be understood on the assumption that the Messiah is the eschatological agent of God.

Paul also uses the unqualified epithet "Lord" in all the undisputed letters. He does so only twice in Galatians. This usage appears twice in Philemon, which is significant, since this letter is only twenty-five verses long. The lone use of "Lord" occurs many times in each of the other letters. Sometimes this epithet clearly refers to God.[1] Most of these are quotations from scripture. But in four instances, it is the context that makes clear that the term refers to God.[2] Most of the time the epithet clearly or most likely refers to Christ, but a number of cases are ambiguous.[3] This state of affairs is interesting. It implies that one of the traditional "names" of the God of Israel, according to the Septuagint, is also applicable to Christ.

This state of affairs is explained in the hymn or prose poem that Paul probably composed to serve his rhetorical purpose in writing to the Philippians. In this passage "Christ Jesus" is praised because he humbled himself and was obedient to the point of death, even death on a cross. He did all this in spite of the fact that he had been "in the form of God." This phrase has often been interpreted to mean that "Christ Jesus" was equal to God before his incarnation. In the context of Second Temple Jewish texts, this reading is highly unlikely. It is also hard to accept that the phrase alludes to Adam being in the image of God, since Paul could have written "image" instead of "form" if that is what he meant. The most likely historical interpretation is that Paul meant that "Christ Jesus" was a preexistent, heavenly being, but not equal to God. The drama and logic of the passage depend upon his being more highly exalted at the end of the process than he was at the beginning.

In another late letter Paul declares, "If you acknowledge Lord Jesus with your mouth and believe in your heart that God raised him from the dead, you will be saved" (Rom 10:9). As in the Philippians poem, the lordship of Jesus is linked to his resurrection and exaltation. An earlier letter may give us a clue as

1. Thirteen times: Rom 4:8; 9:28; 11:3, 34; 12:19; 14:4b, 6, 11; 15:11; 1 Cor 1:31; 3:5; 2 Cor 6:17; 1 Thes 4:6.

2. Rom 14:4b, 6; 1 Cor 3:5; and 1 Thes 4:6.

3. Rom 10:16; 12:11; 1 Cor 2:16; 3:20; 4:19; 7:32–35; 10:26; 11:32; 14:21; 2 Cor 5:11; 10:17, 18; 1 Thes 1:8; 5:2.

to the origin of this link. In that letter he affirms, "But for us there is one God, the Father, from whom all things are and for whom we are, and one Lord Jesus Christ through whom all things are and through whom we are" (1 Cor 8:6). This passage has often been read as referring, in both parts, to the original creation. In this reading, Christ is a preexistent being, like personified Wisdom, through whose agency God creates. Another way to read this passage is to put it in the context of the eschatological expectations of some late Second Temple Jewish texts and groups and especially Paul's idea of a new creation through Christ.

But why is the epithet "Lord" used here? Joseph A. Fitzmyer argued that the "*kyrios*-title was first applied to Jesus of the parousia" and that it was gradually retrojected "to other phases or states of his existence, even to that of his earthly mission."[4] He also notes, however, that the "*kyrios*-title" has regal connotations as applied to Jesus in the passage in which Jesus asks, "How can the scribes say that the Messiah is the son of David?"[5] Even more interestingly, he takes the position that "the entire tradition of the royal character of Yahweh in the OT would seem to be associated with the *kyrios*-title."[6] These observations suggest to me that the origin of the acclamation of Jesus as "Lord" is connected with the belief that he is the Messiah. If this hypothesis is right, it would explain the relationship of "the one God (for us), the Father" and "the one Lord Jesus Christ." It would also explain why the name "Lord" was chosen here. As the Messiah, Christ is God's agent through whom the "new creation" takes place. The latter is a process that begins with people being incorporated "in Christ" and reaches its consummation at the coming of Christ.

In five of his letters, Paul refers to Jesus as the Son of God. Mark 12:35–37 provides evidence that Psalms 110:1 was read in the first century of the Common Era as referring to the Messiah. The Markan Jesus says, "How can the scribes say that the Messiah is the son of David?" If David calls him "Lord," how can he be David's son? The Psalm text refers to God "putting your enemies under your feet." In 1 Corinthians 15, Paul wrote about the resurrection of those who belong to Christ at the time of his coming. He went on to say,

4. Joseph A. Fitzmyer, SJ, Chap. 5, "The Semitic Background of the New Testament *Kyrios*-Title," in *A Wandering Aramean: Collected Aramaic Essays*, repr. in Fitzmyer, *The Semitic Background of the New Testament* (Grand Rapids: Eerdmans, 1997), 115–42; quotation from 129.

5. Mark 12:36 and parallels; Fitzmyer, "Semitic Background," 131.

6. Fitzmyer, "Semitic Background," 132.

"Then comes the end, when he hands over the kingdom to God the Father, when he destroys every rule and every authority and power. For he must reign until 'he places' all 'his enemies under his feet.' The last enemy to be destroyed is Death. The implication is that the primary and fundamental meaning of "Son of God" for Paul is "Messiah."[7]

This reading explains how Paul can write of Christ in the opening passage of Romans, a passage that creates difficulties for the later Christian understanding of Jesus as Son of God. In Romans, Paul speaks of the gospel of God, "concerning his Son, who was descended from David according to the flesh and was appointed Son of God in power according to the Holy Spirit as a result of his resurrection from the dead, Jesus Christ our Lord" (Rom 1:3–4). During his lifetime, Jesus was Messiah only in the sense of descent from David. He was actually installed in the office with full messianic power only on the occasion of his resurrection from the dead.

This clear statement sheds light on how other passages, which seem to speak of Jesus' preexistence as Son of God, ought to be read. Paul also wrote, "God sent his Son in the likeness of sinful flesh and with regard to sin" (Rom 8:3) and "(God) did not spare his own Son but handed him over for us all" (Rom 8:32). In the former passage, God "sends" Jesus in a way analogous to his "sending" of the prophets and John the Baptist.[8] The "likeness of sinful flesh" stands in contrast to the glorified Christ, raised by the power of the spirit. The portrayal of God not sparing his "own" Son evokes a comparison and contrast with the binding of Isaac. Abraham was willing to sacrifice Isaac, but God spared him.

For those used to thinking in Trinitarian terms, one of the peculiar aspects of Paul's letters is the way in which he seems to associate very closely, if not identify, Christ and the Spirit.[9] The most striking instance is 2 Cor 3:17, "The Lord is the Spirit, and the Spirit of the Lord is freedom." This close association may explain a remark in Paul's application of a story about the wandering of Israel in the wilderness to the situation of the Corinthians. Paul says

7. This interpretation also fits 1 Thes 1:10, "and to wait for his Son from the heavens, whom he raised from the dead, Jesus, the one who rescues us from the wrath that is coming." Compare the description of the coming of the Messiah in 4 Ezr = 2 Esdras 13, especially vv. 23–24.

8. Gal 4:4 may be read in the same way: "When the fullness of time had come, God sent his Son, born of woman, born under the law."

9. Gal 4:6; 1 Cor 2:10–16; 15:45; 2 Cor 3:17, 18; Rom 8:9.

that the Israelites drank spiritual drink from the spiritual rock that followed them in the wilderness. He adds, "and the rock was Christ." If it was the Spirit who provided the water from the rock, and Paul closely associates the Spirit with Christ, he can identify the rock with Christ without implying the preexistence of Christ per se.

Another passage that seems to imply the preexistence of Christ occurs in the discussion of the ministry of the new covenant in 2 Corinthians:

> And even if our gospel is veiled, it is veiled among those who are perishing; in their case the god of this age has blinded the minds of the unbelievers so they will not see the light of the gospel of the glory of Christ, who is the image of God.[10]

One way to interpret this passage is to affirm that Paul has identified the preexistent Christ with the wisdom of God, God's agent in creation.[11] Another possibility is that Paul is taking the idea of a new creation seriously here and implying that the resurrection and exaltation of Christ made him equivalent to God's wisdom.[12] According to this reading, the passage signifies that Christ became the image of God when he was raised and exalted to heaven. The latter interpretation is perhaps supported by the context. A little later Paul says, "For it is the God who said, 'Light shall shine out from darkness,' who has shone in our hearts to bring to light the knowledge of the glory of God in the face of Jesus Christ."[13] This passage seems to make an analogy between God's creation of light, on the one hand, and God's self-revelation through Christ in the last days, on the other.

As we have seen, Paul depicts Christ as preexistent in the hymn or poem in Philippians 2. I suggest that the idea of the preexistence of Christ, however, was not a notion of great interest to Paul. Before I turn to the legacy of Paul, I would like to quote a rare Trinitarian formulation from Paul. As it has come down to us, Second Corinthians ends with the following benediction: "May the grace of the Lord Jesus Christ and the love of God and the fellowship of the Holy Spirit be with you all" (2 Cor 13:13).[14]

10. 2 Cor 4:3–4.

11. The role of wisdom in creation is hinted at in Prv 8:22–31 and more fully developed in Ws 7:22–8:1; 9:2; compare Conzelmann, *1 Corinthians*, 144–45. For Wisdom as the image of God, see Ws 7:25–26.

12. On Paul's notion of a new creation in Christ, see 2 Cor 5:16–17; see also Victor Paul Furnish, *II Corinthians*, AB 32A (Garden City, N.Y.: Doubleday, 1984), 222.

13. 2 Cor 4:6.

14. See also 1 Cor 12:4–6.

Paul's Legacy to Trinitarian Theology

As we have seen, Paul wrote ambiguously in the Corinthian correspondence about the nature and work of Christ in relation to the old or the new creation or both. He also described God's intention that Christ be the "firstborn among many brothers" (Rom 8:29). The letter to the Colossians, probably written soon after Paul's death, takes up these themes. In the praise of Christ that follows the opening thanksgiving, the author affirms, "He is the image of the unseen God, the firstborn of all creation" (Col 1:15). It is clear that this language is adapted from speculation about Wisdom in Jewish texts.[15] The following two verses make clear that these epithets, "image" and "firstborn," refer to the original creation, not the new, eschatological creation. To this degree the ambiguity of some Pauline passages is resolved. It is striking, however, that the language about Christ here is as ambiguous in its own way as Paul's language is. How did the preexistent Christ become the "image" of God? Does the term "firstborn" imply that Christ was generated or begotten by God? Or does it mean that Christ was the first of all the creatures of God?

By affirming that Christ is "before all things," Colossians 1:17 seems to imply that "firstborn" does not mean that Christ is the first creature. Rather, it is he in whom "all things exist (or hold together)." The latter formulation is ultimately a philosophical claim about the unity and coherence of the universe, a claim that Jewish writers explained in terms of God's Wisdom and Logos.[16]

Near the end of the passage of praise, it is said concerning Christ, "in him all the fullness was pleased to dwell" (Col 1:19). This elliptical remark is elaborated later in the letter in a polemical context, "in him all the fullness of deity dwells in a bodily way" (2:9). This affirmation is synonymous with the claim that in Christ "all the treasures of wisdom and knowledge are hidden" (2:3). These affirmations are made in order to prevent the audience from being deceived by speciously persuasive speech (2:4) and from being taken captive by deceptive philosophy and human tradition (2:8). All their intellectual and spiritual needs may be amply fulfilled in Christ.

The pastoral epistles continue some Pauline themes and introduce new

15. Eduard Lohse, *Colossians and Philemon,* trans. William R. Poehlmann and Robert J. Karris, ed. Helmut Koester, Hermeneia (Philadelphia: Fortress, 1971), 46–48.

16. Ibid., 52.

ones. The pastoral Paul affirms, "Christ Jesus came into the world to save sinners" (1 Tm 1:15). Like some statements of the historical Paul, it is not clear whether this language implies that a preexistent being came into the world or just that Jesus "came" as did John the Baptist.[17] Similarly, the poetic statement about Christ in 1 Tm 3:16, "he was manifested in the flesh," leaves open whether the preexistence of the redeemer is presupposed. The concept of preexistence is not necessary for this epiphany Christology but is easily combined with it.[18]

In 2 Timothy, the affirmation is made that God's grace "was given to us in Christ Jesus before the ages (began)" (2 Tm 1:9). It is not clear whether this language presupposes the personal preexistence of Christ.[19] Like Paul in the opening of Romans, the author of 2 Timothy contrasts the human state of Jesus as a descendant of David with the stage of his exaltation by resurrection (2 Tm 2:8). Neither passage implies preexistence.[20]

A passage in Titus may represent a striking innovation, depending on how it is read. One reading of 2:13 is, "We await the blessed hope and manifestation of the glory of our great God and Savior, Jesus Christ." The other is, "We await the blessed hope and manifestation of the glory of our great God and of our Savior, Jesus Christ."

In the Apostolic Fathers, triadic formulas become more pronounced and more frequent.[21] As we have seen, Titus 2:13 may refer to Jesus Christ as "God," but the passage is ambiguous. In Ignatius's letter to the Ephesians, the reference to Jesus Christ as "God" is quite clear. In addition, he maintains the tradition that Jesus was a descendant of David but affirms that he was also of the Holy Spirit.[22] Analogously, he teaches that Jesus Christ is both son of man and Son of God.[23]

In contrast, *2 Clement* states that Jesus Christ was first a spirit and then

17. Martin Dibelius and Hans Conzelmann, *The Pastoral Epistles: A Commentary on the Pastoral Epistles*, trans. Philip Buttolph and Adela Yarbro, ed. Helmut Koester, Hermeneia (Philadelphia: Fortress, 1972), 29.

18. Ibid., 63.

19. Ibid., 99n9.

20. Ibid., 108.

21. See *1 Clement* 46:6 (a concise summary of Eph 4:4–6); 58:2; Ignatius, *Magnesians* 13:1–2; *Ephesians* 9:1; see the introduction of Rusch, *Trinitarian Controversy*, 3.

22. Ignatius, *Ephesians* 18:2.

23. Ignatius, *Ephesians* 20:2.

became flesh.[24] In light of Paul's letters, this affirmation can be understood in at least two ways. One way is to read it in connection with 2 Corinthians 3:17. But that passage says, "The Lord is *the* Spirit." Another way is to consider it an interpretation of Philippians 2:6. Being "in the form of God" means being "a spirit." Like 2 Corinthians 3:17, the *Shepherd of Hermas* affirms that the Holy Spirit is the Son of God.[25]

Like Ignatius, Justin Martyr refers to Christ as "God."[26] He argues that Christ is not an aspect of God that returns to the indivisible and inseparable Father. Rather, as some angels at least "always exist and are never reduced to that form out of which they sprang," so also God, the Son and Word of God, "is indeed something numerically distinct"; "this power was begotten from the Father" as a fire is "kindled from a fire, which we see to be distinct from it, and yet that from which many can be kindled is by no means made less, but remains the same."[27] Here we see an early example of a text that understands "Son of God" in a generative way, rather than as the result of resurrection and appointment to the role of Messiah. In a fuller statement of his Christology, Justin declares, "Jesus Christ is the only proper Son who has been begotten by God, being his Word and first-begotten and power."[28]

From a historical point of view, Romans 1:3–4 does not imply preexistence. Colossians 1:14–15, however, clearly does so. In book three of *Against Heresies*, Irenaeus argues against those who contend that Jesus was merely a receptacle for Christ or that Jesus was one and Christ another.[29] By combining Romans 1 and Colossians 1, Irenaeus is able to argue, on the one hand, that the Jesus who was descended from David is the same as the one who was "designated" the Son of God.[30] On the other, Colossians allows him to declare that Jesus Christ, the Son of God, is "the first begotten in all the creation."[31]

Later in the same book, Irenaeus combines Galatians 4:4 with Romans 1:3–

24. *2 Clement* 9:5.

25. *Hermas* 9.9.1.

26. Justin Martyr, *Dialogue with Trypho* 128; ANF, 1.264; see also *Dialogue* 63: "He is witnessed to by Him who established these things, as deserving to be worshipped, as God and as Christ" (ANF, 1.229).

27. Ibid.

28. Justin Martyr, *1 Apology* 23; ANF, 1.170; compare *1 Apol.* 63, where the Son of God is said also to be the first-begotten Word of God and even God; ANF, 1.184.

29. Irenaeus, *Against Heresies* 3.16.1–2.

30. Irenaeus, *Against Heresies* 3.16.3, trans. Unger.

31. Ibid.

4 to argue against those "who assert that He received nothing from the Virgin" and who "reject the likeness [between Him and Adam]."[32] He translates Galatians 4:4 as follows: "God sent His Son, made from a woman," so that he can claim that Paul "says plainly" that Christ recapitulated the creation of Adam.[33] The combination with Romans 1 allows him to affirm that Christ was both "made of the seed of David" and "designated as the Son of God."[34]

In the early third century Hippolytus wrote a work, *Against the Heresy of One Noetus*. According to Hippolytus, this man "alleged that Christ was the Father Himself, and that the Father Himself was born, and suffered, and died."[35] Noetus found support for his view in Romans 9:5, which he translated, "Whose are the fathers, (and) of whom as concerning the flesh Christ came, who is over all, God blessed forever."[36] Modern translations take "who is over all" as modifying "Christ" or "the Messiah." The rest of the verse, however, is taken as a distinct phrase praising God—that is, the Father. Noetus, however, took the word "God" to apply to "Christ" and interpreted "God" as "the Father." The position taken by Noetus is usually designated "monarchism," a term used by ancient Christian writers.[37]

Praxeas taught a similar doctrine. He and his followers were called patripassians because they taught that the almighty creator of the world came down into the virgin, and he suffered. They were also called monarchians because they argued that God was a monad, a unity without distinction. In his work *Against Praxeas*, Tertullian says that the followers of Praxeas admit that there is a distinction between Father and Son but:

> [They] endeavour to interpret this *distinction* in a way which shall nevertheless tally with their own opinions; so that, all in one Person, they distinguish two, Father and Son, understanding the Son to be flesh, that is man, that is Jesus; and the Father to be spirit, that is God, that is Christ.[38]

32. Irenaeus, *Against Heresies* 3.22.1, trans. Unger.

33. Ibid. He takes γενόμενον ἐκ γυναικός as "made of a woman." It may also be translated "born of a woman."

34. Irenaeus, *Against Heresies* 3.16.3, trans. Unger.

35. Hippolytus, *Against Noetus* 1; ANF, 5.223.

36. Hippolytus, *Against Noetus* 7; ANF, 5.224.

37. A similar view was taken by Sabellius, though in a more elaborate and philosophical form; see Epiphanius, *Ref.* 62.1.4; Rusch, *Trinitarian Controversy*, 9.

38. Tertullian, *Against Praxeas* 27; ANF, 3.623.

Against this view Tertullian argued that "the apostle" taught that the Word of God, Jesus, had two substances. That he is flesh is attested by Romans 1:3, "who was made of the seed of David." That he is spirit is proved by Romans 1:4, "Who was declared to be the Son of God, according to the Spirit."[39] The divine substance of Christ was shared with the Father. "Christ is Spirit of Spirit and God of God, as light is kindled."[40] The Three—Father, Son, and Paraclete—are one in "respect of unity of substance, not of singularity of number."[41]

Athanasius is generally recognized as the great defender of the creed of the Council of Nicaea, which affirms that the Son is begotten not made and truly God.[42] He also went beyond Nicaea "in stating the equal status of Father, Son, and Holy Spirit."[43] In his first *Oration against the Arians*, he opposes the Arian view "that 'there was once when the Son was not.'"[44] Like Noetus, Athanasius cited Romans 9:5 and apparently also understood the word "God" as referring to Christ: "Of whom as concerning the flesh is Christ, who is over all, God blessed forever." Athanasius used the verse, however, not to claim that Christ was the Father, but to argue for the eternity of Christ as the Son of God.[45]

Athanasius also argued that "the Holy Spirit must be as divine as Christ if he is to unite individuals with Christ."[46] He interprets the descent of the Holy Spirit upon Jesus at his baptism as "a descent upon us, because of His bearing our body."[47] He contends that the Spirit was not given to Christ for his own improvement, but for our sanctification, and cites 1 Corinthians 3:16 in support of this view: "Do you not know that you are a temple of God, and the Spirit of God dwells in you?"[48]

39. Tertullian, *Against Praxeas* 27; ANF, 3.624.

40. Tertullian, *Apology* 21; ANF, 3.34.

41. Tertullian, *Against Praxeas* 25, ed. and trans. Ernest Evans, in *Tertullian's Treatise against Praxeas* (London: SPCK, 1948).

42. Rusch, *Trinitarian Controversy*, 19, 22.

43. Ibid., 23.

44. Athanasius, *Orations against the Arians* 1.11; NPNF, second series, 4.312; Rusch, *Trinitarian Controversy*, 73.

45. Athanasius also seems to assume that "his eternal power and deity" in Romans 1:20 refers to Christ as the Son.

46. Rusch, *Trinitarian Controversy*, 23; see also Athanasius, *Orations* 3.25.24; NPNF, 4.407. See also the condemnation of "those who say that the Holy Spirit is a creature" in Athanasius, *Letter to the Church in Antioch* 3; NPNF, second series, 4.484. He says that the Synod of Nicaea "upsets those who blaspheme the Holy Spirit, and call Him a Creature"; *Letter to the Bishops of Africa* 11; NPNF, 4.494.

47. Athanasius, *Orations* 1.47; NPNF, 4.333; Rusch, *Trinitarian Controversy*, 110.

48. Athanasius, *Orations* 1.47; NPNF, 4.333; Rusch, *Trinitarian Controversy*, 110.

Jennifer R. Strawbridge

10. THE IMAGE AND UNITY OF GOD

The Role of Colossians 1 in Theological Controversy

Theological disputes in the early church were, more often than not, conflicts over the interpretation of scripture.[1] This struggle over right interpretation was not just "a battle of the books" but "a battle for souls."[2] For example, Colossians 1:15, a text at the center of early Christological disputes, leads to some of the most remarkable declarations and insults in early Christian writings. Based on different understandings of this text, Arius purportedly claims that "there was a time when he was not,"[3] while Tertullian exclaims that he can "more easily find a man born without a heart or without brains, like Marcion, than without a body, like Marcion's Christ."[4]

Like most biblical exegetes, early Christian writers have favorite passages of scripture on which they rely to make their arguments. While Colossians is not cited by early Christian writers as frequently as other New Testament epistles, in a comprehensive survey of the use of Pauline texts in ante-Nicene Christian writings,[5] Colossians 1:15–20 is the passage most utilized, second

1. See Rowan A. Greer, "Applying the Framework," in *Early Biblical Interpretation,* ed. James L. Kugel and Rowan A. Greer (Philadelphia: Westminster, 1986), 185.

2. Tessa Rajak, "Talking at Trypho: Christian Apologetic as Anti-Judaism in Justin's *Dialogue with Trypho the Jew,*" in *Apologetics in the Roman Empire: Pagans, Jews, and Christians,* ed. Mark J. Edwards, Martin Goodman, and Simon Price (Oxford: Oxford University Press, 1999), 80.

3. Rowan Williams, Arius: *Heresy and Tradition* (London: SCM, 2001), 150; Athanasius, *C.Ar.* 1.5–6; 1.9; 2.37.

4. Tertullian, *Marc.* 4.10.16.

5. Early Christian writers assume Pauline authorship of Colossians, and thus any shadows cast by

only to 1 Corinthians 2:6–16.[6] Used for more than declarations and insults, this text is scattered across early Christian preaching, teaching, and apologies. In fact, excerpts from this pericope appear over 670 times in the works of more than fifty ante-Nicene authors. As Lightfoot acknowledges, the "history of patristic exegesis of this [passage] is not without painful interest."[7]

Lightfoot's description of early Christian interest in this passage as "painful," however, speaks to why Colossians 1:15–20 was favored in early Christian writings. As this chapter explores, the phrases from this Colossian pericope and especially Colossians 1:15, make it, at first, the text that best supports theological conclusions about Christ's divine nature and the unity of God.[8] While many other descriptions of Christ—his ascension, miracles, or titles, for example—could have been used to uphold his divine nature, Colossians 1 is the passage that early Christians turn to time and again to defend Christ's divinity. The words of Colossians 1:15 offer a veritable goldmine of references to support emerging doctrinal and Christological claims and are used to emphasize what early Christian writers found to be essential about Christ, "the image of the invisible God" and "first-born of all creation."

Over time, however, arguments for the unity of God and of Christ based on the words of Colossians 1 were achieved through increasingly complex hermeneutical moves. This is true as two limitations of this pericope were exposed: the subordination of God the Son to God the Father and the use of this same passage to question the divinity of the Son as first-born and thus begotten. Excerpts from Colossians 1:15–20, therefore, are no longer easy phrases for defending the divinity of Christ and the unity of God. Rather, now they are favored because they fall at the center of the first major Christological con-

---

modern scholarship on the authenticity of this letter do not affect this chapter's conclusions; see Origen, *Princ.* 2.6.1; Novatian, *Trin.* 3; Alexander of Alexandria, *Ep.Alex.* 6.

6. These two texts are incredibly close in terms of the number of references to each in early Christian writings (fewer than twenty references separate them in the survey). If the timeframe is extended just beyond the ante-Nicene period to include texts from the Nicene controversy, Col 1:15–20 surpasses 1 Cor 2:6–16 in number of occurrences; see Jennifer R. Strawbridge, *The Pauline Effect: The Use of the Pauline Epistles by Early Christian Writers* (Berlin: De Gruyter, 2015).

7. Joseph Barber Lightfoot, *Saint Paul's Epistles to the Colossians and to Philemon: A Revised Text with Introductions, Notes, and Dissertations* (London: Macmillan, 1890), 146. Apart from Lightfoot, few if any modern commentaries on Colossians make reference to early Christian writings, and even then, many simply offer a summary of Lightfoot's work. See Robert McLachlan Wilson, *A Critical and Exegetical Commentary on Colossians and Philemon* (London: T. and T. Clark International, 2005), 135–36.

8. Col 1:15 is cited by pre-Nicene writers more than 210 times.

troversy in the early church—the Arian controversy—where each side sought to claim the words of Colossians 1 and the authority of Paul as their own.

In this chapter, I offer an overview of early Christian use of this most frequently cited Pauline pericope. Finding themselves challenged by notions of a divided Christ (two natures) and a divided God (Father and Son), early Christian writers import phrases from Colossians 1:15 into a wide range of contexts to support a diversity of arguments. Nevertheless, as these same phrases are taken up by opposing sides of the emerging Christological debate, the limitations of Colossians 1:15 are exposed. Therefore, a section of this chapter focuses on the hermeneutical and exegetical effects of these limitations and how the Christological questions raised by the Arian controversy affected early Christian use of Colossians 1.

Colossians 1:15: The First-Born Image

For early Christian writers, the phrases "image of the invisible God" and "first-born of all creation" are central to their understanding of the relationship between God the Father and God the Son.[9] These two phrases are used to describe the incorporeal, undivided nature of God known only through God's "image" Christ and concomitantly to discuss the preexistent nature of the Son as co-creator with God the Father.

Irenaeus

Excerpts from Colossians 1:15 play a central role in Irenaeus's argument for the unity of God the Father and God the Son as he uses this passage to support his doctrine of recapitulation (*anakephalaiosis*).[10] Irenaeus adapts this

9. Other examples of Col 1:15 in early Christian writings include "image of the invisible God," see *Tri.Trac.* 12; *Didas.Silv.*; Irenaeus, *Haer.* 2.6.1–2.6.2; Clement of Alexandria, *Exc.Theod.* 7 and 10. (These sections of Clement's work are attributed to the Valentinian author; see *François Louis Sagnard, Extraits de Théodote, SC 23 (Paris: Cerf, 1948)*, 33–36); Eusebius, *Dem.ev.* 5.4.10. For "first-born of all creation," see Justin Martyr, *Dial.* 84; 100; 125; *A.Petr.* 2; Tatian, *Orat.* 5.2; Melito of Sardis, *Pass.* 82; Dionysius of Alexandria, *Fr.* 204–5, 210; *Six.* 3; Irenaeus, *Haer.* 3.16.3; Theophilus, *Autol.* 2.22.1; Tertullian, *Prax.* 5.19.3–5; 7.1; Origen, *Comm.Jo.* 1.118; 1.192; 1.195; 19.20; 28.18; *Comm.Cant.* Pr.; 1.1; 2.1; *Comm.Matt.* 16.8; *Cels.* 2.25; 2.31; 5.37; 6.17; 6.47–48; 6.63–64; 6.69; 7.16; 7.43; 7.65; 7.70; 8.17; 8.26; *Hom.Gen.* 1.13; *Hom.Jer.* 1.8.1; *Hom.Num.* 3.4; Pamphilus, *Apol.* 45; Novatian, *Trin.* 21.1–6; Eusebius, *Dem.ev.* 4.3–4; 5.1; 7.3.14; *Eccl.theol.* 1.38.

10. *Anakephalaiosis*, meaning a concluding summary, is a term from Greco-Roman rhetoric first used in a Christian context by Irenaeus, drawing on the words of Eph 1:9–10; see Greer, "Applying the Framework," 169; Methodius, *Res.* 1.1.13.

rhetorical concept to argue for the "summing up of all things and all human history under the headship of Christ,"[11] the image of God. He is clear that in Christ all things can be recapitulated so that God in Christ "came to save all through means of himself" by passing through "every age."[12] Irenaeus writes that there is only

> one God the Father and one Christ Jesus, who is coming throughout the whole disposition, and recapitulating all things in himself (*in semetipsum recapitulans*). In this all is a man, the image of God (*plasmatio Dei*) and thus he recapitulated humankind in himself, the invisible becoming visible, the incomprehensible becoming comprehensible (Col 1:15–16: *et hominem ergo in semetipsum recapitulans est, invisibilis visibilis factus, et imcomprehensibilis factus comprehensibilis*), the impassible becoming capable of suffering, and the Word human, thus recapitulating all things in himself.[13]

The word "image" sparks off a series of responses for Irenaeus that focus on the unity of God the Father, the unity of God the Son, and the salvation of all through God in Christ. As Creator, God alone causes everything to exist while remaining uncreated and undivided.[14] For Irenaeus, the unity of God the Father affirms the unity of God the Son, the image of God who is fully human and fully divine. Irenaeus is especially concerned to argue that Christ is one, and his doctrine of recapitulation holds together this view so that everything human and divine is summed up in Christ. Jesus Christ is not comprised of two parts—a passive, visible part and an impassive, invisible part—but is everything that it is to be God and everything that it is to be human.[15] Therefore, by recapitulating all things in himself, including humankind, "the invisible, incomprehensible, impassible Word becomes visible, comprehensible and passible,"[16] becomes human and, in the process, redeems all. As we will see in the final section of this chapter, the importance of humanity's participation in the process of salvation for Irenaeus influences the theology of Athanasius

11. John Behr, "Irenaeus on the Word of God," in *Studia Patristica: Papers Presented at the 13th International Conference on Patristic Studies Held in Oxford 1999*, ed. Maurice F. Wiles and Edward Yarnold (Leuven: Peeters, 2001), 163.

12. Irenaeus, *Haer.* 2.22.4. Similarly, Origen writes that Christ becomes a youth, an elder, and the first fruits of all creation in order to redeem all (*Hom.Jer.* 1.8.5).

13. Irenaeus, *Haer.* 3:16.6; Behr, *The Way to Nicaea* (Crestwood, N.Y.: St. Vladimir's Seminary Press, 2001), 126–27, with adaptations.

14. Irenaeus, *Haer.* 2.2.1.

15. Behr, *Way to Nicaea,* 125.

16. Ibid., 127.

in his argument against the Arians and especially his influential statement that "God became man that man might become God."[17]

Irenaeus's understanding of God as Creator and Christ as fully human and divine is also supported by a second phrase from Colossians 1:15. For Irenaeus, Christ as the "first-born of all creation" is the one through whom all things were made.[18] He connects Colossians 1 with John 1 in order to describe how God, by his Son and Spirit, makes all things, visible and invisible. Irenaeus writes that no other "principle nor power nor pleroma" exists apart from God, "who, by his Word and Spirit, makes and disposes and governs all things and commands all things into existence."[19] For Irenaeus, this understanding of Christ as "first-born of all creation" needs little explanation, because this phrase makes clear that God the Son is one with God the Father in creation through whom, with the Spirit, all things were made. Word and Spirit are inextricably linked to God in the creative process to the degree that Irenaeus writes that, in creation, they are "the hands of the Father."[20] The words of Colossians 1 and John 1 say exactly what he needs in order to argue that the eternal God is the one who made all things in the beginning by his Word without "exception or deduction."[21] Irenaeus has become so used to reading John 1 and Colossians 1 "in a certain way that he cannot see how they could be read differently,"[22] at least until they are read differently by the Arians.

Tertullian

Facing a slightly different challenge, Tertullian uses the phrase "image of the invisible God" to argue against Marcion's claim that Christ is a recent creation who exists only as an image and a phantom of flesh. For Tertullian, both of these arguments threaten Christ's divine nature and the indivisibility of God.[23]

17. Athanasius, *Inc.* 54.3; compare with Irenaeus, *Haer.* 3.19.1; 5.Pr.

18. Irenaeus, *Haer.* 3.11.1 (SC 211); see also Daniélou, *A History of Early Christian Doctrine before the Council of Nicaea,* vol. 3, *A History of Early Christian Doctrine: The Origins of Latin Christianity* (London: Darton, Longman and Todd, 1977), 337–38.

19. Irenaeus, *Haer.* 1.22.1 (SC 264).

20. Irenaeus, *Haer.* 5.6.1 (SC 153).

21. Irenaeus, *Haer.* 1.22.1 (SC 264).

22. David Sedley, "Philosophical Allegiance in the Greco-Roman World," in *Philosophia Togata: Essays on Philosophy and Roman Society*, ed. Miriam Griffin and Jonathan Barnes (Oxford: Clarendon, 1989), 111.

23. Peter Gorday, ed., *Colossians, 1–2 Thessalonians, 1–2 Timothy, Titus, Philemon* (Downers Grove, Ill.: Intervarsity Press, 2000), 10.

Combining excerpts from Philippians 2 and Colossians 1, Tertullian is clear that Christ is undivided and not separated into two beings or forms when he writes that

Of course, the Marcionites suppose that they have the Apostle on their side in the following passage in the matter of Christ's substance (*substantia Christi*), that in Christ there was nothing but a phantom of flesh (*phantasma carnis*).[24] For he says of Christ, that being in the form of God (*in effigie Dei*), he thought it robbery to be equal with God; but emptied himself and took upon him the form of a servant (Phil 2:6–7: *accepta effigie serui*), not the reality, and was made in the likeness of man, not a man, and was found in the form (*figura*) of a man, not in his substance (*substantia*), that is to say, his flesh. Just as if to a substance there did not accrue both form and likeness and fashion (*non et figura et similitudo et effigies substantiae*). It is well for us that in another passage [the Apostle] calls Christ the image of the invisible God (Col 1:15: *imaginem Dei invisibilis*).[25]

Tertullian is eager to claim Paul's authority, since the Marcionites assume Paul is "on their side." Here, the words concerning form and image connect Philippians 2 and Colossians 1 as Tertullian establishes that these words are Pauline, whereas the vocabulary Marcion uses to describe Christ is not. Moreover, Tertullian continues that if Marcion's claim is true that Christ is only a phantom of flesh and therefore not fully human, then an unintended consequence of this position is that Christ is not fully God, either. Following a reference to Colossians 1:15 and arguing that Christ is fully human even as he takes on the form and image of a man, Tertullian writes:

For in both cases the true substance will have to be excluded if form and likeness and fashion shall be claimed for a phantom (*si effigies et similitudo et figura phantasmati uindicabuntur*). But since he is, in the form and image of God (*in effigie et in imagine Dei*), as the Son of the Father, truly God, in the form and image of humankind (*in effigie et imagine hominis*), he has already been judged, as the son of man, to be found as truly man.[26]

Disturbed by Marcion's Christology, Tertullian argues that while Pauline texts such as Colossians 1 and Philippians 2 could support the distinction between God the Father and God the Son, this distinction is superficial. Using Co-

24. For other examples of Marcion's description of Christ's body as *phantasma*, see Tertullian, *Carn.Chr.* 1.2; *Marc.* 3.10.11; 4.7.1–5; 5.8.3.

25. Tertullian, *Marc.* 5.20.3–4 (*CCL* 1); see also *Prax.* 10.

26. Tertullian, *Marc.* 5.20.4 (translation adapted *CCL* 1; Evans, 639).

lossians 1 as a proof text to correct Marcion's misinterpretation of Philippians 2, Tertullian seeks to reclaim both passages. He uses both of these Pauline excerpts to describe the connection between the humanity of Jesus and the divinity of Christ as undivided so that Paul could not have called God the Son, Jesus Christ, obedient unto death, if he had not been made in the image of God and as God, found in the fashion and image of humankind. Moreover, substance (*substantia*) is central to Tertullian's understanding of how the Father and the Son, and elsewhere in his writings, the Spirit, are related to one another. So he writes that the Father, Son, and Spirit are one "not in condition, but in degree, not in substance, but in form, not in power, but in aspect, yet of one substance and of one condition and of one power."[27] Tertullian uses Colossians 1:15 to determine that substance is what unifies the Father and the Son, despite the Son being an image, so that God the Father and God the Son are inseparable in a unity that is "a unity of substance, not a singularity of number."[28] He also includes rhetorical questions directed at Marcion that demonstrate the sarcastic regard with which he held his opponent as he reclaims the language of Colossians 1:15 and Philippians 2. Here he proclaims the insult with which we began, that one may "more easily find a man born without a heart or without brains, like Marcion, than without a body, like Marcion's Christ."[29]

Clement of Alexandria

Clement uses Colossians 1:15 in his *Exhortation* both to ridicule Greek deities and to teach that God is a transcendent unity who can only be known through the Son. He asks the "heathen," to whom his treatise is addressed,

> Who breathed into life? Who bestowed righteousness? Who promised immortality? The creator of all things alone; the great artist and Father has formed us, such a living glory as humankind is. But your Olympian, the image of an image (εἰκόνος εἰκὼν), greatly out of harmony with truth, is the work of dull Attic hands. For the image of God is his word (Col 1.15: Εἰκὼν μὲν γὰρ τοῦ θεοῦ ὁ λόγος αὐτοῦ), and the gen-

27. Tertullian, *Prax.* 2; see also *Apol.* 21.12 and *Prax.* 25.

28. Christopher J. Stead, "Divine Substance in Tertullian," *Journal of Theological Studies NS* 14, no. 1 (1963): 46, 55; see also Eric Francis Osborn, *Tertullian, First Theologian of the West* (Cambridge: Cambridge University Press, 1997), 132; Tertullian, *Prax.* 25.

29. Tertullian, *Marc.* 4.10.16 (CCL 1), and Ehrman, *Lost Christianities: The Battles for Scripture and the Faiths We Never Knew* (Oxford: Oxford University Press, 2003), 191.

uine son of mind the divine word, the archetypal light of light; and the image of the word (εἰκὼν δὲ τοῦ λόγου) is the true person, the mind which is in humankind, who is therefore said to have been made in the image and likeness of God (Gn 1:27: ὁ κατ' εἰκόνα τοῦ θεοῦ καὶ καθ' ὁμοίωσιν).[30]

With a focus on the word "image," Clement claims that the Olympian Zeus "is only an image of an image," far removed from reality, whereas the divine Logos is the direct image and Son of God. As Clement argues, to be created in the image of God the Son is to be created not as an "image of an image" but in the very image of God himself.[31] At stake for Clement is the reality that God the Father alone is the living God who gives life to his image. Clement uses this phrase from Colossians to describe how a living image (humankind) implies a living original (God). Connecting the "image of the invisible God" from Colossians 1:15 with the image of God found in Genesis, Clement takes "image" to be an entity that expresses or communicates something. Therefore Christ, as the Word of God and image of God's nature and likeness, takes on the very nature and likeness of God. As he tries to work out how the Father and the Son are one, Clement describes how God the Father can only be known through his image, the Son. And the Son is not only the image of God, but also the mind and light. Here, as in his *Stromata*, God the Son as "both a unity and a plurality, contains the Father's ideas and the forces by which the Father animates the world.... The Word is essentially one with him."[32]

Origen

At stake for Origen in his use of Colossians 1:15 is a defense of the incorporeal and invisible nature of God as revealed only in Jesus Christ. He writes, in an argument similar to Clement before him, that

Scripture clearly says that God is incorporeal (ασώματόν). That is why no one has ever seen God (Jn 1:18: θεὸν οὐδεὶς ἑώρακε πώποτε), and the first-born of all creation is said

30. Clement of Alexandria, *Prot.* 10.23–26 (translation adapted SC 2; LCL 92).

31. The use of the phrase "image of an image (εἰκὼν εἰκόνος)" is also found in the works of Philo of Alexandria and his use of Plato to describe both the cosmos and humans as those made after the image of God (*Tim.* 92c); see Geurt Hendrik van Kooten, *Paul's Anthropology in Context: The Image of God, Assimilation to God, and Tripartite Man in Ancient Judaism, Ancient Philosophy and Early Christianity* (Tübingen: Mohr Siebeck, 2008); Behr, *Asceticism and Anthropology*, 139–41; Philo, *Conf.* 97; *Somn.* 1.139–40; *Spec.* 3.207.

32. Rusch, *Trinitarian Controversy*, 12; see Clement of Alexandria, *Strom.* 1.156.1–2.

to be an image of the invisible God (Col 1:15: εἰκὼν λέγεται εἶναι τοῦ ἀοράτου θεοῦ ὁ πρωτότοκος πάσης κτίσεως), using invisible in the sense of incorporeal.[33]

This use of John 1 and Colossians 1 together leads Origen elsewhere to explain how important it is to distinguish between seeing and knowing when speaking about the image of God. He writes that Paul, when discussing Christ,

> says that he is the image of the invisible God, the first-born of all creation (Col 1:15: *qui est imago invisibilis Dei, primogenitus omnis creaturae*). Not, as some suppose, that the nature of God is visible to some and invisible to others, for the Apostle does not say the image of God invisible to humankind or invisible to sinners (*imago invisibilis Dei hominibus aut invisibilis peccatoribus*), but with unvarying constancy pronounces on the nature of God saying, the image of the invisible God (*imago invisibilis Dei*). Moreover, John in his Gospel, saying that no one has seen God at any time (John 1:18), manifestly discloses to all who are capable of understanding, that there is no nature to which God is visible, not as if he were a being who was visible by nature and merely escaped or baffled the view of a frailer creature.[34]

Origen is particularly concerned with those who assume from the words "he is the image of the invisible God" that this means God is corporeal. Furthermore, he has to balance this phrase with the words of John 1:18 that God cannot be seen. For Origen, Christ as the image of the invisible God holds together this tension and enables him to declare that the invisible God is incorporeal, while at the same time God may be seen and known through his image, Christ. Origen is clear that his opponents do not understand the distinction between seeing and knowing and with this, the primary place of Christ in the cosmic hierarchy with God the Father. He continues, "It is one thing to see (*videre*), and another to know (*cognoscere*); to see and to be seen is a property of bodies, to know and to be known is an attribute of intellectual being."[35] The only appropriate attributes of the divine—the Father and the Son—are those of knowing and being known, and one can only know God, incorporeal and invisible, by seeing his image, Jesus Christ.[36] Origen can therefore declare that anyone

33. Origen, *Cels.* 7.27 (SC 150; Chadwick, 416). See also Origen, *Cels.* 6.69; *Princ.* 1.2.6; *Comm.Jo.* 32.29, and *Hom.Gen.* 1.13, where Col 1:15 is cited with Jn 14:9 ("He who has seen God has seen the Father").

34. Origen, *Princ.* 1.1.8 (translation adapted from GCS 22 and *On First Principles*, trans. G. W. Butterworth (Gloucester, Mass.: Peter Smith, 1973); see also *Princ.* 2.4.3. Origen's texts are in Greek and Latin, since some of his works are only extant because they were preserved in the later Latin writings of Rufinus.

35. Origen, *Princ.* 1.1.8 (GCS 22).

36. Origen, *Princ.* 2.4.3.

who has understood how we must think of the only-begotten God, the Son of God (μονογενοῦς θεοῦ υἱοῦ τοῦ θεοῦ), the first-born of all creation (Col 1:15: τοῦ πρωτοτόκου πάσης κτίσεως), and how the *logos* became flesh will see that anyone will come to know the Father and maker of this universe by looking at the image of the invisible God (Col 1:15: τὴν εἰκόνα τοῦ ἀοράτου θεοῦ).[37]

For Origen, "image" is of particular significance because Christ as the image of God makes possible the knowledge of God as God himself becomes visible in Christ, his image. Grillmeier writes, "Christ as image of God is therefore the revelation and the representation of God," and in this way "the cosmological significance of Christ as the image of God comes to the forefront."[38] God is not corporeal, but rather, on the contrary, Origen is clear that Colossians 1:15 holds together the "majesty, unchangeability, and invisibility of God with the divinity of the Son" in order to counter the building consensus of his opponents that only God the Father possessed full divine attributes.[39]

In his argument against Celsus, Origen uses Colossians 1:15 to focus on another aspect of Christ's divinity—namely, the preexistent, eternal nature of Christ as "first-born of all creation." Celsus claims that Christians worship a creature who has recently come into existence,[40] and Origen is anxious to show that Christ is not novel. In a culture and context where history and tradition lend authority to argument, the accusation of novelty is a serious one. Origen writes that

even if the first-born of all creation (Col 1:15: ὁ πρωτότοκος πάσης κτίσεως) seems to have become man recently, yet he is, in fact, not new on that account. For the divine scriptures know that of all created things, he is oldest, and that to him God said of the creation of humankind, let us make humankind in our image and likeness (εἰκόνα καὶ ὁμοίωσιν).[41]

Making clear his intention to defend Christ as fully God and present with God the Father at the creation of humankind, Origen emphasizes the status of

37. Origen, *Cels.* 7.43 (translation adapted SC 150; Chadwick).

38. Alois Grillmeier, *Christ in Christian Tradition: From the Apostolic Age to Chalcedon (451)*, trans. John Bowden (London: Mowbray, 1965), 25.

39. See Gorday, *Colossians*, xxvii; Christopher M. Tuckett, *Christology and the New Testament: Jesus and His Earliest Followers* (Edinburgh: Westminster John Knox, 2001), 6; Guy G. Stroumsa, "*Caro salutis cardo*: Shaping the Person in Early Christian Thought," *History of Religions* 30, no. 1(1990): 30.

40. See Origen, *Cels.* 5.37; 6.17; 6.47; 6.64; *Comm.Jo.* 1.18; 19.20; 28.18; *Comm.Matt.* 16.8.

41. Origen, *Cels.* 5.37 (translation adapted SC 147; Chadwick). Tertullian makes a similar argument in *Prax.* 1; 8; 19.

Christ as the "oldest." Here, he holds together createdness and temporal eternity. For Origen, the Word is created in the image of God and is the one after whom all rational beings are made. At the same time, this created Word participates in all aspects of God, since the Word was created in eternity. As he writes in *First Principles*, the Word as Wisdom "was generated before any beginning that can be either comprehended or expressed."[42] In other words, the createdness of the Word is eternal in the sense that it is a continuous creation or generation. In a way, Origen argues almost exactly the opposite of Arius, when he is clear that there is *not* a time when Christ was not.[43] The preexistent Christ eternally generated "before any beginning" that Origen finds in Colossians 1 means that everything revealed in creation is made manifest in the person of Christ.[44] Connecting Christ with the figure of Wisdom, Origen also draws on the words of Proverbs 8, using Wisdom to confirm Christ's cosmic role in creation. Origen asserts that the Son of God

> is termed Wisdom (*sapientia*), according to the expression of Solomon about the person of Wisdom: the Lord created me, the beginning of his ways, among his works before he made any other thing. Before the ages he founded me. In the beginning, before he made the earth, before he brought forth the fountains of waters, before the mountains were made strong, before all the hills, he brought me forth (Prv 8:22). He is also called first-born (*primogenitus*), as the Apostle has declared, who is the first-born of all creation (Col 1:15: *qui est primogenitus omnis creaturae*). However, first-born (*primogenitus*) is not by nature a different person from Wisdom (*sapientia*), but one and the same.[45]

For Origen, Christ "is wisdom (*sapientia*), and in wisdom there can be no suspicion of anything corporeal."[46] Similar to the way he used the description of Christ as "image of the invisible God," Origen is concerned to uphold the incorporeal nature of God. The equation he makes between Wisdom and Christ as "first-born of all creation" gives him another way to maintain his defense. Colossians 1:15 lends support to his understanding that God the Son, as the image of God and first-born of all creation, is active in creation with God the Father, who remains invisible and incorporeal. Combining excerpts from

42. Origen, *Princ.* 2.1.2 (SC 253).
43. See also Origen, *Princ.* 1.2.4.
44. Origen, *Princ.* 2.1.2, (SC 253).
45. Origen, *Princ.* 1.2.1 (GCS 22; Butterworth).
46. Origen, *Princ.* 1.2.6 (GCS 22; Butterworth).

Colossians 1 and Proverbs 8, Origen claims that Christ is "*both* to be identified as the divine Wisdom, i.e. none other than the one creator God active in creation and now in redemption, *and* to be distinguished from the Father, not as in dualism whereby two gods are opposed, nor as in paganism where two gods are distinguished and given different (and in principle parallel) tasks."[47] For Origen, the Son as Wisdom and Word is therefore "always with God as an effect of the eternal will of God; thus, Origen may say that the Son has no beginning because he began in the Father."[48]

Novatian

Novatian, similar to Clement and Origen, uses excerpts from Colossians 1:15 and John 1 to describe and defend the relationship between God the Father and God the Son. However, Novatian offers a different understanding of "image" and suggests an interpretation of Colossians 1:15 closely related to the Christological arguments of Irenaeus and Tertullian.[49] In his treatise on the Trinity, he asks,

> If God cannot be seen, how is it that he was seen [referring to Gn 12:7 and God's appearance to Abraham]? If he has been seen, how is it that he cannot be seen? For John also says, no one has ever seen God (Jn 1:18). And the Apostle Paul says, whom no one has seen or can see (1 Tm 6:16). But certainly Scripture does not lie; therefore, God has been seen. Accordingly, this can only mean that it is not the Father who was seen, that is, the one who cannot be seen, but the Son, who is wont both to descend and to be seen, because he descended. He is the image of the invisible God (Col 1:15: *Imago est enim invisibilis Dei*), that our inferior and frail human condition might in time grow accustomed to see God the Father in the image of God (*in imagine Dei*), that is, in the Son of God (*in filio Dei*).[50]

Novatian, similar to Origen, is concerned about the visible nature of the Son and the invisible nature of the Father and how to defend the divine attributes of both God the Father and Son. He also has to balance how scrip-

47. N. T. Wright, "Poetry and Theology in Colossians 1:15–20," *New Testament Studies* 36 (1990): 462–63 (italics in original). Eusebius also connects the preexistent Christ, first-born of all creation, with Wisdom and draws on excerpts from Col 1 and Prv 8; see Eusebius, *Dem.ev.* 5.1.4–8, and Rebecca Lyman, *Christology and Cosmology: Models of Divine Activity in Origen, Eusebius, and Athanasius* (Oxford: Clarendon, 1993), 71–72.

48. Lyman, *Christology and Cosmology*, 71; see also Origen, *Princ.* 1.2.9.

49. See Daniélou, *Latin Christianity*, 3.

50. Novatian, *Trin.* 18.1–3 (CCL 4; FC 67).

ture can say that God is seen (Gn) and not seen (Jn). Like Origen, he finds a loophole in the words of Colossians 1:15 that allows him to show that "scripture does not lie," since Christ as the "image of the invisible God" means that God the Father remains invisible while also being seen in God the Son. However, Novatian is also careful to affirm the physical substance of the Son of God as God. He expands exegetically upon an inherited tradition from Justin Martyr, Irenaeus, and Tertullian, arguing that appearances of God in the Old Testament were in fact appearances of the preexistent Son of God.[51] Where Origen's Hellenistic background does not allow much room for a physical, corporeal, preexistent God, Novatian reads Colossians 1:15 differently. Against docetic views of Christ, Novatian holds that even before the incarnation, the preexistent Son was present in the visions and visitations of the Old Testament to the point that "it was the Son of God, who is also God, who appeared to Abraham."[52] The description in Colossians 1:15 of God the Son as the image of the invisible God enables Novatian to show that as image, God the Son is not only visible in the incarnation but is the one who is visible as the divine throughout the scriptural record.[53]

Summary

How Colossians 1:15 shaped the arguments of early Christian writers is understood primarily through the ways phrases from this passage were used to address a range of Christological and theological arguments. Christ as "image of the invisible God" is adopted by early Christians to defend the invisible and incorporeal nature of God the Father and the visible and corporeal nature of God the Son. "Image" takes on slightly different meanings to support arguments about the preexistence of Christ and the relationship between God the Father and God the Son. Additionally, this phrase helps early Christians navigate through the tensions they find within scripture, especially as they attempt to reconcile the visible incarnate Son of God with the phrase from John 1:18 that God cannot be seen. Christ as "first-born of all creation" is adapted primarily within texts that focus on creation and God as creator. Also used to support claims of Christ's preexistence, the focus of early Christians who

51. See also Tertullian, *Prax.* 14.1–4.

52. Novatian, *Trin.* 18 (CCL 4).

53. Daniélou, *Latin Christianity*, 3. See also Tertullian, *Prax.* 14; 16; Justin Martyr, *Dial.* 56, 60–61.

adapt this excerpt is on the creative acts of God and on Christ as one who has been present from the beginning and active as creator. The interpretation of Colossians 1:15, therefore, influences the emerging doctrine of the Trinity, as the Son's eternal relationship with God the Father is inseparable from the Son's salvific work as fully human and fully divine. Early Christian writers are thus able to adapt Colossians 1:15 to a number of arguments, including times when they needed to be "anti-Arian ... to argue for the full divinity of the Son from before all creation" or "anti-Gnostic ... to argue for the powerful and full involvement of the Son in the origination, unfolding and renewal of the material universe."[54]

However, the adaptability of the words of Colossians 1:15 is not only a blessing but also a curse, as the opponents of these proto-orthodox writers take up this same passage, challenging (and frustrating!) early Christians in their scriptural interpretation.[55] Thus, we begin to glimpse some of the limitations of this passage and the challenges that it presents on at least two fronts. On the one hand, the focus of early Christian writers to ensure Christ's place in the beginning with God but without worrying about the emphasis on Christ as one "born" or created serves as an implicit endorsement of the Arian position—namely, the understanding of Jesus Christ as a creature who cannot be fully divine.[56] On the other hand, Christ as eternally generated co-creator produces the situation where God the Son is the one in and through whom God the Father acts, yet this Son is subordinate to the Father. Wiles clarifies that "in the ante-Nicene period the subordinationist implications of the text are accepted as entirely natural; they appear for the most part to be accepted as something requiring neither to be pressed nor to be explained away."[57] Among pre-Nicene writers, subordinationism was "the common position,"[58] especially when speaking of the relation between God the Son and God the

54. Gorday, *Colossians,* xxviii.

55. See the frustration expressed in Irenaeus, *Haer.* 3.15.1, and Tertullian, *Marc.* 4.4.1.

56. See also L. G. Patterson, "Methodius, Origen, and the Arian Dispute," in *Studia Patristica XVII,* ed. E. A. Livingstone (Oxford: Pergamon, 1982), 917–21.

57. Maurice Wiles, *The Divine Apostle: The Interpretation of St. Paul's Epistles in the Early Church* (Cambridge: Cambridge University Press, 1967), 88. For a similar argument, see Mark J. Edwards, *Origen against Plato* (Aldershot: Ashgate, 2002), 70.

58. David Rankin, *From Clement to Origen: The Social and Historical Context of the Church Fathers* (Farnham: Ashgate, 2007), 136n54; see also Joseph W. Trigg, *Origen*, Early Church Fathers (New York: Routledge, 1998), 23.

Father.[59] Nevertheless, this same argument can be discerned in the works of Marcellus and the later Arians as they claim that the Son was subordinate to God the Father and thus, once again, the Son cannot be fully divine.

Given these new challenges, early Christian writers adapted their interpretation of Colossians 1:15 as their opponents exposed the limits of this passage. Because a definitive rebuttal of their opponents is difficult to make on the basis of *sola scriptura*, early Christians mounted ingenious interpretative strategies to support their arguments for Christ's preexistence and divinity and to claim the right interpretation of each Pauline phrase. This is especially true when their opponents are using the same texts. Up to this point early Christian writers used the words of Colossians 1 to argue for the divine and preexistent nature of Christ and to dismiss the arguments of their opponents without worrying about the implications of the subordination of God the Son to God the Father. This argument no longer works, however, when their opponents claim the same passage to argue that Jesus Christ is not fully divine. In the final section of this chapter, therefore, the timeframe of this study is extended into the post-Nicene period in order to examine more fully how the interpretation of Colossians 1:15 shaped early Christian writers and their doctrine, especially as they describe and defend Christ's nature and unity in one of the first major conflicts facing the early church: the Arian controversy.

The Arian Controversy and Colossians 1:15

Shortly before 320 C.E., Arius became a leading figure in a Christological controversy that divided the church for most of the fourth century.[60] As Stead remarks, "There is no need to argue the crucial importance of the Arian controversy in the early development of Christian doctrine," since it was from this controversy that the first creedal statement to demand universal assent was formed.[61] Despite scholarly endorsements of the influence of Arius and the Arian movement on early Christian writings and doctrine, very little of Arius's own writings have survived. Thus, the writings that are extant must be treated with caution and the recognition that "divorced from their own

59. Wiles, *Divine Apostle*, 89.

60. Williams, *Arius,* 1. For a history of scholarship on Arius and Arianism, see ibid., 2–25.

61. Christopher J. Stead, "Arius in Modern Research," *Journal of Theological Studies NS* 45, no. 1 (1994): 24.

original literary context, they are, in the works in which they are now found, very far from presenting to us the systematic thought of Arius as he himself saw it."[62] According to Williams, "'Arianism' as a coherent system, founded by a single great figure and sustained by his disciples, is a fantasy—more exactly, a fantasy based on the polemic of Nicene writers, above all Athanasius."[63] Nevertheless, while a coherent system might not be entirely definable, some of the beliefs and doctrinal arguments attributed to Arius and his followers are possible to identify.

Essentially, Arius's thesis is that God the Son is a creature, begotten from God the Father. Consequently, he denies the full divinity of God the Son. Drawing on the same expressions found in Colossians 1 that early Christian writers used to defend the Son's divinity, especially Christ as the first-born of all creation, Arius argues that it is impossible for God the Son as a created being to be preexistent and consubstantial with God the Father. As Lightfoot observes, the Arian controversy "gave a different turn to the exegesis" of Colossians 1:15 as the Arians focused on the expression "first-born of all creation" and concluded from it that God the Son was a created being.[64] This, for Arius, protects the transcendence and incorporeal nature of God. At the heart of this debate, however, is not simply Arius's denial of the full divinity of Christ and his advocacy of Christ's nature as that of a creature, but more crucially the fact that Arius was using scripture—and especially Colossians 1:15—to reach these conclusions.

Within their arguments, the Arians relied on scriptural texts that they understood to assert the created nature of Christ—namely, Proverbs 8:22 and Colossians 1:15. These passages supported their conclusions about both the unbegotten nature of God the Father and the begotten nature of God the Son, who is the form and image of God. For Arius, "image" is not the same as the archetype who is God, and thus Christ is not fully God but rather reflects and reveals God as his image.[65] In this way, "for Arius, Christ is God not by nature, but by being the reflection of the Father who alone is true God," and

62. Williams, *Arius,* 95; see also Charles Kannengiesser, *Athanase d'Alexandrie, évêque et écrivain: Une lecture des traités Contre les Ariens* (Paris: Beauchesne, 1983), 457.

63. Williams, *Arius,* 82.

64. Lightfoot, *Colossians,* 146.

65. J. Warren Smith, "Trinity in the Fourth-Century Fathers," in *The Oxford Handbook of the Trinity,* ed. Giles Emery and Matthew Levering (Oxford: Oxford University Press, 2011), 118.

thus, "Christ is ontologically subordinate to the Father."[66] Certainly, preexistence is an issue for the Arians, just as it was for early Christian writers. Except that the question of Christ's preexistence was solved by the Arians by denying the full divinity of Christ (and, as a consequence, that of the Holy Spirit), who as a creature and a created being cannot be of the same substance as God and thus cannot exist with God before being created. Arius agrees with early Christian conclusions that God the Father is necessarily uncreated and unbegotten, and yet, because the Son is created and begotten, as he finds in the words of Colossians 1, the Son cannot truly be God.[67] As Arius purportedly wrote, "There was when he [the Son] was not."[68]

Arius's theology is not based on a new understanding of Colossians 1:15, but rather builds on how this same passage had already been used by early Christian writers. Only now it is used to oppose these earlier works and to claim that the same words from Colossians (and Proverbs) that early Christians used to defend the divinity of God the Son actually point to a Christ who is subordinate to God and thus not fully divine. Rebecca Lyman describes how Origen's explanation of the incarnation of the preexistent divine logos is "one of the first constructive Christologies" and yet, at the same time, its subordinationist tendencies and Origen's language about the preexistent Christ "anticipated many problems in later theology regarding the proper union of divine and human nature."[69] While many early Christians did not have a problem with the subordination of God the Son in their interpretations of scripture, with the Arian interpretation of Colossians 1:15, proto-orthodox writers like Athanasius must now grapple with the implications of these issues in order to enable the basic insights of the earliest Christological confessions to be expressed aright. These early Christological claims based on an exegesis of Colossians 1 could no longer by themselves address the Arian claims of Christ as a creature, created and begotten in time. Athanasius cannot fathom how Arius can draw the conclusions he does from Colossians 1, and yet he also knows that expressing his incredulity will not solve the deeper interpretative issue at stake. He writes against Arius that

66. Ibid., 118–19.

67. Athanasius, *Dep.Ar.* 70 (NPNF 4); see also *C.Ar.* 2.6–3.1, 3.5–6, and Williams, *Arius*, 97–98.

68. Williams, *Arius*, 150; Riemer Roukema and Saskia Deventer-Metz, *Jesus, Gnosis and Dogma* (London: T. and T. Clark, 2010), 184; and Athanasius, *C.Ar.* 1.5–6; 1.9; 2.37.

69. Lyman, *Christology and Cosmology*, 69.

if the Word was one of the creatures, Scripture would have said of him, that he is first-born of the other creatures (πρωτότοκος τῶν ἄλλων κτισμάτων ἐστί). But now since what the sacred writers actually do say is, that he is the first-born of all creation (Col 1:15: πρωτότοκός ἐστι πάσης τῆς κτίσεως), it is clearly shown that the Son of God is other than all creation and not a creature.[70]

To this defense, he also offers what appears to be an "external hermeneutical principle, namely the fundamental otherness of the divine,"[71] in order to express the divine nature of Christ: *homoousios*. The problem with Colossians 1:15 is that the Arians' interpretation of this passage to defend Christ as creature and not fully divine is entirely plausible, and the problem for Athanasius and his sympathizers is that the basic sense of Colossians 1:15 leads to Arianism.[72]

Exegetes of the second and third centuries set forth the preexistent Christ using Colossians 1:15 and other related texts in order to defend their understanding of Christ as fully human and fully divine, undivided from God the Father. However, after Arius, the hermeneutical moves used by the likes of Origen and Tertullian to make Christological claims stressing the ontological unity of Father and Son no longer worked.[73] Athanasius therefore had to take an approach to exegesis that attended to his understanding of the sense of scripture as a whole as he "sought to reinterpret texts exploited by the opposition in the light of his hermeneutical principles."[74] It is true Athanasius assumes that his expression of the divine nature of Christ is consistent with scripture, but now scriptural texts can only be the beginning point of theological interpretations, and weight is not put on the most basic sense of the biblical words at the expense of the rule of faith.[75]

70. Athanasius, *C.Ar.* 1.63.5 (NPNF 4); see also Khaled Anatolios, *Athanasius* (London: Routledge, 2004), 126. Athanasius cites Col 1:15–20 more than seventy times in his writings.

71. Young, *Biblical Exegesis and the Formation of Christian Culture*, 32; Athanasius, *Decr.* 11.4–6; 10.4–6, 13.

72. Were our study to include the Council of Nicaea, we would see how Arius's claims led to the Nicene statement that God the Son is consubstantial (*homoousios*) with God the Father. This is a move that essentially anathematizes the Arian theology we have described, arguing against Arius for the full divinity of the Son, who is distinct from and yet one with the Father. It is not until the writings of the Cappadocians against the Eunomians (later followers of Arius) that this is worked out in greater detail as they (Cappadocians) reiterate the divinity of the Son as consubstantial with the Father, even as God remains incorporeal and unbegotten.

73. Martin Werner, *The Formation of Christian Dogma: An Historical Study of Its Problem*, trans. S. G. F. Brandon (London: A. and C. Black, 1957), 158.

74. Young, *Biblical Exegesis and the Formation of Christian Culture*, 37.

75. Ibid., 32.

The history of the interpretation of Colossians 1:15 both affects and is shaped by the Arian controversy and early Christian understanding of Jesus Christ, the image of the invisible God and the first-born of all creation. When early Christians wrote about the divine nature of God the Son and the preexistence of Christ, Colossians 1:15 was one of the main Pauline texts to which they turned. The reception of Colossians 1 in early Christian writings, therefore, establishes ways early Christians used Paul's writings to think about the divine nature of Jesus Christ and the unity of God, while at the same time beginning to grapple with the limits of *sola scriptura* in that enterprise.

Christopher A. Beeley

11. THE SPIRIT AND THE LETTER

2 Corinthians 3:6 and the Legacy of Origen in Fourth-Century Greek Exegesis

For much of modern scholarship, the relationship between the Bible and the development of early Christian theology has meant tracing how the apostolic documents eventually contributed to the cardinal doctrines of God, Christ, the Holy Spirit, and the church or to related topics such as the Christian understanding of creation, time, the human person, and society. A second approach, fueled by recent advances in biblical text criticism, has been to note the ways in which the final versions of the canonical texts reflect the theological agenda of early Christian communities, suggesting a kind of reverse, or at least spiraled or circular, influence between the two. Yet there is a third sense, as well, in which the relationship between the scriptures and the development of Christian theology demands our attention, one that many interpreters would argue is fundamental to the other two. Among the core beliefs of early Christians was the view that the Holy Spirit plays the leading role in the composition, reading, and interpretation of scripture and that, accordingly, the way in which Christians understand and respond to the scriptures is itself a theological enterprise and an ongoing source of doctrinal reflection. The early rules of faith and significant portions of second- and third-century literature express the belief that the Spirit inspired the biblical prophets (the scriptures of Israel, soon to be supplemented with apostolic writings) and that the

Spirit continues to teach and guide Christian believers in the present day, particularly in the work of biblical interpretation.[1] This means, in turn, that the church's Spirit-led interpretation of scripture belongs to Trinitarian doctrine properly speaking, not as a remote source, but as an intrinsic element and a constantly determinative method.

A key development in the history of Christian belief in the Holy Spirit and the work of biblical reading occurred in Origen's construction of a "spiritual" method of interpretation, based in his reading of Paul, and its reception by the major theologians of the fourth and early fifth centuries. Through the likes of Didymus the Blind, the Cappadocians, John Chrysostom, Cyril of Alexandria, Ambrose, and Augustine, Origen's understanding of the literal and spiritual senses of scripture eventually came to characterize much of mainstream pneumatology and biblical hermeneutics in the Christian East and West until at least the sixteenth century.[2] The extent of Origen's influence in the fourth century, particularly in Trinitarian doctrine and Christology, is

1. In addition to well-known New Testament texts such as 2 Cor 3, 2 Tm 3:16, and 2 Pt 1:21, see Irenaeus, *Epid.* 6 ("through whom the prophets prophesied"); *AH* 1.10.1 ("who through the prophets predicted the economies of God"); 4.33.7 ("who in each generation discloses publicly among human beings the saving economies of the Father and the Son, as the Father wills"), along with briefer three-article confessions, which simply name the Holy Spirit, and two-article confessions, which omit it. Tertullian tends to concentrate on the Spirit's role in Jesus' conception and on Jesus' sending the Spirit to guide believers (*De praescriptione* 13), although, following a brief statement of the rule in *De virg. vel.* 1, he comments that the Spirit's proper office is "the direction of discipline, the revelation of the scriptures, the reformation of the intellect, the advancement toward the 'better things.'" The Nicene Creed of 381 repeats the notion that the Spirit "spoke through the prophets," and it gives the Spirit the titles "Lord" and "Giver of life," both of which appear in 2 Cor 3, the chapter that contains Paul's paradigmatic statement of spiritual exegesis.

2. The seminal modern studies of Origenist hermeneutics and their legacy are Henri De Lubac, *Histoire et esprit: L'intelligence de l'Écriture d'après Origène*, Théologie 16 (Paris: Aubier, 1950), and *Exégèse médiéval: Les quatre sens de l'Écriture*, 2 vols. Théologie 41 (Paris: Aubier: 1959). Lubac's achievement was to show that what later became the fourfold sense of scripture in the Middle Ages did not derive principally from Augustine or from Eucher or John Cassian, as was commonly thought, but from Origen. The reception of Origen's hermeneutics among the major fathers has yet to receive a substantial, synthetic treatment. Manlio Simonetti's *Profilo Storico dell' Esegesi Patristica*, (English translation *Biblical Interpretation in the Early Church*) gives some attention to spiritual and allegorical exegesis in the New Testament, including 2 Cor 3:6 and Rom 2:28–29, as well as John and Hebrews; and in Origen, he discusses the exegesis of Eusebius and, briefly, the Cappadocians, yet he does not examine the language of the spirit and the letter per se, and he draws different conclusions than those presented here. A pathbreaking study in the early Christian use of Hellenistic scholarly and rhetorical methods came in Frances Young's *Biblical Exegesis and the Formation of Christian Culture* and related articles. The most significant recent work is Margaret M. Mitchell, *Paul, the Corinthians and the Birth of Christian Hermeneutics* (Cambridge: Cambridge University Press, 2010), which concentrates on Paul and Origen and gives sustained attention to later Origenist tradition in Gregory of Nyssa and John Chrysostom.

rapidly gaining recognition among patristics scholars. Looking instead at the work of the Holy Spirit, this chapter examines one aspect of the legacy of Origen's hermeneutics among the Greek theologians of the fourth century: the adoption, and at times the avoidance, of Paul's notion that "the letter kills, but the Spirit gives life" in 2 Corinthians 3:6 as a basic framework for biblical interpretation, together with related statements in Romans 2:29, 7:6, and 7:14, which speak of "letter" and "spirit" in similar ways.[3] Due to constraints of space, we will concentrate on Eusebius of Caesarea, Athanasius, Epiphanius, Didymus the Blind, and the three Cappadocians.[4]

Origen on the Spirit and the Letter

As many have noted, Origen's voluminous and massively influential body of writings centers on the interpretation of scripture.[5] In concert with many of his Christian forebears and contemporaries, Origen believes that, for all their human particularity and historical contingency, the biblical authors composed the scriptures by the inspiration of the Holy Spirit and that the scriptures possess both an obvious and a more hidden meaning (*Princ.* 1, pref. 8).

3. This study is based on TLG searches for γραμμα- + πνευμα- and νόμος + πνευματικός, which cover Rom 2:29, 7:6, and 14, and 2 Cor 3:6; the Biblia Patristica index; the scripture indexes to the relevant Greek editions and English translations; and secondary studies of the relevant works. Passages from the catenae are used sparingly due to the uncertain nature of those sources.

4. Omitting Methodius, Cyril of Jerusalem, Evagrius, and Pseudo-Macarius; excluding spurious works attributed to fourth-century figures; and leaving aside John Chrysostom, Severian of Gabala, Cyril of Alexandria, Theodoret, Theodore of Mopsuestia, and Mark the Hermit as figures who bridge the fifth century. Diodore does not appear in the TLG searches for hermeneutical uses of "spirit" and "letter," nor are there any relevant scripture citations in the new critical edition of Diodore's fragments; John Behr, ed. and trans., *The Case against Diodore and Theodore: Texts and their Contexts*, Oxford Early Christian Texts (Oxford: Oxford University Press, 2011). Likewise, there are no relevant citations in Lietzmann's collection of the fragments of Apollinarius or in Ekkehard Mühlenberg's *Apollinaris von Laodicea* (Göttingen: Vandenhoeck and Ruprecht, 1969), and Apollinarius does not appear in the TLG searches either, with the exception of one fragment from the catena: In his lost *Commentary on Romans*, Apollinarius cites 2 Cor 3:6 and Rom 2:29 in a comment on Rom 7:7. He applies Paul's letter-spirit language chiefly to the abolition of sin and the Christian's transformation from a reliance on human strength to an experience of divine strength and God's "activity (ἐνέργεια) of righteousness" now been revealed in Christ (Frag. on Rom 7:7; Karl Staab, *Pauluskommentare aus der Griechischen Kirche,* 2nd ed., Neutestamentliche Abhandlungen 15 [Münster: Aschendorff, 1984], 65).

5. Brian E. Daley, "Origen's *De Principiis*: A Guide to the Principles of Christian Scriptural Interpretation," in *Nova et Vetera: Patristic Studies in Honor of T. P. Halton*, ed. J. Petruccione (Washington, D.C.: The Catholic University of America Press, 1998), 3–21. On Origen's biblical interpretation, see now Ronald E. Heine, *Origen: Scholarship in the Service of the Church*, Christian Theology in Context (Oxford: Oxford University Press, 2010).

Accordingly, Origen bases his biblical interpretation as a whole on the distinction that he finds in Paul between the "letter" and the "spirit" of scripture,[6] expressed most decisively in 2 Corinthians 3:6, with support from Romans 2:29, 7:6, and 7:14.[7] Origen's many biblical homilies vary in their respective attention to the letter or the spirit of the text at hand, ranging from constant attention to the literal sense of a passage to a nearly exclusive interest in its spiritual meaning.[8] While Origen believes that the spiritual sense of a passage is crucial for enabling the Christian's ascent to God, he works assiduously to establish the literal sense, and he means to anchor his spiritual exegesis firmly in the literal text, however much later readers may believe he succeeded at avoiding arbitrary allegorization.[9] Given his pervasive emphasis on interpretation "according to the Spirit" (Rom 8:5), Origen's hermeneutical method has conveniently been called "spiritual exegesis."

Paul's letter-spirit distinction frames Origen's summary definition of biblical interpretation in book four of *First Principles*. While some readers have concentrated on the three-part model that Origen gives, which distinguishes among spiritual, psychic, and fleshly meanings of scripture (*Princ.* 4.2.4), the two-part distinction between literal and spiritual exegesis remains primary throughout Origen's work, most visibly in his homilies and commentaries.[10] Accordingly, references to 2 Corinthians 3:6 and similar passages recur throughout Origen's corpus.[11] The right way to learn the "mind" of the scriptures, he writes, is to work carefully through the literal sense toward the higher, spiritual meanings of the text (*Princ.* 4.2.4–6).[12]

Origen gives an especially clear indication of his meaning in his *Commentary on Romans*, where the letter-spirit idea of 2 Corinthians 3:6 informs much

6. See, e.g., O'Keefe, "Scriptural Interpretation," in *Westminster Handbook to Origen*, 193–97.

7. Other passages that tend to appear in the same connection are 1 Cor 2:13; 10:1–11; and Gal 4:21–31, along with Heb 10:1.

8. Henri Crouzel, *Origen*, trans. A. S. Worrall (San Francisco: Harper and Row, 1989), 61.

9. As Mitchell ably demonstrates, "'arbitrary' … is the last thing figural exegesis is." The rhetorical quality of most early Christian exegesis, she notes, was normally quite strategic and deliberately adapted to address specific, immediate purposes; Mitchell, *Paul, the Corinthians and the Birth of Christian Hermeneutics*, x and *passim*.

10. Crouzel, *Origen*, 61; Joseph W. Trigg, *Origen: The Bible and Philosophy in the Third-Century Church* (Atlanta: John Knox, 1983), 120; Mitchell, *Paul, the Corinthians and the Birth of Christian Hermeneutics*, 54.

11. The verse is among the most cited, according to the Biblia Patristica index.

12. Biblical references in these sections include, in sequence, 1 Cor 2:6–7; Rom 7:14; Heb 10:1; Rom 2:29; 1 Cor 9:9–10, 10; Heb 8:5; Gal 4:21–24.

of his reading of that letter. Also informing this work, and much of his writing from the last half of his career, which he spent in Palestinian Caesarea, is Origen's sense of a costly, live debate between contemporary Christians and Jews over the right interpretation of the Old Testament, as well as a longer dialog with pagan detractors and Christian heretics.[13] Building on his reading of Paul, Origen teaches that the Mosaic law has two aspects: "The law ... contains both the letter that kills and the Spirit that gives life" (*CRom* 6.11.3; 6.12.2). In its most complete and truest meaning, Origen argues, "the law is spiritual" (Rom 7:14), and the spiritual meaning of scripture requires the gift of the Holy Spirit to perceive. The condition of the believer's relationship to Christ and the Holy Spirit is therefore crucial for the work of biblical interpretation. The law of Moses, and the Old Testament as a whole, "is a spiritual law and a life-giving Spirit for those who understand it spiritually. But the one who understands it in a fleshly way recalls it as a law of the letter and a letter that kills" (*CRom* 6.9.3).

"The letter that kills," or the literal sense of the scripture, Origen associates with Paul's language of "flesh"—such as "the law was weak through the flesh" (Rom 8:3; *CRom* 1.10.2); "living to the flesh" (Rom 8:14; *CRom* 1.10.2)—as well as the idea of boasting through the law of works (Rom 3:27; *CRom* 3.9.8) and the literal observance of the law, such as the detailed commandments regarding the Sabbath, which Origen believes are physically impossible, or the sacrificial system in the absence of a temple in Jerusalem (*CRom* 6.12.2). If one takes the literal sense of scripture as the end of interpretation, so that one fails to move through the letter to the deeper meaning concerning God's heavenly plan in Christ, the literal sense of the law becomes an obstacle to faith and hence "the letter that kills" (*CRom* 6.12.6). By contrast, Origen associates the "spirit" of the law with Paul's phrases "the law of the Spirit of life" (Rom 8:2); "living by the Spirit" (Rom 8:13); "the law of faith" (Rom 3:27); "the law of the Spirit of life" (Rom 8:2; *CRom* 3.9.8); "the circumcision of the heart," which is performed by the Spirit and not in the flesh, or according to the letter (Rom 2:29; *CRom* 2.12.1); and the grace of God, which Origen calls "the law of the Spirit that makes alive" (Rom 6:14; 2 Cor 3:6; *CRom* 6.1.9). What Origen says here concerning the law of Moses and the Old Testament scriptures, following Paul's argument in Romans, he applies to the New Testament as well,

13. In *CRom* Origen comments that the law of Moses stands now between Jews and Christians (*CRom* 6.12.6). On Origen's relationship to contemporary Judaism, especially in Caesarea, and its effect on his outlook and work, see Heine, *Origen*.

so that the scriptures as a whole possess both a literal and a spiritual sense. In this regard Christian heretics, who argue on the basis of both Testaments, possess only the letter that kills (*CRom* 2.14.11). The spiritual meaning of the divine mysteries "in Christ" (2 Cor 3:14) is obviously closer to the literal level of the text in much of the New Testament, where one reads about the realities toward which the shadows and riddles of the Old Testament point (*CJn* 1.6.33–36). Yet, even so, the New Testament also contains mysteries and enigmas that require spiritual interpretation, in addition to the constant problem of the limitations of human language in general, so it too is "a shadow of the good things to come" (Heb 10:1), which are the "eternal gospel" of which John speaks in Revelation 14:6 and which can be perceived only eschatologically (*CJn* 1.7.40; *Princ.* 3.6.8).[14]

For the sake of our comparison with fourth-century authors, it is important to note the rich set of connections that Origen makes in his practice of spiritual exegesis, ranging from the law given to Moses on Mount Sinai and its textual expression and expansion in the pages of scripture, to the person of Christ and the gift of the Holy Spirit, to the flesh of the human body and the way of life that Christians aspire to live "in Christ," to God's eschatological kingdom and the community of the saints in the heavenly Jerusalem. All of these topics are involved in the spiritual interpretation of scripture, according to Origen. The central place that biblical interpretation occupies in Origen's work and the vast influence that he came to have on later ascetics and theologians give us some indication of how important the principles of spiritual exegesis are for patristic theology at large.

Eusebius of Caesarea

Eusebius of Caesarea's theology has only recently begun to receive the scholarly attention that it deserves,[15] mainly due to the informal ecclesiasti-

14. Trigg, "Knowing God in the *Theological Orations* of Gregory of Nazianzus: The Heritage of Origen," in *God in Early Christian Thought: Essays in Memory of Lloyd G. Patterson*, ed. Andrew B. McGowan, Brian E. Daley, SJ, and Timothy J. Gaden, Supplements to Vigiliae Christianae 94 (Leiden: Brill, 2009), 88.

15. See esp. Holger Strutwolf, *Die Trinitätstheologie und Christologie des Euseb von Caesarea: Eine dogmengeschichtliche Untersuchung seiner Platonismusrezeption und Wirkungsgeschichte*. Forschungen zur Kirchen- und Dogmengeschichte 72 (Göttingen: Vandenhoeck and Ruprecht, 1999); the works of Michael Hollerich (notes 18, 21, and 29 in this chapter); Anthony Grafton and Megan Williams, *Christian-*

cal opprobrium under which he lay for centuries, thanks to Athanasius's blanket condemnation of the group of "Eusebians."[16] As a result, several key works have yet to be edited or translated.[17] Eusebius spent much of his adult life as an assiduous Christian scholar working in Origen's library in Caesarea, basing his research on Origen's works and making use of the Hexapla that Origen had prepared for biblical research; Eusebius became a bishop only in his fifties. Given that he was the most notable and accomplished disciple of Origen in the early fourth century,[18] it comes as no surprise that Eusebius would give attention to Paul's spirit-letter distinction and to Origenist spiritual exegesis in general.

For Eusebius, as for Origen, the biblical text has two main types of meaning: the literal sense, which Michael Hollerich defines as "an understanding of the actual words themselves," and the deeper metaphorical or allegorical sense given through symbols, circumstances, key words, or names. Eusebius takes pains to defend the necessity of figurative or allegorical interpretation even in works in which he places great emphasis on the literal sense of the text (*CIsa* pref.; 11.15). The literal and spiritual senses are something like fact versus interpretation or event versus meaning. As Hollerich describes it, Eusebius's hermeneutics blend literal and spiritual interpretation in a way that shows "a dedication to grammatical analysis of the text, an acceptance of the church's traditional apologetic exegesis, a belief in the supernatural inspiration of biblical prophecy, a moderate and cautious exploration of figurative interpretation, and a vivid sense of the hand of God in the events of his own day."[19] Equally

ity and the Transformation of the Book: Origen, Eusebius, and the Library of Caesarea (Cambridge, Mass.: Belknap Press, 2008); and Christopher A. Beeley, *The Unity of Christ*, chap. 2, "Eusebius of Caesarea."

16. On which see Beeley, *The Unity of Christ*, chaps. 2–3.

17. For example, Eusebius's massive *Commentary on the Psalms*, his longest work, is only now being critically edited; and his most significant theological work, the *Ecclesiastical Theology*, has an English translation in preparation.

18. He is "the most prestigious living representative of the Alexandrian tradition"; Michael J. Hollerich, *Eusebius of Caesarea's Commentary on Isaiah: Christian Exegesis in the Age of Constantine*. Oxford Early Christian Studies (Oxford: Clarendon, 1999), 95. Sébastien Morlet argues that, in composing the *Prophetic Eclogues*, Eusebius not only drew profusely on Origen's works via anthologies that he himself prepared (which he later used for the *Dem. ev.* as well), making the work "a kind of *epitome* of Origen's exegesis addressed to the beginners," but that he may have intended the work to serve as an introduction to Origen's commentaries; Morlet, "Origen as an Exegetical Source," in *Eusebius of Caesarea: Tradition and Innovations*, ed. Aaron Johnson and Jeremy Schott, Hellenic Studies 60 (Washington, D.C.: Center for Hellenic Studies, 2013), 224.

19. Hollerich, *Eusebius of Caesarea's Commentary on Isaiah*, 67. On Eusebius's exegetical method,

obvious, however, is the fact that Eusebius gives a new measure of attention to the literal sense in comparison with Origen, a shift that correlates with Eusebius's interest in historical research and the biblical sites of the Palestinian region.[20] While Eusebius carried forward Origen's characteristic attention to spiritual interpretation, arguably the most distinctive feature of his work is his attention to the Bible's historical and literary aspects.[21]

In Eusebius's early historical works the *Church History* and *The Martyrs of Palestine*, Paul's letter-spirit idea appears sparingly but not without significance. In his paean to Origen in book 6 of the *Church History*, Eusebius singles out this description of Paul from book five of Origen's *Commentary on John*: he was "a minister of the New Covenant not of the letter but of the spirit" (2 Cor 3:6; *HE* 6.25.7). In his comments on the canons of Anatolius concerning the date of Easter, Eusebius writes that "those from whom the veil on the Law of Moses has been removed" (2 Cor 3:16) require no proof that the Passover is after the spring equinox, since they reflect Christ with faces unveiled (*HE* 7.32.19). More humanly tangible is Eusebius's account of the Palestinian martyrs, which he again casts in terms of spiritual exegesis. Because the Egyptian martyrs around Pamphylus had changed their names from those of pagan idols to those of biblical prophets, they showed themselves to be Jews inwardly (Rom 2:29), not only in their martyrs' deeds but also "by the literal sense of the words they used." When the martyr in question tells the judge that his city is Jerusalem, Eusebius explains that he means Paul's "Jerusalem that is above" (Gal 4:26; 6:6), even though the judge "had his thoughts fixed on this world here below" and worried about political competition with Rome, for which reason he proceeded to torture Pamphylus's companion (*Mart. Palest.* 11.8–12 [both resc.]; GCS 2.937.3–4). Eusebius again invokes 2 Corinthians 3 in the final account of the work, on John the Egyptian. John demonstrated his confession and character not only through his hideous mutilations, but also by his excellent memory, Eusebius says. For John had "written whole books of the divine Scriptures 'not in tables of stone,' as the divine apostle says, nor even on skins of animals or on paper which moths and time destroy (Lk 12:33), 'but in

see esp. chap. 3. In Eusebius's *Commentary on Isaiah* the literal sense includes both "the ordinary language meaning of the prophetic diction and the actual [future] events it foresaw"; ibid., 96.

20. D. S. Wallace-Hadrill, *Eusebius of Caesarea* (London: A. S. Mowbray, 1960), 97.

21. Hollerich, "Eusebius," in *The New Cambridge History of the Bible: From the Beginnings to 600*, ed. James Carleton Paget and Joachim Schaper (Cambridge: Cambridge University Press, 2012), 629.

tables that are' truly 'hearts of flesh' (2 Cor 3:3)" (*Mart. Palest.* short rescension 13.7–8; GCS 2.948.17–20).[22]

In the two major apologetic works that followed, the theoretical terms of Origenist spiritual exegesis are fairly muted, most likely due to Eusebius's need to defend Christianity from Porphyry's criticisms of the allegorical interpretation of the Old Testament (see *HE* 6.19.4–5; *Dem.* 10.1.3) as well as ongoing competition with Judaism (*Dem.* 1.2.2; 1.8.4).[23] Even so, the letter-spirit idea appears several times. Near the beginning of the *Preparation for the Gospel*, Eusebius describes his overall method in terms that evoke Paul's language. Against Porphyry's charge that Christians hold an unreasoning faith, Eusebius will offer unambiguous proofs in a manner similar to the method that Paul indicated in the Corinthian correspondence, such as his "demonstration of Spirit and power" (1 Cor 2:4), his speaking hidden wisdom among the perfect (1 Cor 3:6), and the sufficiency that he derives solely from God, who made him sufficient as minister of a new covenant (2 Cor 3:5; *Prep.* 1.3.5). In the *Proof of the Gospel*, which is an argument for the truth of the Christian gospel mainly from Old Testament prophecy, Eusebius argues that, in the "new and fresh system" of faith that Christ inaugurated, God has inscribed the ordinances of the prophets not on stone tablets like Moses', nor with ink and parchment, but "on the hearts of his pupils (2 Cor 3:3)" (*Prep.* 1.7.23; 1.8.1). Similarly, the Jews who will be saved will be "all those who represent the Jew [in the text] mystically understood and the true Israel which sees God spiritually," since it is "the secret Jew and the true Israel" (Rom 2:28–29) that will endure (*Prep.* 7.3.46).[24]

Eusebius's lengthy exegetical works, his *Commentary on Isaiah* and *Commentary on the Psalms*, give us the clearest indication of his exegetical practice at the height of his career. Over time Eusebius continued to show an interest in spiritual interpretation, even as he concentrated more on the literal sense. Of particular interest is the fact that Eusebius makes no reference to 2 Corin-

22. Eusebius of Caesarea, *Ecclesiastical History* (*H.E.*), ed. Eduard Schwartz, SC 31, 41, 51, 73; English trans. *The Ecclesiastical History and the Martyrs of Palestine*, trans. Hugh Jackson Lawlor and John Ernest Leonard Oulton, 2 vols. (London: SPCK, 1954), 1:398.

23. Hollerich, "Eusebius," 641, 643.

24. Eusebius of Caesarea, *The Proof of the Gospel, Being the Demonstratio evangelica of Eusebius of Cæsarea*, trans. W. J. Ferrar, 2 vols. (London: SPCK, 1920), 1:92–93. Contra the Biblia Patristica index, Eusebius's oblique contrast of the sacraments of new covenant with those of the old covenant (*Dem.* 8.2.118) and "the new law and word of the new Covenant" (*Dem.* 8.3.12) do not constitute references to 2 Cor 3.

thians 3:6 in either work and that the *Commentary on Isaiah*, written shortly after the Council of Nicaea in 325,[25] lacks any reference to the language of the spirit and the letter in any of the verses normally associated with spiritual interpretation.[26] In this work Eusebius avoids the term "allegory" as well, and prefers to describe the alternative to the literal sense (πρὸς λέξιν) as a more hidden meaning (πρὸς διάνοιαν, also Origenist terms), which the prophet sometimes conveys through symbolism or other complex ways of speaking (*CIsa* 3.1–9).[27] The reason for this practice, again, may well be Eusebius's determination to oppose the criticisms of Porphyry and certain Jews.

Yet the *Commentary on the Psalms*, which Eusebius wrote several years later, in the 330s,[28] refers to the spirit and the letter several times, although by way of Romans 2:29 instead of 2 Corinthians 3:6.[29] Rather than declaring his hermeneutical procedure in summary fashion, Eusebius simply performs a spiritual interpretation of the Psalms in order to apply them to the present-day church. This purpose leads him to appeal to Paul's statement in Romans 2:28–29 to clarify who is meant by "Israel," "Judea," and the like in the psalter. For example, on Ps 75:2 (LXX), "God is known in Judea; in Israel his name is great," Eusebius argues on the basis of Romans 2:28–29 that the true Israel and the true Jerusalem are not those according to flesh and blood, which exist in the region of Palestine, any more than the seed of Abraham is the offspring of his flesh (PG 23.876C–77A).[30] While he does not cite 2 Corinthians 3:6, Eusebius nevertheless employs Paul's letter-spirit idea in order to apply the text of the Psalms to the church and to identify the biblical referent as Chris-

25. Hollerich, "Eusebius," 641.

26. Jn 6:63; Rom 2:29; 7:6, 14; 2 Cor 3:6. There are slight references to 2 Cor 3:12 (1x) and 3:17 (2x).

27. Hollerich, "Eusebius," 648–49. These terms are not unconventional, and they also appear in Origen.

28. Ibid.

29. Rom 2:29 (4x); Rom 7:14 (2x). Eusebius's *Commentary on the Psalms* has not yet been critically edited; it currently exists in Migne in a version that is only moderately stable; see Hollerich, "Eusebius' Commentary on the Psalms," 151–68; in Johnson and Schott, *Eusebius of Caesarea*.

30. Similar arguments occur in PG 23.720D–21A on Ps 67:34–36 ("Give glory to God; his magnificence is over Israel"), with reference to Rom 2:29 and 9:6–8; 23.1172D on Ps 91:2–4, another appeal to Rom 2:29; and 24.36B on Ps 135:23 ("because in our humiliation the Lord remembered us"): "Israel" means not merely those from the race of the Jews, but whoever lives a pious life with God, again quoting Rom 9:6 and 2:28–29. Hollerich argues that the *PsCom* contains proportionally less Origenist spiritual exegesis than the *IsaCom*, since prophetic fulfillment is itself "historical" for Eusebius ("Eusebius's Commentary on the Psalms," in Johnson and Schott, *Eusebius of Caesarea*, 156); but Eusebius's employment of the letter-spirit language could make the case otherwise.

tians rather than contemporary Jews. Eusebius's late *Against Marcellus* and *Ecclesiastical Theology* employ fewer ideas of spiritual exegesis, no doubt due to the fact that Eusebius is responding to Marcellus, who avoids them entirely. However, when Eusebius criticizes Marcellus for interpreting biblical proverbs on the model of Greek proverbs, he adds the comment that only "spiritual people" can receive the Spirit of God (*C. Marcel.* P30/R11/K124).[31]

Across his works Eusebius practices a moderate form of Origenist spiritual exegesis, gradually moving away from the text of 2 Corinthians 3:6 itself as he gives increasing attention to matters of literal interpretation. Yet it is important to keep in mind that both senses were of concern to Origen, making Eusebius's practice a type of Origenist exegesis. By contrast, Eusebius's onetime associate Asterius shows even less evidence of using the terminology of the spirit and the letter of scripture.[32] In his use of the letter-spirit idea, Eusebius's main concern is to define the characteristic identity of Christians, whether against pagan persecutors or contemporary Jews; otherwise, he shows a smaller range of topical interconnection by comparison with Origen. In doing so Eusebius attenuates the role of the Holy Spirit in the work of biblical interpretation and the place of spiritual exegesis within his theological program, although without denying them entirely.

Athanasius

Athanasius stands out among the major fourth-century fathers for how little use he makes of Origenist hermeneutical principles. He is the exception that proves the rule of Origen's pervasive influence on fourth-century Christian theology. In his detailed study of Athanasius's exegesis, James Ernest ob-

31. Brief reference to Jn 6:63 occurs in *C.Marcel.* 210.9 (Nr. 117/Re 104) and 211.13 (Nr. 118/Re 105); and to 2 Cor 3:17 in *Eccl.Th.* 1.20. See also *Quaestiones ev. ad Steph.*, 28, ref. to Rom 2:29.

32. In the thirty-one *Homilies on the psalms*, there is only one slight mention of the letter and the spirit of the text; In: *ComPss* 18.17, (Marcel Richard, in *Asterii Sophistae Commentariorum in Psalmos quea supersunt: Accedunt aliquot homiliae anonymae*, Symboae Osloenses, Fasc. suppl. 16 [Oslo: A. W. Brøgger, 1956]), and none in the published *Fragments* (Asterius the Sophist, *Fragments*, ed. Markus Vinzent, *Die theologischen Fragmente: Einleitung, kritischer Text, Übersetzung und Kommentar*, Supplements to Viviliae Christianae 20 [Leiden: Brill, 1993], despite the fact that Asterius's doctrine is recognizably Origenist on other points: see the list of items (on each of which Eusebius agrees) given in Mark DelCogliano, "Eusebius of Caesarea on Asterius of Cappadocia in the Anti-Marcellan Writings: A Case Study of Mutual Defense within the Eusebian Alliance," in Johnson and Schott, *Eusebius of Caesarea.*

serves that Athanasius was reluctant to identify himself as an Alexandrian biblical interpreter in the mold of Philo or Origen.[33] The most likely reasons for this choice are Athanasius's vehement opposition to the group of theologians that he grouped together as "Eusebians" (named after the bishop of Nicomedia) and later "Arians,"[34] some of whom proudly carried forth the legacy of Origen (as Arius did not), as well as Athanasius's intellectual disposition to eschew the sort of sophisticated research and reasoning that Origen modeled.[35] Accordingly, the language of Origenist spiritual exegesis hardly appears in Athanasius's work.[36] The phenomenon is all the more striking when we note that Athanasius's early mentor, Bishop Alexander, was a thoughtful Origenist;[37] Athanasius speaks laudably of the great teachers of the Christian past (*C.Gent.* 1); he once quotes Origen to defend his own argument, calling him one of the "fathers" (*decr.* 27); and he adopts a few points of Origen's Christology.[38]

Athanasius's first documented use of Pauline hermeneutical terms appeared in 347, nearly twenty years after his emergence as a public theologian. In the first phase of his career (pre-339),[39] Athanasius participated in the Council of Nicaea as a deacon before devoting his attention to consolidating the disparate and schismatic Egyptian church under his authority as a new bishop. During this period Athanasius does use the language of shadow and reality from Hebrews 10:1 to set Christianity apart from contemporary Judaism. In his first *Festal Letter*, from 329, he argues that the physical city of Je-

33. James D. Ernest, *Bible in Athanasius of Alexandria*, 159.

34. "The traditional trappings of Alexandrian biblical interpretation, including the image of the erudite Bible teacher, are in [Athanasius's] mind tainted by Arian use"; Ernest, *Bible in Athanasius of Alexandria*, 163.

35. The fact that Athanasius received little formal education like Origen, Didymus the Blind, or the Cappadocians (Timothy D. Barnes, *Athanasius and Constantius: Theology and Politics in the Constantinian Empire* [Cambridge, Mass.: Harvard University Press, 2001]; Ernest, *Bible in Athanasius of Alexandria*, 159–60) does not explain the matter, since a lack of advanced theological training could be an excellent reason to make as much use of earlier Christian teachers as possible.

36. For example, the noun *allegoria* does not appear at all, and the verb appears only twice, both times negatively. *Tropologia* does not appear, either, and he never speaks of the "letter" versus the "spirit" of scripture. For a detailed discussion of each term, see Ernest, *Bible in Athanasius of Alexandria*, 160 and notes.

37. Beeley, *Unity of Christ*, 114–17.

38. Ibid., 126–28, 159–61.

39. For an account of the three main stages of the development of Athanasius's Christology, see Beeley, *Unity of Christ*, 124–70.

rusalem is like the figure that had to be "laid waste" in order for the truth of Christianity to shine forth. Although he connects the idea of "passing beyond the time of shadows" with turning to the Lord, who is "spirit" (2 Cor 3:18; *Ep.* 1.9), he makes no use of Paul's hermeneutical argument from the same chapter of 2 Corinthians.

Early in the second phase of his career (339–62), Athanasius entered into a fateful association with Marcellus of Ancyra, whom he met in Rome during Athanasius's second exile from Alexandria. Marcellus was a determined anti-Origenist in his own right, which may explain why there are no references to 2 Corinthians 3 in any of the remaining fragments of Marcellus's works. It was Marcellus who taught Athanasius the chief exegetical and polemical strategies that he later deployed in his three *Orations Against the Arians*, including the idea of calling all his enemies "Arians." The fact that Athanasius makes no appeal to Pauline hermeneutics in his heavily exegetical *Orations against the Arians* (c. 340) is significant in itself.

The first glimpse that we have of Paul's letter-spirit distinction comes in Athanasius's *Festal Letter* 19 from the year 347. This appears to be the only passage in Athanasius's corpus where he employs Paul's language to mean the text of the Old Testament versus its true meaning. In another anti-Jewish passage, Athanasius argues that, although the law was given for the people's instruction and to prefigure Christ (Gal 3:23–24), the Jews did not understand it but walked in darkness, "feeling for, but not touching, the truth in the law, which we [Christians] possess. They conformed to the letter but did not submit to the spirit. And when Moses was veiled they looked on him, but they turned their faces away from him when he was uncovered; for they did not know what they read" (*Ep.* 19.2).[40]

Athanasius next addresses Paul's letter-spirit distinction in two texts from the late 350s. In his *Letters to Serapion* on the Holy Spirit, Athanasius catalogs the various meanings of "spirit" in scripture in order to counter his opponents' argument from Amos 4:13, which states that God "creates spirit," that the Holy Spirit must therefore have been created. As the final meaning of the term, Athanasius writes that the scriptures use the word "spirit" to denote "the meaning which is in the divine words themselves." Whatever can be spoken is called the "letter," but "the meaning in it is called its 'spirit,'" with reference to

40. *Festal Letter*, NPNF trans. adapt.

2 Corinthians 3:6 and the related verses Romans 7:6, and 7:14, plus Romans 7:25–8:2, and the less expected Acts 8:30, Numbers 14:24, and Ezekiel 18:31 (*Serap.* 1.8.1). Although Athanasius defines the letter-spirit idea as meaning an utterance or text versus its meaning, he does not apply the notion to the scriptures, as he did in *Letter* 19.[41] He makes no other use of the letter-spirit idea in the *Letters to Serapion*, despite the fact that their topic is the Holy Spirit.[42]

Slightly later, in *On the Councils of Ariminum and Seleucia* (359–61), Athanasius makes a glancing, and somewhat ironic, reference to 2 Corinthians 3:6. In order to argue for substantial agreement among theologians and councils despite the "literal" differences among their doctrinal formulations concerning the term *homoousios*, Athanasius appeals to Paul's different uses of the word "law." While using the same word, Paul teaches the Romans and others "to turn from the letter to the spirit," while he teaches the Hebrews and Galatians "to place their hopes not in the law, but in the Lord who had given the Law." Ironically, Athanasius does not apply 2 Corinthians 3:6 itself to the matter at hand, as we might expect: he does not argue that the "spirit" or meaning of the term *homoousios* is the same, even though some might oppose it according to the letter, as did the Council of Antioch in 269, which condemned Paul of Samosata (*syn.* 45). This passage is additionally ironic in that Athanasius is making a case for broad agreement among the "fathers," all the while insisting on a very particular adherence to the term *homoousios* and denying the consensus of a substantial group of mainstream theologians.[43]

A further, nontheological reference to 2 Corinthians 3 comes in *Letter* 55 to Bishop Rufinianus, whom Athanasius regards as a father figure. Although he might write to Rufinianus like a son, he refrains from doing so lest his testimony should be made known by writing: "For you are my letter, as it is written (2 Cor 3:2), known and read in the heart" (*Ep.* 55).[44] With one rare exception

41. Ernest, *Bible in Athanasius of Alexandria*, 161 n100: here Athanasius "is interested only in illustrating diverse biblical uses of the word πνεῦμα."

42. His only other reference to 2 Cor 3 in the *Letters* is to verse 17 as an example of the use of the word "spirit" to refer to the Holy Spirit (*Serap.* 1.6.8). Years earlier, in *Contra Arianos* 1.11, Athanasius had cited 2 Cor 3:16–17 to argue for the eternity of the Son, in contrast to his use of the passage in *Serap.* 1.8.1 to argue for that of the Spirit; Michael Haykin, *Spirit of God: The Exegesis of 1 and 2 Corinthians in the Pneumatomachian Controversy of the Fourth Century*, Supplements to Vigiliae Christianae 27 (Leiden: Brill, 1994), 68n60.

43. See Beeley, *Unity of Christ*, 124–25, on Athanasius, *syn.* 47.

44. See also, possibly, *Ep.* 65.1 to Jovian: the true faith has become manifest, both "known and read" from the divine scriptures (2 Cor 3:2).

in *Letter* 19, then, Athanasius never employs Paul's letter-spirit distinction to identify the true or deeper meaning of the scriptures. Origen's Pauline hermeneutics play virtually no role in Athanasius's theology. His polemical stance and intellectual disposition led him to avoid the magisterial legacy of Origen in this and several other respects.

Epiphanius

Epiphanius has long been known for his virulent opposition to Origen and his legacy, a stance that helped to fuel the Origenist controversy of the late fourth century. While his biblical interpretation, like most of his writing, is often regarded as bluntly uncritical and opposed to sophisticated reasoning, Andrew Jacobs argues that what appears literalist and reactionary in Epiphanius's exegesis can best be described as an imperial antiquarian style.[45] Nevertheless, in spite of himself, Epiphanius occasionally engages in allegorical exegesis in his treatise *On Weights and Measures*, which also discusses the canon and translation of the Old Testament.

Epiphanius's first major work, the *Ancoratus* (374), gives extended attention to the Holy Spirit.[46] Epiphanius wrote the work in order to counter supposedly heretical teaching on the Spirit by Pneumatomachoi at the request of certain presbyters and monks in Pamphylia who, it appears, had previously found help in Athanasius's *Letters to Serapion*.[47] Yet his wariness of Origenist tradition makes Epiphanius reticent to adopt the methods of spiritual exegesis, much as Athanasius was. Several sections of the work (*Anc.* 52–55, 58–63) argue in favor of straightforward versus allegorical interpretation of scripture, and his use of Paul's letter-spirit idea is minimal.

Epiphanius employs Paul's letter-spirit idea once, in a passage concerning the Trinity. In order to defend the uncreated status of the Holy Spirit, Epipha nius contrasts the Father, Son, and Spirit with the angels. Whereas the angels are created, the Father, Son, and Holy Spirit are uncreated, and whereas the Father, Son, and Spirit all choose to bring about the final day of judgment,

45. Andrew Jacobs, "Epiphanius of Salamis and the Antiquarian's Bible," *Journal of Early Christian Studies* 21, no. 3 (2013): 437–64.

46. Epiphanius, *Ancoratus*, trans. Young Richard Kim, Fathers of the Church 128 (Washington, D.C.: The Catholic University of America Press, 2014), 4, 7.

47. Athanasius had died on May 3, 373.

the angels do not know when that will be. To the predictable objection that in Matthew 24:36 Jesus says "only the Father [knows], neither the angels *nor* the Son," Epiphanius appeals to the letter-spirit distinction: one should "think on the meaning of the scripture, in order that the letter might not be death for us." The letter of the text contains life, he continues, so long as one "receives the Spirit" and approaches the Bible with the true understanding that the Spirit reveals in the letter of the text—a description not far from Origen's approach. Yet, ironically for such a staunch anti-allegorist, Epiphanius's exegesis in this case is rather stretched. He claims that Jesus' statement means simply that the Father and Son do know the day and the hour, but the Son has not yet accomplished it. (He does not elect to apply the statement to Jesus' human existence in the economy, as other interpreters did.) Epiphanius's interpretation, which runs not merely beyond but straight against the literal meaning of the text—a flight of fancy that even the allegorizing Origen would not have countenanced—enables him to maintain the shared knowledge and "harmony" of the Trinity, from which the angels are excluded (*Anc.* 22.2–7). Aside from this passage, Epiphanius makes no hermeneutical use of any of the verses commonly associated with Origenist spiritual exegesis, again like Athanasius's.[48]

In the *Panarion* Epiphanius's anti-Origenism intensifies. Among several lengthy passages against Origen quoted from Methodius and Proclus (*Panar.* 64.21.1–64.62.65), Epiphanius concurs with Methodius's assessment: "In his position on doctrines, and about faith and higher speculation, [Origen] is the wickedest of all before and after him, except for the shameless behavior of the sects" (*Panar.* 64.5.7).[49] Included in the scandalous excerpts from Methodius is Origen's reference to Romans 7:14 in connection with the spiritual condition of the resurrected body (*Panar.* 64.56.8).

Didymus the Blind

If Athanasius and Epiphanius studiously avoided Origen's hermeneutics, the opposite is true of the Alexandrian teacher Didymus the Blind. The flowering of Origenist hermeneutics in the late fourth century began with Didymus.

48. Rom 2:29 and 2 Cor 3:18 figure in a long list of verses on the Spirit that prove that the Spirit "serves with Christ"; Epiphanius, *Ancoratus*, FC 68–69.

49. Epiphanius, *Panarion,* trans. Williams, 136.

Athanasius nowhere mentions Didymus, and the relationship between the two has confounded scholars.[50] In his own time Didymus was regarded as a magisterial scholar of the Bible: Jerome praises him as "the foremost Christian scholar of his era in Alexandria" (*Os.* 1.prol.),[51] and Rufinus traveled to Alexandria to study with him for several years. Richard Layton characterizes Didymus's exegetical work and his general intellectual activity, as evidenced in the commentaries and notes found in the Tura papyri, as "scholastic Origenism." In Layton's reconstruction, Didymus oversaw a local Christian school that practiced Christian scholarship on par with elite rhetorical and philosophic studies. The entire enterprise was founded on Origen's exegesis.[52]

Didymus's biblical interpretation concentrates on elucidating the letter and the spirit of the biblical text. For Didymus, literal interpretation consists in what Layton calls "the clarification of difficulties that a reader might encounter," while spiritual interpretation aims to disclose "the interior meaning of the text."[53] As for Origen, Didymus believed that the Holy Spirit coauthored the Bible, producing both kinds of meaning. For the former, Didymus employs the usual grammatical arts, such as the identification of the speaker, word usage, literary and rhetorical devices, and analysis of verse divisions and punctuation, as Frances Young identified in much patristic exegesis.[54] It was the literal level of interpretation that provided Didymus's students with the tools they needed to defend the integrity of the text and to counter heretical teachings by Eunomians and Apollinarians, based in a "science" (ἐπιστήμη) of scripture that includes rational principles based on common notions (κοινάι ἔννοιαι) and the logical rules found in Aristotle.[55] Yet the real "fruit" of interpretation (see Ps 1:3) remains "the mystic and spiritual understanding of the Scriptures" (*ad Ps.* 1.3).[56]

50. Ernest speculates that Athanasius must have appointed him to a formal teaching post (*Bible in Athanasius of Alexandria*, 163n105); however, Richard Layton argues that Didymus probably did not head the catechetical school but instead led a private scholastic enterprise, whose connection with Bishop Athanasius is unclear at best; Layton, *Didymus the Blind and His Circle in Late-Antique Alexandria: Virtue and Narrative in Biblical Scholarship* (Urbana: University of Illinois Press, 2004), 160.

51. Layton, *Didymus the Blind*, 166 n1.

52. Ibid., 160.

53. Ibid., 26–27.

54. Ibid., 26, following Young, *Biblical Exegesis*, 76–96.

55. Layton, *Didymus the Blind*, 27–28.

56. Mühlenberg, *Apollinaris von Laodicea*, Fr. 4; Layton, *Didymus the Blind*, 27.

In his early work *On the Holy Spirit*, from c. 360 to 365,[57] Didymus characterizes the church's life after the sending of the promised Holy Spirit in terms of Paul's letter-spirit distinction. In a long unit on John 16:12–15 (*Spir.* 146–74), Didymus writes that, when Jesus said that he had many more things to tell the disciples that they could not yet bear (Jn 16:12), it was because they were still "serving a shadow and copies" (Heb 8.5) and a type of the law, unable to look on the truth and "to bear the weight of spiritual things." But when the Spirit came to guide the disciples into all truth (Jn 16:13), it conveyed believers "from the death of the letter to the Spirit that gives life (see 2 Cor 3:6)," for in the Spirit alone resides "all the truth of Scripture" (*Spir.* 150). Near the end of the work, Didymus gives an account of the various meanings of the word "spirit," much as Athanasius had done, only with a richer understanding of the spirit as the meaning of scripture. The sixth and most important meaning of the term, Didymus says, is "the deeper and mystical sense in the Holy Scriptures," as stated in 2 Corinthians 3:6. Didymus then describes what he takes Paul to mean: "The letter is the simple and obvious narrative in accordance with the historical sense," while "the spirit gives knowledge of what is holy and spiritual in the text read." Christians are the true circumcision because they "serve the Lord in the spirit and place no trust in the flesh" (Phil 3:3; *Spir.* 249). They circumcise their hearts through the Spirit, making them Jews in secret (Rom 2:29) and true Israelites without guile (Jn 1:47). They "pass beyond the shadows and images of the Old Testament (see Heb 8:5)" and are true worshippers, and they "adore the Father in spirit and in truth" (Jn 4:24) because they "have passed beyond all bodily and lowly realities" and "have left behind the types, shadows, and copies, and come to the substance of Truth itself." They have, in fine, "scorned the lowly and bodily simplicity of words … and attained knowledge of the spiritual law (Rom 7:14)" (*Spir.* 250). Other sections of 2 Corinthians 3 appear as well.[58]

Nearer the end of Didymus's career, the *Commentary on Zechariah* (c. 388), which Didymus wrote at the request of Jerome, shows the full extent to which Origenist spiritual exegesis informed Didymus's work. With its strong apocalyptic themes and obvious Christian prophecies, the book of Zechariah

57. Didymus the Blind, *On the Holy Spirit*, ed. Louis Doutreleau, SC 386, trans. DelCogliano, Radde-Gallwitz, and Ayres, PPS 43, 42.

58. See 2 Cor 3:15 as an example of when Moses is named in place of the law (*Spir.* 225); 2 Cor 3:17 as a verse where the Son is called "spirit," as Athanasius also interpreted the verse (*Spir.* 236, 252).

offers an ideal case for the development of spiritual interpretation.[59] Examples are numerous and run throughout the commentary. We can appreciate the centrality of spiritual exegesis to Didymus's work by the way in which he defines the progress and end of the Christian life in terms of the letter-spirit idea. A particularly telling statement comes in Didymus's comment on Zechariah 13:1: "On that day every place will be open in the house of David and the inhabitants of Jerusalem for transformation and aspersion." The place opened to the house of David, Didymus says, is the divinely inspired scripture itself, especially the Old Testament, and the place opened to Jerusalem is the Jerusalem on high and the "heavenly city of the living God" (Gal 4:26).[60] The opening of these places involves "a transformation from the letter to the spirit (2 Cor 3:6) and from the shadow to the reality (Heb 10:1)," a change that occurs as well "from the temporal to the eternal and from the visible and earthly to the lofty and invisible" as a result of the sprinkling of the savior's blood (see 1 Pt 1:2, *CZech* 4.280).[61]

In several passages Didymus coordinates Paul's letter-spirit idea with his own Christological program. For example, Didymus argues that Christ is Lord specifically of those who are Jews beneath the surface, in spirit but not in the letter (2 Cor 3:6), circumcised not in the flesh but in the heart (Rom 2:29; *CZech* 3.56, on Zec 8:23).[62] Similarly, God's commands "under the law of the Spirit" (Rom 8:2) are faithful and unchangeable, whereas those "under the shadow of the law" are subject to being "changed from letter to spirit and from shadow to reality" (*CZech* 1.243, on Zec 3:8–9).[63] Again, the spiritual interpretation of scripture corresponds with the mission of Christianity throughout

59. Robert Hill describes Didymus's exegesis in the *CZech* as kaleidoscopic, by contrast with the more focused approach of the Antiochenes; Didymus the Blind, *Commentary on Zechariah*, trans. Robert C. Hill, Fathers of the Church 111 (Washington, D.C.: The Catholic University of America Press, 2006), 12.

60. See also *CZech* 1.342 (1.374 SC; §4, FC 99): the "spiritual law" (Rom 7:14) is "the mystical understanding of the inspired Scriptures" that is indicated by the "sons of plenty" (Zec 4:11–14), and by the "living water that will come out from Jerusalem" (Zec 14:8–9a)—which Didymus calls an anagogical rather than a physical interpretation (*CZech* 5.82 [3.1014 SC; §14, FC 332–33]).

61. 3.948 SC; §13, FC 307. See also *CZech* 3.301: after fleeing from Egypt and Assyria, the Israelites/true fathers God leads "into Gilead and Lebanon," and 266 (3.774 SC; §10, FC 246–47): Christians have passed from sin to righteousness, "from elements of instruction to further advancement," and "from the shadow of the law to its reality by those who bypass the death-dealing letter and reach the life-giving Spirit (2 Cor 3:6)."

62. 2.644 SC; §8, FC 198.

63. 1.318 SC; §3, FC 77, Hill trans. adapt.

the world. Now that true worship has spread to the whole world, the life-giving Spirit enables one to read the Old Testament no longer "in letter and shadow" (2 Cor 3:6; Heb 10:1) and "in a veiled fashion" (2 Cor 3:14–15). By the Holy Spirit one can now pray, "Unveil my eyes, and I shall understand your marvels from your Law" (Ps 118:18 LXX), with the full meaning of scripture clarified. In this way the nations will be brought into "the mystical and spiritual courts of Jesus" to hear and understand the scriptures, unlike the outsiders whom Jesus said could not understand his teachings (Mt 13:11). At that time God will dwell in Jerusalem and the Temple be filled with his glory (*CZech* 2.299).[64]

Although Didymus does not systematically present his hermeneutical theory or his ascetical and dogmatic theology, through a rich practice of Origenist spiritual exegesis,[65] he communicates Christian doctrine and practice by interpreting biblical narratives in such a way that they produce a spiritual journey toward union with the divine life.[66] While the literal sense of scripture is necessary and requires its own disciplined labor,[67] it is the spiritual meaning that ultimately yields the knowledge of Christ and the spiritual transformation that accompanies it, just as in Origen's case. For Didymus the Holy Spirit makes the letter of scripture what Hugues Agbenuti calls "an occasion for an encounter between God and the human" and "a means for progressing in the knowledge and communion of the divine" within the context of the paschal mystery.[68]

Basil of Caesarea

The full extent of the Cappadocians' knowledge of Didymus is unclear.[69] All four theologians studied the work of Origen, and each reflects Origen's hermeneutics to a significant degree, albeit in different ways. Modern scholar-

64. 2.572 SC; §8, FC 171.

65. Simonetti notes the Origenist "gusto" of the *Commentary on Zechariah*; Simonetti, "Lettera e allegoria," 350; trans. Hill, 111, FC 15n47.

66. Layton, *Didymus the Blind*, 161.

67. In his edition of the *CZech*, Doutreleau defends Didymus's attention to the literal sense, against presumed critique that he is allegorizing the scriptures without a proper connection to the literal text (1.53 SC).

68. Hugues Agbenuti, *Didyme d'Alexandrie: Sense profond des Écritures et pneumatologie*. Cahiers de Biblia Patristica 11 (Strasbourg: Université de Strasbourg, 2011), 323.

69. Mark DelCogliano has recently argued that Basil drew on Didymus's *De Spiritu Sancto* for his own work on the Spirit, rather than on Athanasius, as has often been assumed; DelCogliano, "Basil of

ship has not painted a uniform picture of Basil's hermeneutics. Long associated with Gregory Nazianzen as an editor of the *Philokalia* of Origen's writings, Basil regards moral growth as necessary for the interpretation of the deeper meanings of scripture (*Adul.* 2.6), much as Origen did, although his view of this growth gives less place to the work of the Holy Spirit and relies more on philosophically informed ethics (*Ep.* 2) and a fairly direct application of the Bible to Christian behavior.[70] Although he did practice spiritual exegesis in the tradition of Origen, on the whole Basil preferred a moral to a spiritual or mystical interpretation, and he often favored straightforward interpretation over too-frequent allegory.[71] In his late *Hexaemeron* Basil advocated for the simple (ἁπλοῦς), literal sense of the text over allegory (*Hex.* 2.5; 9.1), following the common use of the words (*Hex.* 8.3).[72] Yet in many passages in his *Homilies* on the Psalms written before the *Hexaemeron*, Basil undertakes spiritual exegesis in ways that are similar to Origen's exegesis, for example, referring the psalms to Christ, the Holy Spirit, the Christian way of life, the soul, and the church,[73] although he employs the explicit language of spirit and letter only once.[74] Basil's shift of tone from the *Homilies* to the *Hexaemeron* requires further explanation, and his correspondence with Diodore of Tarsus, the founder of the Antiochene school of exegesis, which strongly opposed Origenist allegory, cannot be ruled out.[75]

If we consider his corpus as a whole, it is evident that Basil employs the letter-spirit idea with seriousness, although to a lesser extent than either of the two Gregories. In Basil's earliest work, the *Contra Eunomium*, the themes of Paul's argument appear only slightly. One likely reason is that Eunomius has not made the terms central to his own argument, to which Basil is respond-

Caesarea, Didymus the Blind, and the Anti-Pneumatomachian Exegesis of Amos 4:13 and John 1:3," *Journal of Theological Studies* n.s. 61, no. 2 (2010): 644–58.

70. Philip Rousseau, *Basil of Caesarea*, Transformation of the Classical Heritage 20 (Berkeley: University of California Press, 1994), 51–52, 80–81.

71. Simonetti, *Biblical Interpretation*, 64–65.

72. Rousseau, *Basil of Caesarea*, 323.

73. Richard Lim, "The Politics of Interpretation in Basil's 'Hexaemeron,'" *Vigiliae Christianae* 44 (1990): 351–70; and Hildebrand, *Trinitarian Theology of Basil of Caesarea*, 127–33.

74. Basil of Caesarea, *Hom. Ps.* 32 (PG 29.328.19 = *Hom.* 15 in FC 46, at 230), quoting from Rom 7:6 to comment on Ps 32:3 (the reference is not cited as such in the English translation).

75. Hildebrand's argument that Basil's exegesis "remained basically the same" (*Basil of Caesarea*, 138), i.e., a form of spiritual interpretation, is partly correct, in that the *Hexaemeron* does contain some figural readings; however, it minimizes the recognizable differences between that text and Basil's earlier exegesis.

ing.[76] Nevertheless, Basil briefly argues, in defense of the Son's divinity, that it should be evident that it was the Only-Begotten who declared himself to Moses as "He who is" (Ex 3:14) to anyone who does not "have the veil of the Jews on his heart 'when he reads Moses' (2 Cor 3:15)" (*Eun.* 2.17). Basil also cites 2 Corinthians 3:17, "The Lord is the Spirit," to argue that the Holy Spirit is not a creature (*Eun.* 3.3), as Athanasius and Didymus had done, although this citation does not bear on hermeneutical questions. Otherwise, themes of spiritual exegesis appear little in the work.

Yet by the mid-370s Paul's hermeneutical argument has gained in Basil's attention. In *On Baptism* (c. 372–75), in the course of outlining what it means to have new life in Christ, Basil identifies Paul's term "letter" with the law and "spirit" with the Christian gospel and the doctrine of Christ in general. Thus he reads Paul in connection with John, arguing that by "spirit" Paul means "the Lord's doctrine, for the Lord himself said: 'My words are spirit and life' (Jn 6:64)," another verse commonly associated with the Pauline texts on letter and spirit in Origenist tradition. Likewise the Christian life involves moving away "from all sin and also from justice according to the law." Christians must serve God "in newness of spirit and not in the oldness of the letter" (see Rom 7:6), and for this reason Paul repudiates Christians who still seek justice according to the law and other human traditions. (*Bap.* 1.2.19).[77] In addition to these programmatic statements, Basil appeals to 2 Corinthians 3 to note that the glory of Moses has been superseded by the superior glory of the new covenant (2 Cor 3:10, *Bap.* 1.2.5) and to mount a defense of biblical authority, so that Christians must obey "every word that proceeds from the mouth of God (Dt 8:3)" in scripture (*Bap.* 2.4).

In *On the Holy Spirit*, from roughly the same period (375), Basil uses Paul's terms with similar force. While the work deals mainly with the glorification of the Holy Spirit in the doxology and with the Spirit's uncreated status, hermeneutical themes appear in significant ways. Basil argues that the scriptures call the Spirit "Lord" in 2 Corinthians 3:17–18, likening the Pneumatomachians' doctrine to Jewish interpretations through a veil. He then comments that the letter of the Old Testament, which is "the bodily observance of the law," ceas-

76. There is no mention of Rom 2 or 7; Gal 3; 1 Cor 15:45. Jn 6:63 is noted only for the title "Spirit that gives life" (*Eun.* 3.6).

77. Elsewhere Basil associates 2 Cor 3:6 with Rom 7:6 and Jn 6:63 (*Bap.* 1.2.13f).

es with the coming of Christ, after which "the types [the prophets] are to be exchanged for the truth," just as lamps are no longer needed in the presence of the sun. The "spirit" of scripture, which is the truth of Christ, thus involves looking into "the depths of the meaning of the law, and passing through the obscurity of the letter as through a veil, so to enter the mysteries," just as Moses himself did. By turning to the Lord, the Spirit (2 Cor 3:18), in this way, one will attain spiritual vision and become similar to Moses (*Spir.* 21.52). The respective glories of the covenants (2 Cor 3:8–9) figure as well, as does Paul's statement that with the Spirit there is freedom (2 Cor 3:17; *Spir.* 24.55).

Although they are few in number, these passages reveal the seriousness with which Basil considered these Pauline themes. Nonhermeneutical references to 2 Corinthians 3 and Romans 2:29 appear briefly in *On Faith* (Basil's preface to the *Morals*)[78] and the *Morals*.[79] Basil is interested in both the purely hermeneutical and the law-gospel dimension of the letter-spirit idea. The odd exception in his later thematic works is the *Hexaemeron*. Yet we may also note that the language of the spirit and the letter and related Pauline verses figures little in Basil's actual preaching. In sum, Origen's notion of the letter and the spirit of scripture was important in some, but not all, of Basil's theological and ascetical works, but it was a less central or pervasive theme than it was for either Gregory.[80]

Gregory of Nazianzus

By contrast with Basil's occasional use of Origenist spiritual exegesis, both Gregories make extensive mention of the spirit and the letter of scripture. Of the three Cappadocians, Gregory Nazianzen is the most explicitly reflective on the process and the language of spiritual exegesis. The notion of the spirit versus the letter of scripture frames much of Gregory's doctrinal and herme-

78. Dated 365–72; Paul J. Fedwick, "A Chronology of the Life and Work of Basil of Caesarea," In *Basil of Caesarea, Christian, Humanist, Ascetic: A Sixteen-Hundredth Anniversary Symposium*, 1:1–19, ed. Paul J. Fedwick (Toronto: Pontifical Institute of Mediaeval Studies, 1981). Basil quotes 2 Cor 3:5–6 to justify his confidence in sending a profession of faith as requested (*De fide* 1; prol. 8).

79. *Reg. mor.* 43, cap. 1 (PG31.761.47, FC 120) quotes Rom 2:28–29 in full. *Reg. mor.* 23, cap. 1 (PG 31.741.46, FC 104–5), on Rom 7:14–20, concentrates on the persistence of human sin rather than on the spiritual nature of the law.

80. If we were to include Amphilochius, as well, we would find a single passage where he makes theological use of the terms of 2 Cor 3:6 (*Or.* 6.42–44, Datema).

neutical project, involving topics that range from hermeneutics and theological method to Christology, pneumatology, and pastoral theory, thus showing a breadth like that of Didymus, only in a more comprehensive and systematic form. Like Didymus, Gregory received high praise from Jerome for his exegetical abilities. Despite the fact that some have considered Gregory's exegesis uninteresting (or inaccessible), presumably because he did not produce discrete biblical homilies and commentaries like his two colleagues, recent scholarship has shown that Gregory's use of the Bible in his carefully crafted rhetoric is, in fact, quite deliberate, consistent, and sophisticated.[81]

Paul's letter-spirit distinction informs Gregory's treatment of biblical interpretation and theological method in several major passages that focus on the figure of Moses. In Gregory's paradigmatic description of Moses' ascent up Mount Sinai to receive the law in the second *Theological Oration* (Ex 19–24; *Or.* 28.2–3), Gregory himself figuratively ascends the mount in the persona of Moses in order to demonstrate for his hearers the nature of Christian doctrine and the knowledge of God. Gregory comments that the law given to Moses, and by extension the Old Testament as a whole, has a dual nature: it is engraved on both sides of the tablets, "because the law has an obvious and a hidden aspect." In the imagery of the Exodus passage, the obvious meaning is for the crowd below, while the hidden meaning is for the few who ascend the mount (*Or.* 28.2).[82] The clearer level of meaning is available to a wide variety of hearers, while the deeper levels of meaning are accessible only to those who are purified and are being transformed into God's being and likeness. Gregory applies this distinction to the Christian gospel and his own doctrine, as well. Like the Mosaic law, Gregory's teaching in the *Theological Orations* is engraved on both sides of the "stone tablets" of his oral and written orations. The Christian gospel, too, stands either as "the law of the letter" or "the law of the Spirit," depending on one's spiritual condition (*Or.* 28.3).

Gregory then takes the further step of elucidating how the letter-spirit dy-

81. See Christopher A. Beeley, *Gregory of Nazianzus on the Trinity and the Knowledge of God: In Your Light We Shall See Light*, Oxford Studies in Historical Theology (New York: Oxford University Press, 2008), and Ben Fulford, *Divine Eloquence and Human Transformation: Rethinking and History through Gregory of Nazianzus and Hans Frei*, Emerging Scholars (Minneapolis: Fortress, 2013).

82. See also *Or.* 2.29: Moses received the tables that are of the letter for the multitude, but of the spirit for those above the many; *Or.* 43.72: "Moses ... legislated the double law, the outward law of the letter as well as an inward law of the Spirit"; and *Or.* 20.2.

namic holds implications for the knowledge of God. One approaches the divine nature, which transcends bodily knowledge and the reach of sinful existence, by moving from the letter to the spirit of scripture through a process of purification and illumination. According to the spirit, one comes to understand that we can see God only to the extent that God reaches down to us and that the divine nature can never be fully grasped, as the Eunomians believed it could (*Or.* 28.3).[83] By grace alone God is seen by human beings in the mount of divine knowledge because God has descended from on high to draw us up to himself, "so that the incomprehensible may be in some degree, and as far as is safe, comprehended by a mortal nature" (*Or.* 45.11). In addition to the letter-spirit idea, this key passage in the second *Theological Oration* and others like it have the additional resonance that Gregory is seeking to confirm his own authority as a theological teacher, much as Paul does in 2 Corinthians 3.

In a second major application of the idea, Gregory applies the Spirit's precedence over the letter of scripture to the incarnation of Christ, again echoing a related theme in 2 Corinthians 3: Paul's connection of the lifting of Moses' veil with what it means to be "in Christ" (2 Cor 3:14). In a festal sermon for the Epiphany, Gregory proclaims that, in the incarnation, "the letter gives way and the Spirit comes to the fore. The shadows flee away, the Truth comes in upon them (Heb 10:1)" (*Or.* 38.2), so that Christ fulfills and is the end of the spiritual Law (Rom 7:14; *Or.* 2.23). Moreover, Gregory argues that orthodox Christology itself is the direct result of the spiritual interpretation of scripture. In the rule of Christological exegesis that Gregory gives near the end of the third *Theological Oration*, he characterizes the Eunomians as being tripped up by the letter of scripture (*Or.* 29.18). By contrast, the spiritual interpretation of the scriptures about Christ recognizes that all biblical statements about Jesus are real and true descriptions of him and should not be rationalized away in one fashion or another, either by assuming that the lowly statements are in conflict with the lofty ones (Eunomius) or by dividing both sets of statements between two different referents (Diodore). Instead, the orthodox interpretation of Christ refers the lofty statements to the divine Son of God pure and simple, whether apart from the economy or in his involvement with it, and the lowly statements to the same divine Son of God in his created, human form in the economy (*Or.* 29.18). By taking the *communicatio idiomatum* of

83. See Beeley, *Gregory of Nazianzus*, 90.

scripture at face value Gregory demonstrates how the "spirit" of scripture derives from the "letter" and does not subvert or circumvent it. In this way the orthodox doctrine of Christ is the direct result of spiritual exegesis. The aim and result of the spiritual interpretation of Christ is that the interpreter will ascend with Christ to God by passing through the lowly and the lofty titles of the same, one Lord: "to ascend from below to become God" through the divine names of Christ given in scripture (*Or.* 30.21). This spiritual-exegetical ascent is for Gregory the pinnacle of all biblical interpretation according to the spirit (*Or.* 2.97–98), and it makes Christ's life, death, and resurrection a pattern for imitation, though not an exact resemblance (*Or.* 40.30).[84]

Similarly, Gregory believes that the orthodox doctrine of the Holy Spirit is likewise the product of interpreting the scriptures about the Spirit "according to the Spirit." Gregory charges the Pneumatomachians with denying the Spirit's divinity out of their love for the letter of scripture alone (*Or.* 31.3), whereas, if one looks beneath the letter of scripture into its inner meaning, the Spirit's divinity is plainly demonstrated throughout (*Or.* 31.21). The inner spiritual meaning of the biblical teaching about the Holy Spirit is the Spirit's direct witness to its own divinity in the Christian experience of baptismal deification (*Or.* 31.28/29).[85]

Finally, Gregory appeals to 2 Corinthians 3 to speak of the pastoral ministry of the church. In his first oration Gregory tells the church of Nazianzus that Christ has given them a pastor whose sermons the Holy Spirit will engrave in their hearts "not with ink, but with grace" (see 2 Cor 3:3; *Or.* 1.6). He then describes the appropriate condition of the Christian priest in terms of Origenist spiritual exegesis and ascent (*Or.* 2.94–99), again pointing to the example of Moses (*Or.* 2.92–93). And the sort of biblical reading that is necessary to bring about the spiritual transformation required of a priest is the one in which the believer "escapes from the oldness of the letter and serves the newness of the spirit (2 Cor 3:6)" by cleaving to the truth that biblical figures signify. In this way the true pastor moves from the law to grace (*Or.* 2.96–97),[86] a transfor-

84. See also *Or.* 38.4, 18.

85. See Beeley, *Gregory of Nazianzus*, 174–80.

86. A crescendo of several Pauline motifs: thus one attains the mind of Christ (1 Cor 2:16) and is admitted to the secret treasures that are normally hidden, "comparing spiritual things with spiritual" (1 Cor 2:13), and one becomes a temple of God (2 Cor 2:16) and the dwelling place of Christ in the Spirit (Eph 2:22). This transformation enables one to "speak the hidden wisdom of God in a mystery" (1 Cor 2:17) like Paul (*Or.* 2.99).

mation that, again, centers on the contemplation of the names and powers of Christ (*Or.* 2.98). In his memorial oration for his former friend, Gregory describes Basil in glowing spiritual-exegetical terms (*Or.* 43.65), offering a characterization that reflects Gregory's own stance more than Basil's, as we have seen.[87]

Gregory Nazianzen's application of Paul's letter-spirit distinction informs his hermeneutical and theological system throughout, much as it did for Origen and Didymus. In sum, the spiritual interpretation of scripture yields the theology of the Trinity and the spiritual growth that is meant to accompany it. In Gregory's usage, the letter-spirit idea combines the hermeneutical principle of obvious versus hidden meanings with that of the law versus the gospel so that, in light of the gospel of Christ, Christians are able to perceive the true meaning of the law beyond its mere literal significance, which on its own can only kill, and by the Spirit they come to know the divine life of God, Christ, and the Holy Spirit.

Gregory of Nyssa

Gregory of Nyssa's reputation as a biblical interpreter is, in a sense, the reverse of his brother Basil's. If Basil is known for his suspicion of allegorical exegesis in the late *Hexaemeron*, Gregory is even more famous for the sweeping allegorical interpretation of his *Homilies on the Song of Songs*, which directly carries forward a tradition of commentary stemming from Origen. Yet, despite their similarities, Gregory's practice of spiritual exegesis differs in noticeable ways from Origen's. With reference to Gregory's early treatise *On the Inscriptions of the Psalms* (pre-379),[88] Marie-Joseph Rondeau draws attention to the way in which Gregory regards the single aim (σκόπος) of the psalter to be the believer's ascent to beatitude through growth in virtue, a theme not unknown to Origen, even if Gregory gives it a special emphasis. Ronald Heine has since shown that, in this and other respects, Gregory was influenced not only by Origen, but equally by the neo-Platonist exegete Iamblichus, who places a strong

87. See Beeley, *Gregory of Nazianzus*, 260–61.

88. Gregory of Nyssa, *On the Inscriptions of the Psalms*, ed. J. A. McDonough, *Gregorii Nysseni Opera* 5.24–175 (Leiden: Brill, 1986); *Gregory of Nyssa's Treatise on the Inscriptions of the Psalms*, intro., trans., and notes by Ronald E. Heine, Oxford Early Christian Studies (Oxford: Clarendon, 1995), 11.

emphasis on the aim and sequence (ἀκολουθία) of texts.[89] For all his allegorizing of the Song, Gregory makes less frequent use of Paul's letter-spirit idea in his biblical interpretation than Didymus or Gregory Nazianzen did. In her major study of Gregory's exegesis, Mariette Canévet notes that Gregory makes more use of 2 Corinthians than he does of Romans and 1 Corinthians and that 2 Corinthians 3:6 is among the most cited portions of the letter, along with the images of removing the veil of the flesh and the mirror of the soul (2 Cor 3:16, 18).[90] Yet, whereas Didymus and Gregory Nazianzen employ the letter-spirit idea for a wide range of dogmatic and ascetical purposes, Gregory of Nyssa focuses more exclusively on hermeneutical matters pertaining to anagogical and allegorical interpretation and a select number of dogmatic themes.[91]

In the early *Against Eunomius* Gregory applies the letter-spirit idea exclusively to hermeneutical and linguistic matters. In opposition to Eunomian exegesis, he argues that the scriptures contain the message of the Holy Spirit and are of benefit to humankind (2 Tm 3:16) only if one perceives the deeper meaning of the text beneath its superficial form: "the divine intention is hidden under the surface of the text," like a screen concealing the real meaning (*Eun.* 3.5.162–64). This deeper meaning is the "spirit" of scripture in Paul's terms. For Gregory, the spirit of scripture chiefly has a moral-ascetical focus: it contains "rules for the perfection of virtue [that takes place] through the total escape of human beings from passions." Gregory adds that this higher (or deeper) kind of meaning Paul calls its "sovereign" or "lordly" (*kurios*) meaning (2 Cor 3:16–17), so that one must avoid slavery to the letter and follow the lordship of the Spirit (2 Cor 3:18; *Eun.* 3.5.164).

The problem that Gregory has in view is that some of the historical narratives and commandments (mainly in the Old Testament) are less than exemplary: they convey "incongruous things" that "concur with the natural passions" (*Eun.* 3.5.163). The historical sense of the text and even certain divine commandments represent the "bodily" aspect of scripture, and those who focus on that aspect have a veil over their hearts (2 Cor 3:18). They are "unable to see through to the glory of the spiritual law," whereas, "for those who turn

89. Heine, *Gregory of Nyssa's Treatise*, 29–49, building on the work of Rondeau, Alain Le Boulluec, and Jean Daniélou.

90. Mariette Canévet, *Grégoire de Nysse et l'herméneutique biblique: Étude des rapports entre le langage et la connaissance de Dieu* (Paris: Études augustiniennes, 1983), 198.

91. Ibid., 199.

their thoughts to what is intelligible, … the glory inhering in the letter is exposed to view." For Gregory, "the letter that kills" is the morally questionable quality of the historical and moral sense of the Old Testament (2 Cor 3:6, *Eun.* 3.5.162). The biblical narrative, certain commands, and even the words themselves are therefore distracting, and those who concentrate on them are reading with a veil over their understanding. Yet the problem does not apply to the Old Testament alone; even Jesus' words "are Spirit and Life" (Jn 6:63) only when they are stripped of their bodily veil (*Eun.* 3.5.165). Gregory of Nyssa's hermeneutical approach focuses not on the relation between law and gospel or the fulfillment of the covenants in Christ, but rather on the nature of language itself in comparison with God's nature and way of communicating. The idea that God could speak in human sentences or "spell out his thoughts in sound and speech" Gregory calls "Jewish opinion" through which "the letter kills" (*Eun.* 2.282–83). To illustrate his point Gregory observes that words and naming are mentioned in Genesis 1:11–12 before rational man had yet been created, from whom actual human speech comes (*Eun.* 2.196). As an example of avoiding Eunomian slavery to the letter, Gregory offers the Christological meaning of Proverbs 8:22, which, he says, cannot refer to Wisdom's eternal generation but must refer to the incarnation (*Eun.* 3.1.21–22), an economic interpretation that Origen, Alexander, and Eusebius had avoided because it stretches any claim to faithfulness to the literal text, but which by this time has become commonplace among pro-Nicene theologians.

Near the end of his career Gregory of Nyssa gave a famous allegorical interpretation of the Song of Songs (post-391), in which he further articulates his method of biblical interpretation in largely Origenist terms. At this point, several years after the Theodosian settlement and the victory of the Antiochene faction at the council of 381,[92] Gregory addresses certain ecclesiastics who are defending the letter of scripture against undue allegorizing in what appears to be Antiochene fashion (*HomSg*, pref. 4).

In order to interpret as Christian scripture the marriage song, with all of its vivid sexual imagery, it is imperative, Gregory says, to "cleanse the text of its obvious literal sense" by purifying the interpreter of all indecent or passionate thoughts. Only in this way, he says, can one gaze on undefiled Beauty (*HomSg*, pref. 4). In his account Gregory identifies a number of Pauline state-

92. See Beeley, *Unity of Christ*, 198–99.

ments about exegetical method,[93] arguing that they all refer to a single form of instruction—namely, the method of spiritual exegesis summarized in the saying "the letter kills, but the spirit gives life" (2 Cor 3:6).[94] Since the letter is sometimes positively unhelpful, the interpreter must move beyond the letter to "an understanding that concerns the immaterial and intelligible" (*HomSg*, pref. 7), noting that the useful, spiritual sense of scripture includes the literal sense whenever it contains something useful already (*HomSg*, pref. 5). The discernment of higher meanings Gregory also calls "philosophy" (*HomSg*, pref. 4, 11), which he likens to the preparation of raw grain for human consumption. The letter alone is like unprepared grain, which is food for animals; but the spiritual meaning is a careful preparation by "a properly subtle and discerning inquiry." Again, spiritual interpretation is like the winnowing fork that clears the threshing floor of the grain while the chaff is blown away (*HomSg*, pref. 12). Interpreters like Paul thus "grind up the divine mysteries" like teeth, to make them edible for the church (*HomSg* 7.226).[95] This "spiritual" method of reading justifies the anagogical, tropological, or allegorical method (the terms do not matter) that Gregory proposes to offer in his homilies. It applies to the New Testament as well as the Old, since Jesus too speaks in parables, dark sayings, and aphorisms, and the New Testament contains plenty of figurative images, such as bread from heaven (Jn 6:50–51) and the stone that the builders rejected (Mk 12:10). In a rare Christological connection, Gregory notes that the incarnation itself is "the unveiling of the hidden thoughts contained in the law" (*HomSg*, pref. 7–8). In the fifth *Homily*, we read that spiritual interpretation produces "the exalted gospel," which surpasses "the shadowy teaching that comes through types and symbols" (*HomSg* 5.161), much as Origen had taught. And, giving some attention to the notion of law versus gospel, Gregory adds that the Christian gospel involves the rejection of the corporeal observance of the law, which must be transposed to the spiritual and intelligible plain. In this sense the gospel itself is spiritual, while the law is of the earth (*HomSg* 5.162–63).

This approach is borne out as well in Gregory's *Life of Moses*, even though

93. E.g., that the Old Testament was "written for our sakes" (1 Cor 9:9–10); Paul's varying manner of speech (Gal 4:20); his use of the terms "allegory," "types" (Gal 4:24; 1 Cor 10:11), "mirror," and "enigma" (1 Cor 13:12), and the removing of a veil (2 Cor 3:16) (pref. 5, 7).

94. Here Gregory also cites Rom 7:14, that "the law is spiritual."

95. With reference to Origen, *HomEx.* 10.4, on Ex 21:23.

he does not employ the language of spirit and letter to any noticeable extent. In a pair of allegorical interpretations, Gregory compares God's inscription of the tablets with his finger to the creation of the soul (*Mos.* II.215) and the incarnation (*Mos.* II.216). In keeping with his usual themes, the upshot of the work is that one should "have but one purpose in life: to be called servants of God by virtue of the lives we live" (*Mos.* II.315), and "to carve in our own heart the divine oracles which you receive from God" (*Mos.* II.316).[96]

With a few exceptions, Gregory of Nyssa applies the letter-spirit idea either to the Christian pursuit of virtue or to a set of ontological and linguistic themes concerning divine darkness and unknowability, the limitation of language, the scale of beings, and epectasy.[97] Gregory's allegorical exegesis serves to map biblical language onto an ontological-linguistic paradigm and an ethical program that are more independent and self-contained that what we find in either Basil or Gregory Nazianzen.[98] By virtue of his popularity in the twentieth century, many have had the impression that most fourth-century theologians employed Paul's letter-spirit idea to make similar allegorical assignments, when in fact Gregory's exegesis was fairly idiosyncratic.[99]

Conclusion

From this survey of major figures, it is evident that Origen's programmatic use of the letter-spirit distinction from 2 Corinthians 3:6 not only formed a major part of late fourth-century Greek theology and hermeneutics, but that it did so in a variety of ways. To begin with the negative cases, the opposition to Origenist hermeneutics—and consequently to several key Pauline ideas—by Athanasius and Epiphanius (and several Antiochene theologians) stands out in hindsight as exceptional to broader currents in catholic theology. Taken

96. See also Gregory of Nyssa, *HomSg.* 14.414.

97. Canévet, *Grégoire de Nysse*, 249–65.

98. Canévet faults Gregory of Nyssa for opting instead for a confirmation of the necessity of allegorical exegesis because "the teaching of scripture is hidden, following Origen, substituting for the historical judgment of Paul his own theory of language (Ibid., 199).

99. E.g., Margaret Mitchell takes Gregory of Nyssa's use of 2 Cor 3:6 in the prologue to Gregory's Song homilies as the paradigmatic/exemplary early Christian use of Paul; Mitchell, *Paul, the Corinthians*, 1–4 and passim. On Gregory's unique theological viewpoint, by contrast with Origen's, see also Morwenna Ludlow, "Theology and Allegory: Origen and Gregory of Nyssa on the Unity and Diversity of Scripture," *International Journal of Systematic Theology* 4, no. 1 (2002): 45–66.

together, the anti-Origenist contingent makes for one of the most significant countercurrents in fourth-century theology and one that corresponds in some respects with the course of other theological developments, particularly the emerging Christological controversy that will come to a head in the dispute between Diodore, Apollinarius, and Gregory Nazianzen by the 370s.

Positively speaking, Origenist spiritual exegesis is a central and formative element in the theological and ascetical work of its two most devoted fourth-century adherents, Didymus and Gregory Nazianzen. In Didymus's case, Origen's hermeneutics essentially is the program, whereas for Gregory, it contributes significantly to a theological system of more advanced design—much of which, as it happens, will set the terms for orthodoxy in later generations of Eastern theology. If Didymus most directly and accurately repeats Origen's original project, it was Gregory who gave it its most systematic and wide-ranging application, albeit one that revised Origen's doctrine on several key points of Christology and pneumatology. Of the three Cappadocians, Basil's exegesis shows the least influence by Origen's approach. The difference is most visible in Basil's tendency to favor straightforward moral interpretation and in his straightforward identification of the letter of scripture with the Old Testament law and the spirit with the Christian gospel. By literalizing the law-gospel motif Basil foregoes the twin notions that the law itself has a spiritual meaning and that the New Testament also has a literal sense that will be fulfilled only in the eschaton. On the other hand, running against the grain of these broader tendencies, in the mid-370s Basil employs two characteristically Origenist motifs that also appear in Gregory Nazianzen, at a time when the two were still active colleagues, but that recede in Basil's late *Hexaemeron*, after his falling out with Gregory just after 375 and as Diodore becomes more influential in the Antiochene church. It is worth pondering to what extent the two Cappadocians' collaboration might have supported Basil's embracing this element of Origen's hermeneutics and whether the differences between them bear on the question of who edited the *Philokalia* of Origen's writings on biblical interpretation and the freedom of the will. Gregory of Nyssa, then, makes for a third option. For the younger Gregory, Origen's notion of the spirit and the letter of scripture for the most part reinforces Gregory's moral theology and his idiosyncratic ontological program.

Not surprisingly, the hermeneutical choices that different authors make correspond, in often complex ways with their broader doctrinal and ecclesial commitments, and it would be worth considering those relationships in greater detail. This study has made clear that Origen's understanding of the spirit and the letter of scripture influenced the development of Christian theology and spirituality in ways that extend far beyond matters of hermeneutics alone.

Mark E. Weedman

12. AUGUSTINE'S MOVE FROM A JOHANNINE TO A PAULINE TRINITARIAN THEOLOGY

My purpose in this essay is to explore the effects of Augustine's turn to Paul on his Trinitarian theology. I argue that when Augustine turned to Paul, he did so in ways that shaped his Trinitarian theology to such a degree that this might be a way of tracing the development of his Trinitarian theology as a whole. In particular, I will show that by turning to Paul, Augustine abandons a Trinitarian model that emphasizes the role of the Logos as revealer, whose appearance restores humanity's ability to see God. This is an idea that figured prominently in early Trinitarian theology, and it derived heavily from a reading of John's Gospel, especially the prologue. By the time he wrote *De Trinitate*, however, Augustine had come to a Trinitarian model that emphasized the Son as the mediator of human redemption and resurrection. This move, I will argue, corresponds with (or reflects) Augustine's turn to Paul.

I should be clear at this point that my question is not whether Augustine used exegesis of Paul (or John) to formulate his Trinitarian theology. He used both Pauline and Johannine texts early in his writing career, and he continued to do so in his more mature writings. The question for this essay is whose scheme, or whose account of what the Trinitarian event means for human-divine relations, Augustine employs. By sorting out how Augustine used the perspectives of the two biblical texts, what I am calling the Pauline and Johannine perspective, we gain a clearer sense of how Augustine exegeted various biblical passages and, more generally, how Augustine developed his encounter with Paul in his theology as a whole. Studies on Augustine and Paul have concentrated almost exclusively on how Paul shaped Augustine's theological anthropology, but the Pauline influence on Augustine's theology extended well beyond his account of human depravity. Another goal is for this argument to illustrate the reception of Paul in the early church. By reading how Augustine used Paul, we can at some point return to the Pauline texts and gain a clearer conception of how Paul's thought was perceived by fourth-century theologians and why a fourth century pro-Nicene might have turned to Paul in the first place.

I will use some key passages from Augustine's *De Trinitate* to illustrate what I will call Augustine's "Pauline Trinitarian theology." But before turning to *De Trinitate*, we have to consider the background both of Augustine's use of Paul and of his Trinitarian theology as a whole. We are greatly aided here by a series of studies of Augustine and Paul by William Babcock.[1] As Babcock shows, that Augustine would turn to Paul early in his career is not unusual, because concern for Paul was rampant among Latin theologians in the late 300s, not least—but not entirely—because of the prominent place that the Manichees gave to Pauline exegesis.[2] If *why* Augustine would be interested in Paul is relatively straightforward, however, the question of *when* Augustine first turned to Paul is somewhat less obvious. The problem is that much of our information about Augustine's early career comes from the *Confessions*, which presents us with a stylized and not necessarily historically accurate account of his early influences. If we were to judge solely from the account of his conversion in the *Confessions*, it would seem that Paul has played a decisive role in Augustine's conversion, which implies that Augustine had been deeply engaged with Paul's writings before his conversion. A survey of Augustine's writings immediately after his conversion does not bear this out, however. In fact, it is not until 394, nearly six years after his conversion (and after his ordination) that we can find Augustine working with Paul in a substantial way and in ways that correspond to his exegesis of Paul in the *Confessions*.[3]

Babcock's concern is with Augustine's theological anthropology and with

1. See especially, William Babcock, "Augustine's Interpretation of Romans, A.D. 394–396," *Augustinian Studies* 10 (1979): 55–74.

2. Ibid., 56.

3. Ibid., 60.

the ways that Augustine used Paul to support his more revolutionary ideas about the role of grace and free will in the experience of salvation. It is possible that were we to examine Augustine's use of Paul in Trinitarian contexts during this early period, we *might* come to a different conclusion about when Paul began to influence Augustine. Nevertheless, Babcock gives us a useful starting place for evaluating how Augustine adapted Pauline categories in his Trinitarian thought. If Babcock is right that Augustine's real engagement with Paul does not begin until the mid-390s, then it is in the years just prior to that time that we might establish a baseline Trinitarian theology that we can test against the later *De Trinitate* to see if Augustine's use of Paul has also affected his approach to the Trinity. The texts from this era are important because they show Augustine as he was starting to come to grips with what Trinitarian theology was all about. Augustine's early attempts at Trinitarian theology were halting and largely superficial. As Lewis Ayres has shown, however, during this period around 390, Augustine began to engage with the pro-Nicene theology of his Latin heritage. He apparently had read and thought about Latin Trinitarian theologians such as Hilary and Ambrose, and we start to see this reflected in his writing of that time.[4]

One especially interesting work of this era is Epistle 11, to Nebridius, written around 390.[5] Nebridius had written to Augustine asking why the Son had become incarnate and not the Father. Augustine wonders why Nebridius had not asked about the Holy Spirit, too, because—and this is the beginning of Augustine's answer—whatever is done by the Trinity must be regarded as being done by the Father, and by the Son, and by the Holy Spirit together. Augustine believes that this is the basis of Latin Catholic (pro-Nicene) Trinitarianism, and he asserts it here as a matter of principle: what one does, they all do.[6] Augustine follows this argument with a short philosophical discourse on the nature of substances, but it's the end of the letter that is interesting for our question. The reason the Son became incarnate, says Augustine, was because we needed training.

This is why a certain rule and standard of reasoning had first to be proved. This has been accomplished by that dispensation of the Incarnation, which is properly to be at-

4. For discussion, see Ayres, *Augustine and the Trinity*, 72–92.

5. For the dating of this epistle, see ibid., 59.

6. Augustine, Epistle 11.2; CCSL 31.

tributed to the Son, so that there proceeds from the Father Himself, as from the single principle from whom are all things, both understanding through the Son, and a certain interior and ineffable sweetness and delight in that understanding.... Therefore, although all these operations occur with the most complete union and inseparability, they nevertheless had to be proved separately, by reason of our weakness through which we have fallen from unity into multiplicity. For no-one raises another to the place where he is, without stooping somewhat to the place where the other is.[7]

This is not an entirely satisfactory answer to Nebridius's question, because it does not show *why* the Son was incarnated and not the Father or Spirit, but as an explanation of what the incarnation was for and how only one person of the Trinity could be incarnated, which is the point of the three aspects of talk of substance; there is much of interest here. Augustine's argument is that the nature of the human fall means that we are unable to see and know God, which means that God, as the incarnated Son, has to appear and show us how to have knowledge of God. In other words, it is our weakness, Augustine believes, that both requires the incarnation and that forces us to first encounter God through the apparently diverse operations of Father, Son, and Spirit.

Augustine does not refer to John's Gospel to authorize his account of the Son's visibility, although, as we will see, such a move would have been natural in late fourth-century Latin pro-Nicene Trinitarian theology. Nevertheless, Augustine is clearly explaining the Trinitarian character of the incarnation in such a way as to emphasize the Son's revelatory role. In *De Fide et Symbolo*, however, written only two or three years after Epistle 11 (c. 393), Augustine explores a similar idea with an explicit reference to the prologue of John. In his discussion of the line from the creed that refers to belief in the "only Son of God," Augustine frames the creedal confession of the Son as belief in the divine Word. The transition is, in fact, jarring. Augustine moves directly from quoting the creed to saying that "this Word however, we ought not to apprehend merely in the sense in which we think of our own words." It is not until a few lines later that we get a sense for why he has invoked the Son as *verbum*. According to Augustine,

He is also called the Word of the Father because it is through him that the Father is made known. In giving utterance to the truth we aim to disclose our thoughts to the

7. Augustine, Epistle 11.4; CCSL 31; English translation in *Saint Augustine: Letters, Volume 1 (1–82)*, Fathers of the Church 12, trans. Sr. Wilfrid Parsons, SND (Washington, D.C.: The Catholic University Press, 2010), 1:30.

hearer by words and to bring to the knowledge of another through such signs which we hold hidden away in our heart. Similarly, that Wisdom which God the Father begot is most fittingly styled His Word since it is through Him that the inner most nature of the Father is revealed to worthy souls.[8]

Augustine goes on to argue that there is great utility in calling the Son the Word. Just as humans only speak (unless we are lying!) in order to be understood, so too with God. When God begets the Word, he does so in such a way that he can make himself known in the highest way to minds that are "designed to obtain knowledge" of God.[9]

This passage famously marks the first time that Augustine ventures into Logos theology, but the significance of this move has as much to do with his Trinitarian emphasis on the Son as the revealer as it does with the formal mechanics of Logos as a theological or philosophical principle. Or, perhaps more accurately, Augustine has figured out that the exegetical basis for the traditional Latin pro-Nicene belief that the Word reveals the Father is the prologue to John. Augustine's Logos theology changes as he goes forward, and we will have occasion to observe those changes in greater detail shortly. For now, it is enough to note that Augustine's early Trinitarian theology is designed to defend the notion that the incarnate Son reveals the Father and that Augustine (eventually) recognizes that this notion has an exegetical basis in John's Gospel, especially the Prologue.[10]

Augustine's early use of John's Gospel and his emphasis on the epistemological function of the incarnation have deep roots in his Latin Trinitarian heritage; concern for John's Gospel is one of the most consistent through-themes of early Latin Trinitarian theology.[11] Augustine had access to this tradition through Hilary of Poitiers, who flourished in the late 350s and early 360s.

8. Augustine, *De Fide et Symbolo*, 3.4; CSEL 41. English translation in *Saint Augustine: Treatises on Marriage and other Subjects*, trans. Robert P. Russell, OSA, Fathers of the Church 27 (Washington, D.C.; The Catholic University of America Press, 1955), 319–20.

9. Ibid.

10. It is important to note that Augustine's emphasis on the Son's visibility remains important to his Trinitarian theology and extends beyond the themes I have identified here. See especially Michel R. Barnes, "Visible Christ and the Invisible Trinity," 329–55. Barnes shows that in Augustine's later explicit polemic against Homoian theology, which is not present in the earlier texts being discussed here, Augustine employs an exegesis of Mt 5:8 to affirm the Son's visibility—and that in doing so, he draws from his Latin predecessors, including Hilary.

11. See Mark Weedman, "Finding the Form of God in Philippians 2: Gregory of Nyssa and the Development of Pro-Nicene Exegesis," *Journal of Theological Interpretation* 2, no. 1 (2008): 23–41.

There is evidence that Augustine has already begun reading Hilary during this early period in his own development, which is significant because Hilary also gives special attention to John's Gospel in his own *De Trinitate* and so provides an important witness to the place of John in Latin pro-Nicene Trinitarian theology.[12] Interestingly, Hilary also seems to have had to learn about the importance of John's Gospel, but once he did, he quickly moved exegesis of John to the center of his theological method.[13] Indeed, the earliest strata of his pro-Nicene period, what we now have as *De Trinitate* 2–3, is almost entirely a verse-by-verse exegesis of the prologue to John and John 17. Hilary concentrates his exegesis on the "Trinitarian" implications of John's language—that is, he spends a lot of time on how the Word being both "with" God and the one "though whom all things were made" means that the Son is both equal to and distinct from the Father. However, Hilary is aware of the epistemological focus of pro-Nicene Christology, and at several key moments he describes the effect of the Incarnation in ways that anticipate Augustine—and reflect this pro-Nicene emphasis on the Son's visibility. In 3.9, for example, Hilary declares that the Son became a human "first of all, in order that he might be believed, in order that as one of ourselves he might be a witness for us concerning the things of God, and in the weakness of our human flesh might proclaim God as his Father to us frail and carnal mortals."[14] A few chapters earlier, Hilary again asserts that the "glory which the Father receives from the Son consists in this, that He must be perceived by us."[15] Outside of books 2–3, Hilary continues to refer back to John's Gospel, and even in places where he is not talking about Christ, his concern for the visibility of the Son continues to show up, as, for example, in book 5, where Hilary comments, almost in passing, that "God, in accordance with the weakness of our nature, assumed the form of a man who can be seen."[16]

12. Augustine refers to Hilary by name in *De Trinitate* 6.4, but Ayres finds at least one other allusion to Hilary in Augustine's *De Moribus*; see Ayres, *Augustine and the Trinity*, 58. One of the sub-arguments of this essay is that Augustine's appropriation of the Latin theological traditional represented by Hilary is very deep, especially in his early Trinitarian theology.

13. See Carl Beckwith, *Hilary of Poitiers on the Trinity: From De Fide to De Trinitate* (Oxford: Oxford University Press, 2008), 196.

14. Hilary of Poitiers, *De Trinitate* 3.9; CCL 62; English translation in Stephen McKenna, *Hilary of Poitiers: On the Trinity* (Washington, D.C: The Catholic University of America Press, 1954), 71.

15. Hilary of Poitiers, *De Trinitate* 3.1; CCL 62; McKenna, 75.

16. Hilary of Poitiers, *De Trinitate* 5.17; CCL 62; McKenna, 147.

To be sure, Hilary has many other concerns in *De Trinitate*, and I do not want to give the impression that his use of John and his reliance on the "revelatory" motif is the only theme in that work. I have, in fact, argued elsewhere that Hilary undergoes a "turn to Paul" of his own, eventually coming to read the Gospel of John through the lens of the Christ Hymn of Philippians 2.[17] Still, Hilary's interest in John and his insistence on the epistemological function of the Word survives even the final revision of his *De Trinitate*. Hilary wrote the prologue for that work to introduce this final revision, and he includes in it his own spiritual autobiography. Hilary describes his conversion to catholic Christianity as a journey from a pagan philosophy that was driven by his anxiety over the fate of his body; he believed in God, but he could not shake his fear that he was "destined for destruction." It was only after he read the prologue to the Gospel of John—which he quotes in full—that Hilary gained some assurance about his fate. This assurance comes in part because John's Gospel confirms some things about God the Creator that Hilary already believed. But it also comes because Hilary learns from John that it is possible "to obtain a heavenly regeneration," a theme that does appear in the Johannine text. Hilary goes on to say that he could not have come to this realization on his own, because knowledge of how God will renew creation is "beyond the range of the human mind." As a result, Hilary concludes, "the Word made flesh dwelt among us because [the mind] could not understand."[18]

We are now in a position to return to Augustine and ask how his turn to Paul changed his conception of what it means for the Son to be fully divine. We can date Augustine's turn to Paul fairly precisely. As William Babcock has shown, prior to his deep engagement with Paul, Augustine believed that it was possible to attain a linear progression toward God, and he optimistically believed that a human mind could recognize the Good and—perhaps taught by Christ—orient its will toward that Good.[19] His Trinitarian exegesis of John during this period conforms to that scheme. In these early texts, the problem is pride, and the Word was made flesh to show us how to attain humility and so progress to God. After he begins to engage with Paul seriously, however, Augustine begins to make a distinction between the human who is *sub lege* and

17. Weedman, "Finding the Form of God," 28–33.

18. Hilary of Poitiers, *De Trinitate* 1.12; CCL 62; McKenna, 13.

19. Babcock, "Augustine's Interpretation," 59.

sub gratia, and he contends that the only way to move from one state to the other is through the direct action of God.[20] Thus in the *Confessions* Augustine can attain a vision of God, but he is unable to sustain it because of the weight of his sin, and it is not until that direct action of God relieves him of that weight that he can truly convert.

We can see how this turn to Paul influences his Trinitarian theology by examining two places in *De Trinitate* where Augustine discusses the prologue of John. The first place is *De Trinitate* IV. This book, along with its second half, book XIII, gets us very close to the heart of Augustine's Trinitarian project because it's here that Augustine connects the Trinitarian economy—the Word becoming flesh—with his analysis of the human condition. And so, in IV.2, Augustine asserts that humans had to be persuaded "how much God loved us," just as we had to be shown "what sort of people we are that he loves." Just when Augustine has us primed to hear about the Word become visible so that we could learn about God, however, he makes a somewhat startling detour into Paul. He quotes 1 Corinthians 12:9 ("My grace is enough for you, strength is made perfect in weakness") and Romans 8:31 ("God showed the quality of his love for us in that Christ died for us while we were still sinners") in order to emphasize the voluntary nature of God's action in Christ—that what humanity receives in the Son is an act of grace, one that reminds us not to rely on our own strength.[21]

It is here that Augustine begins his initial exegesis of John 1:1–14. Augustine quickly makes it plain why he quoted those Pauline texts. When John says that "the light shines in the darkness," Augustine interprets "darkness" as "the foolish minds of men, blinded by depraved desires and unbelief."[22] This is what the Word became flesh to cure, but whereas before Augustine described the effects of the incarnation in terms of training or enlightenment, he now focuses exclusively on curing humans of that "darkness." Augustine now maintains that "enlightenment" is to participate in the Word, but we are incapable of that participation because of our sin, which means that the only way we could attain that participation is if the Word cleanses us from that sin. The reason the Word had to become flesh, therefore, was so that, by taking on the

20. Ibid., 61.

21. Augustine, *De Trinitate*, 4.2; CCL 50.

22. Augustine, *De Trinitate*, 4.3; CCL 50; English translation in Augustine, *The Trinity*, trans. Edmund Hill, 2nd ed. (New York: New City Press, 2012), 143.

human condition, he could make us "partakers in his divinity," which included his healing both the body *and* the soul.[23]

Augustine continues this line of thinking in *De Trinitate* XIII. Like book IV, book XIII is about the incarnation and its place in the Trinitarian economy, and as we might expect from his earlier writing, Augustine frames the book as an extended exegesis of John 1:1–14: he quotes the entire prologue at the beginning of the book, and he returns to John's text throughout his discussion. Augustine does gesture toward the epistemological dimension of John 1 here. As Lewis Ayres has shown, Augustine is especially interested in how the two parts of the prologue correspond to the two natures of Christ and how the two natures of Christ make possible (or authorize) the spiritual journey from the *scientia* (knowledge) of natural things to the *sapientia* (wisdom) of divine things.[24] Nevertheless, Augustine's exegesis of John in book XIII is driven by his reading of Paul. He authorizes his reading of John's prologue with a citation from a Pauline text, Colossians 2:1, "in whom are hidden all the treasures of wisdom and knowledge."[25] Then, as in book IV, Augustine establishes his ongoing concern for the role of the incarnation in human redemption, and in the end, both *scientia* and *sapientia* have to do with the resurrection. The presence of both *scientia* and *sapientia* in the Word does indeed give us confidence in the ability of natural things to lead us toward true wisdom. But even more importantly, Augustine believes that the purpose of the incarnation was to activate (or personify?) the faith that is necessary to purify the heart, forgive sins, and ultimately lead us to true beatitude.[26] In other words, for all of his talk about moving from knowledge to wisdom, the goal here is not epistemological enlightenment, but purification and redemption by faith.

In conclusion, I would like to make four points. The first is that it does seem likely that Augustine's Trinitarian theology was influenced by his turn to Paul. This is not surprising given the significance of that turn for Augustine, but by thinking about its influence on his Trinitarian theology we can get a better sense of how deeply that turn to Paul permeated the broader scope of his entire corpus. It may be, in fact, that in this turn we have a kind of through-theme for reading the diversity of Augustine's writings. For example, scholars have no-

23. Augustine, *De Trinitate*, 4.4; CCL 50.

24. Ayres, "The Christological Context of Augustine's De Trinitate XIII: Toward Relocating Books VIII–XV," *Augustinian Studies* 29 (1998): 111–41.

25. Augustine, *De Trinitate*, 13.24; CCL 50.

26. Augustine, *De Trinitate*, 13.25; CCL 50A.

ticed the similarities between the *Confessions* and *De Trinitate*, especially in their common reliance on neo-Platonic categories. In light of the evidence I have presented here, I would argue that the real similarity between the two works is their common soteriology—that is, their sense that the only way to participate in the divine life is by means of God's action in the Word made flesh.

Second, recognizing the Pauline turn in *De Trinitate* (and the *Confessions*) gives us a different perspective on that turn. The studies on Augustine's turn to Paul, including those I have cited here, almost always focus on his theological anthropology and his development of "grace" as a central theological category. By turning to works like *De Trinitate*, however, Augustine's stress on the resurrection comes into sharper focus. Augustine was not just interested in the effect of grace on original sin. He was also intensely interested in how the entire Christ-event made it possible to overcome the corruption of the flesh along with the will and what healing might mean for the Christian life. An opportunity to extend this line of investigation, in fact, might be to trace how Augustine's theology of the resurrection corresponds to his turn to Paul.

Third, the distinctive elements in Augustine's Trinitarian theology now seem to me to reflect his turn to Paul. This has implications for how we understand the neo-Platonic character of Augustine's Trinitarian theology, which is the most common way of evaluating Augustine's Trinitarian contribution. But I also wonder if Augustine's growing awareness of what it meant to be a pro-Nicene Trinitarian, which is something that happened to him during the course of his career, doesn't correspond to his turn to Paul, and if at least part of his Trinitarian project was to integrate the insights from his Pauline turn into Latin pro-Nicene Trinitarian theology. If so, then Augustine's true contribution to Western Trinitarian theology may well be the way that he brought together his insights about grace and the human problem with his Latin Trinitarian heritage.

Fourth, it is not clear how well Augustine has read Paul. My sense is that he has not read him particularly well, in fact, especially given recent contributions to Pauline scholarship by movements such as the New Perspective. More interesting to me, at least, is what this study suggests about how Augustine and other early Christian theologians used scripture to construct a grammar that they then used to read scripture. Paul gave Augustine the theological grammar that he used to shape his exegesis and so construct his theologies of the Trinity, the resurrection, and other major topics.

BIBLIOGRAPHY

Ancient Sources

Only translations that have been quoted are listed here.

Alexander of Alexandria. *Letter to Alexander of Byzantium* (*He philarchos*). Edited by Hans-Georg Opitz. *Athanasius Werke* 3.1.19–29. Berlin: De Gruyter, 1934–35. Translated by J. B. H. Hawkins. ANF 6:291–96.

———. *Urkunde* 4b and 14. Edited by Hans-Georg Optiz. *Athanasius Werke*, 3.1. Berlin: De Gruyter, 1934–35.

Ambrose of Milan. *De Excessu Fratris*. Edited by O. Faller. CSEL 73. Translated by J. J. McGuire. FC 22.

———. *De fide*. Edited by O. Faller. CSEL 78.

———. *De Spiritu Sancto*. Edited by O. Faller, CSEL 79. Translated by R. J. Deferrari. FC 40.35–213.

Amphilochius of Iconium. *Orations*. Edited by Cornelis Datema. CCSG 3.

Aphrahat. *Demonstrations*. Edited by R. Graffin. *Patrologia Syriaca* 1. Paris: Firmin-Didot, 1894.

Apostolic Constitutions. Edited by Marcel Metzger. SC 320, 329, 336.

The Ascension of Isaiah. Translated by Jonathan Knight. Sheffield: Sheffield Academic Press, 1995.

Asterius the Sophist. *Fragments*. Edited by Markus Vinzent. *Die theologischen Fragmente: Einleitung, kritischer Text, Übersetzung und Kommentar*. Supplements to Viviliae Christianae 20. Leiden: Brill, 1993.

———. *Homilies on the Psalms*. Edited by Marcel Richard. *Asterii Sophistae Commentariorum in Psalmos quea supersunt; accedunt aliquot homiliae anonymae*. Symboae Osloenses. Fasc. supplet. 16. Oslo: A. W. Brøgger, 1956.

Athanasius of Alexandria. *Against the Pagans*. Edited and translated by Robert W. Thomson. *Contra Gentes and De Incarnatione*. Oxford: Clarendon, 1971.

———. *Festal Letters*. PG 26.1351–1444. Syriac version edited by William Cureton. *The Fes-*

tal Letters of Saint Athanasius. London: Society for the Publication of Oriental Texts, 1848. Translated by Henry Burgess. NPNF 4.506–553.

———. *Letter to the African Bishops*. Edited by Annette von Stockhausen. *Athanasius von Alexandrien Epistula ad Afros: Einleitung, Kommentar, und Übersetzung*. Patristische Texte und Studien 56. Berlin: De Gruyter, 2001.

———. *Letter to Rufianus*. PG 26.1179–82.

———. *Letters to Serapion concerning the Holy Spirit*. Edited by J. Lebon. SC 15. Translated by C. R. B. Shapland. London: Epworth, 1951.

———. *On the Councils of Ariminum and Seleucia*. Edited by Hans-Georg Opitz. *Athanasius Werke* 2.1.231–78. Translated by John Henry Newman and A. Robertson. NPNF 2.4.448–80.

———. *On the Decrees of Nicaea*. Edited by Hans-Georg Opitz. *Athanasius Werke* 2.1.1–45. Translated by John Henry Newman and A. Robertson. NPNF 2.4.150–72.

———. *On the Incarnation*. Edited and translated by Robert W. Thomson. *Contra Gentes and De Incarnatione*. Oxford: Clarendon, 1971.

———. *On the Sayings of Dionysius*. Edited by Hans-Georg Opitz. *Athanasius Werke* 2.1.46–67. Translated by A. Robinson. NPNF 2.4173–87.

———. *Orations against the Arians*. Edited by Karin Metzler, revised by Kyriakos Savvidis. *Athanasius Werke* 1.1.2–3. Berlin: De Gruyter, 1998. Translated by John Henry Newman and A. Robertson. NPNF 2.4.303–447.

———. *Tome to the Antiochenes*. Edited by Hans-Georg Opitz. *Athanasius Werke* 1.1.8. Translated by H. Ellershaw. NPNF 2.4.481–86.

Augustine of Hippo. *Against Maximinus, an Arian*. PL 42.669–78.

———. *The City of God*. Edited by Bernhard Dombart and Alphons Kalb. CCSL 47–48.

———. *Confessions*. Edited by M. Skutella, revised by L. Verheijen. CCL 27. Translated by Maria Boulding. Hyde Park, N.Y.: New City Press, 1997.

———. *Letters*. Edited by A. Goldbacher. CSEL 34, 44, 57. In *Saint Augustine: Letters, Volume 1 (1–82)*. Fathers of the Church 12. Translated by Sr. Wilfrid Parsons, SND. Washington, D.C.: The Catholic University Press, 2010.

———. *On the Catholic and the Manichean Ways of Life (De moribus)*. CSEL 90.

———. *On the Faith and the Creed (De Fide et Symbolo)*. CSEL 41. In *Saint Augustine: Treatises on Marriage and other Subjects*. Fathers of the Church 27. Translated by Robert P. Russell, OSA. Washington, D.C.: The Catholic University of America Press, 1955.

———. *On the Literal Interpretation of Genesis*. Edited by Joseph Zycha. CSEL 28.1.

———. *Teaching Christianity (De doctrina Christiana)*. CSEL 80.

———. *The Trinity*. Edited by J. Mountain. CCL 50, 50A. Augustine, *The Trinity*, translated by Edmund Hill, 2nd ed. New York: New City Press, 2012.

Basil of Caesarea. *Against Eunomius*. Edited by Bernard Sesboüé, Georges-Matthieu de Durand, and Louis Doutreleau. SC 299, 305. Translated by Mark Del Cogliano and Andrew Radde-Gallwitz. FC 122.

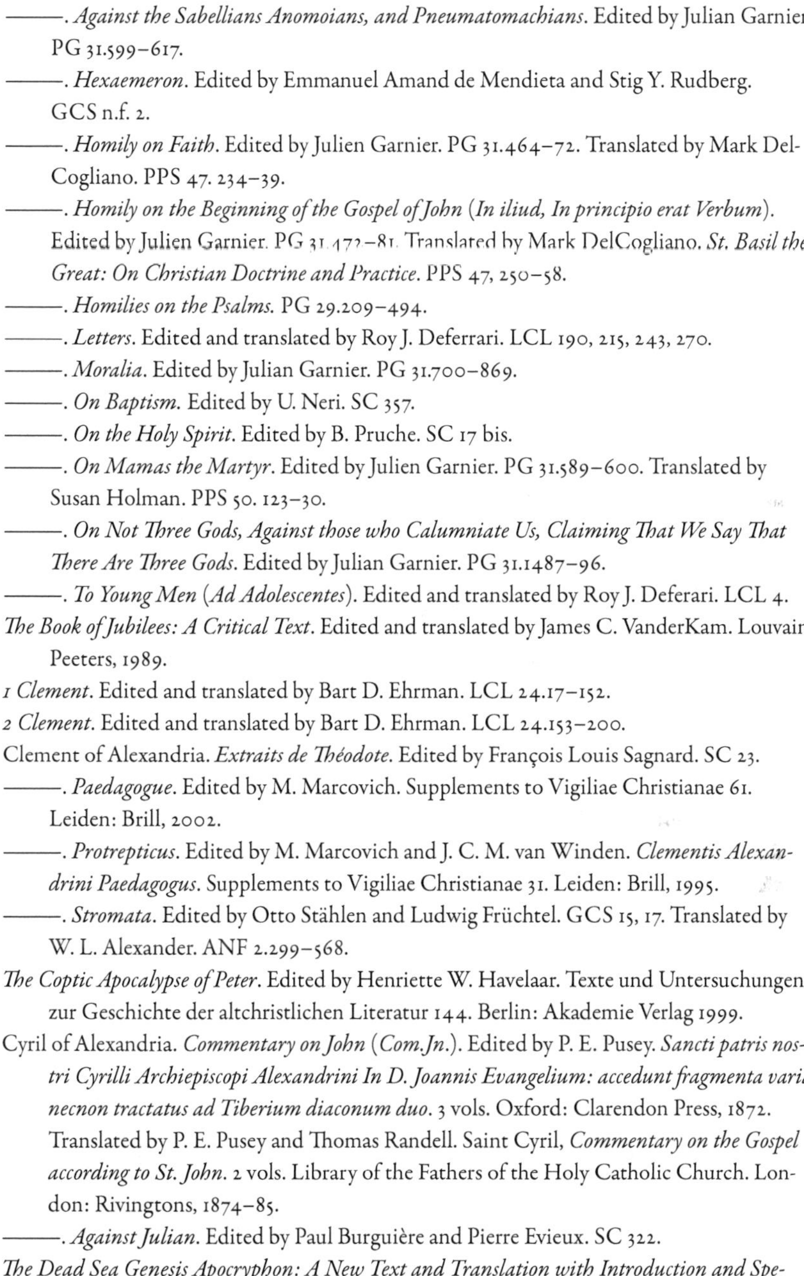

———. *Against the Sabellians Anomoians, and Pneumatomachians*. Edited by Julian Garnier. PG 31.599–617.

———. *Hexaemeron*. Edited by Emmanuel Amand de Mendieta and Stig Y. Rudberg. GCS n.f. 2.

———. *Homily on Faith*. Edited by Julien Garnier. PG 31.464–72. Translated by Mark DelCogliano. PPS 47. 234–39.

———. *Homily on the Beginning of the Gospel of John* (*In iliud, In principio erat Verbum*). Edited by Julien Garnier. PG 31.472–81. Translated by Mark DelCogliano. *St. Basil the Great: On Christian Doctrine and Practice*. PPS 47, 250–58.

———. *Homilies on the Psalms*. PG 29.209–494.

———. *Letters*. Edited and translated by Roy J. Deferrari. LCL 190, 215, 243, 270.

———. *Moralia*. Edited by Julian Garnier. PG 31.700–869.

———. *On Baptism*. Edited by U. Neri. SC 357.

———. *On the Holy Spirit*. Edited by B. Pruche. SC 17 bis.

———. *On Mamas the Martyr*. Edited by Julien Garnier. PG 31.589–600. Translated by Susan Holman. PPS 50. 123–30.

———. *On Not Three Gods, Against those who Calumniate Us, Claiming That We Say That There Are Three Gods*. Edited by Julian Garnier. PG 31.1487–96.

———. *To Young Men* (*Ad Adolescentes*). Edited and translated by Roy J. Deferari. LCL 4.

The Book of Jubilees: A Critical Text. Edited and translated by James C. VanderKam. Louvain: Peeters, 1989.

1 Clement. Edited and translated by Bart D. Ehrman. LCL 24.17–152.

2 Clement. Edited and translated by Bart D. Ehrman. LCL 24.153–200.

Clement of Alexandria. *Extraits de Théodote*. Edited by François Louis Sagnard. SC 23.

———. *Paedagogue*. Edited by M. Marcovich. Supplements to Vigiliae Christianae 61. Leiden: Brill, 2002.

———. *Protrepticus*. Edited by M. Marcovich and J. C. M. van Winden. *Clementis Alexandrini Paedagogus*. Supplements to Vigiliae Christianae 31. Leiden: Brill, 1995.

———. *Stromata*. Edited by Otto Stählen and Ludwig Früchtel. GCS 15, 17. Translated by W. L. Alexander. ANF 2.299–568.

The Coptic Apocalypse of Peter. Edited by Henriette W. Havelaar. Texte und Untersuchungen zur Geschichte der altchristlichen Literatur 144. Berlin: Akademie Verlag 1999.

Cyril of Alexandria. *Commentary on John* (*Com.Jn.*). Edited by P. E. Pusey. *Sancti patris nostri Cyrilli Archiepiscopi Alexandrini In D. Joannis Evangelium: accedunt fragmenta varia necnon tractatus ad Tiberium diaconum duo*. 3 vols. Oxford: Clarendon Press, 1872. Translated by P. E. Pusey and Thomas Randell. Saint Cyril, *Commentary on the Gospel according to St. John*. 2 vols. Library of the Fathers of the Holy Catholic Church. London: Rivingtons, 1874–85.

———. *Against Julian*. Edited by Paul Burguière and Pierre Evieux. SC 322.

The Dead Sea Genesis Apocryphon: A New Text and Translation with Introduction and Spe-

cial Treatment of Columns 13–17. Edited and translated by Daniel A. Machiela. Leiden: Brill, 2009.

Didymus the Blind. *Commintary on the Psalms*. Edited by Louis Doutreleau, Adolphe Gesché, and Michael Gronewald. *Psalmenkommentar (Tura-Papyrus)*. Papyrologische Texte und Abhandlungen 4, 6, 7, 8, 12. Bonn: R. Habelt, 1968–70.

———. *Commentary on Zechariah*. Edited by Louis Doutreleau. SC 83–85. Translated by Robert C. Hill. FC 111. Washington, D.C.: The Catholic University of America Press, 2006.

———. *On the Holy Spirit*. Edited by Louis Doutreleau. SC 386. Translated by Mark DelCogliano, Andrew Radde-Gallwitz, and Lewis Ayres. PPS 43.

Diogenes Laertius. *Lives of Eminent Philosophers*. Translated by R. D. Hicks. LCL 184–85.

Dionysius of Alexandria. *Fragments*. Edited by Charles Lett Feltoe. *The Letters and Other Remains of Dionysius of Alexandria*. Cambridge Patristic Texts. Cambridge: Cambridge University Press, 1904.

3 Enoch; or, The Hebrew Book of Enoch. Edited and translated by Hugo Odeberg. New York: Ktav, 1973.

Epictetus. *Discources*. LCL 131, 218.

Epiphanius. *Anchoratus*. Edited by Karl Holl. GCS 25. Translated by Young Richard Kim. FC 128. Washington, D.C.: The Catholic University of America Press, 2014.

———. *On Weights and Measures*. Edited and translated by James Elmer Dean. *Epiphanius' Treatise on Weights and Measures: The Syriac Version*. Studies in Ancient Oriental Civilizations 11. Chicago: University of Chicago Press, 1935.

———. *Panarion*. Edited by Karl Holl. GCS 25, 31, 37. Translated by Frank Williams. *The Panarion of Epiphanius of Salamis*. 2nd rev. ed., Nag Hammadi and Manichean Studies 63 and 79. Leiden: Brill, 2009, 2013.

The Epistle of the Apostles. Edited and translated by Julian V. Hills. Early Christian Apocrypha 2. Santa Rosa: Polebridge Press, 2009.

The Ethiopic text of 1 Enoch. Edited by August Tillman. Eugene, Ore.: Wipf and Stock, 2005.

Eunomius of Cyzicus. *Apology* (*Apol.*). Edited and translated by Richard Paul Vaggione. *The Extant Works*, 43–75. Oxford Early Christian Texts. Oxford: Clarendon, 1987.

Eusebius of Caesarea. *Against Marcellus* (*C.Marcel.*). Edited by Erich Klostermann and Günter Christian Hansen. GCS 14.

———. *Commentary on Isaiah*. Edited by J. Ziegler. GCS 60.

———. *Commentary on the Psalms*. PG 23; 24.9–76.

———. *Ecclesiastical History* (*H.E.*). Edited by Eduard Schwartz. SC 31, 41, 51, 73. Translated by Hugh Jackson Lawlor and John Ernest Leonard Oulton. *The Ecclesiastical History and the Martyrs of Palestine*. 2 vols. London: SPCK, 1954.

———. *Ecclesiastical Theology* (*E.Th.*). Edited by Erich Klostermann. GCS 4b.60–182.

———. *Gospel Questions and Solutions Addressed to Stephanus* (*Quaestiones ev. ad Steph.*). PG 22.880–936.

———. *The Martyrs of Palestine* (*Mart.Pal.*). Edited by E. Schwartz. GCS 9.2. Translated by Hugh Jackson Lawlor and John Ernest Leonard Oulton. *The Ecclesiastical History and the Martyrs of Palestine*. 2 vols. London: SPCK, 1954.

———. *Preparation for the Gospel* (*Prep.*). Edited by E. des Places, J. Sirinelli, G. Schroeder, G. Favrelle, and O. Zink. SC 206, 215, 228, 262, 266, 292, 307, 338, 369. Translated by Edwin Hamilton Gifford. Oxford: Clarendon, 1903.

———. *Proof of the Gospel* (*Proof*). Edited by I. A. Heikel. GCS 23. Translated by W. J. Ferrar. 2 vols. Translations of Christian Literature Series 1. London: SPCK, 1920.

———. *Prophetic Eclogues*. Edited by Thomas Gaisford. In *Eusebii Pamphili episcopi Caesariensis eclogae propheticae*. Oxford: Oxford University Press, 1842.

The Gospel of Truth. Translated by Harold Attridge and George W. MacRae. In *Nag Hammadi Codex I (the Jung Codex): Introductions, Texts, Translations, Indices*. Nag Hammadi Studies 22. Leiden: Brill, 1985.

Gregory of Nazianzus. *Orations* 1–3. Edited by Jean Bernardi. SC 247.

———. *Orations* 20–23. Edited by Justin Mossay and Guy Lafontaine. SC 270.

———. *Orations* 27–31 (*The Theological Orations*). Edited by Paul Gallay. SC 250.

———. *Orations* 38–41. Edited by Claudio Moreschini. SC 358.

———. *Orations* 42–43. Edited by Jean Bernardi. SC 384.

———. *Orations* 44–45. Edited by Armand Benjamin Caillau. PG 36.

Gregory of Nyssa. *Against Eunomius*. Edited by Werner Jaeger. *Gregorii Nysseni Opera*, vols. 1–2. Leiden: Brill, 1952.

———. *Homilies on the Song of Songs*. Edited by H. Langerbeck. *Gregorii Nysseni Opera*, vol. 6. Leiden: Brill, 1960.

———. *The Life of Moses*. Edited by Jean Daniélou. SC 1 bis.

———. *On the Inscriptions of the Psalms*. Edited by J. A. McDonough. *Gregorii Nysseni Opera* 5.24–175. Leiden: Brill, 1986. Translated by Ronald E. Heine. *Gregory of Nyssa's Treatise on the Inscriptions of the Psalms*. Oxford Early Christian Studies. Oxford: Clarendon, 1995.

Hilary of Poitiers. *The Trinity*. Edited by Pieter Smulders. SC 443, 448, 462. Translated by Stephen McKenna. In *Hilary of Poitiers: On the Trinity*. Fathers of the Church 25. Washington, D.C: The Catholic University of America Press, 1954.

Hippolytus. *Blessing of Jacob*. Edited by Maurice Brière, Louis Mariès et B.-Ch. Mercier. Patrologia Orientalis 27. Paris: Firmin-Didot, 1957.

———. *Against Noetus*. Edited by Robert Butterworth. London: Heythrop College, University of London, 1977.

———. *On the Antichrist*. Edited by H. Achelis. GCS 1–2.

———. *Refutation of All Heresies*. Edited by Maroslav Marcovich. Berlin: De Gruyter, 1986.

Homer. *Iliad*. LCL 170–71.

Ignatius of Antioch. *Letters*. Edited and translated by Bart D. Ehrman. LCL 24.201–322.

Irenaeus of Lyons. *Against the Heresies*. Edited by A. Rousseau, L. Doutreleau, B. Hemmerdinger, and C. Mercier. SC 100, 152, 153, 210, 211, 263, 264, 293, 294.

———. *Demonstration of the Apostolic Preaching*. Edited and translated by Adelin Rousseau. SC 406.

Jacob of Serug. *Homilies*. Edited by P. Bedjan, suppl. Sebastian P. Brock. 6 vols. Piscataway, N.J.: Gorgias Press, 2006.

John Chrysostom. *Against the Theater*. PG 56.541–54.

———. *Homilies on Genesis*. Edited by Laurence Brottier. SC 433.

Josephus. *Jewish Antiquities*. Edited and translated by Henry St. John Thackeray et al. LCL 242, 281, 326, 365, 410, 433, 456.

Justin Martyr. *Apologies*. Edited and translated by Denis Minns and P. M. Parvis. In *Justin, Philosopher and Martyr: Apologies*. Oxford Early Christian Texts. Oxford: Oxford University Press, 2009.

———. *Dialog with Trypho*. Edited by Miroslav Marcovich. Berlin: De Gruyter, 1997. Translated by Thomas B. Falls and Thomas P. Halton. FC 3.

Maximus the Confessor. *Questions to Thalassius*. Edited by Carl Laga and Carlos Steel. CCSG 7, 22.

Melito of Sardis. *On Pascha*. Edited and translated by Stuart George Hall. Oxford Early Christian Texts. Oxford: Clarendon, 1979.

Midrash. Edited by Reuven Hammer. *The Classic Midrash: Tannaitic Commentaries on the Bible*. Mahwah, N.J.: Paulist Press, 1995.

Novatian. *The Trinity*. Edited by G. F. Diercks. CCSL 4. Translated by R. J. DeSimone. FC 67.

Origen. *Commentary on the Gospel of John* (*Com.Jn.*). Edited by C. Blanc. SC 120, 157, 222, 290, 385. Translated by Ronald E. Heine. Fathers of the Church 80, 89. Washington, D.C.: The Catholic University of America Press, 1989.

———. *Commentary on the Song of Songs* (*Com.Song*). Edited by Luc Brésard, Henri Crouzel, and Marcel Borret. SC 375–76. Translated by R. P. Lawson. Origen. ACW 26.

———. *Contra Celsum*. Translated by Henry Chadwick. *Origen: Contra Celsum*. Cambridge: Cambridge University Press, 1965.

———. *On First Principles*. Edited by Henri Crouzel and Manlio Simonetti. SC 252–53, 268–69, 312. Translated by G. W. Butterworth. Gloucester, Mass.: Peter Smith, 1973.

———. *Homilies on Genesis* (*Hom.Gen.*). Edited by L. Doutreleau. SC 7. Translated by Ronald Heine. FC 71.

———. *Homilies on the Song of Songs*. Edited by W. Baehrens. GCS 33.

———. *Homilies on Leviticus* (*Hom.Lev.*). Edited by M. Borret. SC 286–87. Translated by Gary Wayne Barkley. FC 83.

Pausanias. *Description of Greece*. Translated by W. H. S. Jones. LCL 272.

Philo. *Liber antiquitatum Biblicarum*. Edited by Guido Kisch. University of Notre Dame Publications in Medieval Studies 10. Notre Dame, Ind.: University of Notre Dame Press, 1949.

———. *On God*. Translated by F. H. Colson and G. H. Whitaker. LCL 247.

———. *On the Cherubim*. Translated by F. H. Colson and G. H. Whitaker. LCL 227.

———. *On the Change of Names*. Translated by F. H. Colson and G. H. Whitaker. LCL 275.

———. *On the Creation of the World*. Translated by F. H. Colson and G. H. Whitaker. LCL 226.

———. *On the Decalogue*. Translated by F. H. Colson. LCL 320.

———. *On the Life of Abraham*. Translated by F. H. Colson. LCL 289.

———. *On the Sacrifices of Abel and Cain*. Translated by F. H. Colson and G. H. Whitaker. LCL 227.

———. *On the Special Laws*. Translated by F. H. Colson. LCL 320.

———. *Questions and Answers on Genesis*. Translated by Ralph Marcus. LCL 380.

Plato. *Theaetetus*. Edited and translated by Harold Fowler. LCL 123.

———. *Timaeus*. Edited and translated by R. G. Bury. LCL 234.

Plutarch. *The E at Delphi*. Edited and translated by Frank Cole Babbitt. LCL 306.

Procopius of Gaza. *Commentary on Genesis*. PG 87.21–512.

Prudentius. Days Linked by Song. Edited and translated by Maurice Lavarenne. *Cathemerinon liber* (*Livre d'heures*). Paris: Belles letters, 1943.

Quintilian. *The Orator's Education* (*Institutio oratoria*). Edited and translated by Donald A. Russell. LCL 124–27, 494.

Romanos. *Hymns*. Edited by Paul Maas and C. A. Trypanis. *Sancti Romani Melodi Cantica*. Vol. 1. *Cantica genuina*. Oxford: Clarendon, 1963.

La Sainte Bible qui contient le Vieux et le Nouveau Testament. Edited by David Martin. Brussels: La société biblique britannique et étrangère, 1851.

Socrates. *Ecclesiastical History*. Edited by Günther Christian Hansen. GCS n.f. 1. Translated by A. C. Zenos. NPNF 2.2.1–178.

The Shepherd of Hermas. Edited and translated by Bart D. Ehrman. LCL 25.161–474.

Stoicorum veterum fragmenta. Edited by Hans von Arnim. 4 vols. Leipzig: Teubner, 1903–24.

The Talmud. Edited and translated by Heinrich W. Guggenheimer. *The Jerusalem Talmud: Edition, Translation, and Commentary*. Berlin: De Gruyter, 2000–.

Tatian. *Diatessaron*. Edited and translated by Carmel McCarthy. *Saint Ephrem's Commentary on Tatian's Diatessaron: An English Translation of Chester Beatty Syriac MS 709 with Introduction and Notes*. Oxford: Oxford University Press, 1994.

Tertullian. *Against Marcion*. Edited by A. Kroymann. CSEL 47.290–650. Translated by P. Holmes. ANF 3.271–474. Edited and translated by E. Evans. Oxford: Oxford University Press, 1972.

———. *Against Praxeas*. Edited and translated by Ernest Evans. *Tertullian's Treatise against Praxeas*. London: SPCK, 1948.

———. *Against Hermogenes*. Edited by A. Kroymann. CSEL 47.126–176. Translated by P. Holmes. ANF 3.477–502.

———. *Apology*. Edited by H. Hoppe. CSEL 69. Translated by S. Thelwall. ANF 3.17–55.

——. *On the Flesh of Christ*. Edited by A. Kroymann. CSEL 70.189–250. Translated by P. Holmes. ANF 3.521–42.

———. *The Resurrection of the Flesh*. Edited by A. Kroymann. CSEL 47.25–125. Translated by P. Holmes. ANF 3.545–594.

Theodoret of Cyrus. *Questions on the Octateuch*. Edited by Fernández Marcos and A. Sáenz-Badillor, revised by John Petruccione. Translated by Robert C. Hill. LEC 1–2.

———. *Ecclesiastical History*. Edited by F. Scheidweiler. GCS 44. Translated by Blomfield Jackson. NPNF 2.3.33–159.

Theophilus of Antioch. *To Autolycus*. Edited and translated by Robert M. Grant. Oxford Early Christian Texts. Oxford: Clarendon Press, 1970.

Tyndale's New Testament. Edited by Priscilla Martin. Ware, Hertfordshire: Wordsworth, 2002.

Modern Sources

Adelman, Rachel. *The Return of the Repressed: Pirqe De-Rabbi Eliezer and the Pseudepigrapha*. Leiden: Brill, 2009.

———. "Can We Apply the Term 'Rewritten Bible' to Midrash? The Case of Pirqe de-Rabbi Eliezer." In *Rewritten Bible after Fifty Years: Texts, Terms, or Techniques?: A Last Dialogue with Geza Vermes*, edited by J. Zsengellér, 295–317. Leiden and Boston: Brill, 2014.

Agbenuti, Hugues. *Didyme d'Alexandrie: Sense profond des Écritures et pneumatologie*. Cahiers de Biblia Patristica 11. Strasbourg: Université de Strasbourg, 2011.

Alexander, Philip S. "Retelling the Old Testament." In *It Is Written: Scripture Citing Scripture: Essays in Honour of Barnabas Lindars*, edited by D. A. Carson and H. G. M. Williamson. Cambridge: Cambridge University Press, 1988.

"Allegoria." In *Dizionario patristico e di antichità cristiane*, edited by Angelo Di Berardino, 1: 140–41. Casale Monferrato: Marietti: 1983.

Altaner, Berthold. *Patrologie: Leben, Schriften und Lehre der Kirchenväter*. 2nd ed. Herders theologische Grundrisse. Freiburg: Herder, 1950.

Anatolios, Khaled. *Retrieving Nicaea: The Development and Meaning of Trinitarian Doctrine*. Grand Rapids: Baker, 2001.

———. *Athanasius*. London: Routledge, 2004.

Anderson, Janice Capel, and Stephen D. Moore, eds. *Mark and Method: New Approaches in Biblical Studies*. 2nd ed. Minneapolis: Fortress, 2008.

Anderson, Paul N. "The Cognitive Origins of John's Christological Unity and Disunity." *Horizons in Biblical Theology* 17 (1995): 1–24.

———. *The Christology of the Fourth Gospel.* Wissenschaftliche Untersuchungen zum Neuen Testament, vol. 2, series 78. Tübingen: J. C. B. Mohr, 1996.

———. "The Sitz im Leben of the Johannine Bread of Life Discourse and Its Evolving Context." In *Critical Readings of John 6*, ed. R. Alan Culpepper, 1–59. Biblical Interpretation Series 22. Leiden: Brill, 1997.

———. "The Having-Sent-Me Father: Aspects of Agency, Encounter, and Irony in the Johannine Father-Son relationship." Semeia 85 (1999): 33–57.

———. *Navigating the Living Waters of the Gospel of John: On Wading with Children and*

Swimming with Elephants. Pendle Hill Pamphlet 352. Wallingford: Pendle Hill Press, 2000.

———. "Mark and John—the Bi-Optic Gospels." In *Jesus and the Johannine Tradition*, edited by Robert Fortna and Tom Thatcher, 175–88. Philadelphia: Westminster/John Knox Press, 2001.

———. "Interfluential, Formative, and Dialectical—A Theory of John's Relation to the Synoptics." In *Für und wider die Priorität des Johannesevangeliums: Symposion in Salzburg am 10. März 2000*, edited by Peter Hofrichter, 19–58. Theologische Texte und Studien 9. Hildesheim, Zürich, and New York: Georg Olms Verlag, 2002.

———. *The Fourth Gospel and the Quest for Jesus: Modern Foundations Reconsidered*. Library of New Testament Studies 321. London: T. and T. Clark, 2006.

———. "Bakhtin's Dialogism and the Corrective Rhetoric of the Johannine Misunderstanding Dialogue: Exposing Seven Crises in the Johannine Situation." In *Bakhtin and Genre Theory in Biblical Studies*, edited by Roland Boer, 133–59. Society of Biblical Literature Semeia Studies 63. Atlanta: SBL Press, 2007.

———. "On Guessing Points and Naming Stars—The Epistemological Origins of John's Christological Tensions." In *The Gospel of St. John and Christian Theology*, edited by Richard Bauckham and Carl Mosser, 311–45. Grand Rapids: Eerdmans, 2007.

———. "The Origin and Development of the Johannine Egō Eimi Sayings in Cognitive-Critical Perspective." *Journal for the Study of the Historical Jesus* 9 (2011): 139–206.

———. *The Riddles of the Fourth Gospel: An Introduction to John*. Minneapolis: Fortress, 2011.

———. "Mark, John, and Answerability: Interfluentiality and Dialectic between the Second and Fourth Gospels." *Liber Annuus* 63 (2013): 197–245.

———. "On 'Seamless Robes' and 'Leftover Fragments': A Theory of Johannine Composition; Structure, Composition, and Authorship of John's Gospel." In *The Origins of John's Gospel*, edited by Stanley E. Porter and Hughson Ong, 169–218. Leiden: Brill, 2015.

———. "The Johannine *Logos*-Hymn: A Cross-Cultural Celebration of God's Creative-Redemptive Work." In *Creation Stories in Dialogue: The Bible, Science, and Folk Traditions*, Radboud Prestige Lecture Series by Alan Culpepper, edited by R. Alan Culpepper and Jan van der Watt, 219–42. Biblical Interpretation Series 139. Leiden: Brill, 2016.

Ashton, John. "Breaking Away: Three New Testament Pictures of Christianity's Separation from the Jewish Communities." In *"To See Ourselves as Others See Us": Christians, Jews, "Others" in Late Antiquity*, edited by Jacob Neusner and Ernest S. Frerichs, 93–115. Scholars Press Studies in the Humanities. Chico: Scholars, 1985.

———, ed. *Interpretations of the Fourth Gospel.* London: SPCK; Philadelphia: Fortress, 1986.

Attridge, Harold W. "Thematic Development and Source Elaboration in John 7," *Catholic Biblical Quarterly* 42 (1980): 160–70.

———. "Argumentation in John 5." In *Rhetorical Argumentation in Biblical Texts: Essays from the Lund 2000 Conference*, edited by Anders Eriksson, Thomas H. Olbricht, and Walter Übelacker, 188–99. Emory Studies in Early Christianity 8. Harrisburg, Pa.: Trinity Press International, 2002.

———. "Heracleon and John: Reassessment of an Early Christian Hermeneutical Debate." In *Biblical Interpretation, History, Context, and Reality*, edited by Christine Helmer and Taylor G. Petrey, 57–72. Society of Biblical Literature Symposium series 26. Leiden: Brill, 2005.

———. "Philo and John: Two Riffs on one Logos." *Studia Philonica Annual* 17 (2005): 103–17.

———. *Essays on John and Hebrews*. Wissenschaftliche Untersuchungen zum Neuen Testament 264. Tübingen: Mohr Siebeck, 2010.

Auerbach, Erich. "Figura." In *Scenes from the Drama of European Literature*, translated by Ralph Manheim, 11–78. Minneapolis: University of Minnesota Press, 1984.

Auvray, Paul. "Qu'est-ce que la typologie?" In *L'Ancien Testament et les Chrétiens*, ed. Paul Auvray et al., 199–205. Paris: Cerf, 1951.

Ayres, Lewis. "The Christological Context of Augustine's De Trinitate XIII: Toward Relocating Books VIII– XV." *Augustinian Studies* 29 (1998): 111–41.

———. *Nicaea and Its Legacy: An Approach to Fourth-Century Trinitarian Theology*. Oxford: Oxford University Press, 2004.

———. *Augustine and the Trinity*. Cambridge: Cambridge University Press, 2014.

Babcock, William. "Augustine's Interpretation of Romans, A.D. 394–396." *Augustinian Studies* 10 (1979): 55–74.

Bammel, C. P. "Ignatian Problems." *Journal of Theological Studies* 33 (1982): 62–97.

Barnes, Michael René. "The Fourth Century as Trinitarian Canon." In *Christian Origins: Theology, Rhetoric, and Community*, edited by Lewis Ayres, 47–67. New York: Routledge, 1998.

———. "Exegesis and Polemic in Augustine's *De Trinitate* I." *Augustinian Studies* 30, no. 1 (1999): 43–60.

———. *The Power of God: Δύναμις in Gregory of Nyssa's Trinitarian Theology*. Washington, D.C.: The Catholic University of America Press, 2001.

———. "The Visible Christ and the Invisible Trinity: Mt. 5:8 in Augustine's Trinitarian Theology of 400." *Modern Theology* 19, no. 3 (2003): 329–55.

Barnes, Timothy D. *Athanasius and Constantius: Theology and Politics in the Constantinian Empire*. Cambridge, Mass.: Harvard University Press, 2001.

———. "Review: Constantine and Christendom. The Oration to the Saints. The Greek and Latin Accounts of the Discovery of the Cross. The Edict of Constantine to Pope Silvester." *Journal of Theological Studies* 55, no. 1 (2004): 351–55.

———. "The Date of Ignatius." *Expository Times* 120, no. 3 (2008): 125–26.

Barrett, C. K. "The Dialectical Theology of St John." In *New Testament Essays*, edited by C. K. Barrett, 49–69. London: SCM, 1972.

———. "'The Father is Greater than I' (John 14:28): Subordinationist Christology in the

New Testament." In *Neues Testament und Kirche, für Rudolf Schnackenburg*, edited by J. Gnilka, 144–59. Freiburg: Herder, 1974.

———. *Essays on John*. Philadelphia: London: SPCK, 1982.

Bauckham, Richard J. "The Worship of Jesus in Apocalyptic Christianity." *New Testament Studies* 27 (1981): 322–41.

———. "The Worship of Jesus." In *The Climax of Prophecy: Studies on the Book of Revelation*, edited by Richard Bauckham, 118–49. Edinburgh: T. and T. Clark, 1993.

———. *God Crucified: Monotheism and Christology in the New Testament*. Carlisle: Paternoster, 1998.

———. *Jesus and the God of Israel: God Crucified and Other Studies on the New Testament's Christology of Divine Identity*. Grand Rapids: Eerdmans, 2008.

Beckwith, Carl. *Hilary of Poitiers on the Trinity: From De Fide to De Trinitate*. Oxford: Oxford University Press, 2008.

Beeley, Christopher A. *Gregory of Nazianzus on the Trinity and the Knowledge of God: In Your Light We Shall See Light*. Oxford Studies in Historical Theology. New York: Oxford University Press, 2008.

———. *The Unity of Christ: Continuity and Conflict in Patristic Tradition*. New Haven: Yale University Press, 2012.

Behr, John. *Asceticism and Anthropology in Irenaeus and Clement*. Oxford Early Christian Studies. Oxford: Oxford University Press, 2000.

———. "Irenaeus on the Word of God." In *Studia Patristica: Papers Presented at the 13th International Conference on Patristic Studies held in Oxford 1999*, edited by Maurice F. Wiles and Edward Yarnold, 163–67. Leuven: Peeters, 2001.

———. The Way to Nicaea. Crestwood, N.Y.: St. Vladimir's Seminary Press, 2001.

———. *Formation of Christian Theology*. Vol. 2, *The Nicene Faith*. New York: SVS Press, 2004.

———. ed. and trans. *The Case against Diodore and Theodore: Texts and their Contexts*. Oxford Early Christian Texts. Oxford: Oxford University Press, 2011.

Bennema, Cornelis. "The Giving of the Spirit in John's Gospel: A New Proposal?" *Evangelical Quarterly* 74 (2002): 195–214.

———. *The Power of Saving Wisdom: An Investigation of Spirit and Wisdom in Relation to the Soteriology of the Fourth Gospel*. Wissenschaftliche Untersuchungen zum Neuen Testament, vol. 2, series 148. Tübingen: Mohr Siebeck, 2002.

Bernardi, Jean. *La prédication des pères cappadociens*. Publications de la Faculté des lettres et sciences humaines de l'Université de Montpellier 30. Paris: Presses universitaires de France, 1968.

Betz, Otto. *Der Paraklet: Fürsprecher im Häretischen Spätjudentum, im Johannes-Evangelium und in Neugefundenen Gnostischen Schriften*. Arbeiten zur Geschichte des Spätjudentums und Urchristentums 2. Leiden: Brill, 1963.

Blank, Josef. *Krisis: Untersuchungen zur johanneischen Christologie und Eschatologie*. Freiburg im Breisgau: Lambertus Verlag, 1964.

Blowers, Paul M., ed. and trans. *The Bible in Greek Christian Antiquity*. The Bible through the Ages 1. Notre Dame, Ind.: University of Notre Dame Press, 1997.

Bockmuehl, Markus N. A. *Seeing the Word: Refocusing New Testament Study*. Studies in Theological Interpretation. Grand Rapids: Baker Academic, 2006.

Boismard, M. E. *Moses or Jesus: An Essay in Johannine Christology*. Minneapolis: Fortress; Leuven: Peeters, 1993.

Borgen, Peder. "God's Agent in the Fourth Gospel." In *The Interpretation of John*, edited by John Ashton, 83–96. 2nd ed. (Oxford: Clarendon, 2007).

Boring, M. Eugene. "The Influence of Christian Prophecy on the Johannine Portrayal of the Paraclete and Jesus." *New Testament Studies* 25 (1978–79): 113–23;

Boulnois, Marie-Odile. "'*Trois hommes et un Seigneur': Lectures trinitaires de la théophanie de Mambré dans l'exégèse et l'iconographie.*" *Studia Patristica* 39 (2006): 194–201.

Breck, John. *Spirit of Truth: The Holy Spirit in Johannine Tradition*. Vol. 1, *The Origins of Johannine Pneumatology*. Crestwood, N.Y.: St. Vladimir's Seminary Press, 1991.

Breytenbach, Cilliers, and Henning Paulsen, eds. *Anfänge der Christologie: Festschrift für Ferdinand Hahn zum 65. Geburtstag.* Göttingen: Vandenhoeck und Ruprecht, 1991.

Brown, Raymond E. "The Paraclete in the Fourth Gospel." *New Testament Studies* 13, no. 2 (1967): 113–32.

———. *The Gospel According to John (xiii–xxi)*. Garden City, N.Y.: Doubleday, 1970.

Buch-Hansen, Gitte. *"It Is the Spirit That Gives Life": A Stoic Understanding of Pneuma in John's Gospel*. Beihefte zur Zeitschrift für die neutestamentliche Wissenschaft 173. Berlin: de Gruyter, 2010.

Bucur, Bogdan G. "Theophanies and Vision of God in Augustine's De Trinitate: An Eastern Orthodox Perspective." *St. Vladimir's Theological Quarterly* 52, no. 1 (2008): 67–93.

———. "The Mountain of the Lord: Sinai, Zion, and Eden in Byzantine Hymnographic Exegesis." In *Symbola caelestis: Le symbolisme liturgique et paraliturgique dans le monde chrétien*, edited by B. Lourié and A. Orlov, 129–72. Piscataway, N.J.: Gorgias, 2009.

———. "'Early Christian Binitarianism': From Religious Phenomenon to Polemical Insult to Scholarly Concept." *Modern Theology* 27, no. 1 (2011): 102–20.

———. "Vision, Exegesis, and Theology in the Reception History of Hab 3:2 (LXX)." In *"What Does the Scripture Say?": Studies in the Function of Scripture in Early Judaism and Christianity*. Vol. 2, *The Letters and Liturgical Traditions*, edited by Craig A. Evans and H. Daniel Zacharias, 134–46. London and New York: T. and T. Clark International, 2011.

———. "*I Saw the Lord*: Observations on the Early Christian Reception of Isaiah 6." *Pro Ecclesia* 23 (2014): 309–30.

———. "Christophanic Exegesis and the Problem of Symbolization: Daniel 3 (the Fiery Furnace) as a Test Case." *Journal of Theological Interpretation* 10 (2016): 227–44.

Bühner, Jan-A. Der *Gesandte und sein Weg im 4. Evangelium: Die kultur- und religionsgeschichtlichen Grundlagen der johanneischen Sendungschristologie so wie ihre traditions-*

geschichtliche Entwicklung. Wissenschaftliche Untersuchungen zum Neuen Testament, vol. 2, series 2. Tübingen: J. C. B. Mohr, 1977.

Bultmann, Rudolf. *The Gospel of John: A Commentary*. Translated by G. R. Beasley-Murray, R. W. N. Hoare, and J. K. Riches. Johannine Monograph Series 1. Eugene, Ore.: Wipf and Stock, 2014. Originally published in 1971.

Bunge, Gabriel. *The Rublev Trinity: The Icon of the Trinity by the Monk-Painter Andrei Rublev*. Crestwood, N.Y: St. Vladimir's Press, 2007.

Burge, Gary M. *The Anointed Community. The Holy Spirit in the Johannine Tradition*. Grand Rapids: Eerdmans, 1987.

Burgess, Stanley M. *The Holy Spirit: Eastern Christian Traditions*. Peabody, Mass.: Hendrickson, 1989.

Burgon, R. W. *The Causes of the Corruption of the Traditional Text of the Gospels*. New York: Cosimo, 2007. Originally published in 1896.

Burton-Christie, Douglas. *The Word in the Desert: Scripture and the Quest for Holiness in Early Christian Monasticism*. New York: Oxford University Press, 1993.

Capes, David B. *Old Testament Yahweh Texts in Paul's Christology*. Wissenschaftliche Untersuchungen zum Neuen Testament, vol. 2, series 47. Tübingen: J. C. B. Mohr, 1992.

Capes, David. B., A. D. DeConick, H. K. Bond, and T. A. Miller. *Israel's God and Rebecca's Children: Christology and Community in Early Judaism and Christianity*. Waco: Baylor University Press, 2007.

Canévet, Mariette. *Grégoire de Nysse et l'herméneutique biblique: Étude des rapports entre le langage et la connaissance de Dieu*. Paris: Études augustiniennes, 1983.

Casurella, Anthony. *The Johannine Paraclete in the Church Fathers: A Study in the History of Exegesis*. Beiträge zur Geschichte der biblischen Exegese 25. Tübingen: Mohr, 1983.

Chester, Andrew. *Messiah and Exaltation: Jewish Messianic and Visionary Traditions and New Testament Christology*. Tübingen: J. C. B. Mohr, 2007.

Childs, Brevard S. *Introduction to the Old Testament as Scripture*. London: SCM, 1979.

Clark, Elizabeth A. *Reading Renunciation: Asceticism and Scripture in Early Christianity*. Princeton: Princeton University Press, 1999.

———. *History, Theory, Text: Historians and the Linguistic Turn*. Cambridge, Mass.: Harvard University Press, 2004.

Collins, Raymond F. *First Corinthians*. Sacra Pagina. Collegeville, Minn.: Liturgical Press, 1999.

Colpe, Carsten. "Von der Logoslehre des Philo zu der des Clemens von Alexandrien." In *Kerygma und Logos: Beiträge zu den geistesgeschichtlichen Beziehungen zwischen Antike und Christentum; FS für Carl Andresen zum 70 Geburtstag*, edited by A. M. Ritter, 89–107. Göttingen: Vandenhoeck and Ruprecht, 1979.

———.*Der Siegel der Propheten: Historische Beziehungen zwischen Judentum, Judenchristentum, Heidentum und frühen Islam*. Berlin: Institut Kirche und Judentum, 1990.

Conzelmann, Hans. *1 Corinthians: Hermeneia Commentary*. Philadelphia: Fortress, 1975.

Crouzel, Henri. "La distinction de la 'typologie' et de 'l'allégorisme.'" *Bulletin de littérature ecclésiastique* 65 (1964): 161–74.

———. *Origen*. Translated by A. S. Worrall. San Francisco: Harper and Row, 1989.

Daley, Brian E., SJ. "Origen's De Principiis: A Guide to the Principles of Christian Scriptural Interpretation." In *Nova et Vetera: Patristic Studies in Honor of T. P. Halton*, edited by J. Petruccione, 3–21. Washington, D.C.: The Catholic University of America Press, 1998.

Daniélou, Jean. "Traversée de la Mer Rouge et baptême aux premiers siècles." *Recherches de Science Religieuse* 33 (1946): 402–30.

———. "Typologie et allégorie chez Clément d'Alexandrie." *Studia Patristica* 4 (1961): 50–57.

———. *Theology of Jewish Christianity*. Translated by John A. Baker. London: Darton, Longman and Todd, 1964.

———. *A History of Early Christian Doctrine before the Council of Nicaea*. Vol. 3, *A History of Early Christian Doctrine: The Origins of Latin Christianity*. London: Darton, Longman and Todd, 1977.

d'Alès, Adhémar. "La théophanie de Mambré devant la tradition des Pères." *Recherches de Science Religieuse* 20 (1930): 150–60.

Davis, Carl J. *The Name and Way of the Lord: Old Testament Themes; New Testament Christology*. Supplement series 129 (1996): 103–40.

Dawson, David. *Allegorical Readers and Cultural Revision in Ancient Alexandria*. Berkeley: University of California Press, 1992.

———. *Christian Figural Reading and the Fashioning of Identity*. Berkeley: University of California Press, 2002.

DelCogliano, Mark. "Basil of Caesarea on Proverbs 8:22 and the Sources of Pro-Nicene Theology." *Journal of Theological Studies* 59 (2008): 183–90.

———. "Basil of Caesarea, Didymus the Blind, and the Anti-Pneumatomachian Exegesis of Amos 4:13 and John 1:3." *Journal of Theological Studies* n.s. 61, no. 2 (2010): 644–58.

———. *Basil of Caesarea's Anti-Eunomian Theory of Names: Christian Theology and Late-Antique Philosophy in the Fourth-Century Trinitarian Controversy*. Supplements to Vigiliae Christianae 103. Leiden: Brill, 2010.

———. "The Influence of Athanasius and the Homoiousians on Basil of Caesarea's Decentralization of 'Unbegotten.'" *Journal of Early Christian Studies* 19 (2011): 197–233.

———. "Tradition and Polemic in Basil of Caesarea's Homily on the Theophany." *Vigiliae Christianae* 66 (2012): 30–55.

———. "Eusebius of Caesarea on Asterius of Cappadocia in the Anti-Marcellan Writings: A Case Study of Mutual Defense within the Eusebian Alliance." In *Eusebius of Caesarea: Tradition and Innovations*, edited by Aaron Johnson and Jeremy Schott, 263–88. Washington, D.C.: Center for Hellenic Studies, 2013.

———. *St. Basil the Great: On Christian Doctrine and Practice*. Popular Patristics 47. Crestwood, N.Y.: St. Vladimir's Seminary Press, 2013.

DelCogliano, Mark, and Andrew Radde-Gallwitz. *St. Basil of Caesarea: Against Eunomius.* The Fathers of the Church 122. Washington, D.C.: The Catholic University of America Press, 2011.

Dibelius, Martin, and Hans Conzelmann. *The Pastoral Epistles: A Commentary on the Pastoral Epistles.* Translated by Philip Buttolph and Adela Yarbro. Edited by Helmut Koester. Hermeneia. Philadelphia: Fortress Press, 1972.

di Bernardino, Angelo, ed. *Dizionario patristico e di antichità cristiane.* 2 vols. Rome: Institutum patristicum Augustianum, 1983–84.

Dietzfelbinger, Christian. "Paraklet und theologischer Anspruch im Johannesevangelium." *Zeitschrift für Theologie und Kirche* 82, no. 4 (1985): 389–408.

Dowling, Maurice. "Proverbs 8:22–31 in the Christology of the Early Fathers." *Perichoresis* 8 (2010): 47–65.

Drecoll, Volker Henning. *Die Entwicklung der Trinitätslehre des Basilius von Cäsarea: Sein Weg vom Homöusianer zum Neonizäner.* Forschungen zur Kirchen und Dogmengeschichte 66. Göttingen: Vandenhoeck and Ruprecht, 1996.

Dunn, James D. G. *Did the First Christians Worship Jesus? The New Testament Evidence.* London: SPCK, 2010.

———. *Jesus, Paul and the Gospels.* Grand Rapids: Eerdmans, 2011.

Ebeling, Gerhard. *Word and Faith.* Translated by James W. Leitch. Philadelphia: Fortress, 1963.

Edwards, Mark J. "Ignatius and the Second Century: An Answer to R. Hübner." *Zeitschrift für Antikes Christentum* 2 (1998): 214–26.

———. *Origen against Plato.* Aldershot: Ashgate, 2002.

———. *John through the Centuries.* Oxford: Blackwell, 2003.

———. "Orthodox Corruption? John 1:18." *Studia Patristica* 44 (2010): 201–7.

———. "How to Refute an Arian: Ambrose and Augustine." In *Le "De Trinitate" de Saint Augustin: Exégèse, logique et noétique,* edited by Emmanuel Bermon and Gerard O'Daly, 29–42. Paris: Institut des Études Augustiniennes, 2012.

Ehrman, Bart D. *The Orthodox Corruption of Scripture: The Effect of Early Christological Controversies on the Text of the New Testament.* New York: Oxford University Press, 1993.

———. *Lost Christianities: The Battles for Scripture and the Faiths We Never Knew.* Oxford: Oxford University Press, 2003.

Erasmus, Desiderius. *Erasmus' Annotations on the New Testament: The Gospels; Facsimile of the Final Latin Text (1535) with All Earlier Variants (1516, 1519, 1522, and 1527).* Edited by Anne Reeve. London: Duckworth, 1986.

Ernest, James D. *The Bible in Athanasius of Alexandria.* Bible in Ancient Christianity 2. Boston: Brill, 2004.

Evans, Craig A. *Word and Glory: On the Exegetical and Theological Background of John's Prologue.* Journal for the Study of the New Testament Supplement series 89. Sheffield: Sheffield Academic Press 1993.

Fatehi, Mehrdad. *The Spirit's Relation to the Risen Lord in Paul: An Examination of Its Chris-*

tological Implications. Wissenschaftliche Untersuchungen zum Neuen Testament, vol. 2, series 128. Tübingen: Mohr Siebeck, 2000.

Fedwick, Paul J. "A Chronology of the Life and Work of Basil of Caesarea." In *Basil of Caesarea, Christian, Humanist, Ascetic: A Sixteen-Hundredth Anniversary Symposium*, 1:1–19. Edited by Paul J. Fedwick. 2 vols. Toronto: Pontifical Institute of Mediaeval Studies 1981.

Fee, Gordon D. *Pauline Christology*. Peabody, Mass.: Hendrickson, 2007.

Fennema, D. A. "John 1.18: 'God the Only Son.'" *New Testament Studies* 31, no. 1 (1985–86): 124–35.

Fitzmyer, Joseph A., SJ. Chap. 5, "The Semitic Background of the New Testament Kyrios-Title." In *A Wandering Aramean: Collected Aramaic Essays*. Reprinted in *The Semitic background of the New Testament*, edited by Joseph A. Fitzmeyer, 115–42. Grand Rapids: Eerdmans, 1997.

Fossum, Jarl. "In the Beginning Was the Name: Onomatology as the Key to Johannine Christology." In *The Image of the Invisible God: Essays on the Influence of Jewish Mysticism on Early Christology*, edited by Jarl Fossum, 117–33. Freiburg: Universitätsverlag and Vandenhoeck and Ruprecht, 1995.

Fowler, James F. *Stages of Faith: The Psychology of Human Development and the Quest for Meaning*. New York: HarperCollins, 1981.

Fraade, Steven D. "Rewritten Bible and Rabbinic Midrash as Commentary." in *Current Trends in the Study of Midrash*, edited by Carol Bakhos, 59–78. Leiden: Brill, 2006.

Franck, Eskil. *Revelation Taught: The Paraclete in the Gospel of John*. Coniectanea Biblica; New Testament Series 14. Lund: Gleerup, 1985.

Fredriksen, Paula. "Mandatory Retirement: Ideas in the Study of Christian Origins Whose Time Has Come to Go." *Studies in Religion–Sciences Religieuses* 35 (2006): 231–46.

Friesen, Steven J. *Imperial Cults and the Apocalypse of John: Reading Revelation in the Ruins*. New York: Oxford University Press, 2001.

Fulford, Ben. *Divine Eloquence and Human Transformation: Rethinking and History through Gregory of Nazianzus and Hans Frei*. Emerging Scholars. Minneapolis: Fortress, 2013.

Furnish,Victor Paul. *II Corinthians*, AB 32A. Garden City, NY: Doubleday, 1984.

Gadamer, Hans-Georg. *Truth and Method*. Translated by Joel Weinsheimer and Donald G. Marshall. 2nd. rev. ed. New York: Crossroad, 1989.

Gamble, Harry Y. *Books and Readers in the Early Church: A History of Early Christian Texts*. New Haven: Yale University Press, 1995.

Gerhardsson, Birger. "The Shema' in Early Christianity." In *The Four Gospels 1992: Festschrift Frans Neirynck*, edited by F. van Segbroeck, C.M. Tuckett, G. van Belle, and J. Verheyden, 275–93. Leuven: Leuven University Press, 1992.

Giblin, Charles H. "Three Monotheistic Texts in Paul." *Catholic Biblical Quarterly* 37 (1975): 528–47.

Gieschen, Charles. "The Real Presence of the Son Before Christ: Revisiting an Old Approach to Old Testament Christology." *Concordia Theological Quarterly* 68 (2004): 103–26.

Gorday, Peter, ed. *Colossians, 1–2 Thessalonians, 1–2 Timothy, Titus, Philemon*. Downers Grove, Ill.: Intervarsity Press, 2000.

Gore, Charles, ed. *Lux Mundi: A Series of Studies in the Religion of the Incarnation*. 4th ed. London: J. Murray, 1890.

Grafton, Anthony, and Megan Williams. *Christianity and the Transformation of the Book: Origen, Eusebius, and the Library of Caesarea*. Cambridge, Mass.: Belknap Press, 2008.

Grant, Robert M. *The Letter and the Spirit*. London: SPCK, 1957.

Green, Joel B., and M. Turner, eds. *Jesus of Nazareth: Lord and Christ; Essays on the Historical Jesus and New Testament Christology*. Grand Rapids: Eerdmans, 1994.

Greer, Rowan A. *The Captain of Our Salvation: A Study in the Patristic Exegesis of Hebrews*. Beiträge zur Geschichte der biblischen Esegese 15. Tübingen: Mohr, 1973.

———. "Applying the Framework." In *Early Biblical Interpretation*, edited by James L. Kugel and Rowan A. Greer, 177–99. Philadelphia: Westminster Press, 1986.

Gruenler, Royce Gordon. *The Trinity in the Gospel of John: A Thematic Commentary on the Fourth Gospel*. Grand Rapids: Baker, 1986.

Gribomont, Jean. "La tradition johannique chez Saint Basile." In *Saint Basile Évangile et Église: Melanges*,1:209–28. Bégrolles-en- Mauges: Abbaye de Bellefontaine, 1984.

Grillmeier, Alois. *Christ in Christian Tradition: From the Apostolic Age to Chalcedon (451)*. Translated by John Bowden. London: Mowbray, 1965.

Grypeou, Emmanouela, and Helen Spurling. "Abraham's Angels: Jewish and Christian Exegesis of Genesis 18–19." In *The Exegetical Encounter Between Jews and Christians in Late Antiquity*, edited by Emmanouela Grypeou and Helen Spurling, 181–200. Leiden: Brill, 2009.

Guillet, Jacques. "Les *exégèses* d'Aléxandrie et d'Antioche: Conflit ou malentendu?" Recherches de science religieuse 34 (1947): 257–302

Haenchen, Ernst. *John: A Commentary on the Gospel of John*. 2 vols. Edited by Ulrich Busse. Translated by R. W. Funk. Hermeneia. Philadelphia: Fortress, 1984.

Hakola, Raimo. *John, the Jews and Jewishness*. Leiden: Brill, 2005.

Hanson, Anthony Tyrrell. *Jesus Christ in the Old Testament*. London: SPCK, 1965.

Hanson, R. P. C. *The Search for the Christian Doctrine of God: The Arian Controversy 318–381*. Edinburgh: T. and T. Clark, 1988.

Hardy, E. R. *Christology of the Later Fathers*. Philadelphia: Westminster, 1954.

Harnack, Adolf von. *History of Dogma*. Translated by Neil Buchanan. New York: Dover Publications 1961. Originally published in 1900.

Harvey, A. E. *Jesus on Trial*. Atlanta: John Knox, 1976.

———. "Christ as Agent." In *The Glory of Christ in the New Testament: Studies in Christology in Memory of George Bradford Caird*, edited by L. D. Hurst and N. T. Wright, 239–50. Oxford: Clarendon Press, 1987.

Hayman, Peter. "Monotheism—A Misused Word in Jewish Studies?" *Journal of Jewish Studies* 42 (1991): 1–13.

Heine, Ronald E. *Origen: Scholarship in the Service of the Church*. Christian Theology in Context. Oxford: Oxford University Press, 2010.

Heiser, Michael S. "The Divine Council in Late Canonical and Non-Canonical Second Temple Jewish Literature." Ph.D. diss., University of Wisconsin-Madison, 2004.

———. "Monotheism, Polytheism, Monolatry, or Henotheism? Toward an Assessment of Divine Plurality in the Hebrew Bible." *Bulletin for Biblical Research* 18 (2008): 1–30.

Hengel, Martin. "The Prologue of the Gospel of John as the Gateway to Christological Truth." In *The Gospel of John and Christian Theology*, edited by Richard Bauckham and Carl Mosser, 265–94. Grand Rapids: Eerdmans, 2008.

———. *The Son of God: The Origin of Christology and the History of Jewish-Hellenistic Religion*. Philadelphia: Fortress; London: SCM, 1976.

———. *Studies in Early Christology*. Edinburgh: Clark, 1995.

Hildebrand, Stephen M. *The Trinitarian Theology of Basil of Caesarea: A Synthesis of Greek Thought and Biblical Truth*. Washington D.C.: The Catholic University of America Press, 2007.

Hill, Charles E. *The Johannine Corpus in the Early Church*. Oxford: Oxford University Press, 2004.

Hollerich, Michael J. *Eusebius of Caesarea's Commentary on Isaiah: Christian Exegesis in the Age of Constantine*. Oxford Early Christian Studies. Oxford: Clarendon Press, 1999.

———. "Eusebius." In *The New Cambridge History of the Bible: From the Beginnings to 600*, edited by James Carleton Paget and Joachim Schaper, 629. Cambridge: Cambridge University Press, 2012.

———. "Eusebius' Commentary on the Psalms and its Place in the Origins of Christian Biblical Scholarship." In *Eusebius of Caesarea: Tradition and Innovations*, edited by Aaron Johnson and Jeremy Schott, 151–68. Washington, D.C.: Center for Hellenic Studies, 2013.

Hübner, R. "Thesen zum Echtheit und Datierung der sieben Briefe des Ignatius von Antiochien." *Zeitschrift für Antikes Christentum* 1 (1997): 44–72.

Hurst, Lincoln D., and N. T. Wright, eds. *The Glory of Christ in the New Testament: Studies in Christology*. Oxford: Oxford University Press, 1995.

Hurtado, Larry W. "First Century Jewish Monotheism." *Journal for the Study of the New-Testament* 71 (1998): 3–26.

———. *At the Origins of Christian Worship: The Context and Character of Earliest Christian Devotion*. Grand Rapids: Eerdmans, 2000. Originally published in 1999.

———. "The Binitarian Shape of Early Christian Worship." In *The Jewish Roots of Christological Monotheism*, edited by Carey C. Newman, James R. Davila, and Gladys S. Lewis, 187–214. Supplements to the Journal for the Study of Judaism 63. Leiden: Brill, 1999.

———. *Lord Jesus Christ: Devotion to Jesus in Earliest Christianity*. Grand Rapids: Eerdmans, 2003.

———. *How on Earth Did Jesus Become a God? Historical Questions about Earliest Devotion to Jesus*. Grand Rapids: Eerdmans, 2005.

———. *God in New Testament Theology*. Nashville: Abingdon Press, 2010.

———. "Monotheism, Principal Angels, and the Background of Christology." In *Oxford Handbook to the Dead Sea Scrolls*, edited by J. J. Collins and T. H. Lim, 546–64. Oxford: Oxford University Press, 2010.

———. "The Origins of Jesus-Devotion: A Response to Crispin Fletcher-Louis." *Tyndale Bulletin* 61 (2010): 1–20.

———. "Monotheism." In *The Eerdmans Dictionary of Early Judaism*, edited by J. J. Collins and Daniel Harlow, 961–64. Grand Rapids: Eerdmans, 2011.

———. "'Ancient Jewish Monotheism' in the Hellenistic and Roman Periods." in the Hellenistic and Roman Periods. *Journal of Ancient Judaism* 4 (2013): 379–400.

———. *One God, One Lord: Early Christian Devotion and Ancient Jewish Monotheism*. 2nd ed. T. and T. Clark, 1998. Originally published in 1988. Third edition published in London by Bloomsbury T. and T. Clark, 2015.

Irvine, Martin. *The Making of Textual Culture: Grammatical and Literary Theory 350–1100*. Cambridge: Cambridge University Press, 1994.

Jackson, F. J. Foakes, and Kirsopp Lake, eds. *The Acts of the Apostles*. 5 vols. London: Macmillan, 1920–33.

Jacobs, Andrew. "Epiphanius of Salamis and the Antiquarian's Bible." *Journal of Early Christian Studies* 21, no. 3 (2013): 437–64.

Jähnichen, Traugott. "Seeberg, Reinhold." In *Biographisch-Bibliographisches Kirchenlexikon*, 1307–10. Band 9. Bautz: Herzberg, 1995.

Jauss, Hans-Robert. "Literary History as a Challenge to Literary Theory." In *Theory and History of Literature*, vol. 2, *Toward an Aesthetic of Reception*, edited by Hans-Robert Jauss, translated by Timothy Bahti, 3–45. Minneapolis: University of Minnesota Press, 1982.

Jeanrond, Werner G. *Text und Interpretation als Kategorien Theologischen Denkens*. Hermeneutische Untersuchungen zur Theologie 23. Tübingen: Mohr Siebeck, 1986.

Jenkins, Philip. *Jesus Wars: How Four Patriarchs, Three Queens, and Two Emperors Decided What Christians Would Believe for the Next 1,500 Years*. New York: HarperCollins, 2010.

Jewett, Robert. *Romans: A Critical Commentary*. Hermeneia. Minneapolis: Fortress, 2007.

Joubert, Joseph. *Dictionnaire françois et latin*. Lyon: L. and H. Declaustre: 1710.

Kannengiesser, Charles. *Athanase d'Alexandrie, évêque et écrivain: Une lecture des traités Contre les Ariens*. Paris: Beauchesne, 1983.

———. "Lady Wisdom's Final Call: The Patristic Recovery of Proverbs 8." In *Nova doctrina vetusque: Essays on Early Christianity in Honor of Fredric W. Schlatter, S.J.*, edited by Douglas Kries and Catherine Brown Tkacz. New York: Peter Lang, 1999.

———. *Handbook of Patristic Exegesis*. 2 vols. Bible in Ancient Christianity 1. Leiden: Brill, 2004.

Käsemann, Ernst. *The Testament of Jesus: A Study of the Gospel of John in the Light of Chap-*

ter 17. Translated by G. Krodel. Johannine Monograph Series 6. Philadelphia: Fortress, 1968. Reprinted Eugene, Ore.: Wipf and Stock, 2017.

———. "The Structure and Purpose of the Prologue to John's Gospel." In *New Testament Questions of Today*. London: SCM, 1969, 138–67.

Kelly, J. N. D. *Early Christian Doctrines*. London: Longman, 1972.

Keresztes, Paul. *The Imperial Roman Government and the Christian Church*. Vol. 1, *From Nero to the Severi*. Aufstieg und Niedergang der römischen Welt. 2:23, 247–315. Berlin: De Gruyter, 1980.

Kirchschläger, W. "επικαλεω." *Exegetical Dictionary of the New Testament*, edited by Horst Balz and Gerhard Schneider,2:28–29. Grand Rapids: Zondervan, 1993.

Kloos, Kari. *Christ, Creation, and the Vision of God: Augustine's Transformation of Early Christian Theophany Interpretation*. Leiden: Brill, 2011.

Klumbies, Paul-Gerhard. "Der Eine Gott des Pa—Röm 3:21–31 als Brennpunkt paulinischer Theologie." *Zeitschrift für die Neutestamentliche Wissenschaft und die Kunde der Älteren Kirche* 85 (1994): 192–206.

Koester, Craig. *Symbolism in the Fourth Gospel: Meaning, Mystery, Community*. 2nd ed. Minneapolis: Fortress, 2003. Originally published in 1995.

Kooten, Geurt Hendrik van. *Paul's Anthropology in Context: The Image of God, Assimilation to God, and Tripartite Man in Ancient Judaism, Ancient Philosophy and Early Christianity*. Tübingen: Mohr Siebeck, 2008.

Kopecek, Thomas A. *A History of Neo-Arianism*. Patristic Monograph Series 8. Cambridge: Philadelphia Patristic Foundation, 1979.

Köstenberger, Andreas J., and Scott R. Swain. *Father, Son, and Spirit: The Trinity and John's Gospel*. Downers Grove, Ill.: Intervarsity, 2008.

Kugel, James L., and Rowan A. Greer. *Early Biblical Interpretation*. Edited by Wayne A. Meeks. Philadelphia: Westminster, 1986.

Kurz, William S. "The Johannine Word as Revealing the Father: A Christian Credal Actualization." *Perspectives in Religious Studies* 28 (2001): 67–84.

Kysar, Robert. "Christology and Controversy: The Contributions of the Prologue of the Gospel of John to New Testament Christology and Their Historical Setting." *Currents in Theology and Mission* 5, no. 6 (1978): 348–64.

Laato, Antti, and Jacques van Ruiten, eds. *Rewritten Bible Reconsidered: Proceedings of the Conference in Karkku, Finland, August 24–26, 2006*. Studies in Rewritten Bible 1. Åbo, Finland: Åbo Academy University Press; Winona Lake, Ind.: Eisenbrauns, 2008.

Lake, Kirsopp. "The Unknown God." In *The Beginnings of Christianity*, edited by Kenneth Foakes Jackson and Kirsopp Lake, 5:240–46. London: Macmillan, 1933.

Lampe, G. W. H. "The Reasonableness of Typology." In *Essays On Typology*, edited by G. W. H. Lampe and K. J. Woollcombe, 9–38. Studies in Biblical Theology 22. Naperville: Allenson, 1957.

Layton, Richard. *Didymus the Blind and His Circle in Late-Antique Alexandria: Virtue and Narrative in Biblical Scholarship*. Urbana: University of Illinois Press, 2004.

Leonhardt-Balzer, Jutta. "Der Logos und die Schöpfung: Streiflichter bei Philo (Op 20–25) und im Johannesprolog (John 1:1–18)." In *Kontexte des Johannesevangeliums: Das vierte Evangelium in religions- und traditionsgeschichtlicher Perspektive*, edited by Jörg Frey and Udo Schnelle, 295–320. Wissenschaftliche Untersuchungen zum Neuen Testament 175. Tübingen: Mohr Siebeck, 2004.

Levison, John R. *Filled with the Spirit*. Grand Rapids: Eerdmans, 2009.

Lienhard, Joseph T. *Contra Marcellum: Marcellus of Ancyra and Fourth-Century Theology*. Washington, D.C.: The Catholic University of America Press, 1999.

Lightfoot, Joseph Barber. *The Apostolic Fathers*. Part 2, *Ignatius and Polycarp*. Vol. 2. London: Macmillan, 1889.

———. *Saint Paul's Epistles to the Colossians and to Philemon: A Revised Text with Introductions, Notes, and Dissertations*. London: Macmillan, 1890.

Lim, Richard. "The Politics of Interpretation in Basil's 'Hexaemeron.'" *Vigiliae Christianae* 44 (1990): 351–70.

Lindbeck, George A. *The Nature of Doctrine: Religion and Theology in a Postliberal Age*. Louisville: Westminster John Knox Press, 2009.

Loader, William R. G. *The Christology of the Fourth Gospel: Structure and Issues*. 2nd ed. Beiträge zur biblischen Exegese und Theologie 23. Frankfurt: Peter Lang, 1992.

Loder, James. *The Transforming Moment: Understanding Convictional Experiences*. New York: Harper and Row, 1981.

Lohse, Eduard. *Colossians and Philemon*. Translated by William R. Poehlmann and Robert J. Karris. Edited by Helmut Koester. Hermeneia. Philadelphia: Fortress, 1971.

Louth, Andrew. *Discerning the Mystery: An Essay on the Nature of Theology*. Oxford: Clarendon, 1983.

———. "The Oak of Mamre, the Fathers and St. Andrei Rublev: Patristic Interpretation of the Hospitality of Abraham and Rublev's Icon of the Trinity." In *The Trinity-Sergius Lavra in Russian History and Culture*, edited by Vladimir Tsurikov, 90–100. Jordanville, N.Y.: Holy Trinity Seminary Press, 2005.

Lubac, Henri de. "'Typologie' et 'allégorisme.'" *Recherches de Science Religieuse* 34 (1947): 180–247.

———. *Histoire et esprit: L'intelligence de l'Écriture d'après Origène*. Théologie 16. Paris: Aubier, 1950.

———. *Exégèse médiéval: Les quatre sens de l'Écriture*. 2 vols. Théologie 41. Paris: Aubier: 1959.

Ludlow, Morwenna. "Theology and Allegory: Origen and Gregory of Nyssa on the Unity and Diversity of Scripture." *International Journal of Systematic Theology* 4, no. 1 (2002): 45–66.

Lyman, Rebecca. *Christology and Cosmology: Models of Divine Activity in Origen, Eusebius, and Athanasius*. Oxford: Clarendon Press, 1993.

Mach, Michael. *Entwicklungsstadien des jüdischen Engelglaubens in vorrabinischer Zeit*. Texte und Studien zum Antiken Judentum 34. Tübingen: J. C. B. Mohr, 1992.

MacIntyre, Alasdair. *After Virtue*. 3rd ed. Notre Dame, Ind.: University of Notre Dame Press, 2007.

Marrou, H. I. *A History of Education in Antiquity*. Translated by George Lamb. Madison: University of Wisconsin Press, 1956.

Martens, Peter W. "Revisiting the Allegory/Typology Distinction: The Case of Origen." *Journal of Early Christian Studies* 16, no. 3 (2008): 283–317.

Martin, Dale. *Pedagogy of the Bible: An Analysis and Proposal*. Louisville: Westminster John Knox Press, 2008.

Martyn, J. Louis. "Apocalyptic Antinomies." In Martyn, *Theological Issues*, 111–23. 1997.

———. "Epistemology at the Turn of the Ages." In Martyn, *Theological Issues*, 89–110. 1997.

———. *History and Theology in the Fourth Gospel*. Rev. ed. Nashville: Abingdon, 1979. Reprinted Louisville: Westminster John Knox, 2003. Originally published in 1968.

———. *Theological Issues in the Letters of Paul*. Edinburgh: T. and T. Clark, 1997.

McCarron, Richard E. "An Epiphany of Mystical Symbols: Jacob of Sarug's Mêmrâ 109 on Abraham and His Types." *Hugoye* 1 (1998): 57–78.

McGowan, Andrew. "God in Early Latin Theology: Tertullian and the Trinity." In *God in Early Christian Thought: Essays in Memory of Lloyd G. Patterson*, edited by Andrew McGowan, Brian E. Daley, and Timothy J. Gaden, 73–82. Boston: Brill, 2009.

McGrath, James. *The Only True God: Early Christian Monotheism in Its Jewish Context*. Champaign: University of Illinois Press, 2009.

Meeks, Wayne A. *The Prophet-King: Moses Traditions and the Johannine Christology*. Supplements to Novum Testamentum 14. Leiden: Brill, 1967. Reprinted in Johannine Monograph Series 5. Eugene, Ore.: Wipf and Stock, 2017.

"The Man from Heaven in Johannine Sectarianism." *Journal of Biblical Literature* 91, no. 1 (1972): 44–72. Reprinted in Ashton, *Interpretations of the Fourth Gospel*, 141–73 (1986).

———. "Breaking Away: Three New Testament Pictures of Christianity's Separation from the Jewish Communities." In *"To See Ourselves as Others See Us": Christians, Jews, "Others" in Late Antiquity*, edited by Jacob Neusner and Ernest S. Frerichs, 93–115. Chico, Calif.: Scholars, 1985.

Menken, Maarten J. J. "The Christology of the Fourth Gospel: A Survey of Recent Research." In *From Jesus to John: Essays on Jesus and New Testament Christology in Honour of Marinus de Jonge*, edited by Martinus de Boer, 292–320, Supplements to the Journal for the Study of Judaism 84. Sheffield: Sheffield Academic Press, 1993.

Menzies, Robert P. *The Development of Early Christian Pneumatology with Special Reference to Luke-Acts*. Journal for the Study of the New Testament Supplement 54. Sheffield: Sheffield Academic Press, 1991.

Meredith, Anthony. "Proverbes, VIII:22 chez Origène, Athanase, Basile et Grégoire de Nysse." In *Politique et théologie chez Athanase d'Alexandrie*, edited by Charles Kannengiesser, 349–57. Paris: Éditions Beauchesne, 1974.

Metzger, Bruce. *A Textual Commentary on the Greek New Testament*. London: United Bible Societies, 1975.

Mitchell, Margaret M. *Paul, the Corinthians and the Birth of Christian Hermeneutics*. Cambridge: Cambridge University Press, 2010.

"Monotheism: The Doctrine or Belief That There Is Only One God." TheFreeDictionary.com. http://www.thefreedictionary.com/monotheism. Accessed July 15, 2015.

Mortley, Raoul. *Connaissance religieuse et herméneutique chez Clément d'Alexandrie*. Leiden: Brill, 1973.

Moreland, Bishop Moore, and Milton C. Moreland. "Historical Criticism." In *The Oxford Encyclopedia of Biblical Interpretation*, edited by Steven L. McKenzie. 2 vols. New York: Oxford University Press, 2014.

Morlet, Sébastien. "Origen as an Exegetical Source." In *Eusebius of Caesarea: Tradition and Innovations*, edited by Aaron Johnson and Jeremy Schott, 207–38. Hellenic Studies 60. Washington, D.C.: Center for Hellenic Studies, 2013.

Mühlenberg, Ekkehard. *Apollinaris von Laodicea*. Göttingen: Vandenhoeck and Ruprecht, 1969.

Mütschler, Bernhard. *Das Corpus Johanneum bei Irenäus von Lyon: Studien und Kommentar zum dritten Buch von Adversus Haereses*. Wissenschaftliche Untersuchungen zum Neuen Testament 189. Tübingen: Mohr Siebeck, 2006.

Najman, Hindy. *Seconding Sinai: The Development of Mosaic Discourse in Second Temple Judaism*. Boston: Brill, 2003.

Neuschafer, Bernhardt. *Origenes als Philologe*. 2 vols. Basel: Friedrich Reinhardt, 1987.

Neyrey, Jerome. *An Ideology of Revolt: John's Christology in Social-Science Perspective*. Philadelphia: Fortress, 1988.

———. *The Gospel of John in Cultural and Rhetorical Perspective*. Grand Rapids: Eerdmanns, 2009.

Norris, Richard A. Jr. *The Christological Controversy*. Philadelphia: Fortress, 1980.

———. "Typology." In *The Westminster Handbook to Origen*, edited by J. A. McGuckin, 209–11. Louisville: Westminster John Knox Press, 2004.

Oeming, Manfred. *Contemporary Biblical Hermeneutics: An Introduction*. Translated by Joachim F. Vette. Aldershot: Ashgate, 2006.

O'Keefe, John. "Allegory." In *The Westminster Handbook to Origen*, edited by John A. McGuckin, 49–50. Louisville: Westminster John Knox Press, 2004.

———. "Scriptural Interpretation." In *The Westminster Handbook to Origen*, edited by John A. McGuckin, 193–97. Louisville: Westminster John Knox Press, 2004.

O'Keefe, John J., and J. J. Reno. *Sanctified Vision: An Introduction to Early Christian Interpretation of the Bible*. Baltimore: The Johns Hopkins University Press, 2005.

Osborn, Eric Francis. *Tertullian, First Theologian of the West*. Cambridge: Cambridge University Press, 1997.

Paget, James Carleton, and Joachim Schaper, eds. *The New Cambridge History of the Bible*. Vol. 1, *From the Beginnings to 600*. Cambridge: Cambridge University Press, 2013.

Painter, John. "Rereading Genesis in the Prologue of John." In *Neotestamentica et Philonica: Studies in Honor of Peder Borgen*, edited by David E. Aune, Torrey Seland, and Jarl Henning Ulrichsen, 179–201. Supplements to Novum Testamentum 106. Leiden/Boston: Brill, 2003.

Parsenios, George L. *Departure and Consolation: The Johannine Farewell Discourses in Light of Greco-Roman Literature*. Supplements to Novum Testamentum 117. Leiden: Brill, 2005.

———. *Rhetoric and Drama in the Johannine Lawsuit Motif.* Wissenschaftliche Untersuchungen zum Neuen Testament 258. Tübingen: Mohr Siebeck, 2010.

Patterson, L. G. *Methodius, Origen, and the Arian Dispute*. Edited by E. A. Livingstone, 912–23. *Studia Patristica*, series 17, vol. 2. Oxford: Pergamon, 1982.

Pearson, John. *Vindiciae epistolarum S. Ignatii*. 2 vols. Oxford:, J. H. Parker, 1852.

Peers, Glenn. "Angelophany and Art after Iconoclasm." *Deltion tes Christianikes Archaiologikes Hetaireias* 26 (2005): 339–44.

Pendrick, Gerard. "Monogenes." *New Testament Studies* 41, no. 4 (1995): 587–600.

Peterson, Erik. *Ειϛ Θεοϛ*. Forschungen zur Religion und Literatur des Alten und Neuen Testaments 23. Göttingen: Vandenhoeck and Ruprecht, 1926.

Pollard, T. E. *Johannine Christology and the Early Church*. Society for New Testament Studies Monograph Series 13. Cambridge: Cambridge University Press.

Quasten, Johannes. *Patrology*. 4 vols. Utrecht: Spectrum, 1950–86.

Radde-Gallwitz, Andrew. *Basil of Caesarea, Gregory of Nyssa, and the Transformation of Divine Simplicity*. Oxford: Oxford University Press, 2009.

Rainbow, Paul. "Jewish Monotheism as the Matrix for New Testament Christology: A Review Article," *Novum Testamentum* 33 (1991): 78–91.

Rajak, Tessa. "Talking at Trypho: Christian Apologetic as Anti-Judaism in Justin's Dialogue with Trypho the Jew." In *Apologetics in the Roman Empire: Pagans, Jews, and Christians*, edited by Mark J. Edwards, Martin Goodman, and Simon Price, 59–80. Oxford: Oxford University Press, 1999.

Rankin, David. *From Clement to Origen: The Social and Historical Context of the Church Fathers*. Farnham: Ashgate, 2007.

Rauschen, Gerhard. *Patrologie: Die Schriften der Kirchenväter und ihr Lehrgehalt*. Revised by Berthold Altaner. 8th, 10th and 11th eds. Freiburg: Herder, 1931.

Reinhartz, Adele. "Jesus as Prophet: Predictive Prolepses in the Fourth Gospel." *Journal for the Study of the New Testament* 36 (1989): 3–16.

Richardson, Neil. *Paul's Language about God*. Sheffield: Sheffield Academic Press, 1994.

Ricoeur, Paul. "The Canon between the Text and the Community." In *Philosophical Hermeneutics and Biblical Exegesis*, edited by Petr Pokorny and Jan Roskovec, 7–26. Wissenschaftliche Untersuchungen zum Neuen Testament 153. Tubingen: Mohr, 2002.

Ridderbos, Herman. *The Gospel of John: A Theological Commentary*. Grand Rapids: Eerdmans, 1997.

Roukema, Riemer, and Saskia Deventer-Metz. *Jesus, Gnosis and Dogma*. London: T. and T. Clark, 2010.

Rousseau, Philip. *Basil of Caesarea*. Transformation of the Classical Heritage 20. Berkeley: University of California Press, 1994.

Rowe, C. Kavin. "Romans 10:13: What Is the Name of the Lord?" *Horizons in Biblical Theology* 22 (2000): 135–73.

———. "Seeing the Word: Refocusing New Testament Study." Review. *Pro Ecclesia* 18, no. 1 (2009): 111–15.

Rowe, J. N. "Origen's Subordinationism as Illustrated in His Commentary on St. John's Gospel." *Studia Patristica* 11, no. 2 (1972): 222–28.

Rowland, Christopher, and Ian Doxall. "Reception Criticism and Theory." In *The Oxford Encyclopedia of Biblical Interpretation*, edited by Steven L. McKenzie, 206–15. Oxford: Oxford University Press, 2013.

Rusch, William G. *The Trinitarian Controversy*. Philadelphia: Fortress, 1980.

Sanday, W. R., and C. H. Turner. *Novum Testamentum sancti Irenaei episcopi lugdunensis*. Oxford: Clarendon Press, 1923.

Schaff, Philip. *The Creeds of Chistendom*. 3 vols. Grand Rapids: Baker, 1977. Originally published in 1931.

Schmemann, Alexander. *For the Life of the World*. Crestwood, N.Y.: St. Vladimir's Seminary Press, 1973.

———. *The Eucharist: Sacrament of the Kingdom*. Translated by Paul Kachur. Crestwood, N.Y.: St. Vladimir's Seminary Press, 1988.

———. "Symbol and Symbolism in the Byzantine Liturgy: Liturgical Symbols and Their Theological Interpretation." In *Liturgy and Tradition: Theological Reflections of Alexander Schmemann*, edited by Thomas Fisch, 115–28. Crestwood: St. Vladimir's Seminary Press, 1990.

Schmidt, K. L. "επικαλεω." *Theological Dictionary of the New Testament*, edited by Gerhard Kittel, 3:496–500. Grand Rapids: Eerdmans, 1964–76.

Schnackenburg, Rudolf. *The Gospel according to St. John*. Vol. 3, *Commentary on Chapters 3–21*. New York: Crossroad, 1982.

———. "'Der Vater, der mich gesandt hat': Zur johaneischen Christologie." In *Anfänge der Christologie: Festschrift für Ferdinand Hahn zum 65. Geburtstag*, edited by Cilliers Breytenbach and Henning Paulsen, 275–91. Göttingen: Vandenhoeck and Ruprecht, 1991.

Schneiders, Sandra M. *The Revelatory Text: Interpreting the New Testament as Sacred Scripture*. 2nd ed. Collegeville, Minn.: Liturgical Press 1999.

———. "'Der Vater, der mich gesandt hat': Zur johaneischen Christologie." In *Anfänge der Christologie: Festschrift für Ferdinand Hahn zum 65. Geburtstag*, edited by Cilliers Breytenbach and Henning Paulsen, 275–91. Göttingen: Vandenhoeck and Ruprecht, 1991.

Schnelle, Udo. *Antidocetic Christology in the Gospel of John*. Translated by Linda M. Maloney.

Minneapolis: Fortress, 1992. English translation of *Antidoketische Christologie im Johannesevangelium*, Forshungen zur Religion und Literatur des Alten und Neuen Testament 144. Göttingen: Vandenhoeck and Ruprecht, 1987.

Schoedel, W. R. *Ignatius of Antioch: A Commentary on the Letters*. Hermeneia. Philadelphia: Fortress, 1985.

Schrage, Wolfgang. *Unterwegs zur Einzigkeit und Einheit Gottes: Zum "Monotheismus" des Paulus und seiner alttestamentlich-frühjudischen Tradition*. Neukirchen-Vluyn: Neukirchener Verlag, 2002.

Scott, Kenneth. *The Imperial Cult under the Flavians*. New York: Arno, 1975. Originally published in 1936.

Sedley, David. "Philosophical Allegiance in the Greco-Roman World." In *Philosophia Togata: Essays on Philosophy and Roman Society*, edited by Miriam Griffin and Jonathan Barnes, 97–119. Oxford: Clarendon Press, 1989.

Seeberg, Reinhold. *Lehrbuch der Dogmengeschichte*. 2 vols. Erlangen: A. Deichert, 1895–98.

Segal, Alan F. "'Two Powers in Heaven' and Early Christian Trinitarian Thinking." In *The Trinity: An Interdisciplinarry Symposium on the Trinity*, edited by Stephen Davis, Daniel Kendall, and Gerald O'Collins, 73–95. Oxford: Oxford University Press, 1999.

Segal, Michael. "Between Bible and Rewritten Bible." In *Biblical Interpretation at Qumran*, edited by Matthias Henze, 10–28. Grand Rapids: Eerdmans, 2005.

Seibt, Klaus. *Die Theologie des Markell von Ankyra*. Arbeiten zur Kirchengeschichte 59. Berlin: De Gruyter, 1994.

Sekki, Arthur Everett. *The Meaning of Ruah at Qumran*. Society of Biblical Literature 110. Atlanta: Scholars Press, 1989.

Sesboüé, Bernard. *Saint Basile et la Trinité: Un acte théologique au IVe siècle*. Paris: Descleé, 1998.

Sesboüé, Bernard, Georges-Matthieu de Durand, and Louis Doutreleau. *Basile de Césarée: Contre Eunome suivi de Eunome Apologie*, SC 299 and 305. Paris: Cerf, 1982–83.

Shelfer, Lochlan. "The Legal Precision of the Term 'πάράκλητος.'" *Journal for the Study of the New Testament* 32, no. 2 (2009): 131–50.

Siegert, Folker. *Philon von Alexandrien: Über die Gottesbezeichnung "wohltätig verzehrendes Feuer" (De Deo) / Rückübersetzung des Fragments aus dem Armenischen, deutsche Übersetzung und Kommentar von Folker Siegert*. Tübingen: Mohr, 1988.

———. "Homerinterpretations, Tora-Unterweisung, Bibelauslegung: Vom Ursprung der patristischen Hermeneutik." *Studia Patristica* 25 (1993): 159–71.

———. "Der Logos, 'älterer Sohn' des Schöpfers und 'zweiter Gott': Philons Logos und der Johannesprolog." In *Kontexte des Johannesevangeliums: Das vierte Evangelium in religions- und traditionsgeschichtlicher Perspektive*, edited by Jörg Frey and Udo Schnelle, 277–94. Wissenschaftliche Untersuchungen zum Neuen Testament 175. Tübingen: Mohr-Siebeck, 2004.

Simonetti, Manlio. "Sull' interpretazione patristica di Proverbi 8:22." In *Studi sull' Arianesimo*, edited by Manlio Simonetti, 9–87. Rome: Editrice Studium, 1965.

———. *Profilo storico dell'esegesi patristica*. Rome: Istituto Patristico Augustinianum, 1981.

———. *Lettera e/o allegoria: Un contributo alla storia dell'esegesi patristica*. Rome: Institutum Patristicum "Augustinianum," 1985.

———. *Biblical Interpretation in the Early Church: An Historical Introduction to Patristic Exegesis*. Translated by John A. Hughes. Edinburgh: T. and T. Clark, 1994.

Slater, Thomas B. "The Paraclete as Advocate in the Community of the Fourth Gospel." *Ashland Theological Journal* 20 (1991): 101–8.

Smalley, Stephen S. "'The Paraclete': Pneumatology in the Johannine Gospel and Apocalypse." In *Exploring the Gospel of John: In Honor of D. Moody Smith*, edited by R. Alan Culpepper, and C. Clifton Black, 289–300. Louisville: Westminster John Knox Press, 1996.

Smith, J. Warren. "Trinity in the Fourth-Century Fathers." In *The Oxford Handbook of the Trinity*, edited by Giles Emery and Matthew Levering, 109–17. Oxford: Oxford University Press, 2011.

Souverain, Matthieu. *Platonism Unveil'd, or, An Essay Concerning the Notions and Opinions of Plato and Some Antient and Modern Divines, his Followers, in Relation to the Logos, or Word in Particular, and the Doctrine of the Trinity in General*. London: 1700.

Spellman, Ched. *Toward a Canon-Conscious Reading of the Bible: Exploring the History and Hermeneutic of the Canon*. Sheffield: Sheffield Phoenix Press, 2014.

Staab, Karl. *Die Pauluskatenen nach den handschriftlichen Quellen*. Scripta Pontificii instituti biblici. Rome: Verlag des Päpstlichen Bibelinstituts, 1926.

———. *Pauluskommentare aus der Griechischen Kirche*. 2nd ed. Neutestamentliche Abhandlungen 15. Münster: Aschendorff, 1984.

Stead, Christopher J. "Divine Substance in Tertullian." *Journal of Theological Studies* 14, no. 1 (1963): 46–66.

———. "Arius in Modern Research." *Journal of Theological Studies* 45, no. 1 (1994): 24–36.

Steenson, Jeffrey N. "Basil of Ancyra and the Course of Nicene Orthodoxy." Ph.D. diss., Oxford University, 1983.

Strawbridge, Jennifer R. *The Pauline Effect: The Use of the Pauline Epistles by Early Christian Writers*. Berlin: De Gruyter, 2015.

Stroumsa, Guy G. "Caro salutis cardo: Shaping the Person in Early Christian Thought." *History of Religions* 30, no. 1 (1990): 25–50.

Strutwolf, Holger. *Die Trinitätstheologie und Christologie des Euseb von Caesarea: Eine dogmengeschichtliche Untersuchung seiner Platonismusrezeption und Wirkungsgeschichte*. Forschungen zur Kirchen- und Dogmengeschichte 72. Göttingen: Vandenhoeck and Ruprecht, 1999.

Stuckenbruck, Loren T. *Angel Veneration and Christology*. Wissenschaftliche Untersuchungen zum Neuen Testament, vol. 2, series 70. Tübingen: J. C. B. Mohr Siebeck, 1995.

Studer, Basil. *Zur Theophanie-Exegese Augustins: Untersuchung zu einem Ambrosius-Zitat in der Schrift "De Videndo Deo."* Rome: Herder, 1971.

Swetnam, James, SJ. "Bestowal of the Spirit in the Fourth Gospel." *Biblica* 74, no. 4 (1993): 556–76.

Thatcher, Tom. *The Riddles of Jesus in John: A Study in Tradition and Folklore*. Society of Biblical Literature Monograph Series 53. Atlanta: Society of Biblical Literature, 2000.

Thiselton, Anthony C. *New Horizons in Hermeneutics*. Grand Rapids: Zondervan, 1992.

———. *The First Epistle to the Corinthians*. New International Greek Testament Commentary. Grand Rapids: Eerdmans, 2000.

———. *The Living Paul*. Downers Grove, Ill.: IVP, 2009.

Thompson, Marianne Meye. *The God of the Gospel of John*. Grand Rapids: Eerdmans, 2001.

Thunberg, Lars. "Early Christian Interpretation of the Three Angels in Gen. 18." *Studia Patristica* 7 (1966): 560–70.

Tilling, Chris. *Paul's Divine Christology*. Tübingen: Mohr Siebeck, 2012.

———. "Ephesians and Divine-Christology." In *The Spirit and Christ in the New Testament and Christian Theology: Essays in Honor of Max Turner*, edited by I. Howard Marshall, Cornelis Bennema, and Volker Rabens, 177–97. Grand Rapids: Eerdmans, 2012.

Trigg, Joseph W. *Origen: The Bible and Philosophy in the Third-Century Church*. Atlanta: John Knox Press, 1983.

———. *Origen*. Early Church Fathers. New York: Routledge, 1998.

———. "Knowing God in the *Theological Orations* of Gregory of Nazianzus: The Heritage of Origen." In *God in Early Christian Thought: Essays in Memory of Lloyd G. Patterson*, edited by Andrew B. McGowan, Brian E. Daley, SJ, and Timothy J. Gaden, 83–104. Supplements to Vigiliae Christianae 94. Leiden: Brill, 2009.

Tuckett, Christopher M. *Christology and the New Testament: Jesus and His Earliest Followers*. Edinburgh: Westminster John Knox Press, 2001.

Turner, Max. "The Spirit of Christ and Christology." In *Christ the Lord: Studies Presented to Donald Guthrie*, edited by H. H. Rowdon, 168–90. Leicester: InterVarsity, 1982.

———. "The Spirit of Christ and 'Divine' Christology." In *Jesus of Nazareth, Lord and Christ*, edited by Joel B. Green and Max Turner, 413–36. Grand Rapids: Eerdmans, 1994.

Uhrig, Christian. *"Und das Wort ist Fleisch geworden": Zur Rezeption von Joh 1:14a und zur Theologie der Fleischwerdung in der griechischen vornizänischen Patristik*. Münsterische Beiträge zur Theologie 63. Münster: Aschendorff, 2004.

Vaggione, Richard Paul. *The Extant Works*. Oxford: Oxford University Press, 1987.

———. *Eunomius of Cyzicus and the Nicene Revolution*. Oxford: Oxford University Press, 2000.

Vermes, Geza. *Scripture and Tradition in Judaism: Haggadic Studies*. Leiden: Brill, 1961.

Vinzent, Markus. *Markell von Ankyra: Die Fragmente [und] Der Brief an Julius von Rom*. Supplements to Vigiliae Christianae 39. Leiden: Brill, 1997.

Viviano, Benedict, OP. "The Spirit in John's Gospel: A Hegelian Perspective." *Freiburger Zeitschrift für Philosophie und Theologie* 43 (1996): 368–87.

von Arnim, Hans Friedrich August. *Stoicorum veterum fragmenta..* Vol. 2. Leipzig: Teubner, 1903–5.

von Rad, Gerhard. *Das erste Buch Mose: Das Alte Testament Deutsch.* Göttingen: Vandenhoeck and Ruprecht, 1953.

von Wahlde, Urban C. *The Earliest Version of John's Gospel: Recovering the Gospel of Signs.* Wilmington: Glazier, 1989.

———. *The Gospel and Letters of John.* 3 vols. Eerdmans Critical Commentary. Grand Rapids: Eerdmans, 2010.

Waaler, Erik. *The Shema and the First Commandment in First Corinthians.* Wissenschaftliche Untersuchungen zum Neuen Testament, vol. 2, series. 253. Tübingen: Mohr Siebeck, 2008.

Walford, Adrian, trans. *Encyclopedia of the Early Church.* Foreword and bibliographic amendments by W. H. C. Frend. Cambridge: James Clarke, 1992.

Wallace-Hadrill, D. S. *Eusebius of Caesarea.* London: A. S. Mowbray, 1960.

Wanamaker, C. A. "Christ as a Divine Agent in Paul." *Journal of Theological Studies* 39 (1986): 517–28.

Weder, Hans. "Deus Incarnatus: On the Hermeneutics of Christology in the Johannine Writings." In *Exploring the Gospel of John: In Honor of D. Moody Smith,* edited by R. Alan Culpepper and C. Clifton Black, 327–45. Louisville: Westminster/John Knox, 1996.

Weedman, Mark. "Finding the Form of God in Philippians 2: Gregory of Nyssa and the Development of Pro-Nicene Exegesis." *Journal of Theological Interpretation* 2, no. 1 (2008): 23–41.

———. "The Polemical Context of Gregory of Nyssa's Doctrine of Divine Infinity." *Journal of Early Christian Studies* 18, no. 1 (2010): 81–104.

Werner, Martin. *The Formation of Christian Dogma: An Historical Study of Its Problem.* Translated by S. G. F. Brandon. London: A. and C. Black, 1957.

Wiles, Maurice F. *The Spiritual Gospel: The Interpretation of the Fourth Gospel in the Early Church.* Cambridge: Cambridge University Press, 1960.

———. *The Divine Apostle: The Interpretation of St. Paul's Epistles in the Early Church.* Cambridge: Cambridge University Press, 1967.

———. "A Textual Variant in the Creed of the Council of Nicaea." *Studia Patristica* 26 (1993): 428–33.

Williams, Rowan. *Arius: Heresy and Tradition.* London: SCM Press, 2001.

Wilson, M. P. "St. John, the Trinity and the Language of the Spirit." *Scottish Journal of Theology* 41, no. 4 (1988): 471–83.

Wilson, Robert McL. *A Critical and Exegetical Commentary on Colossians and Philemon.* London: T. and T. Clark International, 2005.

Windsich, Hans. *The Spirit-Paraclete in the Fourth Gospel.* Translated by James W. Cox. Facet Books Biblical Series 20. Philadelphia: Fortress, 1968.

Wittgenstein, Ludwig. *On Certainty*. Edited by G. E. M. Anscombe and G. H. von Wright. Translated by Denis Paul and G. E. M. Anscombe. Oxford: Blackwell, 1969.

Wright, N. T. "Poetry and Theology in Colossians 1:15–20." *New Testament Studies* 36 (1990): 444–68.

Yeago, David. "The New Testament and Nicene Dogma: A Contribution to the Recovery of Theological Exegesis." In *Pro Ecclesia* 3 (1994): 152–64. Reprinted in *The Theological Interpretation of Scripture: Classic and Contemporary Readings*, edited by Stephen Fowl, 87–102. Oxford: Blackwell, 1997.

Young, Frances M. *Biblical Exegesis and the Formation of Christian Culture*. Cambridge: Cambridge University Press, 1997.

———. "Interpretation of Scripture." In *The Oxford Handbook of Early Christian Studies*, edited by Susan Ashbrook Harvey and David G. Hunter, 846–63. Oxford: Oxford University Press, 2008.

CONTRIBUTORS

Paul N. Anderson, professor of Biblical and Quaker Studies at George Fox University, is the author of *The Fourth Gospel and the Quest for Jesus* (2008) and *Riddles of the Fourth Gospel: An Introduction to John* (2011), among many other works. He is a founding member of the Society of Biblical Literature John, Jesus, and History Project and coeditor of the Biblical Interpretation book series from Brill Publishers.

Harold W. Attridge is Sterling Professor of Divinity and the former dean of Yale Divinity School. Among his numerous publications on the New Testament and early Christianity are *Hebrews: A Commentary on the Epistle to the Hebrews*, *Essays on John and Hebrews* (2010), and *Nag Hammadi Codex I: The Jung Codex* (1985). He is the general editor of the revised edition of the HarperCollins Study Bible (2006).

Christopher A. Beeley, Walter H. Gray Associate Professor of Anglican Studies and Patristics at Yale Divinity School, is the author of *The Unity of Christ: Continuity and Conflict in Patristic Tradition* (2012) and *Gregory of Nazianzus on the Trinity and the Knowledge of God: In Your Light We Shall See Light* (2008), which won a John Templeton Award for Theological Promise. He is the editor of Christianity in Late Antiquity, the official book series of the North American Patristics Society (California).

Bogdan G. Bucur, associate professor of theology at Duquesne University, is the author of *Angelomorphic Pneumatology: Clement of Alexandria and Other Early Christian Witnesses* (2009) and numerous articles on early Christian biblical exegesis and doctrinal development.

Adela Yarbro Collins is Buckingham Professor Emerita of New Testament Criticism and Interpretation at Yale Divinity School and the former president of the Society of New Testament Studies. Her many works in New Testament Studies include *The Combat Myth in the Book of Revelation* (1976), *Cosmology and Eschatology in Jewish and Christian Apocalypticism* (1996), and *Mark: A Commentary,* Hermeneia Series (2007).

Mark DelCogliano, assistant professor of theology at the University of St. Thomas, is the author of *Basil of Caesarea's Anti-Eunomian Theory of Names: Christian Theology and Late-Antique Philosophy in the Fourth-Century Trinitarian Controversy* (2010) and the translator of *St. Basil the Great: On Christian Doctrine and Practice* (2012), *Gregory the Great on the Song of Songs* (2012), and several other patristic texts.

Mark J. Edwards, professor of Early Christian Studies in the University of Oxford, is the author of *Origen against Plato* (2002), *John through the Centuries,* Blackwell Biblical Commentaries (2003), *Catholicity and Heresy in the Early Church* (2009), and *Image, Word and God in the Early Christian Centuries* (2012) and is the translator of several classical and early Christian texts.

Stephen E. Fowl, professor of theology at Loyola University Maryland, is the author of *The Story of Christ in the Ethics of Paul: An Analysis of the Function of the Hymnic Material in the Pauline Corpus,* JSOT (1990), *Engaging Scripture: An Essay in Theological Interpretation* (1998), and commentaries on Philippians (2005) and Ephesians (2012).

Larry W. Hurtado is emeritus professor of New Testament Language, Literature, and Theology and founding director of the Centre for the Study of Christian Origins at the University of Edinburgh. He is the author of *Text-Critical Methodology and the Pre-Caesarean Text: Codex W in the Gospel of Mark* (1981), *One God, One Lord: Early Christian Devotion and Ancient Jewish Monotheism* (1998), and *Lord Jesus Christ: Devotion to Jesus in Earliest Christianity* (2003), among many other works of New Testament criticism.

Jennifer R. Strawbridge is associate professor in New Testament at the University of Oxford. She is the author of *The Pauline Effect: The Use of the Pauline Epistles by Early Christian Writers* (2015), which won the inaugural Society for Biblical Literature–De Gruyter Prize for Biblical Studies and Reception History, and several articles on early Christian biblical interpretation.

Marianne Meye Thompson is the George Eldon Ladd Professor of New Testament at Fuller Theological Seminary. Her many works include *The God of the Gospel of John* (2001), *A Commentary on Colossians and Philemon*, Two Horizons Commentary, *1–3 John*, New Testament Commentary (2011), and *John: A Commentary*, New Testament Library (2015).

Mark E. Weedman, professor of philosophy and ethics at Johnson University, is the author of *The Trinitarian Theology of Hilary of Poitiers* (2007) and several articles on early Christian theology and exegesis.

GENERAL INDEX

INDEX OF BIBLICAL CITATIONS

Also in the series

CUA STUDIES IN EARLY CHRISTIANITY

GENERAL EDITOR

Philip Rousseau

To Train His Soul in Books: Syriac Asceticism in Early Christianity

Robin Darling Young and Monica J. Blanchard, editors

Re-Reading Gregory of Nazianzus: Essays on History, Theology, and Culture

Christopher A. Beeley, editor

Breaking the Mind: New Studies in the Syriac "Book of Steps"

Kristian S. Heal and Robert A. Kitchen, editors

Group Identity and Religious Individuality in Late Antiquity

Edited by Éric Rebillard and Jörg Rüpke

The Bible and Early Trinitarian Theology
was designed and typeset in Garamond by Kachergis Book Design of Pittsboro, North Carolina. It was printed on 60-pound Sebago IV B18 Cream and bound by Maple Press of York, Pennsylvania.